Lincoln the Citizen,
February 12, 1809 to March 4, 1861

THE UIS CENTER FOR
LINCOLN STUDIES SERIES

Series Editor
Michael Burlingame

*For a list of books in the series, please see
our website at www.press.uillinois.edu.*

Lincoln the Citizen, February 12, 1809 to March 4, 1861

THE COMPLETE VERSION

Henry C. Whitney

Edited and with an introduction by
Michael Burlingame

© 2025 by the Board of Trustees
of the University of Illinois
All rights reserved
Manufactured in the United States of America
C 5 4 3 2 1
♾ This book is printed on acid-free paper.

Library of Congress Cataloging-in-Publication Data

Names: Whitney, Henry Clay, 1831–1905, author.
| Burlingame, Michael, 1941– editor, writer of
introduction.
Title: Lincoln the citizen, February 12, 1809 to March 4,
1861 : the complete version / Henry C. Whitney ; edited
and with an introduction by Michael Burlingame.
Description: Urbana : University of Illinois Press, [2025]
| Series: The UIS Center for Lincoln Studies | Includes
index.
Identifiers: LCCN 2024029673 (print) | LCCN
2024029674 (ebook) | ISBN 9780252046384 (cloth) |
ISBN 9780252047671 (ebook)
Subjects: LCSH: Lincoln, Abraham, 1809–1865. | Lincoln,
Abraham, 1809–1865—Childhood and youth. | Lincoln,
Abraham, 1809–1865—Political career before 1861. |
Presidents—United States—Biography. | Legislators—
Illinois—Biography. | Illinois—Biography.
Classification: LCC E457.3 .W58 2025 (print) | LCC E457.3
(ebook) | DDC 973.7092 [B]—dc23/eng/20250105
LC record available at https://lccn.loc.gov/2024029673
LC ebook record available at https://lccn.loc.gov/2024029674

For Lloyd

Henry C. Whitney on his relations with Lincoln:

"I have had the pleasure of intimate association with Mr. Lincoln in every sort of primitive and humble condition in village inns—in wayside farm houses—in village country taverns, in rude courthouses, at country mass-meetings, at picnic dinners, and I have associated with him at the White House when the cares of the nation were pressing him sorely."

"I traveled the circuit with him for seven years and was constantly with him, sleeping or waking, for five months in each year."

"We walked till early bedtime, during which he told me of his early adventures in both Macon and Sangamon counties, the Hanks family, etc.; also his early struggles in life."

Contents

Acknowledgments. ix

Introduction xi

Editorial Method. xxvii

    I Lineage, Parentage, and Childhood .1

   II Youth. 25

  III Lincoln as a Laborer 46

  IV The Romance of New Salem. 67

   V Lincoln as a Storekeeper 71

  VI Soldier, Surveyor, and Postmaster. 83

 VII Lincoln's Early Love Romance. 94

VIII State Legislator. 106

  IX Congressman 127

   X Citizen and Neighbor. 135

  XI Lawyer 144

 XII Lincoln's Religion 168

XIII Lincoln's Mental and Moral Natures 174

XIV Free-Soil Advocate 205

 XV Attainment of the Presidency. .216

XVI Inauguration as President. 249

Index. 263

Acknowledgments

I am grateful to Lawrence Mott, archivist at the Abraham Lincoln Library and Museum, a department of Lincoln Memorial University in Harrogate, Tennessee. He kindly had the handwritten manuscript of Whitney's biography scanned. That somewhat jumbled document was then painstakingly transcribed by the indefatigable Sheila Sullivan of Springfield, Illinois, who skillfully met the challenge of making sense of it. The costs involved were covered by the research fund of the Chancellor Naomi B. Lynn Distinguished Chair in Lincoln Studies at the University of Illinois Springfield, which I have the honor to hold and which is generously underwritten by the philanthropist Val Vaden.

I am also grateful to the exceptionally knowledgeable outside reviewers who vetted the manuscript for the University of Illinois Press. They went over it with a fine-toothed comb and made numerous invaluable suggestions, dramatically improving the final version.

The index has been prepared by Dr. Glenna Schroeder-Lein, a Lincoln scholar in her own right as well as a historian of the Civil War era, a documentary editor, and a conscientious, accomplished indexer.

The dedicatee is my older brother, who over many decades has provided support, encouragement, friendship, hospitality, and laughter, enriching my life immeasurably.

Thanks, thanks to all.

Introduction

Of all the books about Abraham Lincoln written by his friends, only those of William H. Herndon and Henry C. Whitney are "intimate, realistic and convincing," as the Lincoln scholar Paul M. Angle aptly observed.[1] The other such volumes tend to be dry, matter-of-fact narratives, offering little in the way of reminiscence and character analysis. *Herndon's Lincoln* is well known, as is (to a lesser extent) Whitney's *Life on the Circuit with Lincoln*, but the latter author's *Lincoln the Citizen* has been largely overlooked by historians. It is not even mentioned in surveys of important books about the sixteenth president, like Merrill D. Peterson, *Lincoln in American Memory*,[2] Michael Burkhimer, *One Hundred Essential Lincoln Books*,[3] Thomas R. Flagel, *Lincoln in Lists: The Civil War President in Twenty-five Lists*,[4] and Benjamin P. Thomas, *Portrait for Posterity: Lincoln and His Biographers*.[5] Mark E. Neely's entry on Whitney in *The Abraham Lincoln Encyclopedia* contains no allusion to his biography of Lincoln.[6] Scholars evidently thought that *Lincoln the Citizen* simply rehashes earlier biographies (which it does to some extent) or that it contains little of importance that was not already included in *Life on the Circuit with Lincoln*.[7] But in fact, *Lincoln the Citizen*, written in 1892 and published posthumously fifteen years later in a truncated edition, contains much important information that Lincoln confided to Whitney.[8] The present version restores passages that the book's editor, Marion Mills Miller, omitted from the original 1907 edition. The portion left on the cutting room floor amounts to about one-sixth of the original manuscript.

As the publisher of that work asserted, readers "will find in this character study a personal view of that most human of great men, which is second in general interest only to the life of Lincoln by his law partner, William H. Herndon, and surpasses this in many particular points of keen insight and generous appreciation."[9] In fact, though *Lincoln the Citizen* does not rank as high as *Herndon's Lincoln* as an essential book for students of Lincoln's pre-presidential years, Whitney's volume significantly complements Herndon's biography. Both attorneys were intimately acquainted with Lincoln. Benjamin Thomas described Whitney as one of "the six or seven men who could truthfully claim to have known Lincoln well."[10] Herndon knew him better, to be sure, and his book is invaluable, though the University of Illinois Press's publication in 1998 of *Herndon's Informants: Letters, Interviews, and Statements about Abraham Lincoln* makes it less important to scholars than it once was. That volume, containing over 600 letters and interviews by people who knew Lincoln, is a cornucopia of information that formed the basis of *Herndon's Lincoln.* There is no such compilation of similar statements made to Whitney, on which this volume partially rests, along with his own observations and, most significantly, what Lincoln told him about his experiences between 1809 and 1854.

Justifying the publisher's claim about *Lincoln the Citizen* are Whitney's treatment not only of Lincoln's character (about which Whitney offers keen insights) but also of his youth and adolescence in Indiana; of his parents; of his flatboat voyages to New Orleans; of his New Salem years; of his relations with women, especially Ann Rutledge; of his first year in Illinois; of his legal career; of his leadership role in the antislavery movement from 1854 to 1860; of his 1858 campaign against Stephen A. Douglas; of his nomination at the 1860 Republican National Convention; of his relationship with fellow townsmen in Springfield; of his distribution of patronage; of his train journey from Springfield to Washington in 1861; and of his physical appearance.

Over the years spent conducting research on Lincoln's life for several books (including the only cradle-to-grave, multi-volume biography of the sixteenth president by a professionally trained historian),[11] I have stumbled across unknown or unrecognized original sources that proved useful for my work and that I have made available in scholarly documentary editions.[12] Some of them are, like the present volume, fuller versions of previously published works to which I added new original material. Among those are William O. Stoddard, *Inside the White House in War-Times;*[13] Jesse W. Weik, *The Real Lincoln: A Portrait;*[14] Walter B. Stevens, *A Reporter's Lincoln;*[15] John Hay, *Lincoln and the Civil War in the Diaries and Letters of John Hay;*[16] and Henry Villard, *Lincoln on the Eve of '61: A Journalist's Story.*[17] When I realized the importance of *Lincoln the Citizen,* I not only incorporated into *Abraham Lincoln: A Life* many things described therein by Whitney but I also resolved to edit the present volume as yet another contribution to the original-source Lincoln literature, a project that began as a spinoff of my first book, *The Inner World of Abraham Lincoln* (Urbana: University of Illinois Press, 1994). When I began work on that volume forty years ago, I had assumed that I could offer no new facts about Lincoln but would present fresh interpretations of familiar material. To my astonishment, I discovered much new information about Lincoln at repositories in Washington, Springfield, Providence, and elsewhere, including Harrogate, Tennessee, home of Lincoln Memorial University, whose library houses a valuable collection of Lincolniana, including Whitney's handwritten manuscript of *Lincoln the Citizen*.

In addition to valuable information not found elsewhere, Whitney's biography offers some psychological insights in its poignant depiction of Lincoln as a man of sorrows. For instance, in accounting for Lincoln's fondness for lugubrious poetry like Oliver Wendell Holmes's "The Last Leaf," Whitney plausibly suggests that such verse brought back painful memories "of the grave [of his mother] at Gentryville or of that [of Ann Rutledge] in the bend of the Sangamo." Those deaths also predisposed him to depression throughout his life.[18] Elsewhere, Whitney also shrewdly commented on the importance of Lincoln's marriage, speculating plausibly that thanks to his many years of dealing with such a difficult, imperious wife as Mary Todd, the long-suffering Lincoln developed preternatural patience and forbearance. Such "domestic discipline" equipped him well to cope with the challenges he faced as president: "we find the great emancipator possessed of an equanimity and patience, which captivated the masses, while it tired out petulant grumblers, like [Horace] Greeley, [Wendell] Phillips, etc., which enabled him to force unwelcome policies on his cabinet, on Congress and on the nation; which allowed him to bear his 'faculties with meekness,' and finally to restore peace to his bleeding country, and give physical freedom to the blacks and political freedom to the whites. Had [President] Andy Johnson, with his unbridled temper, attempted this, he would not have got through the first year of the war, and but for the domestic discipline which Mr. Lincoln underwent, he too might have failed as signally. That the nation is largely indebted to Mary Todd Lincoln for its autonomy, I do not doubt."[19]

Born in Detroit, Maine, in 1831, Whitney received a classical education (which he flaunts in these pages) at colleges in Kentucky and Ohio. Though twenty-two years younger than Lincoln, he became his "intimate and close friend" starting in 1854, when the two men first met in Urbana, the small Illinois town where Whitney settled that year. It "seemed as if he wooed me to close intimacy and familiarity, at once," Whitney recalled.[20] They were colleagues at the bar as well as political allies, participating together in seventy-one cases, usually representing the same clients (most often the Illinois Central Railroad).[21] Whitney was therefore well positioned to describe Lincoln's life between 1854 and 1861 with the authority of a contemporary witness. As he wrote in a passage of the manuscript omitted by editor Miller, "I have had the pleasure . . . of intimate association with Mr. Lincoln in every sort of primitive and humble condition in village inns—in wayside farm houses—in village country taverns, . . . in rude courthouses, at country mass-meetings, at picnic dinners, and I have associated with him at the White House when the cares of the nation were pressing him sorely."[22] Elsewhere, Whitney wrote of Lincoln: "I traveled the circuit with him for seven years and was constantly with him, sleeping or waking, for five months in each year."[23] In 1887, Whitney asserted that "I remember a great deal about Lincoln and shall never forget it: and I have an idea . . . that Lincoln confided his opinions about men to me more fully than he did to most of his friends." He added: "I suppose even such gossip as I could narrate would be quite acceptable to the public."[24] In addition to opinions about contemporaries, Lincoln shared his sorrows with Whitney, who in the present volume reports that once "on the steps of the War Department, he confided one of his minor sorrows to me to secure my sympathy apparently. I tried to make him relinquish it; he listened assentingly to my casuistry, but dismissed the subject with the conclusion, 'I know all that as well as you do, but I can't get over it.' And he turned sadly away."

Whitney was not the only fellow attorney to whom Lincoln spoke of his sorrows. Even though Lincoln was notoriously "shut-mouthed" about his private life, Orville H. Browning recalled that during the Civil War the president often told him "about his domestic troubles" and "that he was constantly under great apprehension lest his wife should do something which would bring him into disgrace."[25] Similarly, Lincoln was in all likelihood the source for the following interpretation of Mrs. Lincoln's behavior reported in this volume: Lincoln had agreed to run for a seat in the Illinois General Assembly in 1854, hoping thereby to boost the candidacy of his friend Richard Yates, then seeking reelection as a congressman.[26] When Mary Lincoln saw her husband's name listed in a newspaper as a candidate for the State House of Representatives, she instructed the paper's editor to remove his name. That was done, prompting Lincoln's friend William Jayne to ask him to restore his name to the slate of candidates. When making that appeal, Jayne found Lincoln deeply upset: "I went to see him in order to get his consent to run. This was at his home. He was then the saddest man I ever saw—the gloomiest. He walked up and down the floor almost crying, and to all my persuasions to let his name stand in the paper, he said, 'No, I can't; you don't know all. I say you don't begin to know one-half, and that's enough.' I did go, however, and have his name reinstated."[27] The explanation for Lincoln's distress, according to Whitney, was his wife's behavior: "It is scarcely necessary to say that it was Mrs. Lincoln's opposition which so much disturbed him. *She* insisted in her imperious way that he must now go to the United States Senate, and that it was a degradation to run him for the legislature." According to Whitney, Lincoln sought high elective office "to gratify his ambitious wife."[28] Whitney does not identify the source for his assertion, but it may well have been Lincoln himself.

As Mark E. Neely observed apropos of *Life on the Circuit with Lincoln*, "for the years 1854 to 1861, when Whitney repeatedly saw Lincoln, his memory produced many rich, and original anecdotes" that "gave an authentic flavor of life on the Eighth Judicial Circuit and believable appraisals of Lincoln's lawyerly and personal manner available nowhere else."[29] That description also fits *Lincoln the Citizen*, which contains much more than gossip, for Whitney reported not only what he knew firsthand about Lincoln between 1854 and 1861 but also—and most importantly—what Lincoln shared about his pre-1854 life. In addition, Whitney included information gleaned from some of the sixteenth president's other friends and political allies, including Robert L. Wilson, William G. Greene, Parthena Nance Hill, James Matheny, Jesse K. Dubois, Alexander Sympson, William D. Somers, and Henry L. Webb.

It was not unprecedented for Lincoln to reminisce with fellow attorneys as they traversed Illinois's Eighth Judicial Circuit. In 1853, while he and Leonard Swett were riding from Clinton toward Champaign, Lincoln regaled his companion with the story of his early life.[30] Around that same time he confided to William H. Herndon revelations about his mother as they made their way from Springfield to Petersburg.[31]

Whitney related in *Life on the Circuit* that "I was with Lincoln upon terms of the closest intimacy" when in May 1856 they were traveling together toward Bloomington. While laying over in Decatur, they wandered about town, halting before the courthouse, where Lincoln said, partly to himself and partly to Whitney: "Here is the exact spot where I stood by our wagon when we moved from Indiana twenty-six years ago." In a nostalgic mood, Lincoln went on to describe "his early adventures in both Macon and Sangamon counties, the Hanks family, etc.; also his early struggles in life."[32] (In addition, Whitney informed a genealogist that Lincoln "told me much of his kinfolk.")[33]

In *Lincoln the Citizen*, Whitney poignantly recounted some of those early struggles as well as subsequent ones in his friend's "melancholy journey of life," a "solemn and sober procession" across which "lay shadows, sometimes baleful, always gloomy."[34] For the most part, Lincoln's "inner life was a blank, dreary desert of sorrow," making him "an extremely sad and melancholy man." Within "the realms of his diseased fancy, the heavens were always hung in funereal black." In a paragraph omitted by editor Miller, Whitney wrote that such sorrow was especially acute during "three eras of unusual hardship and misery." The first was "the period between the death of his mother [in 1818] and the arrival of [his stepmother] Sallie Bush Lincoln in the wretched house [in 1819]. Misery more abject, childish grief more poignant, privation more pronounced than presided over that rude Indiana home without a mother it would be difficult to conceive." The second "era of more than normal misery was the first year in Illinois [1830]." Finally, in 1835 there was a period of acute depression following "the premature death of Ann Rutledge," his sweetheart.

Whitney's portrayal of Lincoln's childhood, youth, and adolescence tracks closely the one depicted in *Herndon's Lincoln*: "Many of our great men and our statesmen, it is true, have been self-made, rising gradually through struggles to the topmost round of the ladder; but Lincoln rose from a lower depth than any of them from a stagnant, putrid pool, like the gas which, set on fire by its own energy and self-combustible nature, rises in jets, blazing, clear, and bright."[35] That negative, downbeat interpretation of Lincoln's early life has been termed the "dung hill thesis" as opposed to the more positive, upbeat "chin-fly thesis."[36] Champions of the former include Herndon and Albert J. Beveridge, while the latter interpretation was popularized by Carl Sandberg and Ida Tarbell. Modern scholarship has confirmed the soundness of the former school of thought.[37] Similarly, Whitney's generally unflattering depiction of Lincoln's father Thomas is supported by abundant evidence unearthed recently.[38] (In a passage deleted by editor Miller, Whitney wrote of Thomas: "From his father, he [Abraham] only obtained the boon of *being*. From him he inherited only 'infancy, ignorance, and indigence.'")[39] Despite the painstaking research conducted by modern scholars, some authors continue defending Thomas Lincoln as if portraying him unfavorably constituted a "legend that libels Lincoln."[40]

To William Herndon's coauthor, Jesse W. Weik, Whitney expressed skepticism about the reliability of some Lincoln reminiscences: "I notice that often men with quite as good a capacity as I had to acquire information cannot narrate it either from treacherous memories[,] inattention[,] or some other cause."[41] But Whitney's own trustworthiness as a source has been challenged.[42] "Like many other recollective writers," Don E. Fehrenbacher and Virginia Fehrenbacher noted, "Whitney tended to exaggerate the degree of his intimacy with Lincoln, and to remember past events with mingled accuracy and inaccuracy."[43] Paul M. Angle, one of the most thoughtful of Whitney's critics, cited among other things his implausible version of Lincoln's 1856 "lost speech."[44] Whitney claimed that he reconstituted it from notes he had purportedly taken forty years earlier, but his version of the speech tellingly does not jibe with two brief contemporary press accounts, which report that Lincoln addressed topics unmentioned in Whitney's version.[45] The skeptical John G. Nicolay noted that the speech as restored by Whitney contains anachronistic references to events that took place after 1856 and that Whitney did not mention in *Life on the Circuit with Lincoln* that he had made notes of the Bloomington speech.[46] Many men present at the 1856 convention where Lincoln delivered that speech pooh-poohed Whitney's version. Moreover, that reconstruction "contains a number of assertions which it is difficult to believe were actually uttered by him," as Angle noted.[47]

One such assertion dealt with racial equality, a subject Lincoln treated cautiously, never stating that he thought African American people were inferior to White people except in one respect—color—by which he evidently meant to satirize bigots. He did not say or write anything resembling a statement that Whitney alleged he made in the speech: "the government was made by white men, and they were and are the superior race. This I admit."[48] To the contrary, Lincoln opened the campaign of 1858 against Stephen A. Douglas with a ringing endorsement of racial egalitarianism: "Let us discard all this quibbling about this man and the other man, this race and that race and the other race being inferior, and therefore they must be placed in an inferior position. . . . Let us discard all these things, and unite as one people throughout this land, until we shall once more stand up declaring that all men are created equal."[49] Moreover, time and again Lincoln emphatically rejected Douglas's contention that the American government was made by and for White men.

Whitney also misrepresented Lincoln's racial views in *Lincoln the Citizen*, where he alleged that his friend entertained "no feelings of philanthropy toward the black race."[50] (In *Life on the Circuit with Lincoln*, he made a similar observation: "On the vital subject of providing for the negro, his mind was beclouded with anxiety . . . ; he had great faith and unlimited confidence in his own race; but he rated the negro at his worth, and by the Ethiopian record of thousands of years."[51]) In fact, Lincoln felt deep empathy for African Americans and, as Frederick Douglass observed, he "was the first American President who . . . rose above the prejudices of his times, and country."[52] In an 1855 letter to his best friend, Joshua Speed, Lincoln articulated his compassion for African Americans. Calling himself one "who abhors the oppression of negroes," he expressed revulsion for the way that escaping slaves were treated: "I hate to see the poor creatures hunted down, and caught, and carried back to their stripes, and unrewarded toils." (*Hate* was a word Lincoln seldom employed to describe his feelings.) He reminded Speed of a river journey they had taken fourteen years earlier: "In 1841 you and I had together a tedious low-water trip, on a Steam Boat from Louisville to St. Louis. You may remember, as I well do, that from Louisville to the mouth of the Ohio there were, on board, ten or a dozen slaves, shackled together with irons. That sight was a continual torment to me; and I see something like it every time I touch the Ohio, or any other slave-border. It is hardly fair for you to assume, that I have no interest in a thing which has, and continually exercises, the power of making me miserable."[53]

Whitney wrongly attributed to Lincoln his own racist views as revealed in the manuscript of *Lincoln the President*, issued in 1908 as the companion volume to *Lincoln the Citizen*. There Whitney devoted an entire chapter to the supposed inferiority of Black people, arguing that innumerable studies showed how "the Ethiopian, the Congo, Kaffir, Hottentot and negro are alike, savages and barbarians; and, that, left to themselves, they make no progress toward civilization; and that even when semi-civilized by attrition [i.e., association] with other races, when this attrition ceases, the barbarian instinct commences to make inroads on the instilled and adventitious civilization, and ultimately regains the hunt, the jungle and the human sacrifice."[54] Whitney quoted from many sources at great length to clinch his argument. (Such blatantly racist passages do not appear in the published version of *Lincoln the President*.)

In *Life on the Circuit with Lincoln*, Whitney viewed race relations through the lens of Social Darwinism: "The law of the survival of the fittest is a providential and unerring decree, and while the negro and his partisans clamor and make the universe vocal with complaints, and for laws to make him equal to the white, they will yet learn that the only vital right which either the white or black man is entitled to at the hands of society is (as Lincoln puts it) a *'right to be the equal of every other man';*[55] and that nothing but effort and achievements will place the negro on the same moral and social plane with the Caucasian; and the sooner he follows the example of the white man, and works six days in the week, instead of five; the sooner he does honest work instead of seeking to eke out the hours in semi-idleness; the sooner he leaves off his political aspirations for which he is not, by the cast and structure of his mind, or his education, adapted; the sooner he abandons the idea of obtaining forty acres and a mule without earning them, the nearer will he be to a condition of self-support and independence."[56]

Moreover, Whitney's treatment of Lincoln's marriage is contradicted by what he told William Herndon about that subject. In *Lincoln the Citizen* he maintained that "no man thought more of his wife" than he did, and in *Life on the Circuit with Lincoln*, he claimed that "Lincoln thoroughly loved his wife." He added that it "is rare that a man so thoroughly intellectual as Mr. Lincoln, makes a good husband, but there was no flaw in his conduct in this respect."[57] Yet Whitney insisted to Herndon that Lincoln was a poor husband: "so great & peculiar a man as Lincoln could not make any woman happy," for "he was too much allied to his intellect to get down to the plane of the domestic relations." Whitney went on to speculate that "Lincoln would have greatly enjoyed married life if he had [wed?] either Ann Rutledge or Miss [Matilda] Edwards. I think he would have been very fond of a wife" if "he had one to suit."[58]

These inconsistencies cast doubt on Whitney's reliability, but, as Paul Angle noted apropos of *Life on the Circuit with Lincoln*, "much of Whitney's book compels acceptance," for it is "surprisingly accurate."[59] The same could be said of *Lincoln the Citizen*. Its portrayal of Lincoln's life as a sad one, especially in his early years, rings true, given what the sixteenth president said

Introduction xix

about himself and about happiness in general. According to his close friend Joseph Gillespie, he "felt very strongly that there was more of discomfort than real happiness in human existence under the most favorable circumstances."[60] A Springfield neighbor heard Lincoln declare, "I have seen a good deal of the back side of this world."[61] Mary Lincoln's dressmaker, Elizabeth Keckly, who observed Lincoln closely during his presidency, told a journalist about his state of mind just before the assassination: "I know, and I know it well, that so unhappy was that great man, so tired of life and its burdens, that if he could have expressed an opinion concerning the work of the assassin, he would have said: 'I am glad that it is all over.' He was always ready for death, and I knew him so well that I have always felt that death was welcome to him when it came."[62]

Whitney's fellow circuit-riding attorney and good friend Leonard Swett offered a markedly different version of Lincoln's early years. In 1853, the future president allegedly told Swett that he had enjoyed a "happy childhood."[63] But Swett's report of that conversation clashes with Lincoln's own writings and his conversations with Whitney and other friends like Joseph Gillespie, William Herndon, and John Locke Scripps, as well as with the recollections of Springfield neighbors, among them Noyes Miner, and relatives, including John Hanks, Sophie Hanks, Dennis Hanks, and John J. Hall.[64] Moreover, in another version of that 1853 conversation, Swett does not mention Lincoln's purported assertion that his childhood was "happy."[65] In addition, Swett's account contains errors that undermine its credibility.[66] Nonetheless, some biographers still mistakenly claim that Lincoln's youth was a happy one.[67]

Whitney's claim that at Decatur in 1856 he heard Lincoln reminisce about his life is supported by the account of a fellow townsman, Joseph O. Cunningham,[68] who later wrote: "The afternoon was spent by Mr. Lincoln in sauntering about the town [of Decatur] and in talking of his early experiences there twenty-five years before."[69]

Much of what Whitney relates about Lincoln's "early adventures in both Macon and Sangamon counties, the Hanks family, etc.; also his early struggles in life," as well as about Lincoln's legal career and political activity between 1854 and 1861, constitutes high-grade ore for the historian's smelter as well as an intimate portrait of the sixteenth president. Many other passages contain information not found in other sources and may well be equally valuable contributions to the biographical record. Readers may judge for themselves what parts of Whitney's account of Lincoln's pre-1854 life report what Lincoln confided to him, what is based on previously published sources, and what Whitney may have invented.

Also noteworthy is Whitney's character sketch of Lincoln, whom he regarded as "one of the most interesting men I ever saw," someone who "had no envy, malice, or spite—no ill-feeling of any kind toward anybody." Lincoln "was deferential but not obsequious; he made no sarcastic remarks and made no one a butt for an ill-natured joke. He employed no social tyranny to one in his power; he had no angularity except physically; . . . was generous and forgiving to a fault. He was not only sincere and candid, but he assured you by his conduct that he was so; his actions towards men symbolized his belief that the greatest of the social virtues was charity." On the legal circuit, some attorneys "seemed to consider that the dignity of the profession required that they should erect some sort of a social fence or barrier between themselves and the masses that we would meet, but there was none of this attempt at exclusiveness with Lincoln." It was not uncommon "to see him, while court was engaged in something which did not concern him, sitting on a store box on the sidewalk either entertaining, or being entertained by, some of our villagers, nor was there any affectation or demagogical art in this; it was in accordance with his plain, unaffected, undramatic style."

Whitney is especially informative about Lincoln's shyness and awkwardness around women. As he recalled, Lincoln was "extremely bashful" and shunned "the society of females with the greatest particularity." As a young man in New Salem, "he avoided waiting on women at the stores or meeting them casually. Once a family of ladies stopped at the hotel while he was a boarder there, and he failed to appear at the public table while they were there." Later, as a circuit lawyer, he "shone resplendently in an association . . . with men, but not in a general company, which likewise included the fair sex." Now and then on the circuit, "we would be invited out to some social gatherings, and sometimes we would force Lincoln along." On those occasions "he would be ill at ease," for the "presence of females he was not familiar with abashed him extraordinarily, especially if they had on extra frills or tuckers."

Also noteworthy is Whitney's assessment of Lincoln as a lawyer who "was preeminently a man of peace," one who "discountenanced all litigation" rooted in "vengeance or ill feeling." He "favored all compromises" but "fought to the bitter end all contested cases not susceptible of accommodation." His strength "lay in his analytical and reasoning faculties," for he possessed a powerful logical mind, honed by his study of Euclid's geometry. He "showed great analytical skill" and a marked "ability to separate important and controlling matters from those which were secondary."

Above all, Lincoln as a lawyer sought "to achieve justice, equity, and fair dealing by the shortest and least embarrassed mode." He "abhorred that style of practice which attributed unworthy motives to an adversary or enforced technicalities to the exclusion of justice." In preparing a case, "he gave little attention to technicalities," for his "guiding star was not expediency but principle," not "technicalities but right and equity."

Introduction xxi

Whitney described himself unfavorably at the time he began working with Lincoln. "I was an extremely poor and careless lawyer" who "often drew down upon myself the reproofs of older colleagues, but never from Lincoln." In their many joint efforts at the bar, Lincoln "did the best he could for the case in hand, *plus* the difficulty caused by my affirmatively bad management."

But Lincoln too had weaknesses that led Whitney to call him "an uneven lawyer" who "was not well grounded in the principles of law" or "well-read" in legal literature. Lincoln was, in sum, "not great" and "made no pretensions to anything beyond circuit court ability." Within that narrow realm, however, he excelled, attaining success largely because of his "candor and honesty." All things considered, Lincoln "had probably only one superior as a lawyer in our circuit, viz.: Stephen T. Logan."

This expanded version of *Lincoln the Citizen* is a further contribution to the University of Illinois Press's landmark series of scholarly editions of Lincoln reminiscences. Meticulously edited by Knox College professors Douglas L. Wilson and Rodney O. Davis, those editions include the indispensable 827-page compilation, *Herndon's Informants: Letters, Interviews, and Statements about Abraham Lincoln*; the classic biography, *Herndon's Lincoln* (which *Lincoln the Citizen* neatly complements); and *Herndon on Lincoln: Letters*.[70] They form part of the press's larger series generated by the Knox College Lincoln Studies Center, whose valuable work, thus far so nobly advanced, is being carried on by the Center for Lincoln Studies at the University of Illinois Springfield.

Michael Burlingame
May 2024

NOTES

1. Paul M. Angle's introduction to Henry Clay Whitney, *Life on the Circuit with Lincoln, with Sketches of Generals Grant, Sherman and McClellan, Judge Davis, Leonard Swett, and Other Contemporaries* (1892; Caldwell, Idaho: Caxton Printers, 1940), 20. For an overview of Whitney's connection with Lincoln, see Benjamin P. Thomas, *Portrait for Posterity: Lincoln and His Biographers* (New Brunswick, NJ: Rutgers University Press, 1947), 165–77.

2. New York: Oxford University Press, 1994.

3. Nashville: Cumberland House, 2003.

4. Guilford, CT: Stackpole Books, 2021.

5. New Brunswick, NJ: Rutgers University Press, 1947.

6. Neely, *The Abraham Lincoln Encyclopedia* (New York: McGraw-Hill, 1982), 335–36.

7. Some of the material in the earlier portion of *Lincoln the Citizen* is clearly based on previous biographies (especially those by Herndon and Ward Hill Lamon),

xxii *Introduction*

though much of it may well be based on what Lincoln told Whitney. Moreover, some (but not all) of the chapter on Lincoln's law career repeats information that had first appeared in *Life on the Circuit with Lincoln*. In the present volume, Whitney occasionally refers the reader to that earlier work.

8. Henry Clay Whitney, *Lincoln the Citizen: February 12, 1809 to March 4, 1861*, vol. 1 of *The Centenary Edition of the Life and Works of Abraham Lincoln*, ed. Marion Mills Miller (9 vols.; New York: Current Literature Publishing, 1907). It was republished a year later as a separate work by the New York firm of Baker & Taylor, along with a companion volume, *Lincoln the President*, which is based almost entirely on secondary accounts and thus does not qualify as an original source. (Whitney last saw Lincoln in October 1861.) Together those two books were titled *A Life of Lincoln*.

9. Whitney, *Lincoln the Citizen*, viii.

10. Thomas, *Portrait for Posterity*, 165.

11. *Abraham Lincoln: A Life* (2 vols.; Baltimore: Johns Hopkins University Press, 2008).

12. Most notably, they include writings by Lincoln's three principal White House secretaries: John Hay's complete Civil War diary, his unpublished letters and essays, and his unknown pseudonymous journalism datelined Washington during the war; John G. Nicolay's interviews with people who knew Lincoln, his letters to his fiancée written from the White House, and his unpublished essays about Lincoln; and William O. Stoddard's uncollected recollections appearing in a newspaper shortly after the war as well as his many dispatches written from the White House for the *New York Examiner*.

13. Stoddard, *Inside the White House in War Times: Memoirs and Reports of Lincoln's Secretary* (1890; Lincoln: University of Nebraska Press, 2000).

14. Weik, *The Real Lincoln: A Portrait* (1922; Lincoln: University of Nebraska Press, 2002).

15. Stevens, *A Reporter's Lincoln* (1916; Lincoln: University of Nebraska Press, 1998).

16. Tyler Dennett, ed., *Lincoln and the Civil War in the Diaries and Letters of John Hay* (New York: Dodd, Mead & Company, 1939). I published the diary and letters as separate volumes: *Inside Lincoln's White House: The Complete Civil War Diary of John Hay, 1861–1864*, co-edited by John R. Turner Ettlinger (Carbondale: Southern Illinois University Press, 1997); *At Lincoln's Side: John Hay's Civil War Correspondence and Selected Writings* (Carbondale: Southern Illinois University Press, 2000).

17. Villard, *Lincoln on the Eve of '61: A Journalist's Story*, ed. Harold G. & Oswald Garrison Villard (New York: A. A. Knopf, 1941). I published a version of Villard's dispatches appearing not only in the New York *Herald* but also in the Cincinnati *Commercial* and the San Francisco *Bulletin: Sixteenth President-in-Waiting: Abraham Lincoln and the Springfield Dispatches of Henry Villard, 1860–1861* (Carbondale: Southern Illinois University Press, 2018).

18. Burlingame, *The Inner World of Abraham Lincoln* (Urbana: University of Illinois Press, 1994), 92–113.

Introduction   **xxiii**

19. Whitney, *Life on the Circuit with Lincoln, with Sketches of Generals Grant, Sherman and McClellan, Judge Davis, Leonard Swett, and Other Contemporaries* (Boston: Estes and Lauriat, 1892), 99. When citing this work, I refer to this 1892 original edition except when referring to Paul M. Angle's introduction in the edition he edited.

20. Whitney, *Life on the Circuit with Lincoln*, 31.

21. John A. Lupton, "Abraham Lincoln and His Informal Partners on the Eighth Judicial Circuit," *Lincoln and His Contemporaries: Papers from the Fourteenth Annual Lincoln Colloquium, Springfield, 1999* (Springfield: Lincoln Home, n.d.), 97–98.

22. This is from a loose page filed with the text of what became *Lincoln the Citizen* but which may have been intended for inclusion in *Lincoln the President*.

23. Undated manuscript by Whitney pitching several possible magazine articles, Whitney Collection, New York Public Library. The editors rejected his proposals. Whitney was so disappointed at the lack of financial success he enjoyed with his Lincoln writings that he "was sorry that he 'ever invested' in the Lincoln business." Neely, *Lincoln Encyclopedia*, 336.

24. Whitney to Jesse W. Weik, Chicago, 17 September 1887, *Herndon's Informants: Letters, Interviews, and Statements about Abraham Lincoln*, ed. Douglas L. Wilson and Rodney O. Davis with the assistance of Terry Wilson (Urbana: University of Illinois Press for the Knox College Lincoln Studies Center, 1998), 643.

25. Browning interviewed by John G. Nicolay, Springfield, 17 June 1875, in Michael Burlingame, ed., *An Oral History of Abraham Lincoln: John G. Nicolay's Interviews and Essays* (Carbondale: Southern Illinois University Press, 1996), 3.

26. Lincoln's friend Richard Yates (1818–1873) of Jacksonville represented his district in the U.S. House of Representatives (1851–1855) and served as governor of Illinois during the Civil War.

27. Wilson and Davis, *Herndon's Informants*, 266.

28. Whitney, *Life on the Circuit with Lincoln*, 65.

29. Neely, *Lincoln Encyclopedia*, 335.

30. Leonard Swett, "Lincoln's Story of His Own Life," in Allen Thorndike Rice, ed., *Reminiscences of Abraham Lincoln by Distinguished Men of His Time* (New York: North American Review, 1886), 467–80.

31. Herndon to Ward Hill Lamon, Springfield, 6 March 1870, Douglas L. Wilson and Rodney O. Davis, eds., *Herndon on Lincoln: Letters* (Urbana: University of Illinois Press for the Knox College Lincoln Studies Center, 2016), 100.

32. Whitney, *Life on the Circuit with Lincoln*, 19, 73, 74.

33. Whitney to Caroline Hanks Hitchcock, n.p., 17 January 1895, copied in "Hanks Family Notes," vol. 1, p. 102, unpublished typescript, Hanks Family Papers, New England Historic Genealogical Society, Boston.

34. These observations appear in a passage omitted from the published 1907 version.

35. William H. Herndon and Jesse W. Weik, *Herndon's Lincoln*, ed. Douglas L. Wilson and Rodney O. Davis (1889; Urbana: University of Illinois Press for the Knox College Lincoln Studies Center, 2006), 4.

xxiv *Introduction*

36. Mark E. Neely Jr., "Escape from the Frontier: Lincoln's Peculiar Relationship with Indiana" (booklet; Fort Wayne, Indiana: Lincoln National Life Insurance Company, 1983). The term is based on Ida Tarbell's observation: "The horse, the dog, the ox, the chin fly, the plow, the hog, these companions of his youth became interpreters of his meaning, solvers of his problems in his great necessity of making men understand and follow him." Tarbell, *In the Footsteps of the Lincolns* (New York: Harper, 1924), 137.

37. Neely, "Escape from the Frontier" and Michael Burlingame, *Abraham Lincoln: A Life* (2 vols.; Baltimore: Johns Hopkins University Press, 2008), 1:1–51.

38. Wayne C. Temple, "Thomas and Abraham Lincoln as Farmers" (booklet; Racine, Wisconsin: Lincoln Fellowship of Wisconsin, 1996); John Y. Simon, "House Divided: Lincoln and His Father" (booklet; Fort Wayne, Indiana: Louis A. Warren Lincoln Library and Museum, 1987); Rodney O. Davis, "Abraham Lincoln: Son and Father" (booklet; Galesburg, Illinois: Knox College, 1997); Burlingame, *Inner World of Lincoln,* 20–42.

39. The words quoted by Whitney are from Henry Clay's description of his own paternal inheritance, uttered during a congressional debate, where in response to criticism by Senator John Randolph, Clay had said: "I was born to no proud patrimonial estate; from my father I inherited only infancy, ignorance, and indigence." Calvin Colton, ed., *Works of Henry Clay* (7 vols.; New York: Henry Clay Publishing Co., 1897), 1:45.

40. Montgomery S. Lewis, *Legends That Libel Lincoln* (New York: Rinehart, 1946), 36–84; Charles and Mary Coleman, *Thomas Lincoln: Father of the Sixteenth President* (Bloomington, IN: iUniverse, 2015); Richard E. Hart, *Thomas Lincoln Reconsidered* (Springfield, IL: privately printed, 2021).

41. Wilson and Davis, *Herndon's Informants*, 643.

42. David W. Hill, "Henry Clay Whitney: A Reliable Source for Lincoln Research?" *Lincoln Herald* 102 (2000): 177–84.

43. *Recollected Words of Abraham Lincoln*, ed. Don E. Fehrenbacher and Virginia Fehrenbacher (Stanford, CA: Stanford University Press, 1996), 490. The Lincoln quotes reproduced in that volume from *Lincoln the Citizen* all receive the Fehrenbachers' seal of semi-approval, a grade of C, which is awarded to "a quotation recorded noncontemproaneously," and not a D ("a quotation about whose authenticity there is more than average doubt") or an E ("a quotation that is probably not authentic").

44. That highly suspect version of Lincoln's May 29, 1856, speech was included in the nine-volume edition of Lincoln's works published in 1907, volume 1 of which was *Lincoln the Citizen.* The editors of the modern edition of Lincoln's works dismissed Whitney's reconstruction as not "worthy of serious consideration." Roy P. Basler et al., eds., *Collected Works of Abraham Lincoln* (8 vols. plus index; New Brunswick, NJ: Rutgers University Press, 1953–55), 2:34n. In the 1908 edition of *Lincoln the Citizen,* published by Baker & Taylor, the speech was incorporated as an appendix. It originally appeared as "Lincoln's Lost Speech," in the September 1896 issue of *McClure's Magazine*, whose editor paid Whitney $500 for it. For other reasons to doubt the authenticity of Whitney's version of the "lost speech," see

Elwell Crissey, *Lincoln's Lost Speech: The Pivot of His Career* (New York: Hawthorn Books, 1967), and Bill Kemp, "Rediscovery of Lost Speech Debunked," Bloomington, Illinois, *Pantagraph*, 17 July 2016.

45. "Lincoln's Lost Speech," *Bulletin of the Abraham Lincoln Association*, no. 21 (December 1930), 3–5; Belleville *Weekly Advocate*, 4 June 1856; Alton *Weekly Courier*, 5 June 1856.

46. Nicolay to Robert Underwood Johnson, Washington, 6 January 1897, "One Biographer about Another," *Abraham Lincoln Quarterly* 1 (1940): 161–62.

47. Angle's introduction to *Life on the Circuit with Lincoln*, 23–26.

48. Whitney, *Lincoln the President* (New York: Baker & Taylor, 1908), 334.

49. Basler, *Collected Works of Lincoln*, 2:501.

50. Whitney, *Lincoln the Citizen*, 28, 174.

51. *Life on the Circuit with Lincoln*, 398.

52. Frederick Douglass, eulogy for Lincoln, 1 June 1865, manuscript, Douglass Papers, Library of Congress. On Lincoln's empathy for African Americans, see Michael Burlingame, *The Black Man's President: Abraham Lincoln, African Americans, and the Pursuit of Racial Equality* (New York: Pegasus Books, 2021).

53. Basler, *Collected Works of Lincoln*, 2:320–323.

54. *Lincoln the President*, Chapter XVII, "The 'Bete Noir' of the Nation," manuscript, Lincoln Memorial University, Harrogate, Tennessee. Chapter XVIII repeats part of this material, expands on it somewhat, and contains a long, unflattering account of the role Black people played during the era of Reconstruction.

55. "We have, as all will agree, a free Government, where every man has a right to be equal with every other man." Basler, *Collected Works of Lincoln*, 7:505.

56. Whitney, *Life on the Circuit with Lincoln*, 339–40.

57. Whitney, *Life on the Circuit with Lincoln*, 97, 98.

58. Wilson and Davis, *Herndon's Informants*, 616, 617.

59. Angle's introduction to Whitney, *Life on the Circuit with Lincoln*, 28. Merrill D. Peterson, however, called *Life on the Circuit with Lincoln* "a book of rambling reminiscences, Herndonian in spirit, often unreliable, and virtually unreadable." Peterson, *Lincoln in American Memory*, 135.

60. Wilson and Davis, *Herndon's Informants*, 185.

61. Noyes Miner, "Personal Reminiscences of Lincoln," ed. James Cornelius, *Journal of the Abraham Lincoln Association* 44 (2023): 51.

62. Washington letter by Smith D. Fry, n.d., *Deming Herald* (New Mexico), 13 August 1901. This piece appeared in many other papers.

63. "Mr. Lincoln told this story as the story of a happy childhood. There was nothing sad nor pinched, and nothing of want, and no allusions to want, in any part of it. His own description of his youth was that of a joyous, happy boyhood. It was told with mirth and glee, and illustrated by pointed anecdote, often interrupted by his jocund laugh which echoed over the prairies. His biographers have given to his early life the spirit of suffering and want, and as one reads them, he feels like tossing him pennies for his relief. Mr. Lincoln gave no such description, nor is such description true. His was just such life as has always existed and now exists in the frontier States, and such boys are not suffering, but are rather like Whittier's

'Barefoot boy with cheeks of tan,' and I doubt not Mr. Lincoln in after-life would gladly have exchanged the pleasures of gratified ambition and of power for those hours of happy contentment and rest." Rice, ed., *Reminiscences of Lincoln*, 457.

64. These sources are extensively cited in Burlingame, *Lincoln: A Life*, 1:1–51.

65. Undated manuscript marked "Draft of Swett's Mr. Lincoln's story of his own life in A. T. Rice's Reminiscences of Abraham Lincoln (N.Y. 1888)," Swett Papers, Lincoln Presidential Library, Springfield.

66. On Swett's relations with Lincoln, see Robert S. Eckley, "Lincoln's Intimate Friend: Leonard Swett," *Journal of the Illinois State Historical Society* 92 (1999): 274–87; Eckley, *Lincoln's Forgotten Friend, Leonard Swett* (Carbondale: Southern Illinois University Press, 2012).

67. Lincoln "enjoyed a relatively happy Kentucky childhood." William W. Freehling, *Becoming Lincoln* (Charlottesville: University of Virginia Press, 2018).

68. Judge Joseph O. Cunningham (1839–1917) edited the Urbana *Union* in the 1850s and had a law practice for over four decades, starting in 1859.

69. Statement of J. O. Cunningham in Ezra M. Prince, ed., *Meeting of May 29, 1900 Commemorative of the Convention of May 29, 1856 That Organized the Republican Party in the State of Illinois* (Bloomington: Pantagraph, 1900), 91. Cunningham, who had accompanied Lincoln and Whitney on the trip, went on to say: "After a while he proposed going to the woods then a little way south or southwest of the village, in the Sangamon bottoms. His proposition was assented to and all went to the timber. A convenient log by the side of the road, in a patch of brush, afforded seats for the company, where the time was spent listening to the playful and familiar talks of Mr. Lincoln." Whitney does not mention that others in addition to himself heard Lincoln reminisce that day.

70. Wilson and Davis, *Herndon's Informants*; Wilson and Davis, *Herndon's Lincoln*; Wilson and Davis, *Herndon on Lincoln: Letters*. A second volume of *Herndon on Lincoln*, containing his lectures and other writings about his law partner, edited by the same scholars, is being completed by Matthew Norman. *Herndon's Lincoln* was entirely written by Jesse W. Weik, who made extensive use of information that Herndon had provided both orally and in writing, as well as the many other reminiscences that Herndon and Weik collected.

Editorial Method

The editor of *Lincoln the Citizen*, Marion Mills Miller, cut significant portions of Whitney's manuscript, which is preserved at Lincoln Memorial University in Harrogate, Tennessee. When that document went on sale, it was described as "written on one side of about 800 leaves, with numerous corrections, insertions, and annotations. A few leaves [are] either misplaced or missing" (*Lincoln Lore*, no. 735, 10 May 1943). Included in the present volume is the portion of the manuscript covering only Lincoln's pre-presidential life. (The other portion, of equal length, was published in 1908 as *Lincoln the President*, a companion volume to *Lincoln the Citizen*.)

The version in this book is a hybrid, reproducing the text of the 1907 work supplemented with passages deleted by Miller restored in **boldface**. Crossed-out passages in the manuscript have been added when they fit into the narrative and enhance it. Where appropriate, notes Whitney provided are incorporated into the text; otherwise, they are inserted as footnotes and identified as "Whitney's note." Other footnotes have been added by the present editor. When slight variations between the published version and the manuscript occur, the more readable version, in the present editor's judgment, has been chosen. Occasionally editor Miller misread the manuscript (e.g., giving "Hamlin" for "Hunter"). In such cases, the proper reading is silently substituted. Annotations identify, where possible, not only the many literary quotations and allusions liberally sprinkled throughout but also people and events mentioned in the text. Spelling errors (including proper names), as well as mistaken dates, have been silently corrected. Punctuation has been modernized for clarity. Documents that Whitney appended to the original manuscript are not included.

The chapter division has been retained with one exception: the manuscript contains a brief chapter, "The Romance of New Salem," that editor Miller awkwardly tacked on to the preceding chapter ("Lincoln as a Laborer"), which ends in the manuscript with a powerful crescendo, a striking passage omitted by Miller. In the interest of readability, "The Romance of New Salem" is reproduced here as a separate unit. So even though the present edition contains one more chapter than the 1907 volume, almost all of the information in that chapter appears in the book.

Lincoln the Citizen,
February 12, 1809 to March 4, 1861

I

Lineage, Parentage, and Childhood

"There is a child whom genius fires,
Whose every thought the god inspires."[1]

In the year 1622, in the then considerable, rudely built, and socially isolated city of Norwich, the shire town of Norfolk County, England, in one of the humble families, was born a child who, in due course of time received the baptismal appellation of Samuel Lincoln.[2]

During this same year [actually 1619], at Jamestown, a newly formed hamlet in the wilderness of North America, a vessel, in stress of want, cast anchor in the river, and offered in exchange for supplies, as their sole vendible property, sundry human chattels, which the lieutenant governor of the colony, then in command, chiefly from considerations of humanity to the destitute sailors, accepted, and the transaction was deemed of sufficient consequence to be thus jotted down in the sober chronicles of a town gossip: *"About the Last of August came in a Dutch man of warre that sold us twenty negars."*

The vessel, thus relieved, proceeded home; and, coincident with its arrival in Holland, an incident occurred in a neighboring harbor, which is thus narrated by the local historian:

1. "Is there a bard whom genius fires
Whose every thought the god inspires?"
John Gay (1685–1732), *Fable 28: The Persian, the Sun, and the Cloud* (*The Fables*, vol. 1, 1727).

2. Samuel Lincoln (1622–1690) was the president's great-great-great-great-grandfather, who left England in 1637 and settled in Hingham, Massachusetts Bay Colony. Much of what follows is inaccurate. For better accounts of Lincoln's ancestry, see William E. Barton, *The Lineage of Lincoln* (Indianapolis: Bobbs Merrill, 1929); James H. Lea and J. R. Hutchinson, *The Ancestry of Abraham Lincoln* (Boston: Houghton Mifflin, 1909); Waldo Lincoln, *History of the Lincoln Family: An Account of the Descendants of Samuel Lincoln, of Hingham, Massachusetts, 1637–1920* (Worcester, MA: Commonwealth Press, 1923).

2   *Chapter I*

*So they left that goodly and pleasant City of Leyden, which had been their resting place for above eleven years, but they knew that they were pilgrims and strangers here below, and looked not much on these things, but lifted up their eyes to Heaven. Their dearest Country where God had prepared for them a City (Heb. X I.16) and therein quieted their spirits. When they came to Delfs-Haven, they found the ship and all things ready and such of their friends as could not come with them, followed after them, and sundry came from Amsterdam to see them shipt, and to take their leave of them. One night was spent with little sleep with the most, but with friendly entertainment and Christian discourse, and other real expressions of true Christian love. The next day, they went on board and their friends with them, **where truly doleful was the sight of that sad and mournful parting, to hear what sighs and sobs and prayers did sound among them, what tears did gush from every eye, and pithy speeches pierced each other's heart that sundry of the Dutch strangers that stood on the Key as spectators could not refrain from tears**. But the tide (which stays for no man) calling them away that were thus loathe to depart, their reverend pastor falling down on his knees, and they all with him, with watery cheeks, commended them with most fervent prayers unto the Lord and his blessing; and then, with mutual embraces and many tears, they took their leave one of another, which proved to be the last leave to many of them.*

These several events did not appear to have any interrelation, but to be as remote in their moral as in their geographical association; but a retrospective glance reveals the truth that these incidents were acts in the same drama, cantos in the same epic, complementary in the moral world, the bane and antidote of the greatest moral offence of modern days.

When Samuel Lincoln attained the age of eighteen [actually fifteen], he joined in the migration to New England then rife, **and whose pioneers had shipped at Delfshaven**, and landed at Salem in Massachusetts, where he became an apprentice to Francis Lawes, a weaver, remaining until he attained his majority, when he shouldered his bundle and made his way on foot through the wilderness where now are Swampscott, Lynn, Chelsea, Boston, Braintree, and Quincy, to the hamlet of Hingham, which had been founded in the fall of 1635. In this same little hamlet, there was settled, in the year 1636, Thomas Lincoln, the miller; Thomas Lincoln, the cooper; and Thomas Lincoln, the weaver, the latter being a brother to Samuel; and in 1638, Thomas Lincoln, the farmer, and his brother Stephen, settled there. All came from Norfolk County, England; Thomas the weaver from Hingham; Samuel from Norwich; Thomas the farmer and Stephen from Windham.[3]

---

3. Whitney's footnote: "David J. Lincoln of Birdsboro, Pa., says that Abraham Lincoln's grandfather Mordecai emigrated from England to America. He gives no authority, however." David J. Lincoln (1816–1886) was the son of James Lincoln

A great-grandson of Thomas the cooper was Benjamin, a major general in the Revolutionary War, the same who received the surrender of Cornwallis at Yorktown, who also quelled Shays' rebellion in western Massachusetts in 1786, and to whom, when [Henry] Knox retired, was tendered the position of secretary of war in Washington's cabinet, which, however, he declined.[4] Another descendent of Samuel Lincoln was Levi Lincoln, who was a member of Congress and attorney general of the United States in Jefferson's cabinet from March 5, 1801, to December 23, 1805. President Madison appointed him a justice of the Supreme Court of the United States, but Lincoln was obliged to decline the appointment on account of a failure of his eyesight.[5] A son of this Lincoln was named Levi also. He filled many high offices, including that of governor of Massachusetts from 1825 to 1834, and member of Congress from 1835 to 1841, and was prominently mentioned **in responsible circles** as a candidate for president of the United States.[6] He had a brother Enoch, who was a member of Congress from 1818 to 1826, and governor of Maine from 1827 till his death.[7] These illustrious men were cousins of Abraham Lincoln in a remote degree. The similarity of their Hebraic names to those of the immediate ancestry of the president cannot fail to be noticed.

Samuel Lincoln had ten children, one of whom was Mordecai, who was born at Hingham in 1657 and became a blacksmith at Hull, where he married, and in 1704 removed to the neighboring town of Scituate, where he established a furnace for the smelting of ore. He was a man of substance and in his will bequeathed lands in both Hingham and Scituate, a saw- and grist-mill, iron works, and considerable money; he also made provision for a collegiate education for three grandsons.[8] Of his five children, Mordecai Jr., the eldest, removed from Scituate, where his eldest son John was born, to Monmouth County, New Jersey; and afterwards to Chester, Pennsylvania and Berks County in Pennsylvania in due succession.

(Among the "taxable" of Reading Pa. in 1757 is the name of Thomas Lincoln. In 1782, the names of Abraham Lincoln and Mordecai Lincoln are

---

(d. 1860), who stated that the president's great grandfather, known as Virginia John Lincoln, moved to Virginia after hearing Daniel Boone's favorable reports of conditions there. Birdsboro is located in Berks County, near Reading.

4. Benjamin Lincoln (1733–1810) actually did serve as secretary of war (1781–1783) as well as lieutenant governor of Massachusetts (1788–1789).

5. Levi Lincoln Sr. (1749–1820) represented a Massachusetts district in the U.S. House of Representatives (1800–1801).

6. Levi Lincoln Jr. (1782–1868) also served as the mayor of Worcester (1848–1849).

7. Enoch Lincoln (1788–1829) represented a district of Massachusetts and subsequently one of Maine in the U.S. House of Representatives (1818–1826).

8. Mordecai Lincoln (1657–1727) was known as "Mordeek."

among the "taxable." In Union Township, in Berks County, Pa., the name of John Lincoln is among the "taxable" in 1758. The plantation of Mordecai Lincoln was near the town of Exeter, in Berks County, Pennsylvania, and contained one thousand acres. One Abraham Lincoln was a representative in the legislature for the years 1782, 1783, 1784, and 1785. The Boone and Hanks families were the nearest neighbors to Mordecai Lincoln.)

The son John had five sons, named respectively John, Thomas, Abraham, Isaac, and Jacob, together with daughters. In 1758, he removed to the northern part of Augusta County, Virginia, which county was, in 1779, detached and joined to Rockingham County.

The son, Abraham, migrated to the northwest part of North Carolina, to the waters of the Catawba River, where he married Miss Mary Shipley,[9] by whom he had three several sons, named respectively Mordecai, Josiah, and Thomas; and, during or about the year 1780, emigrated with several families of the Berrys and Shipleys to Kentucky, which, though known as "the dark and bloody ground" by reason of the many Indian massacres, was at that time attracting much attention through reports of its extreme fertility **and picturesqueness** made by such explorers as [Daniel] Boone, [Simon] Kenton, and [William] Clark, the exploration of the former commencing in 1769.

There were eight families in all, and these, when they arrived to within twenty-five or thirty miles southeast of Crab Orchard, were attacked by Indians, and some of the party were wounded, and one woman taken prisoner. These immigrants settled in Jefferson and Washington Counties of Kentucky, but the specific settlement of Abraham Lincoln is somewhat obscured by doubt. One excellent biographer fixes the location in Mercer County, but his authority therefor does not appear. Several others, repeating each other, name Floyd's Creek in what is now known as Bullitt County, and, in point of fact, Abraham Lincoln did on May 29, 1780, enter five hundred acres of land on Long Run, a branch of Floyd's fork of Salt River, whence there is reason to suppose that upon that land he made his settlement. Hon. J[ames] L. Nall, a great-grandson of the pioneer and a grandson of his daughter Nancy [Lincoln],[10] who married William Brumfield,[11] avers that his ancestor settled at

---

9. He actually wed Bathsheba Herring (1748–1836), daughter of Alexander Herring and Abigail Harrison. They had seven children.

10. James Luther Nall (1830–1901) represented Hardin County in the Kentucky state legislature and eventually became a merchant in Carthage, Missouri. Louis A. Warren, "James L. Nall," *The Lincoln Kinsman* 44 (February 1942). Nall told W. H. Sweeney, a Louisville attorney: "What I have given you is tradition, handed down from generation to generation; but I am satisfied it is correct. I always took a great deal of pride in keeping posted in the genealogical history of my ancestors and got the above facts from my grandfather and grandmother, who were conversant with them,

the present site of Louisville and adduces in support of his statement the concurrent evidence of his great-grandmother, the wife of the pioneer, and who lived to the great age of one hundred and ten years, and of his grandmother and of his great-uncle, Mordecai Lincoln, all of whom **he remembers well, and all of whom** he has heard talk of the subject frequently.

After settling in Kentucky, there were added to his family two daughters, Mary, who afterward married Ralph Crume,[12] and Nancy, who thereafter married William Brumfield, and in 1784, while he was at work in the clearing, attended only by his youngest son Thomas, the father of the president, he was fatally shot by an Indian, who then attempted to kidnap the little boy. Just as he picked up little Thomas and was starting to make off with his prize, the eldest son Mordecai[13] shot and killed the savage, and so this boy was saved to become father of the president **from the horrors of Indian captivity. In a recent letter to me, Mr. Nall says: "and as to the place where my great-grandfather Abraham was killed, I well know there can be no mistake as to its being where the City of Louisville now stands. I have heard this matter talked over so often by my grandfather and grandmother, who certainly knew what they were talking about, that I was surprised when I heard that the matter was in dispute. My grandmother was in the fort at the time, though small, but remembered the circumstances. Great-uncle Mordecai killed the Indian who killed his father; he died after my recollection, and whenever the families of relatives got together, this thrilling matter was certain to come up. The great-grandfather Abraham was the father of Nancy, who married William Brumfield, who was father of Elizabeth, who married William P. Nall, who was father of the writer."**

At a later date, Mr. Nall thus writes: **"You ask me why my great grandfather's family was in a fort. It was because the Indians were very troublesome at that time (1782) in Ky., and all people had to live either in forts or blockhouses, for safety. The fort my great grandfather was in, and near which he was killed, was called 'Beargrass' Fort and was located near the junction of the Beargrass Creek with the Ohio River, where the city**

---

and with whom the President's grandmother lived and died." Nall was fifteen when his grandmother died in 1845 and twenty-seven when his grandfather died in 1857.

11. Nancy Lincoln, the younger sister of Thomas Lincoln, wed William Brumfield (1778–1858), who owned a large farm near Hardinsburg in Breckinridge County.

12. In 1801, Ralph Crume Jr. (1779–1832) wed Mary Lincoln, the elder sister of Thomas Lincoln.

13. Mordecai Lincoln (1771–1830), an uncle of President Lincoln, who "said that Uncle Mord had run off with all the talents of the family." Usher Linder, *Reminiscences of the Early Bar and Bench of Illinois* (Chicago: Chicago Legal News Company, 1879), 38–39.

of Louisville now stands. The creek there ran into the river much lower down than now, and the fort was near Main and First Streets which was the mouth of the creek."

There is a dispute about the location of the scene of the tragedy. Mr. Nall writes: "The newspaper article stating that my great grandfather Lincoln was killed on Lincoln's Run is altogether wrong; he was killed at 'Beargrass' Fort, as I got it directly from my grandmother, who was in the fort at the time and knew what she was talking about. While he lived in the fort, he entered four hundred acres of land in Floyd's fork of Salt River in what is now Bullitt County Kentucky. . . . My great grandmother, Mary Shipley Lincoln, moved with my grandfather, William Brumfield, who married her daughter Nancy, to Hardin County, Kentucky, and lived the balance of her long life with him, and died, when I was a good big boy, at the age of 110 [actually eighty-eight] years."[14]

The grandmother and great-grandmother were both present at this tragedy, which must have impressed itself deeply upon their minds. So likewise must it have been ever present to the mind of his grand-uncle, Mordecai, who was one of the chief actors in that frontier tragedy; and the writer of the above, a highly intelligent, and in all respects, honorable man, professes to have heard it often talked of in the family circle. Under ordinary circumstances this would be historically conclusive, and certainly as well attested as historical facts usually are, while nobody fixes authoritatively any different locality.[15]

As militating against the above theory is the following: Abraham Lincoln was killed in 1784. In May 1780, the town of Louisville was chartered by the Virginia legislature, and a tract of one thousand acres platted into half-acre lots, the boundaries of the thousand acres being First and Twelfth Streets, and Main and Chestnut Streets. A large number of the lots were immediately sold at auction, and in 1782, there were a hundred householders there, and in 1783, a general store was established. In 1782, a fort was erected and designated "Fort Nelson," but nowhere spoken of as the "Beargrass" Fort; and in all the histories of Louisville, which profess to include all the names of the early pioneers, no mention whatever is made of Abraham Lincoln **although the most elaborate of these histories, a large one, was not published until in the '70s.**

---

14. Whitney footnote: Mary Shipley Lincoln lived and died and was buried at old Mill Creek church after my recollection and I suppose I am the only living person that could find her grave at all!

15. Whitney footnote: S. Bernard Elliot of Pataskala, Ohio, deriving his information from a different source, locates the death of Abraham Lincoln Sr. at Beargrass Fort in the present site of Louisville, Ky.

Another negative is that although Abraham Lincoln himself mentions the fact of the tragedy, which he doubtless obtained from his father, he did not indicate the place, as he doubtless would have done, had it been Louisville.[16] Herndon says that he had often heard President Lincoln describe the tragedy as he had heard it from his father, but Louisville is not mentioned.

The locality of the fort, according to Mr. Nall, was at or about the extreme northeast corner of the town site of Louisville. The histories of Louisville make no mention of any necessity that the inhabitants should remove their families into a fort.

Indeed, in 1784, the date of the pioneer's death, a prosperous village of between 500 and 1000 inhabitants was located near the alleged site of the murder.

The Washington County *Herald* (Springfield, Kentucky), deriving its information from old citizens, fixes the site of the tragedy at "Lincoln's Run," about five miles northwest of Springfield. I incline to think this is correct, although I have great faith in Mr. Nall and his general accuracy about these matters.[17]

The mode of the senior Abraham's death, as understood by Mr. Herndon and Mr. Nall alike, was that he was at work in the clearing near to his cabin, attended by his youngest son Thomas, when an Indian crept up close in the shade of the forest and shot him, and that the little boy, stupefied, sat down beside the dead body, and that Mordecai, the eldest son, seeing the Indian approach the dead body, doubtless for purposes of robbery, took aim and shot him in the heart, while another account is that the Indian was carrying Thomas off, and was shot dead by Mordecai, while thus engaged.

At this time the Virginia law of primogeniture was in force, and the four hundred acres on Floyd's Creek became vested in Mordecai, the eldest son. The widow, with her three sons, Mordecai, Josiah, and Thomas, and two daughters, Mary and Nancy, removed to Washington County, and, settling on a creek which, from that circumstance, took the name of "Lincoln's Run," remained there till all the children reached the age of maturity.

Mordecai, as I was informed by President Lincoln himself, married a Miss Mudd, who belonged to one of the best families of Kentucky.[18] He afterwards became sheriff of Washington County and likewise represented the same

---

16. Basler, *Collected Works of Lincoln*, 3:511, 4:61.

17. The site of the fatal attack was evidently Long Run Road in the Eastwood neighborhood of Louisville.

18. In 1792, Mordecai wed Mary Mudd, daughter of Luke Mudd.

county in the legislature. He then removed to Grayson County, Kentucky, and ultimately to Hancock County, Illinois, where he died.[19] Josiah, the second of the name, removed early in life to Harrison County in southern Indiana, the second county east of that in which his brother Thomas afterwards settled, and there died.[20] The eldest daughter, Mary, married Ralph Crume in Washington County and removed to Breckinridge County in Kentucky, where they finally died. Nancy, the youngest daughter, married William Brumfield in Washington County, Kentucky, and thereafter removed to Hardin County, Kentucky, where they ultimately died.

The widow of Abraham Lincoln Sr. took up her abode with her youngest daughter, Nancy (Lincoln) Brumfield, and removed with her to Hardin County, Kentucky, where she died at the age of one hundred and ten years, being buried at Old Mill Creek burying ground. Mordecai's descendants I have no trace of, except Mrs. Levi Smith, who died a few years since near Springfield, Kentucky, **and** the Hon. J. L. Nall, a grandson of the youngest daughter, Nancy (Lincoln) Brumfield, has been a member of the Kentucky legislature and is now a merchant in southwestern Missouri. A granddaughter of the eldest sister, Mary (Lincoln) Crume, has been an intimate of Mr. Nall's family for thirty-six years past.

While Mr. Lincoln was a member of Congress in 1848, in reply to inquiries made as to his pedigree, he thus wrote to Hon. Solomon Lincoln of Hingham (since deceased):[21] "My Father's name was Thomas. My grandfather's was Abraham, the same as my own. My grandfather went from Rockingham County, in Virginia, to Kentucky about the year 1782, and two years afterwards was killed by the Indians. We have a vague tradition that my great-grandfather went from Pennsylvania to Virginia, and that he was a Quaker. Further than that, I have never heard anything. It may do no harm to say that Abraham and Mordecai are common names in our family."[22] And in a subsequent letter written during the same year, he says: "I have mentioned that my grandfather's name was Abraham. He had, as I think I have heard, four brothers, Isaac, Jacob, Thomas and John."[23] **(It will be seen that this**

19. Whitney footnote: "Old men who personally knew Mordecai said that he was a very smart man and exceedingly popular but was a sporting man and somewhat reckless." J. L. Nall.

20. In 1812, Josiah Lincoln (1773–1835) moved to Indiana, where he purchased a farm near Blue River Township. There he lived the rest of his life.

21. Solomon Lincoln (1804–1881) wrote a history of Hingham.

22. Basler, *Collected Works of Lincoln*, 1:456.

23. Basler, *Collected Works of Lincoln*, 1:459.

corresponds with the account furnished by Samuel Shackford.[24] It also agrees with the research of two others to whom I am indebted for my information. S. Bernard Elliot of Pataskala, Ohio, made a similar research and drew the same conclusion.)

Lineage Parentage and Childhood. Addenda

Through the kindness and courtesy of Mr. Samuel Shackford of Illinois, a descendant of Samuel Lincoln and thus a kinsman of President Lincoln, I append his valuable contribution to history on the important subject of the lineage of his distinguished relation, it being the most reliable and interesting paper extant on that subject.[25]

Thomas Lincoln, the youngest son, who was with his Father when the latter lost his life, was by this circumstance, as well as from the paucity of common schools, deprived of an opportunity to acquire an education, and never attended school in his entire life. The era of childhood was to him one of almost unrestrained liberty, privation, and adventure. He was born and spent his entire life on the frontier—**never saw a larger place than Vincennes, Indiana, a frontier village**; had no culture and was ignorant of the restraints and refinement of enlightened society. He was, however, a man of good native abilities and kindly instincts, but with no system, progress, or natural business qualities; hence he made but little provision for the future and took little thought of the morrow.

"To be content's his natural desire"[26]

William G. Greene, who spent one day with him,[27] and felt interested to make a study of him, avers that he was a man of great native reasoning powers and fine social magnetism, reminding him of his illustrious son; but that, having received no education, drill, or discipline, he knew nothing of

---

24. Samuel Shackford, "The Lineage of President Abraham Lincoln" (pamphlet; Chicago?: Shackford?, 1887, reprint of an article in the *New-England Historical and Genealogical Register*, April 1887). Shackford (1821–1908) was a Chicago businessman and genealogist.

25. Shackford, "The Lineage of President Abraham Lincoln." This item is not included in the present volume.

26. Alexander Pope, "An Essay on Man, Epistle 1: Of the Nature and State of Man, with Respect to the Universe."

27. William G. Greene Jr. (1812–1894) was known as "slicky Bill" because of his "sly schemes for making money, without working for it." He became a close friend of Lincoln in New Salem and later a successful businessman. In 1836, he visited

persistency of effort in a continuous line, nor of the laws of thrift or financial cause and effect; that he evidently was industrious, though shifting rapidly from one thing to another; that he was candid and truthful, popular with his neighbors, and brave to temerity. He was very stoutly built, about five feet ten inches high and weighed nearly two hundred pounds; his desire was to be on terms of amity and sociability with everyone. He had a great stock of border anecdotes and possessed a marvelous proclivity to entertain by "spinning yarns" and narrating his youthful experiences.[28]

He was an inveterate hunter, as, indeed, were most of the pioneers. **It was, in fact, one of the customs of the country**. In both Kentucky and southern Indiana, in the vicinage of his homes, every man and boy owned a rifle, and it was unsafe and also unusual to go through the woods unarmed. Game, particularly deer, was one of the chief staples of existence, **and very much of the larder supplies was obtained in the primitive denizens of the forest and streams.** Before Thomas had attained his majority, he wended his way on foot across the Cumberland Mountains to eastern Tennessee, where he worked on a farm for his uncle Isaac, who had settled on one of the affluents of the Holstein River.[29] Upon his return to Kentucky, he entered as an apprentice to learn the cabinetmaker's trade in the shop of one Joseph Hanks in Elizabethtown,[30] and while thus engaged, he became acquainted with and enamored of a niece of his employer, by the name of Nancy Hanks.

It would appear that there were four families which had been closely and intimately associated in geographical propinquity in at least two States, if not in three or four, and were also equally associated in marital bonds.

Thomas, whose manners he found "Back[w]oodsish" but was "charmed" by his wit and humor and thought him a "mighty hospitable, and a very entertaining host." William G. Greene to Herndon, Tallula, Illinois, 20 December 1865, Wilson and Davis, *Herndon's Informants*, 145; Greene interviewed by George A. Pierce, dispatch dated "on the cars," 12 April, Chicago *Inter-Ocean*, 30 April 1881.

28. Whitney footnote: "I have known several old men who knew Thomas Lincoln intimately. They said he had, as they termed it, good strong horse sense and was an excellent man. He was a cabinet maker and was thrifty when he lived in Kentucky."—[James L.] Nall

29. A brother of grandfather Abraham Lincoln, Isaac (1750–1816) settled in Tennessee in 1775 and prospered. Louis A. Warren, "The Tennessee Lincolns," *The Lincoln Kinsman* 14 (August 1939), 1–4.

30. Joseph Hanks Jr. (1781–1856) wed Mary Young in 1810. According to Dennis Hanks, "Thomas Lincoln learnt his trade as a Carpenter in Hardin Co Ky with my Uncle Joseph Hanks and married Joseph Hanks Niece which was my own cousin." Wilson and Davis, *Herndon's Informants*, 27.

Lineage, Parentage, and Childhood

They were the Lincolns, Hankses, Berrys, and Shipleys.[31] They probably were all of Quaker proclivities, and among that worthy class there is a spiritual intimacy unknown in other clanships. The Lincolns and Hankses had been neighbors in Berks County, Pennsylvania. The Berrys, Shipleys, Lincolns, and Hankses had owned a common tie of spiritual community in Virginia, North Carolina, and Kentucky. One Richard Berry had emigrated from North Carolina to Kentucky in the same party with Abraham Lincoln Sr.[32] They were connected **brothers-in-law** by the fact of both having married sisters of the name of Shipley. A daughter of Richard Berry Sr. had married into the Hanks family in Virginia, the issue being one child, a girl named Nancy. When the father died, the widow—Lucey (Berry) Hanks—migrated with her brothers-in-law to Kentucky, where she married a second time, this husband being one Henry Sparrow,[33] brother to Thomas Sparrow, who had espoused her first husband's sister. Prior to this second marriage, the widow and child had found a temporary home with Thomas Sparrow's family, and after the marriage, Nancy, being greatly endeared to her aunt, continued to live there for a time. Dennis Hanks, a cousin, being a child of still another Hanks, was also an inmate of the same household.[34]

The child Nancy was indifferently called by her married name of Hanks and by her mother's new name, it being also her aunt's name, of Sparrow, and by the latter name both John and Dennis Hanks knew her,[35] and Mrs. Hanaford, in her interesting sketch of Mr. Lincoln's life, so designates her, on the authority of the two Hankses.[36]

31. This account by Whitney is garbled. For a thorough, accurate summary of this tangled network, see Paul H. Verduin, "Brief Outline of the Joseph Hanks Family," Wilson and Davis, *Herndon's Informants*, 779–83.

32. Richard Berry Jr. (1769–1843), guardian of Nancy Hanks, and his wife Polly Ewing Berry (1774–1829) were friends of Thomas Lincoln. At their home, Nancy lived for a while before marrying Thomas; their wedding took place there.

33. Henry Sparrow (1765–1844) wed Lucey Hanks in 1790. It was her first marriage.

34. Lincoln's first cousin once removed, the farmer Dennis Hanks (1799–1892), was an illegitimate son of Charles Friend and Nancy Hanks, an aunt of Lincoln's mother, also named Nancy Hanks. Starting in 1817, Dennis lived for several years with Lincoln's family and was, in effect, an older brother to Abraham. Unlike most of his kin, Dennis was literate.

35. John Hanks (1802–1889), another first cousin once removed of Lincoln, was the son of Joseph Hanks Jr., Nancy Hanks Lincoln's uncle.

36. Phebe Ann Coffin Hanaford (1829–1921) was a Christian Universalist minister and author of *Abraham Lincoln: His Life and Public Services* (Boston: D. Lothrop, 1881).

Chapter I

After living with her Aunt Sparrow for a while she made a visit to her maternal grandfather, Richard Berry, then living at Mattingly's Mills, on Beech Fork, in Washington County, and was induced by him to maintain her abode there, which she did till she was married.

It may be mentioned that, prior to the betrothal of Thomas Lincoln and Nancy Hanks, he had courted another girl in Hardin County, one Sallie Bush,[37] but that for some reason the courtship either did not mature into an engagement or else the engagement was broken off, for both parties entered into other matrimonial alliances. Thomas Lincoln's marriage with Nancy Hanks was a highly respectable one, but that with Sallie Bush, had it gone through, would have been more *recherché* [unusual], for the latter was connected with the elite of that part of Kentucky, as I shall hereafter show. No especial reasons are disclosed by history why Nancy did not make her home with her mother, but it is probable that, when she had so many acceptable homes, she selected that which was most agreeable; that in the depressing poverty incident to the frontier families in those days the stepfather might have found it a relief to be disencumbered of the charge and expense of a child to which he was now bound by only a conventional tie. So it is not strange that this forlorn child, who was **bereft by death of a Father's love before she could know her loss, and deprived of a mother's tender care by circumstance, was being** reared in the home of an aunt, and her grandfather committed her destiny to the keeping of this uncouth apprentice [Thomas Lincoln], who was as ignorant as a caveman of the duties and responsibilities of civilized life. At this time Nancy was in her twenty-third year. She was **about five feet and six inches tall; weighed somewhere about 125 pounds, was spare,** narrow chested, and of consumptive tendencies. Her complexion was sallow, indicative of bad nutrition. Her hair was dark, her eyes were grey, her forehead was high, and her demeanor was reserved and sad, **with an expression of melancholy and a faraway look, as if a vague unrest and a nameless longing filled her breast. A wish that she hardly dared to own for something better than she had known.** Moreover, in that primitive region, where **dense ignorance was the almost inevitable rule, where** there were scarcely any schools even for the better order of people, she had somehow picked up considerable education. She was intellectual in her ambition and tendencies, and she had an excellent memory, good judgment, and a fine sense of propriety. Her nature seems to have been conservative rather than aggressive. Although her ambition was above her surroundings and apparent destiny, she seems to have considered her humble lot and condition in life to

---

37. Sarah Bush Johnston Lincoln (1788–1869) was the second wife of Thomas Lincoln and stepmother of Abraham Lincoln and his sister Sarah.

Lineage, Parentage, and Childhood

be inevitable, and to have made no radical effort to change it, resting content in faithfully performing her wifely and motherly duties.

While biographers have not hesitated to shake the genealogical tree vigorously, in order to bring down all possible fruit availing in connection with the *paternal* ancestry of the martyred president, scarcely more than a passing glance has been bestowed upon the pendent boughs which could illustrate the pedigree of the *maternal* line, the general statement being that the mother's name was Nancy Hanks, a daughter of Lucey Hanks.[38] The president himself states it somewhat differently thus: "My parents were both born in Virginia of undistinguished families—second families perhaps, I should say. My Mother, who died in my tenth year, was of a family of the name of Hanks."[39]

All persons are aware that there is a tendency of adulation or detraction to locate the origin of phenomenal men either in the Elysium of the blest or the limbo of the infernal. In the infinite stretch and realms of the imagination, it is not allowable that a man of unique history should have other than an unique origin. (Romulus and Remus were suckled by a she wolf; Caesar descended from Anchises and Venus; and Napoleon from Agamemnon or Achilles.) Despite all fable, Mr. Lincoln had an origin, on both the maternal and paternal line, common to mankind in general. No act is better avouched than that Richard Berry Sr., the grandfather of the Richard Berry Jr. who became surety on Thomas Lincoln's marriage bond, was also the grandfather of Nancy Hanks.[40] It was so thoroughly well understood in Washington County, Kentucky, as never to have been questioned. It was once disputed whether Abraham Lincoln was born in Washington or Hardin County, but the fact above given was never, and is not now, in question among an entire community who were in a position to know; and if confirmation is needed, the facts that she made her home there as one of the family—that Richard Berry Jr., her cousin, became her guardian and also became surety on the marriage bond—confirm it.

38. Lucey Hanks (ca. 1767–ca. 1833) was Lincoln's maternal grandmother, whom he described as a "halfway prostitute." Wilson and Davis, *Herndon on Lincoln: Letters*, 84. She married Henry Sparrow years after Nancy's birth.

39. Basler, *Collected Works of Lincoln*, 3:511. Whitney footnote: This, in its normal and natural sense, implies that his mother was born in a *family*, of course.

40. According to Lincoln, that grandfather was "some *high blood rake*" in Virginia, who took shameless advantage of poor Lucey Hanks. Wilson and Davis, *Herndon on Lincoln: Letters*, 68. See Paul H. Verduin, "New Evidence Suggests Lincoln's Mother Born in Richmond County, Virginia, Giving Credibility to the Planter-Grandfather Legend," *Northern Neck of Virginia Historical Magazine* 38 (1988): 4354–89 and Verduin, "Plantation Overseers, Patriots, Pioneers: New Light on Lincoln and His Hanks Forbears," unpublished paper delivered at the Lincoln Home, Springfield, 12 February 1992.

14   Chapter I

Equally conclusive is the testimony of Hon. J. L. Nall, a grandson of Thomas Lincoln's sister Nancy, and by far the most intelligent archaeologist and genealogist of that branch of the Lincoln family which includes the president. He says absolutely, and with emphasis and circumstance, that Nancy Hanks was an orphan girl at a tender age, her father being a "Hanks" and her mother a *Berry*, daughter of old Richard Berry. The latter and Abraham Lincoln Sr. married sisters by the name of Shipley, which made the president and his wife their great-grandfather and great-grandmother, having the same remote cousins. Mr. Nall says specifically: "Nancy Hanks' mother was a Berry, and she married a Hanks, who was the father of Nancy; he died in Virginia, and his widow married Sparrow, and Richard Berry raised Nancy. I had an uncle John N. Hill who died in Hardin County in 1883 at the age of one hundred years[41] and he was one of the most intelligent and best posted men in Kentucky history I ever knew in my life, and this was his version of the relationship, as well as that of my grandfather William Brumfield and grandmother Nancy (Lincoln) Brumfield. Uncle Hill was not related to the Lincoln family and, of course, had nothing to cover up or conceal. He lived in Washington County in his younger days, right by the side of the Lincoln and Berry family, and was at the wedding when Thomas Lincoln and Nancy Hanks were married. . . . When Lincoln was nominated for President, there were quite a number of old men living in Hardin County, among whom was old Mr. Riney,[42] to whom the president went to school, and they knew the Lincoln and Berry families and took delight in rehearsing matters they knew in connection with them, and this was their version and understanding. It indeed was not disputed and was not discussed adversly—simply assumed as a well-known fact."

One of the most prominent citizens of Springfield, Kentucky, Squire R[ichard] M[itchell] Thompson, feeling the honor of his own family trenched upon by the innuendo in [Ward Hill] Lamon's *Life of Lincoln*[43] concerning Lincoln's parents, himself searched for and found the marriage certificate of Thomas Lincoln and Nancy Hanks,[44] and, in testifying under oath about it,

41. John N. Hill (1788–1887) wed Fanny Nall in Washington County, Kentucky.

42. Zachariah Riney (1763–1859) was Lincoln's first teacher in Kentucky. Roger H. Futrell, "Zachariah Riney: Lincoln's First Schoolmaster," *Lincoln Herald* 74 (1972): 136–142.

43. Ward H. Lamon, *The Life of Abraham Lincoln: From His Birth to His Inauguration as President* (Boston: James R. Osgood, 1872), was ghostwritten by Chauncey Black.

44. "A cousin of Nancy Hanks Lincoln, Mr. Robert Mitchell Thompson, while on a visit to Larue County, was repeatedly told that Thomas Lincoln and Nancy Hanks were never married, and that Abraham Lincoln was an illegitimate child. Being

Lineage, Parentage, and Childhood

embraced this paragraph: "The mother of Nancy (Hanks) Lincoln, who was the mother of President Abraham Lincoln, was an own cousin of affiant's mother." This was on the theory that she was a Berry. I repeat, the general and particular reputation that Lucey Hanks was a Berry is as firmly grounded as any fact in Washington County. The "Herald" of that county once stated that she was a Shipley. This was a natural mistake, her grandmother being a Shipley and, the Shipleys and Berrys being closely interrelated, her grandmother and President Lincoln's grandmother were sisters, and, of course, their great-grandparents in that time were identical.

I am not unaware that John and Dennis Hanks call her a *Sparrow*, but they also call the President's grandfather *Mordecai*. There is no real basis for either statement, except as I have stated, nor am I unaware that a higher authority than the Hankses does not concur in my arrangement of the pedigree of Nancy Hanks; but it is a notion in equity that "what ought to be done is considered as done," and inasmuch as this statement, well known to close students of Lincolnian biography, ought not to have been made, or, if made, ought not to be printed, it should be treated as not made at all; and besides, however wise or interested a party might be in general, it does not follow that he knew any more (or even as much) about such a matter than others. In addition to all, in a conflict of evidence, that which is most weighty, probable, and convincing, and especially **over that which is not,** if cumulative, should prevail.

The masterpiece of Lincoln biography, **[John] Hay and [John G.]** Nicolay's [*Abraham Lincoln: A History*], accepts Mr. Nall's version of the Lincoln paternal grandmother's identity as conclusive, one that [Navy] Secretary [Gideon] Welles, who was related to the New England branch of the Lincoln family, and by reason of his coign of vantage, should know whereof he affirmed, and this distinguished and accurate kinsman had equal opportunities to know the pedigree in the maternal line, and his comments in that matter are as reliable as are the others. **(In this connection it should be stated that Gideon Welles, Mr. Lincoln's secretary of the navy, and**

---

the kinsman of Nancy Hanks, Mr. Thompson was naturally indignant that such a report should be accepted as true. He had heard of the marriage of Nancy Hanks to Thomas Lincoln at the home of Richard Berry and had heard of it from persons who were guests at the wedding and believed the records of the marriage could be found in the county. Returning home, Mr. Thompson related the story he had heard in Larue County to Mr. W. F. Booker, county clerk, and stated that he remembered the year to have been 1806 when the marriage occurred. As no index of records was kept at that early period the task seemed almost a hopeless one. Mr. Booker's diligent search was rewarded by the discovery of the bond, and the minister's return." Springfield, Kentucky, *News-Leader*, 11 February 1909.

who took an exceptional interest in all that pertained to his great chief, made faithful research on the subject,[45] and came to the conclusion that the president's grandmother was not Mary Shipley of North Carolina, but was Hannah Miller of Rockingham County, Virginia;[46] and if it was not for the circumstantial averments of Mr. Nall to the contrary, he also knowing the person specifically, I should embrace this view, but I have no doubt of Nall's version; still I arrive at an obituary notice taken from a Bellefonte (PA) newspaper which explains itself: "Died in Bellefonte, at the residence of Edwin G. Humes, on Sunday morning the 30th of May 1875. Mrs. Lucy Potter relative of Hon. William W. Potter deceased, aged 84 years, 9 months, and 2 days. Mrs. Potter was a member of a large and rather remarkable family; her father having been born in 1728—married in 1747, died in 1794; children to the number of nineteen having been born to him, the eldest in 1748, the youngest in 1790."

Superimposed upon all is the universal knowledge of the fact at the paternal home of the party herself, and which is cumulative and no wise dependent upon the clear and otherwise derived knowledge of Mr. Nall. I think I have read all that has been published on this subject; and, while it is of none but speculative interest, it is due to history as well as to the memory of a woman who should be revered by the civilized world everywhere, that her own and her mother's honor and reputation should be assured. Mr. Lincoln says his mother was born of an undistinguished *family*, and I claim no more, nor should the world believe any less. [Whitney footnote: Secretary Welles states that he has heard President Lincoln say more than once that when he laid down his official life he would endeavor to trace out his genealogy and family history.[47]] I myself know one member of the family to have been the wife of a United States judge and another to have been the wife of a governor of Kansas and a United States Minister. It was an humble, but respectable, family in all respects.

45. Welles, "Administration of Abraham Lincoln," *The Galaxy* 23 (January 1877), 15–17. Welles said he "had two or three conversations" with Lincoln "concerning his family history." In Lincoln, Welles "saw a craving desire to know something more of his family history." Welles to Robert Todd Lincoln, Hartford, 25 June, 5 July 1875, Nicolay-Hay Papers, Lincoln Presidential Library, Springfield.

46. Hannah Winter Miller (ca. 1748–1823), wife of Henry Miller of Moss Creek, Virginia, was not Lincoln's paternal grandmother, who in fact was Bathsheba Herring, as noted above.

47. Gideon Welles observed that the sixteenth president "knew not his own lineage and connections. . . . The deprivation he keenly felt. I heard him say on more than one occasion that when he laid down his official life he would endeavor to trace out his genealogy and family history." Welles, "Administration of Abraham Lincoln," *The Galaxy* 23 (January 1877): 15.

Lineage, Parentage, and Childhood

All things being ready, as well in the program of Destiny as in the few crude arrangements of the parties directly involved, **who were entering into a mightier contract than they had any idea of,** Thomas Lincoln journeyed in a primitive way to the home of Richard Berry, the prospective bride's grandfather, at Mattingly's Mills, and, together with Richard Berry Jr., cousin to the bride-elect, visited the county seat of Washington County, and executed a marriage bond of the following tenor and import, viz.:

> Know all men by these presents, that Mr. Thomas Lincoln and Richard Berry are held and firmly bound unto his excellency the Governor of Kentucky in the just and full sum of Fifty pounds current money; for the payment of which and truly to be made to the said Governor and his successors, we bind ourselves, our heirs etc., jointly and severally, firmly by these presents. Sealed with our seals and dated this 10th day of June 1806. The condition of the above obligation is such that whereas there is a marriage shortly intended between the above named Thomas Lincoln and Nancy Hanks for which a license has been issued. Now if there be no lawful cause to obstruct the said marriage, then this obligation to be void, else to remain in full force and virtue in law. Thomas Lincoln (seal) Richard Berry (seal)
> Witness: John H. Parrott.

The Rev. Jesse Head, D[eacon] M[ethodist] E[piscopal] C[hurch], certifies that on June 12, 1806, he joined Thomas Lincoln and Nancy Hanks in marriage.[48] According to an article published in *The American*, a Philadelphia magazine published a few years since, it would appear that one *John Hank* lived on what is now the Perkiomen turnpike, six miles east of Reading in Exeter Township in Pennsylvania, and within half a mile of the residence of Mordecai Lincoln, who would be the great-great-grandfather of the president; and that Hank emigrated to Augusta County in Virginia with John Lincoln, the great-grandfather of the president.[49] In 1711, in Berks County,

---

48. Jesse Head (1768–1842) lived in Springfield, Kentucky. The wedding took place in Poortown, also known as Beechland, at the cabin of Richard Berry, who had served as Nancy's guardian.

49. According to an 1883 letter by David Lincoln, John Hank "lived on the Perkiomen turnpike, six miles east of Reading, in Exeter township, and within half a mile of Mordecai Lincoln, great-great-grandfather of the President. This John Hank, with John and Benjamin Lincoln, moved to Fayette county, and from there Mr. Hank went southward. As to a removal, first, to Fayette county, I do not know; but, as has already been noted, John Hank was in Rockingham county, Va., at least as early as 1787, when his daughter Hannah married Asa Lupton. That this John was the one described by Mr. Lincoln is probable, or he may have been a son of the Berks county man, for the latter was in all probability the same John Hank; who was born 1712, the son of the Whitemarsh yeoman and Sarah Evans, of Gwynedd.

PA, John Hank married one Sarah Evans, and they had a son born the next year, who was living as late as 1730, as his father mentions him in his will that year. The Friends' (Quakers') record in Baltimore, still extant, mentions one *John Hanke* as living in Rockingham County, Virginia—probably the same who emigrated from Berks County—and in 1787 Hannah, a daughter of John Hanke, married one Asa Lupton. The only significant fact about this information is that the Lincolns and Hankses were alike Quakers and neighbors, and if this Hanke was the progenitor of Nancy Hanks, it is a coincidence that the ancestors of both should have been close neighbors, and that a century or more afterwards two members of the same families should have united their destinies with such mighty results.[50]

The only basis in my view to avouch this John Hanke as being the progenitor of the president's mother is that the Kentucky Hankses came from Virginia, and the rarity of the name, superadded to the further fact of the Hankses' and Lincolns' intimacy and the quite seeming probability that they might seek the same new home. Thomas Lincoln was a second cousin of his wife, as I show; possibly the families also had in another branch several generations of neighborhood intimacy.

It is a singular fact that to the Kentucky county in which Abraham Lincoln's parents were married, Jefferson Davis came from his home to Louisiana when he was seven years of age, it being just about the time that Lincoln and his father were leaving the state for Indiana. Davis attended the St. Thomas Catholic school, situated near the county seat of that county, and remained there for two years, after which he attended Transylvania University at Lexington. While he was at this institution, Mary Todd, the future wife of Abraham Lincoln, attended a girls' school in Lexington. A chance meeting of the two might have led to a rivalry in love between the future president even more opposite than that which later occurred between Lincoln and Stephen A. Douglas. At least there is basis here for an historical romance.

It has been assumed by biographers generally that immediately upon his marriage, Thomas Lincoln brought his bride to Hardin County, and that in that county all three of their children were born. The president himself, in his brief sketches of his life, says that he was born in Hardin County, **and it is presumable that he got such fact from his father or mother, yet it should be recollected that there was no reason why he should make any critical**

Good-natured, easy-going Thomas Lincoln, of Kentucky, married, for his first wife, Nancy Hank." Howard M. Jenkins, *Historical Collections Relating to Gwynedd* (2d ed.; Philadelphia: the author, 1897), 329.

50. The identity of Nancy Hanks's father is unknown.

Lineage, Parentage, and Childhood

research on that subject; it may simply have been taken for granted or assumed by him, yet he may have been mistaken.

Inasmuch as his earliest recollections were of Hardin County, he may have assumed, without further warrant, that he was born there. His mother died when he was nine years of age and she would not have been likely for any reason now apparent, to impress upon the memory of her child the particular place of his birth. After Mr. Lincoln became famous, a scrutiny would be in the cause, as to the locality of his birth, but no such scrutiny would be probable in the days of his obscurity.

Certain it is that a belief is prevalent and general in Washington County that, after the marriage of Thomas and Nancy, they resided in the same house with the grandfather of his wife until after both Sarah and Abraham were born; and that both of them were born in that house. This belief is derived from the statements of contemporaries of those events. On the other hand, it is averred that immediately after his marriage, Thomas brought his bride to and installed her in a home located in one of the alleys of Elizabethtown, where he resided for two years; and that in this sorry shanty, their daughter, Sarah, was born.[51] And it is further averred that there was also another brother, named William Brumfield Lincoln (after his uncle Brumfield), who died at the age of four or five years and was buried in the Elizabethtown cemetery.[52] It is an undisputed fact that Thomas Lincoln, within a year or so after his marriage, being prompted by a roving disposition, and the land hunger which he had inherited from his forbears, especially his father, **and a desire for change**, removed his family to a patch of ground on which a little clearing had been made and a cabin erected, situated on the south branch of Nolin's Creek, three miles from the

51. Following a brief honeymoon, the newlyweds moved to Elizabethtown, where their first child, Sarah, was born less than eight months after her parents' wedding. Edgar K. Webb, "Lincoln's Birthplace to Be Made a National Park," *The Fresno Morning Republican*, 7 March 1906. In 1865, the circuit court clerk of Elizabethtown, Samuel Haycraft, reported that the "house in which Thomas Lincoln lived in Elizabeth Town is yet standing but has been removed three times—used twice as a slaughter house & now as a stable & within fifty yards of its original locality, about 14 feet square." Wilson and Davis, *Herndon's Informants*, 67. R. Gerald McMurtry claimed that Haycraft confused the cabin of Sarah Bush Johnston with that of the Lincolns. McMurtry, "The Lincolns in Elizabethtown, Kentucky" (pamphlet; Fort Wayne, Indiana: Lincolniana Publishers, 1932), unpaginated.

52. After Abraham was born in 1809, his parents had another son, evidently named for his father, who died in infancy around 1812. When the family moved to Indiana in 1816, they visited the grave of this child. Wilson and Davis, *Herndon's Informants*, 27; Basler, *Collected Works of Lincoln*, 4:61; *Lincoln Lore*, no. 1619 (January 1973). According to Dennis Hanks, Thomas Jr. lived only a few days.

20 Chapter I

present village of Hodgenville, county seat of LaRue County, and that in this rude cabin, in this neglected spot, on the twelfth day of February, 1809, the most illustrious man of his era was born.[53] **Even if the place of his birth is disputed, there is no dispute that the earliest years of his conscious life were spent here.**

The cabin was of the rudest kind even for those days. It is needless to attempt to describe it, for the present comfortably housed generation would deem such description to have been woven in the loom of the imagination. It suffices to say, which I do reverently, that our Saviour, **whose mission was to save the human race and** who was born in **an ox's trough in an Oriental** stable, **and that Abraham Lincoln, who was ordained to rescue imperiled democracy from the destroying hand of anarchy, was born in a Kentucky stable**, had a scarcely less decent birthplace than the typical cabin of the "poor white" of the South a century ago, and that the advents respectively of the **Son of God and of the obscure man charged with a Divine mission—** despised Nazarene and the Kentucky carpenter's son, the one the Saviour of the world, and the other the liberator of a race, were achieved alike amid the most primitive and desolate surroundings, even for the primitive conditions of the time.

In this rude cabin the little stranger lived until he had attained his fourth year. As there were no immediate neighbors, the parents and the two little children were compelled to be company for each other, and we can only imagine—for history was then engaged on statelier themes, such as the career of Napoleon—what their daily life could have arrayed of current happiness, as a solace for prosaic and uneventful poverty and privation. That the mother, with an ambition and enterprise far above her situation, **conditions, or surroundings in life** could read and write, is a basis of fact from which we may reasonably infer that she was wont to gather her little progeny at her knee and instill into their infant minds the rudiments of education **and endeavor to start them on this road** which would lead them to a better condition of life than she had ever known.[54]

I can see, by the aid of a very somber imagination, this sad lonely melancholy woman, who had never known an unadulterated joy in life, call to her side her little son and daughter, and with such rude means as she

---

53. At the end of 1807, Thomas Lincoln moved fourteen miles from Elizabethtown to a site in "the Barrens" on the South Fork of Nolin Creek, known as the Sinking Spring farm, located near the homestead where Thomas and Betsy Sparrow lived with their foster child, Dennis Hanks, and where Nancy's aunt, Polly Hanks Friend, had settled.

54. Nancy Hanks could not write, but she "could read a little." Wilson and Davis, *Herndon's Informants*, 37.

had at command, teach them to trace out the letters of the alphabet or possibly to join two or more words together so as to embody a concrete idea. What sacred and tender memories cluster around the venerated name—*Mother!!*

It is a solemn and impressive thought that the great president, in casting a retrospective glance at these morally dismal and opaque days, in which a mother's love introduced the only shaft of sunshine in the deep gloom of his infant life, should tearfully soliloquize, "God bless my Mother! All that I am or can hope to be, I owe to her."[55] And this was true in a double sense. From his father, he only obtained the boon of *being.* From him he inherited only "infancy, ignorance, and indigence."[56] But from his sainted mother he was endowed with intellect, ambition, aspiration, and from her, likewise, he obtained an introduction into the mysteries of creation which finally unlocked to him the treasures of fame and immortality.

Circumstances rendered it expedient for Thomas Lincoln to remove from this uninteresting place to one more desirable on the banks of Knob Creek, an affluent of Rolling Fork, about six miles distant from Hodgenville, which removal occurred in the spring of 1813, when young Abraham was four years of age. **During their residence of about three years in this place, he grew up to be of some force in the industrial world, for he used to "go to mill" to a little corn cracking establishment, some four or five miles distant. The present generation is unadvised of this house of political economy and sociology, but nothing was more common in rural districts fifty and one hundred years ago. Imagine a rustic household, of an evening, seated in a circle, in the center of which is a grain bag, ready for the reception of shelled corn. Each member of that little group, old and young, has on their laps a pan or dish of some sort, into which, by aid of a cob, each one is shelling corn off the ear. In the fullness of time, the bag would be about half full; then it was closed up and the family would separate for the night. Next morning, bright and early, the small boy of the family would bring his pony to the door. His bag would be loaded on so as to balance,**

55. Herndon contended that although Lincoln was ashamed of his mother and other Hankses, he did praise her one day around 1850 as the two men were riding in a buggy: "All that I am or hope ever to be I get from my mother—god bless her." Wilson and Davis, *Herndon on Lincoln: Letters,* 100. But Herndon was careful to explain that his ambition and intellect came from his unidentified aristocratic grandfather, passed along to him genetically through his mother. Lincoln was not paying the sentimental tribute to motherhood that Whitney describes.

56. This is Henry Clay's description of what he inherited from his father. Calvin Colton, ed., *Works of Henry Clay* (7 vols.; New York: Henry Clay Publishing Co., 1897), 1:45.

and the little boy, mounted, would ride to mill with his grist. Other boys would be there with their grists, and each must take his turn. Such was the most important era in Henry Clay's life as a child, and the epithet "Mill Boy of the Slashes" clung to him through life.[57] It was usually no irksome task to wait, for the boy who got home promptly must betake himself to drudgery, while the boy waiting for his grist would have a "gay old time" fighting, wrestling, swapping knives, jokes etc. Verily, the apotheosis of a farm boy's social life was attained in going to mill, and Abraham was the "mill boy" of this little family when he was six and seven years old.

Both father and mother appreciated the value and necessity of their children's education, the former superficially, the latter substantially and practically, and the only means and opportunities the country afforded for any means of education were eagerly embraced. One Zachariah Riney taught in the immediate neighborhood, and to his school Abraham and his sister faithfully went. He was a man of an excellent character, deep piety, and a fair education. He had been reared as a Catholic, but made no attempt to proselyte, and the still existing town of Rineysville in Hardin County is a tribute to the estimation in which his family is held. He was extremely popular with his scholars, and the great president always mentioned him in later years in terms of grateful respect.[58] At a later period, Caleb Hazel, a youth with a little smattering of education, "took up" a school some four or five miles distant, and the faithful and ambitious mother would fix up her little ones the best she could and send them diurnally on the long journey.[59] She was persistent **and unwavering** in her determination to inculcate education in their youthful minds. The father's enthusiasm was spasmodic and unreliable; still he would occasionally glow with pride in his educational plans for his bright,

---

57. Slashes are tracts of swampy ground.

58. See C. W. Hackensmith, "Lincoln's Family and His Teachers," *Register of the Kentucky Historical Society* 67 (1969): 325. John Locke Scripps, whose 1860 campaign biography is based largely on what Lincoln told him verbally as well as in writing, said that Lincoln attended school with Riney when he was six years old. Scripps, *Life of Abraham Lincoln*, ed. Roy P. Basler and Lloyd A. Dunlap (1860; Bloomington: Indiana University Press, 1961), 27.

59. According to William Makepeace Thayer, whose informants included friends of Lincoln's youth, Caleb Hazel Jr. (1791–1854) was able to read and write, "but beyond this he made a poor figure." Thayer, *The Pioneer Boy and How He Became President* (Boston: Walker, Wise, 1863), 22. A friend said Hazel "could perhaps teach spelling reading & indifferent writing & perhaps could Cipher to the rule of three—but had no other qualifications of a teacher except large size & bodily Strength to thrash any boy or youth that came to his School." Wilson and Davis, *Herndon's Informants,* 67.

intelligent boy.[60] At the age of forty-five Lincoln told [Leonard] Swett[61] that the *summum bonum* of his father's ambition in his behalf was to give his boy **what he considered to be** a *first rate* education, and that his *ne plus ultra* [the absolute best example of its kind] of such an education was to "larn to cipher clean through the 'rithmetic."[62]

I can scarcely imagine a sight in domestic life more tender than that of this melancholy woman of exalted pride and ambition, but of the most meagre resources, fixing up her two little ragged children with a lunch of corn bread and their school appendages and starting them on each morning on their long, lonely tramp to a primitive school, and then at such times as she could seize, examining them, in order to note their progress, and

---

60. Lincoln's father, who "looked upon bone and mussel [as] sufficient to make the man" and thought "that time spent in school [w]as doubly wasted," would "slash" Abe "for neglecting his work by reading." Wilson and Davis, *Herndon's Informants*, 48, 41. Lincoln's stepmother reported things differently. In 1865, she said: "As a usual thing Mr. Lincoln never made Abe quit reading to do anything if he could avoid it. He would do it himself first. Mr. Lincoln could read a little & could scarcely write his name: hence he wanted, as he himself felt the uses & necessities of Education his boy Abraham to learn & he Encouraged him to do it in all ways he could— . . . When Abe was reading My husband took particular Care not to disturb him—would let him read on and on till Abe quit of his own accord." Wilson and Davis, *Herndon's Informants*, 107–08.

61. Attorney Leonard Swett (1825–1889) of Bloomington was one of Lincoln's closest friends and most effective political allies and fellow lawyers.

62. According to Swett, Lincoln said that "My father had suffered greatly for the want of education, and he determined at an early day that I should be well educated. And what do you think he said his ideas of a good education were? We had an old dog-eared arithmetic in our house, and father determined that somehow, or somehow else, I should cipher clear through that book." Swett, "Lincoln's Story of His Own Life," in Rice, *Reminiscences of Lincoln*, 458. In an autobiographical sketch, Lincoln stated that "when I came of age I did not know much. Still somehow, I could read, write, and cipher to the Rule of Three; but that was all." Basler, *Collected Works of Lincoln*, 3:511. Sometimes Thomas hid and even threw out Lincoln's books. Charles T. Baker, "How Lincoln Saved the Farm," Grandview, Indiana, *Monitor*, 14 October 1926, copied from the *Monitor* of 26 August 1920. Cf. Charles T. Baker, "The Lincoln Family in Spencer County," Grandview, Indiana, *Monitor*, 16 February 1928. Based on what he learned from several of the Lincolns' neighbors and friends, J. Edward Murr, a vigorous defender of Thomas Lincoln's reputation, asserted that it was "true beyond all peradventure of a doubt that Tom Lincoln was stoutly opposed to Abe's reading, and in certain stormy ways opposed Abe's habit of borrowing books." Thomas manifested his disapproval of Abe's reading "in an ugly fashion." Murr, "The Wilderness Years of Abraham Lincoln," unpublished typescript, Murr Papers, DePauw University, Greencastle, Indiana, 141–42.

weaving for them in fancy's loom the fabric of a more cheerful destiny than had fallen to her lot.

In 1816, the land hunger which Thomas Lincoln had inherited from his father, the Virginia emigrant, led him to barter his imperfect title to his farm for ten barrels of rye whiskey and twenty dollars in cash, and go to Indiana on a prospecting tour, with a view to emigration. Such is the usual explanation of modern scientific biographers, who find the springs of momentous events in human impulses rather than in divine foreordination. An ancient chronicler would have said: "And the Angel of the Lord came to Thomas **Lincoln as he had come to Joseph before,** and commanded that he take this young child and his mother and depart out of that country."

This humble child of the backwoods—this heir to poverty, privation and sorrow—gazed with wonder at the novel spectacle of his father building a rude boat or raft on the rolling fork of Salt Creek, nearby their home, and, as when launched and loaded, it swung into the current, it bore more than Caesar and his fortunes, for it bears Thomas Lincoln and his fortunes, one item of which was a child who had no equal, and who was matchless and unique among mortal men.

Abraham was now past seven years old. The uneventful and impoverishing epoch of his childhood had come to a close, and now, ready to be ushered upon his life's experiences, was the auroral era of youth and hope.

II

Youth

On the Kentucky shore below Louisville, in the midst of Nature's unkempt, umbrageous, and solemn solitudes, there debouches into the Ohio an affluent [Salt River] whose pellucid waters **and brilliant banks, whether glowing with the emerald verdure of ethereal spring or adorned with the variegated hues of sober autumn,** gave no token of the **rule of the cruel *Genii* of the river, custodians of the** broken hopes, withered ambitions, blasted reputations, and shattered political careers, **and funereal dirges** which its name suggests to the American ear. For this is the **world** renowned **and infamous** Salt River of our political mythology, the stream, to whose headwaters are annually consigned the defeated aspirants for elective office, and which is **the *bete noir* of defeated politicians, than which the fabled Styx does not possess a more melancholy record: and the fiendish glee of the rower, him who molded this force of majorities which echoed through these sylvan glades, and the drear despair of the worried, whose hearts were crushed beneath a weight of adverse votes, formed a staple article of our political journals of half a century ago, heralded by the cabalist's shout of triumph *"Crow, Chapman, Crow!"*[1] And had the journalistic sentences pronounced when the "loved and lost" in our political tourneys been actual, instead of mythical, the wailings of remorse and despair which would have reverberated through these sylvan glades would have equaled the agonizing cries of the chain gang upon a Siberian highway. But all that glitters in newspaper columns is not truth, and the Salt River of newspaper fable is**

---

1. In 1840, Democrat Joseph Chapman of Indiana, while running for a seat in Congress, was ridiculed by the Whigs, but when he managed to win, the Democrats adopted the rooster as their symbol, which was depicted crowing lustily whenever one of the party's candidates won an election.

quite as airy and diaphanous as the political reputations built on nothing, in their columns.

It was on the "rolling fork" of Salt River that Thomas Lincoln, in the fall of 1816, embarked in quest of a new home; and he pursued that stream through its various sinuosities until it joined Salt River proper, **upon whose remorseless tides, as we have seen, so many blasted political careers have been borne, and beneath whose Stygian waters, so many withered and ruined hopes have been inured.** This stream, **thereafter fated to become the Botany Bay of so many political aspirations, was kind to this modern Argonaut who, unconsciously, was sailing in pursuit of an object, to which the golden fleece which Jason and his companions strove for bore no sort of comparison, hardly of contrast; for within the compass of his meanderings, was encountered the lever and fulcrum wherewith the political Archimedes of this century then dawning, was destined to move the moral and political world.** [This stream,] however, had not yet acquired its baleful reputation, and did not have to live up to a bad character. So Thomas Lincoln safely steered himself and cargo down its course to the great Ohio.

Perversely enough, this river belied the favorable name by which the early French *voyageurs* had christened it "La Belle Riviere." Coming out on its turbid tide, Lincoln's boat foundered, and the bulk of his liquid fortune found a watery grave. He rescued a portion of it, however, with much exertion, and, getting afloat again with his cargo of whiskey, succeeded in navigating the Ohio River to a point in Indiana called Thompson's Ferry. Here he left his goods at a cabin and started through the trackless forest on foot, in quest of a site whereupon to found his new home. Sixteen miles distant, he came to a place which suited his fancy, although it is not unlikely that the setting sun and the cravings of hunger, warning him to seek a shelter, had some bearing upon his choice of a location.

The "numbers" of his claim were South West quarter of Section Thirty-Two, Town Four South, Range Five West. The place thus selected was near to both Big and Little Pigeon Creek, in what was then Perry, but thereafter became Spencer County. Having "notched" the trees upon the boundaries of his claim, and made the improvement required by "squatter" law, viz.: to pile up brush at an inchoate clearing; and thus completed his "claim," he returned to Knob Creek on foot. Loading his bedding, kitchen utensils, and other portable property on two borrowed horses, and gathering his little family about him, he then began his *hegira* from a State where the **vulgar** aristocracy of negro ownership was the passport to respectability, to a State where

> The honest man, though e'er sae puir,
> Is king o' men for a' that![2]

---

2. Robert Burns, "A Man's a Man for a' That."

Many scenes, replete with pathos, are presented in the realistic drama of the American pioneer; and this was one of them. The fall had set in; the nights were cold; and the adjuncts to comfort while camping out were meagre. The father and mother were compelled to walk. The two little children, aged respectively nine and seven, were uncomfortably disposed among the packs with which the horses were loaded, **and the little cavalcade presented a pitiful sight to the man of sentiment.**

Arrived at the Ohio River, the horses were sent back and the goods, augmented by those which had been transported by means of the river, were loaded on a hired wagon and hauled out to the claim, where they were deposited, **and [they and] this obscure family were in the forest alone.** Without a single domestic animal, three miles from any neighbor, with no protection from the approaching winter storms **and merciless cold** but the now leafless trees, and no shelter from the rude weather but the few ragged clothes they chanced to bring, and with no defense from the cold but an open brush fire, they present to the imagination a picture more pitiable than that of the Pilgrims on Plymouth Rock, or indeed, of any of the more spectacular scenes of pioneer life.

The first essential enterprise was to construct a shelter for his family, and the father went resolutely at work to fabricate not anything arising to the dignity of a cabin, but a *camp.* The mode and design and style of construction of this were as follows: A slightly sloping patch of ground was selected where two straight trees stood about fourteen feet apart, east and west of each other. The pioneer then cut down a number of small straight trees, **or pollards**, and cut the tops off, so that the finished product would be fourteen feet long. Then the helpful wife would trim off the superfluous branches, and the entire family, two at each end of a log, would somehow tug the logs to the place needed. Two thirds of these logs would be notched at one end **and flattened at the other, and the remaining third would be notched at each end.** The two trees which had been selected as corner posts for the structure were denuded of their bark on the sides facing each other, and the prepared logs placed in position by building three sides of a crib, pinning the flat ends of the logs to the trees by wooden pins, to receive which an augur hole had been previously bored through this log and into the tree itself. Thus the series of three logs superimposed upon each other formed three sides of this primitive camp, leaving the south side exposed to the weather. A roof of small poles and branches, brush, dried grass, and any other suitable material which could be gathered up, completed the camp, into which their little furniture was disposed, and dried leaves gathered and arranged in the two corners for the four occupants to repose on when night should spread her sable mantel on the quiet solitude. The gaps were at leisure filled up with branches, mud, and anything which could be procured. A log fire kindled and kept up, night and day, in front of the camp completed the establishment.

Such an aboriginal structure as this served for an entire year as a home for the family that included the most famous man of modern times.

This species of home was not inapt for a pioneer and his family in the summertime or in good weather, but when drenching storms came, or a south wind drove the smoke into the camp so as to compel evacuation by the inmates, it was extremely uncomfortable, if not, indeed, intolerable.

It was, in fact, a hunter's camp, such as city men even now are wont to occupy for a habitation during a few weeks of good weather for the novelty of a change from civilized life. For a mother and young children during foul and fair weather alike, it was, however, the most cruel travesty of a home that can well be conceived.

Indiana had just been admitted as a State, and the new dignity was alluring settlers from the neighboring States of Kentucky and Ohio. So Thomas Lincoln, the pioneer of [Little] Pigeon Creek, made a journey to Vincennes to make his land entry from the government. He walked all the way, going and coming. Southern Indiana was then a dense virgin forest, having every variety of the hard woods indigenous to that zone. "Varmints," as the early settlers then termed them—wildcats, opossums, racoons &c.—abounded; likewise deer, wild turkeys, grouse, quails, and pheasants. Indeed, most of the animal food was procured by **the seductive wiles of** the rifle **or shotgun**.

Nearby the Lincoln settlement was a famous "deer lick"—a low place where saline water exudes from the ground and to which wild animals were wont to repair for the salt, they themselves forming in turn objects of the hunter's quest. From this lick the Lincolns derived the chief part of their provender. **(Perhaps it is needful to state that a few acre "deer lick" is a low place where brackish water exudes from the ground, or adjacent hillside, to which wild animals in primitive days, and domestic ones in civilization, repair to minister to their appetites for saline relish. I have seen as many as a hundred deer repair to such a place at one time).**

Here, in the forest primeval, in the backwater of civilization, this little family of four pursued their dull round of existence without a solitary bubble of the zest of life. They rose with the robin and commenced their weary rounds of drudgery. The father felled trees; the mother lopped off the branches; the little ones piled brush, hoed away weeds, and walked a mile to the nearest source of water supply, bearing back the heavy burden between them. There was not a pair of shoes among the four. Homemade moccasins served to ward off the snows and frost of winter.

The united efforts of all the members of this little family served to keep the wolf from the door and also to show some progress toward a more comfortable state of existence; and in one year from the date of the first unpromising settlement in this virgin wilderness, a log cabin, situated a few rods distant from the camp, offered a better shelter, and gave token of Thomas Lincoln's ambition, and of his advancement towards a higher condition of life.

Youth

This cabin was formed of undressed logs, about eighteen feet square, with a "stick and mud" chimney; a hole for egress and ingress, in which was hung an untanned deer hide to, in some sort, defend against the assaults of the weather; and the only exterior light was acquired through the imperfect media of the broad chimney floor and the cracks between the logs. The table was the flat surface of a bisected log, termed a *puncheon*, into which were inserted four legs by means of an augur. In lieu of chairs, there were small puncheons resting upon three legs. In lieu of bedsteads, stout poles were inserted in the spaces between the logs which formed the cabin, the two outer ends being supported by a crochet stick, driven into the ground floor of the wretched abode. The bedding and bedclothes, dishes and cooking utensils were in harmony with the cabin and its rustic furniture; and stout pins inserted in the logs constituted a substitute for the staircase or the "elevator" of civilization. This miserable abode was embosomed in brush, and unadorned without any suggestion of refined rusticity or halo of romance.

Lincoln's report of the new country being roseate, more so probably than the facts warranted, induced some of his Kentucky neighbors to migrate thither; and accordingly Mrs. Lincoln's aunt and uncle, Betsy and Thomas Sparrow, arrived at the Lincoln place in November 1817, bringing with them Dennis Hanks, who was a cousin-german [i.e., cousin] to Nancy Hanks Lincoln, and of course, a second cousin [first cousin once removed] to the future president. This family camped in the recently deserted camp of the Lincolns, where they remained until they, too, could get up in the world, as their kinsman had done.

Unless it be dishonorable to be born poor, and in the physical and moral wilderness, and to conform to the genius of the times and *locale*, I fail to see wherein Thomas Lincoln and Nancy Hanks are just objects of aspersion or disparagement. In contrast with the wonderful genius and development of his gifted son, the father appears lamentably lowly and commonplace, but no more so than those who were born to a kindred "low birth and iron fortune."[3] Who knows anything about the father of George Washington or Alexander Hamilton or Shakespeare or Andrew Jackson or James Abram Garfield? Henry Clay said that he inherited from his father naught but "infancy, indigence and ignorance."[4]

Out of the dull mediocrity of Hodgenville and Gentryville and their environs, nothing having the attribute of a supermorality came, except

---

3. Edward Bulwer Lytton, *The Lady of Lyons*, act 3, scene 2: "those twin gaolers of the daring heart, low birth and iron fortune."

4. Henry Clay told his Senate colleagues: "I was born to no proud patrimonial estate from my father. I inherited only infancy, ignorance, and indigence." Calvin Colton, ed., *Works of Henry Clay* (7 vols.; New York: Henry Clay Publishing Co., 1897), 1:45.

Abraham Lincoln; the whole moral surface then was one uniform stagnation; not a single ripple of eminence agitated the calm surface of mediocrity, except our Hero above; had it not been for him, the names of Gentryville, Hodgenville, Pigeon Creek and Thompson's Ferry would have been unknown beyond their own localities. George Washington came from one of the obscurest counties of Virginia. Andrew Jackson came from Waxhaw, but whether it was in North or South Carolina is a mooted point to this day. Henry Clay came from a region so morally opaque as to justify the appellation of the "slashes."

It should not be overlooked that in the days of Thomas Lincoln there were no railways, no common schools; poverty was the normal condition of our people, especially of our pioneers of all but a favored few of whom ignorance was the [doom?]. Education, civilization, and refinement are not compatible with wresting the wilderness from the dominion of nature and the denizens of the forest.

Those who knew Thomas Lincoln personally say that he was an illiterate and uncouth specimen; but nevertheless a man of rude native ability, attractive in conversation and of excellent argumentative prowess. There his style and modes of expression, though uncultured and unrefined, reminded those who knew both of his illustrious son. He was a man of resolute and undaunted courage, and, while peaceably inclined and never provoking a quarrel, was nevertheless always ready to meet all the rude demands of that unkempt society and from these personal encounters always came off conqueror. That fighting is a very ignoble ambition and that seems to our civilization to be clear, it did not so seem to the men of a century since who rescued the forest from the dominion of the buffalo, the bear, and the Indian.

Thomas Lincoln was of the style of man that Daniel Boone, Simon Kenton, Miles Standish, or Captain John Smith were; always to be seen with his rifle on his shoulder; ready for any emergency whether it was a contest with a wild beast of the forest, or an untamed man.

Thomas Lincoln was a man of self-reliance and decisive of character as is exhibited by his leaving the haunts of men and carving out a home in the midst of a howling wilderness. In this day, we cannot realize the amount of courage involved in this enterprise. No man devoid of heroic self-reliance and emphatic decision of character would attempt it, or if he should, would succeed in the attempt. He must be resolute and undaunted.

Catamounts were abundant and panthers not unknown, and not infrequently, a settler in the frontier must defend his claim by force of his own right arm. He must combine within himself the functions of blacksmith, carpenter, shoemaker, farrier, and physician; no one unversed in the experiences of the frontier can imagine the multiform demands which are inevitable to the pioneer in our western wilderness. Thomas Lincoln had been forced by necessity to carve out his own destiny alone and unaided; his elder brother [Mordecai] inherited all the real estate and he simply had as his sole stock in trade an energetic though unstable disposition and an undaunted and tenacious will. He founded and maintained a home apposite to the time and place and reared his children to a better condition than his own.

Finally, to Thomas Lincoln and Nancy Hanks Lincoln are the American nation, the colored race, and humanity in general, indebted for the *being*, the *existence* of *Abraham Lincoln*! And in view, and upon consideration, of that fact alone, no voice but that of respect and consideration should ever repeat their names. Abraham Lincoln always honored his father and mother, and as long as humanity and liberty are esteemed as virtues, to that extent and in that whole scope, should mention of the parents of Abraham Lincoln be made in terms of respect.

As already stated, there was no common-school system either in Kentucky or Indiana in the days of Abraham Lincoln's adolescence. The schoolmaster, a peripatetic pedagogue, was literally abroad then; reading, writing and spelling, the superficial study of Kirkham's[5] or Lindley Murray's grammar,[6] and arithmetic to the "rule of three" comprised the whole curriculum of the best schools, and what schooling was had was the product of fugitive or peripatetic pedagogues.

One of the proclivities of Abraham Lincoln, from the earliest years that one can see by the dim light of early biography, was an inordinate thirst for learning. Thus in a region where education has no vigor of growth, but might be termed a rural Pariah, we find little Abraham at the early age of four or five trudging four miles daily to a feeble school; and from the style of teachers, we cannot suppose he drank deep of the Pierian spring,[7] yet his ambition to learn, and that of his parents to foster and minister to this desire, is shown in a commendable light.

For some time after the settlement in Indiana, there was no school in that primitive, sparsely settled neighborhood, but when Abraham was eleven years of age, there was a school opened in a log shanty about one and a

---

5. Samuel Kirkham Jr. (1799–1843), *Compendium of English Grammar* (Fredericktown, MD: Printed at the Herald Press, by J. P. Thomson, for the author, 1823). Later versions were titled *English Grammar in Familiar Lectures*.

6. In 1795, Lindley Murray (1745–1826) published the bestselling English grammar book of all time, simply called *English Grammar*.

7. "A little learning is a dang'rous thing

Drink deep, or taste not the Pierian spring." Alexander Pope, "An Essay on Criticism."

half miles distant from his home, by one Hazel [actually Azel] Dorsey, the term "Hazel," which formed a component part of this teacher's name, being supposed to refer to a species of twig whose use in the rude school room was ancillary to good scholarship. Andrew Crawford was Abraham's next teacher, his ministrations occurring in the winter of 1822–3, as nearly as can be defined. Finally one [James] Swaney opened a school, pronounced by him *skule*, about five miles from the Lincoln home in 1826, which Lincoln attended for a very short time.[8]

These three schools in Indiana, and two in Kentucky, comprise all that he ever attended. The total time consumed (as Lincoln told Swett) being about five months in all.[9] And such schools! If erudition was ponderable, all that the entire five teachers knew could have been compassed in a thimble. The future President himself said, "there were some schools, so called, but no qualification was ever required of a teacher beyond readin' writin' and cipherin' to the rule of three: if a straggler supposed to understand Latin happened to sojourn in the neighborhood, he was looked upon as a wizard. There was absolutely nothing to excite ambition for education. Of course, when I came of age, I did not know much."[10]

At the time when Thomas Lincoln settled in Indiana, the county was named Perry, and its county seat was known as Troy, on the Ohio River, but the country settled so rapidly that a new county was formed called Spencer, the county seat of which was Rockport. A few years after the advent of the Lincolns, a little trading post was established within less than two miles of their home, which, taking its name from its principal settler, was denominated Gentryville. Corydon, the county seat of Harrison County, was then also the State capital, it having been so selected when the State was admitted into the Union. There was but one county between Harrison and Perry counties.

Although Thomas Lincoln had changed his residence from a *camp* to a *cabin*, it was not an extremely radical change from discomfort to comfort, for the cabin had neither a door nor windows; egress and ingress were had through an opening which was designed ultimately to accommodate a door. The house was likewise innocent of a floor, save the bare and naked earth. These omissions appeared all the more significant and objectionable from

---

8. Crawford, who served as a justice of the peace, was Lincoln's first teacher, probably in the winter of 1819–1820 or 1820–1821. The orphan James Swaney (b. 1800) was the second, and Azel Waters Dorsey (1784–1858), the guardian of Swaney, was the third. Louis A. Warren, "Lincoln's Hoosier Schoolmasters," *Indiana Magazine of History* 27 (1931): 104–18.

9. Swett, "Lincoln's Story of His Own Life," in Rice, *Reminiscences of Lincoln*, 458–59. It was only six weeks, Swett wrote.

10. Basler, *Collected Works of Lincoln*, 3:511.

the better order of things in that line, inherent in the surroundings of other settlers, who were rapidly settling in the neighborhood. Poor children! Young Abe and his sister could not but observe with longing eyes the newly erected cabins of the newcomers rejoicing in puncheon floors, doors from boards hewed out of a straight-grained log, with occasionally a glazed sash to admit light.

This beautiful Pigeon Creek valley, like all sublunary pleasures, had its sting, its fly in the ointment, a disease, equally to be dreaded with the cholera, and very similar alike in its manifestations and fatality, brooded like a spell over it, making it "a valley of the shadow of death."[11] It prevailed in the wooded regions of both Indiana and Illinois, and was called, in the homely and inaccurate vernacular of those regions, "*milk sick.*" It was a mysterious disease, and baffled science and medicine alike. In less than two years from the settlement of Thomas Lincoln on [Little] Pigeon Creek, his wife, and her uncle and aunt, all succumbed to this dread disease and died; and Thomas Lincoln, by the aid of a neighbor, constructed with a whipsaw from the native timber **trunks** coffins for each of these three victims. In the primeval forest, the remains of Nancy Hanks Lincoln were placed in a rude box, made from native lumber, a very much coarser receptacle than fruit trees that are transported in by nurserymen at this day; and in the presence and by the aid of a mere handful of the neighbors, without ceremony, unanointed and unannealed, was committed to the ground. Even the grave remained without the slightest attempt at culture or adornment until 1879, when Mr. P[eter] E. Studebaker of South Bend,[12] Indiana, having heard of it, proposed to Hon. Schuyler Colfax[13] to head a subscription with $50.00 in order to mark the spot with a suitable monument. Colfax assured him that the sum of fifty dollars alone would provide a monument sufficient and in harmony with the surroundings. The philanthropist thereupon caused to be erected a very neat marble monument, although the exact spot where the inanimate body crumbled into dust is involved in some doubt. It bears this inscription: "*Nancy Hanks Lincoln: mother of President Lincoln.* Died October 5th, A.D. 1818, aged 35 years. Erected by a friend of her martyred son, 1879."

The mother thus commemorated was a woman "of sorrows and acquainted with grief."[14] She was a child of the frontier, whose whole brief life was

11. Psalm 23.

12. Peter Studebaker (1836–1897) was treasurer and chairman of the Studebaker wagon business.

13. Schuyler Colfax (1823–1885) of South Bend, Indiana, represented his district in the U.S. House of Representatives (1855–1869) and served as vice president of the United States (1869–1873).

14. Isaiah, 3:53.

employed in removing from one frontier post to another and carving out from the rude wilderness a frontier home.

In the little group which followed the body of this most faithful wife and mother to its last abode was one who was not satisfied with this heathen burial; and he set himself resolutely at work to retrieve this neglect and to secure to the burial of his revered mother an *ex post facto* ceremony and semblance of a Christian interment. In those days, in the frontier, stated and periodical ministrations from the sacred text were not an institution on account of the paucity and poverty of the people. The pioneers, however, were content to accept the pious offices of such migratory clergymen as might chance to sojourn over Sunday in their neighborhood, in their wanderings. And thus a few months after his mother's death, young Abraham with considerable diplomacy for a lad of ten years, contrived to have an itinerant preacher named Daniel Elkin[15] deliver a funeral discourse, commemorative of the merits and humble and unobtrusive virtues of this modern Mary, the mother of one charged with a mission akin to the Divine!

Meanwhile, the **moral** desolation of that little humble household aroused the sympathy of the few neighbors, who "took turns" in aiding the youthful housekeeper [Lincoln's sister Sarah], but a little turned of eleven years of age, to maintain in semi-comfort this semblance of a home. Sarah Lincoln, however, possessed the heroism and resolution of her departed mother and entered with fidelity into the duties of the little household that now increased by the presence of Dennis Hanks, whose home had been broken up by the death of his uncle and aunt.

As must be apparent, a house **destitute of the ordinary appendages to comfortable housekeeping,** presided over by a child of eleven years, could not be expected to be strongly suggestive of home comforts **or ideal housekeeping. The clothing of not only the three children, but of the patriarch of the family as well, must be improvised somehow, within the rude walls of the unostentatious house, and, in view of all things, a "general flavor of mild decay"[16] suggested itself to the view of the observer conversant with this most humble abode.**

That Thomas Lincoln himself was not oblivious of this is evident from the fact that he gathered together what little capital he could, spruced up

15. David Elkin (ca. 1759–1857) was a circuit-riding Baptist minister based in Kentucky.

16. "There are traces of age in the one-hoss shay,
    A general flavor of mild decay,
    But nothing local, as one may say."

Oliver Wendell Holmes, "The Deacon's Masterpiece, or The Wonderful One-Hoss Shay."

Youth 35

a little, and in the ensuing fall, set off on a visit to the scenes of his youth in Kentucky, **That he had an occult purpose in this apparently superficial mission was not disclosed, but in point of fact, the disconsolate widower, having properly endured a decent time of mourning, conceived the purpose, and was self-charged with the mission** to procure a wife to solace his lonely hours and to serve as a mother to his neglected children.

As I have said, when he formed his alliance with Nancy Hanks, he had **as a youth** paid attention to Sallie Bush. Sallie had married one [Daniel] Johnston, who afterward became the jailer of Hardin County, an office then held in higher honor than it is now. Now Mrs. Johnston was not only a rare woman, as the sequel fully attests, but she also was a most excellent housekeeper, and a **most** faithful and devoted mother. Thomas was a shrewd observer, and the death of Mr. Johnston about the time he had lost his own companion giving him opportunity, with characteristic energy and directness of purpose he resolved to lay close siege to the affections of the **now mature** widow and force an early capitulation. Accordingly, upon his arrival in Elizabethtown, he at once repaired to the home of the fair widow who lived with her two girls and one boy, **their father having departed this life**.

Thomas Lincoln was an optimist; his illustrious son got his life's burden of drear despair from the maternal font and so Thomas cheerily and with the air of a conqueror, knocked at the home of his inamorata the next morning, fully assured that his suit was won. He must have arranged matters satisfactorily in one interview, for the next day he married the widow. As a wedding present, he paid all her small debts, the amount being about $12.00**, and they were married on that day. On** the succeeding day the second-hand bride, the second-hand bridegroom, three children, and a comfortable load of furniture and bedding were *en route* to the new home, where the two neglected, motherless, and lonely children were doing the best they could to stem the current of a sad and melancholy life and to painfully wear out the time, till, **as they supposed**, the father should return **and render less dense and opaque their joyless and somber existence,** with the "surprise" that he had probably promised them.

Sallie Bush, who was thus predestined to be a second mother to the great president, came from one of the **most numerous and** most respectable families in that part of Kentucky. One of her nephews is Hon. W[illiam] P[ope] D[uval] Bush, a leading lawyer of Frankfort, Kentucky, who was the State reporter from 1866 to 1878. Another was Hon. S[amuel] W[illiam] Bush, one of the leading lawyers of Hardin County, and a third, Hon. Robert Bush, holding a similar rank at Hawesville.

A niece was the wife of Hon. Martin H. Cofer of Elizabethtown, who was a circuit Judge of that circuit and became judge of the court of appeals in August, 1874, for the term of eight years, serving also as Chief Justice from

1879 till his death. This distinguished family was very devoted to their aunt and also has a high respect for the memory of Thomas Lincoln.

One of them [James L. Nall] is authority for the fact, well known in the "Bush" family, that when the suitor from Indiana came to woo their kinsman, she informed him that while "she would be perfectly willing to marry him as she had known him a long time and felt that the marriage would be congenial and happy, but it would be impossible for her even to think of marrying and leaving the state while in debt."

"Uncle Thomas" told her that this need make no difference, as he had plenty of money for that object and would take care of her financial affairs, and when he had ascertained the amount of her indebtedness, and the names of the parties to whom the money was due, he went around and redeemed and presented to her all her papers; and the marriage was consummated to his satisfaction as well as of her family which, as I have said, was among the most respectable in western Kentucky.

They resent even now any imputation upon the moral worth of Thomas Lincoln. He was not eminent as a financier, so neither was his illustrious son. A granddaughter of one of the Elizabethtown merchants has her grandfather's account books, which attest that Thomas Lincoln was an excellent and prompt customer, if not indeed an extravagant one, for living in a community that used hickory bark for suspenders, he at one time indulged in "one pair silk suspenders $1.50."[17]

Dennis Hanks was no longer an inmate of this little family, and when the father, since little spruced up by additions to his toilet, which he had procured from Troy by the courtesy of a neighbor, bade them "Good Bye," for a few days, and suggested the feasibility of their being "good" children, and stimulating their zeal in that direction by the promise to bring them a *"pretty,"* little did they think of the good fortune in store for them, least of all that the cup of bitterness which they had drained almost to the dregs, should be replaced by one foaming with good cheer, comfort, motherly kindness, and ever-present and exuberant sympathy in their childish woes.

Abraham's inner life was a **blank, dreary** desert of sorrow with an occasional oasis of green fairy land, watered by well-springs of happiness. **But no oasis in his life's parched desert was more welcome than the one that was unfolded to his astonished gaze, and revealed to his sad heart, when he beheld his father,** returning after a week's absence, driving a four horse

---

17. The ledger of the Blakely and Montgomery store in Elizabethtown, Kentucky, contains an entry indicating that Thomas Lincoln purchased a pair of suspenders for nine shillings in 1805. Otis M. Mather, "Thomas Lincoln's Accounts with Elizabethtown Merchants," *The Register of the Kentucky State Historical Society* 28 (1930): 89–95.

team hitched to a heavily loaded wagon, which, on its arrival, disclosed a quantity of homely and substantial household goods, and what was even more joy-inspiring, a considerate, motherly looking woman, who, clasping the neglected boy and girl to her heart and, calling them *Abe* and *Sallie*, and **saying in effect to each, "Child of the lost, the buried, and the sainted, I call thee mine, Till fairer still, with tears and sin untainted, her home be thine"**[18] **and sympathetically and lovingly** told them that henceforth she was to be their mother, and that the three children who had climbed down from the load and were shyly hiding behind her, **sheltering themselves by the bulwark of her shawl and apron,** were also to be their brother and sisters.

How **poor little** Abe's tender heart glowed with gladness and gratitude as he saw feather beds and blankets, coverlids, and tablecloths, chairs and "stand tables" loaded into the small cabin, usurping nearly the whole space! **Unadulterated** joy reigned supreme in the little Lincoln cabin that evening as the augmented **and consolidated** family sat down to their first good meal which had graced the little puncheon table since Nancy Hanks had taken to her bed with the fatal "milk sick." And as, at a late hour, Abe climbed into the loft with a companion [stepbrother] whom he had already learned to call "John," and sank into the tender embrace of the most comfortable bed he had ever known, and compared notes and experiences with his new brother till a late hour, it is safe to assert that no such fine and unadulterated happiness ever visited him afterwards. **No! not even when he slept in the palace of the American Caesars, as the chosen head of the greatest republic of all ages of the world.**

Mr. Lincoln once told me (in 1856) that John D. Johnston **(1810–1854)** his foster brother, was about his own age, and that he loved him as if he had been his own brother; and yet John grew up to be one of the laziest and most shiftless of mortals.[19]

John constantly appealed to Lincoln for aid, for himself and his progeny. I, myself, once strained a point, for Lincoln's sake, to save Johnston's son William from the penitentiary; and it is to the infinite credit of the great president, that he adhered to, and came to the assistance of, not only his father and stepmother, and never deserted them, but that his fidelity even to the utterly worthless child of this remote connection was equally tenacious.[20]

18. Amelia Ball Coppuck Welby, "The Motherless," in Elizabeth Dana, *Sacred and Household Poetry: Gathered from the Highways and Byways* (Newburyport, MA: Moulton & Clark, 1858), 103–104.

19. John D. Johnston was an honest, handsome, kind-hearted, lazy, shiftless, generous, hospitable fellow with a quarrelsome streak.

20. More information about this case appears in Whitney, *Life on the Circuit with Lincoln*, 118, 475–77.

Almost the last act he performed in Illinois was to visit his stepmother. On the morning he started, he urged me to go with him, and in fact, I went with him part way, and I have always since regretted that I did not accompany him during the entire journey.

His deep and earnest affection for his stepmother was returned in full measure by her. "Abe was the *best* boy I ever saw or ever expect to see,"[21] was her summing up of his character. As she parted with him at Charleston on the third day of February, 1861, this **venerable** old lady, whose whole life had been one of unobtrusive goodness, embraced the president-elect, **and as she clasped him to her bosom, convulsing with sobs and emotion,** she had a presentiment that it was their last meeting; she had a premonition which was afterwards so completely fulfilled. She had dimly known by the loose talk in her little rustic neighborhood of the mighty issues involved in her beloved stepson's election, and she already saw, in her prophetic vision, the collision of a mighty people; and in this mighty conflict, she felt that the central and pivotal figure could not escape.

And Abraham Lincoln experienced the maternal solicitude, sympathy, and kindness of his second mother in all ways. This most excellent woman and model stepmother brought comfortable things and essential domestic reforms to pass, without any jar or apparent effort. First a "shutter" appeared in the opening for a door. Next, a puncheon floor was laid, and, anon a half-glazed sash admitted light. Clean beds, clean clothes, clean towels, clean tablecloths were all in place. The wash day came regularly, good fare graced the table, order was enthroned, the family altar was inaugurated, and the family hearth assumed a sacredness begotten of prevalent good cheer, happiness, and the amenities which sweeten existence. The dooryard was cleaned of unsightly litter, a brood of fowls lent animation to the scene, and material comfort dissipated **personal discomfort and** the soul's melancholy. If Nancy Hanks Lincoln were conscious of the rare fidelity with which Sarah Bush Lincoln executed the trust of maternal solicitude to her children, **which had devolved upon her, she would, no doubt, have fervently blessed this glorious gem of such a rare stepmother, who doeth all things well, and** her perturbed spirit would at last have found rest.

New settlers flocked into the neighborhood; a store was instituted nearby; stated religious services followed; systematic social intercourse among the young folks ensued; and ere long, in all directions, the ruddy and cheerful blaze of hearth fires and the animated gleaming through clear window panes instead of oiled paper **supplanted the evanescent and cold glister of the fire fly,** and attested the advent of real civilization.

21. Lamon, *Life of Lincoln,* 39; Wilson and Davis, *Herndon's Informants,* 107.

To the genial requirements of this new order of life, Abraham Lincoln was no delinquent, **debtor or uncomfortable laggard, but the *bonhomie* and** the entertaining qualities which were **so** captivating in his manhood's prime, found exuberant vent in his youthful glow. Boylike, he was frivolous rather than sedate, reckless rather than responsible, and the mental vigor and volume which evolved the Cooper Institute speech[22] or yielded the Emancipation Proclamation were expended in satirical poems and coarse pasquinades, which had no apparent range or objects beyond diversion or petty social revenge, and were confined to the fleeting moment and to the little backwoods coterie which was wont to gather in the store or blacksmith's shop at Gentryville, or in the "corn huskings" or "log rollings" thereabouts.

Abe was no empty-headed country beau, however. He was even then more of a student than gallant. A story is told of a conversation he had, under idyllic circumstances, with a pretty girl of fifteen where his playing the schoolmaster instead of the lover was rather resented by his fair companion.[23] As the two young people sat barelegged on a log and dangled their feet in the limpid waters of Little Pigeon Creek and talked the light and frothy chatter of their age, till the sun sank low in the west and **was in the gloaming, when** the little miss **naively** exclaimed, "See Abe, the sun's going down!" "No," returned Abe with the importance of superior knowledge **and the consciousness that "knowledge is power,"** the "sun doesn't 'go down' it's *we* that do the sinking." But the pert auditor ended the explanation with the conclusive rejoinder, "Abe, you're a fool."

One of Lincoln's peculiarities was his weakness for the fair sex, but in a strictly sentimental and platonic way. In his youthful prime there was little in his appearance or deportment to enthrall the gentler sex, and his affairs of youthful gallantry were not very marked in their episodes or *denouements*. At the age of seventeen, he was six and a third feet high. His feet and hands were unusually large and his legs and arms disproportionately long. His head was small and phrenologically defective; his body very diminutive for one of his height. His walk was awkward, his gestures still more so. His skin was of a dirty yellowish brown and shriveled and baggy, even at that age.

He was attired in buckskin pants which failed to conceal his blue shinbones; his shirt was of a fabric known to pioneers, and to no other life, as linsey-woolsey; and in winter he was clad in what is known as a *warmus*;[24]

22. Address at Cooper Institute, New York, 27 February 1860, Basler, *Collected Works of Lincoln*, 3:523–550.

23. Mrs. Allen Gentry (née Anna Caroline Roby), interview with Herndon, Rockport, Indiana, 17 September 1865, Wilson and Davis, *Herndon's Informants*, 132.

24. A sturdy, coarse, sweater-like garment.

40   *Chapter II*

and finally, a coonskin cap, homemade, and moccasins also homemade, protected and decorated respectively his upper and nether extremities. He was *bizarre* looking, even in that primitive community.

Abraham Lincoln, whether as boy or man, was not enamored of steady, hard work; he preferred a variety of tasks, chiefly mental labor. He was by no means lazy, but was fond of frequent change. Accordingly, throughout his youthful career, he is seen to select such engagements and avocations as allowed him to interweave variety with industry and mental labor or recreation with muscular labor. "Going to mill" was a favorite avocation with him, as it had been with Henry Clay, "the Mill-boy of the Slashes." Abe rode seven miles to a treadmill, into which on his arrival, he put his horse, to furnish the power for grinding. On one of these occasions young Abe's horse kicked him so that he was unconscious for quite a while. On recovering his senses, he completed a sentence that he was in the mist of uttering when the accident took place. In after life he was fond of speculating upon this psychological phenomenon. **Ultimately, another mill was built to run by water, but it was twenty miles distant and to this mill the patronage of Pigeon Creek was transferred, but it not infrequently occurred that the customer would continue one day in carrying his "grist" there, and another day in going after it.**

One of the early settlers paints the rural portrait of this region in the primitive days of its settlement in somber colors. "The settlers were very social and accommodating, but there was more drunkenness and larceny on a small scale, more immorality, less religion, less confidence."[25]

One of Mr. Lincoln's youthful characteristics, and one which adhered to him through life, was his uniform kindness to any and all living things. A favorite pastime with boys of Pigeon Creek was to catch a mud "terkle" **(as they were termed)** and put a live coal on its back in order to enjoy the diversion of watching it writhe with pain. The youthful humanitarian was wont to inveigh, in emphatic terms, against this barbarism, sometimes putting his thoughts and monitions **on the subject** on paper and reading them to the boys. **And he, himself, never indulged in such or any kindred objects.**

Another peculiarity of his youth and manhood alike, was a habit of superficial and desultory reading. A short book he might read entirely through; a long one he would read consecutively for a few chapters and then skim through the rest. Such books as Weems's "Washington" he would read through consecutively, "Robinson Crusoe" he would not read by rote, but would select chapters to suit his fancy, and ultimately perhaps, read all. "Aesop's Fables" and Bunyan's "Pilgrim's Progress" he would read in patches.

---

25. Lamon, *Life of Lincoln*, 24; David Turnham to Herndon, Dale, Indiana, 21 February 1866, Wilson and Davis, *Herndon's Informants*, 217.

He was inordinately fond of books, but was not fond of consuming a great amount of time with any particular one at any one time. A specifically verbose book, he never read clear through, unless at wide intervals of time. He was prone to jot down anything of philosophy, poetry, or history which arrested his attention strongly. This was not done so much to preserve it, as to fix the thought embodied or fact narrated firmly in his memory. After writing it he would study it, then lay it aside for a time, then recur to it; if, on consideration and reconsideration, it struck him as superlatively valuable, he would try to retain it. And he had unused sheets of paper, copybooks, fly-leaves of books, etc., on which, he preserved these memoranda, sticking them in out-of-the-way places.

Books were rare and scarce in the days of his youth. Thomas Lincoln owned literally none but the Bible. His illustrious son's early acquaintance with any literature beyond the domain of primary school books was derived from those which he could borrow from neighbors. The sources of supply, however, were of an extremely attenuated character. A neighbor named Josiah Crawford possessed a copy of Weems's *Washington*, a highly spiced, mendacious and stupid string of anecdotes of the early days in Virginia and elsewhere euphemistically termed "a Life of Washington." Abraham readily borrowed it and read and studied it of evenings. One night it was ruined by rain, and Lincoln at once sought the lender, and reported the loss and the superfluous fact that he had not the wherewithal to pay. An agreement was thereupon made that young Abe should pull fodder for three days in repayment. There does not appear anything out of the way in all this; wages were very low then, and books were very rare; there was no bookstore nearer than Louisville, and the loss of a needed book in that neighborhood was well-nigh irreparable. It is even doubtful if Crawford would voluntarily have exchanged the book for three days' labor of a lad, but Lincoln, somehow, took great umbrage at Crawford's animus **and disposition** in the matter, as well as at the conditions exacted, and thereafter was wont, for the amusement of the neighborhood, to satirize the offender in the coarsest and most suggestive doggerel, using Crawford's physical shortcomings as a text. This reprehensible trait of character did not adhere to Mr. Lincoln beyond his youthful prime; he abandoned it, as he grew and expanded in intellect, together with sundry other foibles, and as a man was as magnanimous and charitable as he was revengeful and satirical as a youth.

Lying down was Lincoln's favorite attitude while reading or studying. This remained a habit with him throughout life. He also was fond of reading while at table. He always enjoyed reading aloud, or commenting on a book to a companion, whoever he might be.

As previously set forth, Lincoln's labors were desultory, he did not like manual labor at all, nor yet uniform, continual mental labor. When he ate,

he wanted a book in his hand, or someone to whom he could intelligently talk. I once knew of his making a pupil of a hostler in his study of Euclid on the circuit. He did not, like Archimedes, run through the streets crying "Eureka!" but he was so joyous at his geometrical lesson that he must share his happiness, even though he could find no better auditor than a stableman.

In his youth, Lincoln might have been encountered in a cabin loft, or under a tree, or anywhere in the shade, or in some out-of-the-way place, intent on his book. He would record his lucubrations on a wooden fire shovel, then shave it off with a draw-knife, and repeat the performance. While in the field at work he would be immersed in deep thought. As soon as he reached his home or his shelter, he would resume his book, if he had one, or his charcoal sketches, if he had none. If he could not obtain manual possession of a book by borrowing, he would repair to the place where it was and thus use it. Among other books which he read in that way was the Statutes of Indiana, **which was his first law book, and** which one [David] Turnham,[26] a constable, possessed, *ex officio.* This gave him an inclination toward the profession of law.

Abraham exhibited a proclivity for public speaking at an early age; anywhere that he could gather a crowd, he was ready with a speech. **Chauncey M. Depew was hardly more eager to get a good dinner free and heave in a speech as payment and a sequel than was the youthful Lincoln to mount a box, or stump, or anything, and venture a talk about something.**[27] His addresses were generally germane to the surrounding conditions, and "sometimes turned out a *song,* and sometimes turned out a sermon."[28] Not infrequently, of a Sabbath when the old folks were at "meetin,'" the youthful orator would edify the young folk at home by an improvised sermon. Upon such occasions, he would adopt the usual order of religious exercises. A hymn would be selected and sung by the petite audience; **the prayer was the only facet of a usual service that was omitted.** His preaching frequently drew tears from his sympathetic auditory, in which occasionally he would join.

In the cornfield, his oratorical powers frequently were in demand. Often, when a resting spell came, Abe would mount half way of the fence, and

26. David Turnham (1803–1884) was a neighbor of the Lincolns.

27. Attorney and raconteur Chauncey M. Depew (1834–1928) represented New York in the U.S. Senate (1899–1911). His after-dinner speeches were numerous and widely read. *Orations and After-Dinner Speeches of Chauncey M. Depew* (New York: Cassell, 1889).

28. "With Dante, life represented the passage of the soul from a state of nature to a state of grace; and there would have been almost an even chance whether (as Burns says) the Divina Commedia had turned out a song or a sermon, but for the wonderful genius of its author, which has compelled the sermon to sing and the song to preach, whether they would or no." James Russell Lowell, *My Study Windows* (Boston: Osgood, 1874), 253.

steadying himself on the remainder, would thrill or amuse his hearers by a speech, sometimes political, sometimes polemical, sometimes jocular. He never failed to create an interest; in fact, his oratory was a great nuisance to employers who were interested that the work should be speedily performed.

Another quality which adhered to him during his entire life was his good humor, leading to a personal popularity with those with whom he came in close contact. Wherever he worked, he would find his way speedily to the kitchen, where he would rock the cradle, or draw water, wash dishes, or empty slops, meanwhile amusing all present with drollery or humor. Some of the men were inimical to him, but there was not a woman but who was extravagant in her laudations, even including Josiah Crawford's wife, whose husband he had so mercilessly lampooned.

His stepmother thought quite as much of him as of her own children; his stepbrother and stepsisters were as devoted to him as to each other, while his own sister idolized him. The closer the attrition with Lincoln, the more ardent and close the cordiality of the friendship. He was ever the best of boys and men, and had always "a tear for pity/ And a hand open as day, for melting charity."[29]

When he was sixteen years old, he entered into the service of [James] Taylor, who owned and operated a ferry franchise across the Ohio at the mouth of Anderson Creek. Here Lincoln remained as a boy of all work, for nearly a year, earning six dollars a month; and at another time, both he and his sister were hired out to Josiah Crawford, the former as a field hand, the latter as kitchen maid. There is hardly a field within a radius of two miles of Gentryville in which the great Emancipator has not wrought at the humblest of labor, for what would now be deemed insignificant wages.

It was noticeable to his companions that when Abraham had attained the age of eleven years or thereabouts, he fell into that habit of abstraction, absentmindedness, and self-introspection which constituted so marked and prominent a feature in his character in his later days. Whereas he presented no appearance of gravity or decorum theretofore, he suddenly, to appearances, awoke to a deep sense of responsibility, **or to its appearance,** and gravity of manner usurped the former characteristic of frivolity and mental vacuity.

Mr. Lincoln was a versatile genius, whether as man or boy. His mind was constantly on the *go*; he hopped about from one thing to another, never adhering to one thing long. He wrote doggerel poetry of no merit whatever; it was sometimes didactic, occasionally philosophical, but generally satirical. A single day's labor was a composite of storytelling, studying all the primitive studies then known to his *locale*, writing chronicles (as he called them) in derision of someone who exhibited ludicrous phases of character, doing

29. Shakespeare, Henry IV, part 2, act 4, scene 2.

chores from choice, and more robust work from compulsion, with occasional lapses into earnest and somber reflection.

Gentryville was a little world by itself. No circus or lecturer ever came within its borders. Its inhabitants simply lived within themselves, and entertained each other the best they could in a social style, and while Lincoln was in great demand as an entertainer and otherwise, he yet had to endure rebuffs which he took as seriously to heart as if he had been fashioned in an ordinary mold of humanity. A noted instance of the truth of the scriptural adage that "the stone which the builders rejected, the same is made the headstone of the corner,"[30] appeared in the great double wedding of two sons of Reuben Grigsby, which important occurrence was closed by a gorgeous infare [reception]. To this great social demonstration Abraham was not invited, although every other young person in the neighborhood, including his own sister, was. And he took a terrible social revenge, for he put in commission his heaviest batteries of wit and satire and churned up a social convulsion whose effects remained, like festering sores for a long time thereafter. Lincoln certainly wielded a *free lance* in those days; an exuberance of animal spirits had to be worked off in some way, and Lincoln was the Douglas Jerrold and Sydney Smith,[31] combined, of the neighborhood about Gentryville.

The satirical element clove to him through life, though he suppressed it generally in his responsible years. I have known him, however, in the privacy of our judicial circle (but very rarely) to impale an object disagreeable to him on a sarcastic lance quite as effectually, and in better style, than in his youthful days.

Although there was little in common between Lincoln and his father, yet they were alike in possessing prodigious strength. The stories which are told of Abraham's power in this line are doubtless exaggerated, but the fact remains that in all the fights in which either he or his father engaged, they prevailed every time, and that Abraham was especially sought for, when feats of muscle were in demand.

Precisely such a condition of society as existed in and about Gentryville would be impossible in the era of steam and a brilliant enlightenment; the outer world was almost a *terra incognita*, while the names of St. Louis, Cincinnati, and New York were sometimes mentioned, no more specific idea of what was signified thereby was impressed in the mind than the mention of a city on Jupiter would be now. Rarely matters outside the

30. Psalm 118:22.

31. Douglas William Jerrold (1803–1857) was an English playwright, journalist, and humorist. Sydney Smith (1771–1845) was an English wit, writer, and Anglican clergyman.

neighborhood were discussed, a feeble glimpse of politics was vouchsafed at each biennial election, and that was all.

Abraham did indeed venture beyond his own bailiwick both in the moral and physical world. Thus he wrote an elaborate essay on "Our Government," when he was but a little turned of seventeen years old, in which he betrayed a knowledge which could hardly be deemed indigenous to Gentryville. He also wrote an article on "Temperance," which was published in a weekly paper.[32]

A village lyceum was one of the institutions of the little hamlet of Gentryville. The sessions were held in [John] Jones's store, where the auditors and disputants sat on the counter, on inverted nail kegs, or lolled upon barrels or bags, while the wordy contest raged. The questions selected for discussion were not concrete. At one time there would be a debate upon the relative forces of wind and water; at another, upon the comparative wrongs of the Indian and the negro, the relative merits of the ant and the bee, also of water and fire.

Then, as later, Lincoln would enforce his views largely by comparison and by illustrations, by sallies of wit and homely anecdotes. It was always understood that fun was ahead when "Abe Linkern" took the floor.

Upon one occasion Abraham walked to Booneville, fifteen miles, to attend a session of the circuit court. One [John] Brackenridge, a lawyer with merely a local fame, made a speech in a murder case which captivated the youthful aspirant, and as he walked home after dark, his vivid fancy wrought like scenes of forensic glory for himself.

32. Lamon, *Life of Lincoln*, 69. Neither of these pieces is known to have survived.

III

Lincoln as a Laborer

As time wore on, and Abraham got from the newspapers and elsewhere an idea firmly lodged in his mind that there was a world outside of and beyond Gentryville, he longed to carry his wits and energy to a larger market. Accordingly, he applied to Mr. William Wood, who was quite willing to aid him, in a recommendation as a hand of some sort on a steamboat. Wood declined doing this favor on the ground that Abe was still in his minority and owed his services to his father. But an opportunity to see the outer world soon offered **itself** in this wise: about March 1, 1828, when Abraham was nineteen years of age, he was in the employment of James Gentry,[1] whose son Allen Gentry was about to start on a flatboat trip to New Orleans to trade off a load of country produce. Needing a hand to aid him, the Gentrys readily induced young Lincoln to go along at eight dollars per month and board. **Abraham felt the spirit of adventure stir within him, as he contemplated the probability of an actual view of places and scenes of which he had discursively read: Evansville, Memphis, Vicksburg, Natchez, Baton Rouge, New Orleans, the Mississippi River, cotton and sugar plantations; and that, on returning, he should experience a ride on a steamboat. With the exterior appearance of the latter he was familiar, having seen them pass and repass frequently while he was attending Anderson's ferry; but to be an actual passenger was an event whose contemplation gave him the liveliest satisfaction, for the boundaries of Gentryville and its neighborhood were altogether too confined for his ambitions, and he longed to see the world beyond, of which he had an exalted, but yet a vague, conception.**

1. James S. Gentry (1778–1840) was a relatively prosperous storekeeper in Gentryville.

The flatboat of early days was simply built of sufficient strength to last one downward trip, after which it would be converted into fuel. Two flat pieces of timber from thirty to fifty feet in length, two to three feet in breadth, and a foot in thickness were hewed out of a poplar log. One edge was level, the other two more beveled at each end. Those were called *gunwales*. Into these gunwales, at suitable distances, were morticed crosspieces of oak, fourteen feet long, six inches wide, and three inches thick, in addition to head blocks at each end, six **or eight** inches square. A stout frame being thus made, two-inch oak plank was fastened longitudinally to the oak crosspieces by means of wooden pins an inch square, systematically cut out from a tough species of timber termed "pin oak," and driven by a heavy maul through an auger hole bored through both planks.

The bottom, consisting of two-inch oak plank, was then fastened on to these longitudinal planks and rabbeted into the gunwales, the same being made watertight by oakum and pitch. Thus far, no iron was used in the construction, and no iron tools employed beyond a crosscut saw, a mill saw, an axe, a broad axe, an auger, and a draw-knife. This boat was launched by simply turning it over by two windlasses and levers so as to lie bottom side down in the river. **After the boat was thus launched and bailed out**, uprights consisting of 4 × 4 scantling were then mortised into the upper edge of the gunwales, and one and one-half inch poplar plank securely fastened longitudinally thereon and the seams caulked with oakum, and pitched. When produce was to be her cargo, a false bottom was put in, as it was impossible to construct such boats so that they would be entirely watertight. Finally, a ridge pole was placed longitudinally, and a roof was added. A cabin was improvised in one corner by the use of rough boards, and four huge oars were rigged, two on the sides, one at the bow, and one at the stern. A "check post" and coil of rope were then provided, and the craft was in commission.

The mode of navigating such an unwieldy craft was thus: Being loaded, the line is cast loose, and impelled as far from shore as is practicable by means of a setting pole, to which the junior navigator sets his shoulder. When that auxiliary fails, then resort is had to the side oars, known otherwise as "sweeps." By their aid, the craft is impelled into the current, which impels it down stream at the rate of four to six miles per hour. Skill is required to pilot the boat around bends in the river, as, left to itself, it would sweep in toward shore, and possibly be beached. This is avoided by the pilot setting the bow toward the center of the stream, and plying the side sweeps, so as to attain and retain that position in the crooked stream. Nevertheless, a severe wind would frequently blow the boat towards the bank, and the crew would be compelled to land, and in such case, the junior navigator must put off in a small boat, as the shore came near, with a rope around his body which he would quickly secure to some riparian object, when the senior navigator would take a turn around the check post, and, by checking the momentum by degrees, finally bring the boat to a stop without disaster. While at shore, a watch is necessary against the incursions of predatory thieves as well as to prevent the boat from grounding by the recession of the river. Sometimes the two navigators would run night and day, in which case but one would be constantly on watch. At night, in addition to keeping the boat in the current, signals must be given to passing steamers, which was done by the waving of a lantern or a firebrand. The cooking usually fell to the lot of the junior. Thus, in one way and another, a flatboat trip, under the management of but two persons, was a constant succession of hardships and novelties. Mr. Lincoln has himself described his flatboat experiences to me. In fact, as I too, once made a flatboat trip, we compared experiences. On Gentry's and Lincoln's trip, they commenced to barter away their load after they had fairly embarked on the Mississippi, receiving cotton, tobacco, and sugar in exchange for potatoes, bacon, apples, and jeans. **Sometimes, however, money would be used both ways.** This sort of river commerce was very common from the year 1820 to the period of the war, and thrives to some extent even now.

Lincoln returned home from this, his first trip, in June 1828, and fell into the same weary round of existence which he had pursued before, but with an evident longing for **some manner of life, and for** pursuits of a more ambitious and dignified character than those to which his existence had theretofore been consecrated.

In two years more, he would arrive at the age of conventional manhood. **When he came into this neighborhood, he was an uncouth, ignorant little boy of seven and a half years of age, a member of a little family of four souls, every one of whom was comparatively helpless, and having, as close neighbors, only catamounts, panthers, wolves, bears, wildcats, and deer. Human existence could not have been borne on a less slender capital than that possessed by the luckless family of which Abraham Lincoln was a sad and melancholy member.** Thomas Lincoln, even with the wages of Abraham and Sarah, had not greatly bettered his condition.

From the humble forest grave of Nancy Hanks Lincoln, to their solitary and cheerless abode, it would have seemed as if to that desolate and stricken family, that "Hope was a stranger and that Mercy never would come." There was not a single oasis in the hardened desert of their existence. The farm (so called) had been purchased entirely on credit, and was then only partially paid for. The father had no title or muniment of title to his farm, only a right to thereafter acquire it, provided he paid for it. From a few lean acres, some corn was gleaned, as the product of the least culture possible. **The scant wages of Abraham reinforced occasionally by the still sorrier earnings of his sister, constituted the mainstay of the little family.** Thomas Lincoln had no vices, nor yet any economic virtues, and he was a poor calculator, and being in the economical "slough of despond,"[2] saw no means by which he might emerge therefrom.

The community of which he formed a part was somewhat more provident but yet very primitive. The most luxuriant **intangible** growth was religion **and worship**; to attend "meetin,'" the settlers would journey eight or ten miles on foot, or horseback, or however they could. The females would be attired in their husbands' overcoats, while the latter would protect themselves from the weather by hunting shirts and moccasins. They met in schoolhouses, private houses, or in the woods. The preachers were apt to be more zealous than consistent, more polemical than charitable. Not only were their "meetin's" employed as an agency by which they might obtain the priceless boon of eternal life, but they served the more worldly and less meritorious object of neighborly reunions, when social amenities were cultivated, friendships cemented, mutual acquaintances fostered, and the general welfare discussed and adjudicated. Instead of formal sanctimony brooding over the gathering, joyousness and *bonhomie* prevailed. They lived too remote from each other to "run in and out" daily, and when they did meet, mix and mingle on the Lord's Day, it was used as a medium by which to secure attrition and hold converse with their kind. The women wore "calash," or scoop-shovel bonnets, linsey-woolsey frocks gathered just under the armpits, coarse underwear, and brogans. The "dress" suit of the men was composed of jeans of close and economical fit, with the waist high up in the back, buckskin trousers, and coonskin cap. Their manners were bluff and hearty; all door strings were hung outside, a sincere welcome was accorded to strangers, locks and bolts were unknown. While entire families were at "meetin'" on Sunday, or at a "hoedown," or "quiltin'" or "corn shuckin'" or "house raisin'" on a weekday, an ill-disposed person might have ransacked the whole neighborhood without let or hindrance. That this never occurred indicates that this neighborhood was a veritable **and living** Arcadia.

While there was no especial spirit of caste, there was, nevertheless, a spirit of criticism and disparagement, and the social gamut had both a bass and treble clef, upon which the merits of all were hung. The conventional standing of Abraham Lincoln was not a product of the family tree. His father's extreme poverty and inability to extricate himself therefrom, prevented any **derivative** social standing, but Abe, by his own individual merit, achieved a place for himself and sister, and likewise for his foster brother and sisters, in the social life of the neighborhood.

Still another mental idiosyncrasy of that primitive community was its proneness to all varieties of superstition; no explanation can be vouchsafed

2. A miry bog into which falls the protagonist of John Bunyan's allegory, *The Pilgrim's Progress* (1678).

why this habit and peculiarity was more rife here than elsewhere under like conditions, but so it was. They performed various matters according to the phases of the moon, planting esculents by the *dark* of this luminary, and products of the vine by its *light*. They dug for water by the guidance of the hazel fork in the hands of the water-witch and had a general belief in witchcraft. They had faith in the healing virtues of the madstone. They believed in dreams, signs, and omens, and were terrified at the chirping of the "death watch." They would commence no journey or undertaking on Friday. They were deceived by charlatans who plied the healing art by means of the secret processes of the cabbala, and saw their future husbands, wives, or destinies in the kaleidoscopic groupings of the tea grounds in their cups.

An accident, which to the unimaginative mind was obviously attributable to improvidence, they assigned to the genus of *bad luck*. A matrimonial match, propitious in its consequences, was made by the angels in the Elysium of light; one unfortunate in its *denouement* was churned up by a dusky crowd in the other place, etc.

The prevalence of these foolish notions exercised a great influence on the plastic and susceptible mind of our hero in the formative stage of his career. His vigor of mind and independence of thought in all other phases and manifestations could not triumph over these mental weaknesses. When his son Robert was bitten by a dog which it was feared was rabid, he journeyed with him, at great discomfort, to Terre Haute, to have a madstone which was there applied to the wound. While in the White House, he was known to steal out furtively and attend spiritualistic *seances*, and consult mediums as to his lines of duty, and to the prognostications of his future.[3]

---

3. Whitney elsewhere wrote that "Mrs. Nettie Maynard has written a book devoted to an enforcement of the statement that Mr. Lincoln was addicted to attending spiritualistic seances while he was in the presidency. I have reflected considerably on the matter, and as a result do not credit the statements, at least not the to the full extent as stated. While I fully believe that Mr. Lincoln would be likely to have a desire to make such investigations, a due sense of propriety would act as a check upon his attempting so radical a departure from the staid ways of life and experience from doing that which would give a radical shock to all of the conservative classes of society. Mr. Lincoln well knew that he stood in the 'wave of light that beats about a throne' and that he must not do any act which would expose him to even unjust criticism, and, as to attempting to do such a thing 'on the sly,' his honest nature and his ordinary sense both remorselessly barred any such deceitful methods. I presume there was a film of basis for the story, as that he met the parties named and gave a courteous reception to their avowals, possibly made some passing inquiries—in short, treated them with interest and possibly advanced some curiosity as to their pretensions. To any adhesion beyond that I decline to believe that he was a party." Whitney, "Lincoln a Fatalist," Rockport, Indiana, *Journal*, 11 February 1898.

He believed in dreams, as Napoleon did; he had faith in destiny. His whole manhood's life was one scene of misery because it was largely filled with dismal and shadowy forebodings.[4]

Among these people, he grew to maturity of manhood, and while there, imbibed and matured an ambition which brought forth fruit after many days.

He lived there from the fall of 1816, when he was seven and a half years old, until the spring of 1830, when he was of age—a physical, political, and conventional man. Almost naked, he came into that region. The value and price of property, and population increased an hundred fold during his stay there, and although the house of "Lincoln" was augmented in substantial wealth by the generous contributions of Sallie Bush Lincoln, yet this family left that region after over thirteen years' sojourn as poor as it came.

Abraham's sister had married Aaron Grigsby[5] at the age of eighteen, and had died, in childbed, within a year [eighteen months] thereafter. It was a sad blow to her brother, **his companion in so much of poverty and childhood hardship**. He reflected upon the preceding burial: he had everything in common with his mother and sister, but little with his father, and as he heard **the dull hollow sound of** the clods reverberate dully from the grave which contained the early companion of his few joys and many sorrows, the pent-up grief of his stricken soul found vent in convulsive sobs which brought tears to the little sympathetic assembly. These were but the least few cords that bound Abraham Lincoln to existence: one of them snapped at the grave of Nancy Hanks Lincoln and yet another at the new-made grave in the weird forest. What have I to live for? he repeated to himself over and over. Even his **two** foster sisters, who had been company and companions to him, were hardly so longer, for Matilda, the eldest, had married his second cousin, Dennis Hanks, and Sarah, the younger, had married another second cousin, Levi Hall;[6] and they each were rearing children. John D. Johnston, his foster brother alone remained, and was only apparently a companion to Abraham, **but no more**. In their common and mutual adolescence, they were closely allied in all things, but as the mind of one delved by self-introspection into the **geological** strata of the moral world, the vacant mind of the other

4. Lincoln told Whitney that in his boyhood, "I used to wander out in the woods all by myself. It had a fascination for me which had an element of fear in it—superstitious fear. I knew that I was not alone just as well as I know that you are here now. Still I could see nothing and no one, but I heard voices. Once I heard a voice right at my elbow—heard it distinctly and plainly. I turned around, expecting to see someone, of course. No one there, but the voice was there." When Whitney asked what the voice said, Lincoln did not reply: "Deep gloom—a look of pain—settled on his countenance and lasted some minutes." Whitney, "Lincoln a Fatalist."

5. Aaron Grigsby (1801–1831), oldest brother of Lincoln's friend Nathaniel Grigsby, wed Lincoln's sister Sarah on August 2, 1826.

6. Levi "Squire" Hall II (1805–1851) married Lincoln's stepsister Sarah.

52   *Chapter III*

remained stranded on the bleak shores of mediocrity, and their intimacy was but of the most superficial character.

Nancy Hanks Lincoln, as has been stated, had an uncle [Joseph] who was a carpenter in Elizabethtown, and with whom Thomas Lincoln "larned" his trade of carpenter. He had a son John, as inflexibly honest and reliable as Abraham Lincoln himself. John had come to the Lincolns' settlement in Indiana, and lived in and about Gentryville for about two years, but during the fall of 1828, he had drifted into Macon County, Illinois, and was comfortably settled there. Thomas Lincoln, ever ready to change his uniformly indigent condition, inquired of John Hanks about the Illinois country, whether it offered sufficiently promising advantages to a poor immigrant such as himself **to justify an experiment in that direction**. To these inquiries, Uncle John (as I always called him) returned very candid, and, on the whole, satisfactory replies, with the result that, during the winter of 1829–30, it was determined in the family councils of the Lincolns to move to Macon County, Illinois, upon the first budding of spring. **Its incubus would follow the star of empire westward and link its destiny with the then rapidly growing state of Illinois.**

The business arrangements were easily and quickly despatched. [James] Gentry, who substantially had a title to the farm, in a mortgage thereon, took over the equity. **The making of the deed was done.** [David] Turnham purchased the few hogs and bought the small remnant of corn for ten cents a bushel. And when the middle of February came, the season was deemed sufficiently advanced for the impatient family to start. There were really three families, to wit: Thomas Lincoln, his wife, Abraham, and John D. Johnston, his foster brother; Levi and Sarah Johnston Hall, and their son; and Dennis **Hanks and his wife** Matilda Johnston Hanks and their four children, thirteen persons in all. The day of departure approached. On the day before the start was to be made, Abraham, Dennis, and John visited the little hamlet of Gentryville and bade adieu to the [James] Gentrys senior and junior, John Baldwin, the blacksmith, who was one of Lincoln's staunchest and most reliable friends, and a man of bluff and sincere manners; [William] Jones, Lincoln's merchant friend;[7] and the various neighbors who were casually there. They then visited and bade goodbye to David Turnham, the constable, at whose house Abe had commenced his studies in law by reading the "Revised Statutes of Indiana," then took affectionate leave of "Uncle" [William] Wood,[8] Stephen McDaniels,

---

7. William Jones (1803–1864) was a prosperous, influential merchant who hired young Lincoln to work in his store. A Whig, he served as a representative in the Indiana legislature (1838–1841).

8. "Squire" William Wood was a judge whose court Lincoln attended as an observer.

John Duthan, Mrs. [Elizabeth] Crawford,[9] the Grigsbys (the *entente cordiale* having been reestablished between them), John Romine,[10] and the rest. As the awkward and uncouth youth, all unconscious of the immortal career for which he was destined, lay down for the last time to sleep in the humble cabin which had sheltered him for thirteen years, we can well imagine that his sensibilities were profoundly stirred and that his feelings found relief in tears. **Reminiscences of those years—the hardships of the camp life, the sad death of his mother and sister, their neglected graves on the blasted hillside, his roguish antics, his rudimentary gallantries, his sincere friend-ships, his attachment to places—preyed upon his fancy. Mired in solemn procession, strong be the cloisters of his memory!**

The example of Thomas Lincoln and his ancestors was not, in any wise, a radical exhibition of the achievements of pioneers. The line of pioneer progression pursued its devious and eccentric course from Plymouth Rock southwardly to New Jersey, westwardly to Pennsylvania, south-wardly to Virginia and North Carolina, and westwardly to Kentucky, where the kinesis of his fate overtook him, and he expiated his heroism of adventure with his life.

The animating principle of Thomas Lincoln's migration is not difficult to divine: the part of Kentucky where manhood found him was sterile at best. The free laborer had little chance for social and material advancement: a *nig-gerless* white was regarded as a social pariah **then**. Thomas Lincoln inherited rigid notions of humanity from a Quaker ancestry, which recognized slavery as a crime, so he did what other conscientious men were doing in similar circumstances; he left a State where *caste* was securely enthroned for a State where social as well as political equality prevailed.

Migration is an American institution. Instances are not rare of men who have actually lived in a dozen different States, and California, Oregon, and Washington are largely peopled by men who commenced their tours of migra-tion in the Atlantic States, and by slow approaches ultimately reached the ultimate limits of Western civilization. Andrew Jackson, William Henry Har-rison, James K. Polk, Zachary Taylor, Andrew Johnson, Ulysses S. Grant, and Benjamin Harrison were emigrants.

Thomas Lincoln likewise had abundant cause to leave Indiana. Milk sick-ness is given as the chief cause by Dennis Hanks. Nancy Hanks Lincoln, and her uncle and aunt had all died of it within two months of each other, and as Dennis naively says: "All of my relatives died of that disease on Little Pigeon

9. Elizabeth Anderson (1806–1889), wife of Josiah Crawford, was a friendly neighbor of the Lincolns.

10. In 1829, John Romine (1806–1888), a near neighbor of the Lincolns, hired Abraham to work on his farm.

Chapter III

Creek, Spencer County. . . . I was determined to leave and hunt a country where milk-sick was not. This is the reason for leaving Indiana."[11]

Activity, bustle, and excitement reigned in and about the Lincoln cabin, near Gentryville, on the morning of February 15, 1830. An early **and informal** breakfast had been hastily despatched by the light of some blazing fagots, by thirteen people, and each of them was engaged in guiding **or in obstructing** events toward an orderly and symmetrical exodus from the scene of so many **of life's chequered and** melancholy experiences.

The two "gals" (as they were called) were tying up rough bedclothes, packing dishes, skillets, pots and pans, and "toting" bundles to an extremely shabby and primitive vehicle, in which the patriarch of the household was awkwardly storing them away. John D. Johnston, Dennis Hanks, and Abraham Lincoln were corralling a few yearling cattle and imposing the yoke upon eight of the least unpromising. Levi Hall was casting a wary eye at the storing of the cargo, tightening a wedge here, tying a bark knot there, or driving a peg yonder, and venturing sundry bits of advice, having in view the proper disposition of the crude freight so as not to endanger the safety of the rude craft. The **good** mother of the tribe was viewing **and superintending** the animated scene with an anxious eye and directing matters with responsible consideration, issuing directions and uttering sundry warnings concerning the task then being wrought out. While the children, **like all others in similar circumstances, were dirty and,** radiant with happiness at the novelty and commotion, were dancing about in everybody's way. **Two or three neighboring women appeared timidly on the scene.**

Finally the four yoke of frisky, half broken steers, after much coercion on the part of four men, **and several failures**, were attached to the wagon; the last rude article was loaded on, stuck in, or tied under the wagon; the good mother, with much protesting, was forced to mount on the load; and the little ones were stored away somewhere in the interstices. The few parting words were said to the few friends who stood tearfully and dejectedly around, and the leader propounded the final interrogatory of, "All ready?" which being answered by half a dozen or more in the affirmative, the leader flourished his ox whip vigorously, at the same time ejaculating "Come *Buck*! You *Bright*! Go 'lang *Jim*!" The team straightened out, the chains were tightly drawn, a creaking sound issued from four rebellious axles, a spasmodic activity was imparted to the load, the old lady clutched uneasily at some means to steady herself, the mercurial and excited youngsters were warned to hang on, the load pitched forward, steadied, careened to one side, righted up, and jolted

---

11. Lamon, *Life of Lincoln*, 74n. The quote from this source is partly verbatim and partly paraphrased.

along to the **harsh music of axles whose asperities had not been mollified by that article so much in demand by aldermen—grease**—dolorous **arthritic, wheezing** creakings of a home-made vehicle. And thus, the Tribe of Lincoln set out on its journey for the Promised Land and thus also, Abraham Lincoln, having been three days a conventional man [i.e., officially an adult], **in the crude and rustic garb of a rude ox driver,** commenced to bear the burden of responsible life as an ox driver.

It is one of the compensations which a beneficent nature in mercy provides, that the hardships and drudgery of emigration are masked and concealed by its novelty, exhilaration, and romance. Among the many homely incidents to be met with on the frontier, none could be conceived of more prosaic, commonplace, less suggestive of the romantic, presenting more elements of the unadorned, than the modern hegira.

Can the imagination of these **epicurean** days of mechanical marvels reconstruct in fancy the rude vehicle which carried the fortunes of Abraham Lincoln from Gentryville, Indiana, to Decatur, Illinois? Will the occupant of the modern railway coach or of an automobile, credit the assertion that not a particle of iron or other metal entered into its composition except the narrow iron bands which bound the periphery of the wheels; that those wheels were solid blocks of wood made approximately circular by the broad axe and drawknife; and that in lieu of bolts, straps, or other fastenings, hickory withes were used? So rude a vehicle does not exist today in any part of the world, not even in Tasmania or Zululand. The cargo consisted of a bureau, a chest of drawers, a table, two chairs bottomed with rawhide, some bundles of bedding, some bundles of clothing, a carpenter's chest of tools and some very rude cooking utensils. The most unpropitious season of year seems to have been selected for such a journey, inasmuch as the road froze at night and thawed by day, causing the heavy wagon to be mired daily.

And thus while the crust would sometimes bear up the cattle, at other times it would break through under their hooves and the draft animals would be heaving and at times would be mired down. A few young cattle were driven behind, and the two daughters very plainly attired and with their skirts bedraggled, picked their way as daintily as they could at the edge of fences, within enclosed fields, or otherwise as they could, occasionally stopping at a wayside house to get water, procure some food or live coals to start the campfire with, etc. etc. The loose cattle were driven and a scrub pony led by some of the party, Abraham remaining the team driver in chief. When night came, a camp would be made preferably by the bank of a creek. The humble meal would be cooked, blessed, and devoured with an appetite and relish which a hard day's tramp and a conscience void of offence toward God and man would soften the labors of prying that wagon out of the mire had induced.

The evening would be spent in making repairs, talking over the day's adventures and simple gossip and when bedtime came, camp beds would be improvised in, under and about the wagon. After an evening series of singing and prayer led by the patriarch, the thirteen human beings would retire to the most primitive of lodgings; and as night drew her sable curtains and shut out these tired and humble nomads of the prairie, no eye but the omniscient one saw in that lowly group one who in a few years was destined to surpass all orators in eloquence, all diplomatists in wisdom, all statesmen in foresight, and the most ambitious in fame.

So, too, the hardships of the journey were greatly increased by the not infrequent crossing of creeks upon whose surface a thin film of ice would generally be formed, and which all parties would be compelled to ford. **And so it was, that when the future president of this great nation crossed the dividing line between Indiana and Illinois, he was probably the most unpromising appearing human being who ever occupied the presidential chair. The exterior condition of this little party was not far above that of the Aboriginees who had not long before preceded them in that primitive region. For thirteen to fifteen weary and uncomfortable days they were** *en route* **and wretched.**

At length the emigrants crossed the Illinois line and struck a north and south trail through the prairie, lying near to, if not, indeed, some of the way upon the location of the main line of the Illinois Central Railway. This ultimately brought them to the then inconsiderable village of Decatur, through whose **dull and** vacant streets they slowly defiled, an object of interest to the few stragglers whom they encountered, as well as to the inhabitants who, from the windows of comfortable rooms, gazed at the uncouth **and squalid** procession, little aware that the tall young ox driver who led it was destined ultimately to shed upon their community its most resplendent lustre—that within that little village, he was to be enthusiastically nominated by delegates from the **whole** State of Illinois as **their choice** candidate for the most exalted office **and honor** on earth, and so cause the name of their then inconsequential village to be handed down in imperishable fame.

Arrived in front of the courthouse, the wagon halted, and the various members of the little ragged and muddy coterie drew together in a circle, while the conventional head of the party went timidly into the courthouse and ventured to enquire of a boy who was recording deeds if he could inform him which road "mout" lead to John Hanks' place on the Sangamo? In point of fact, Hanks lived but four miles northwest of Decatur, and thither the humble procession wended its way, arriving there **just as the sun was setting with a wan, cold disc behind the fringe of lifeless trunks which skirted the river, and reaching the** *ultima thule*[12] **of their long journey, the tired**

---

12. A distant place located beyond the boundaries of the known world.

and worn out travelers at nightfall to receive the heartiest of welcomes from their kinsman, faithful old John Hanks! He had not—could not have—an enemy on earth; he was homespun, matter-of-fact, and dull to a superlative degree, but he was the very soul of generosity, truth, and probity. He made no pretensions to anything beyond mauling rails, plowing, husking corn, and other manual labors.

As shall afterward be related, more than any other friend of Lincoln he aided in his election to the presidency by fixing the epithet of "rail-splitter" upon him—a homely title that struck the popular fancy and attracted ten voters for Lincoln for every one it repelled. And when Lincoln came into his glory, John Hanks displayed a sincerity of nature that only his ignorance saved from being presumption, by applying to the president for an office. Procuring a new suit of blue jeans, he went to Washington and called on his youthful companion, his putative partner in the rail-splitting business, then the dispenser of a munificent patronage. (The prosaic fact is Uncle John split all the *rails*, while Abe cut the logs into rail lengths). "I'll tell ye, Abe, what I come for," he bluntly said: "I want to be a Injun agent; and Dick Oglesby said as how you would give it to me sure." Lincoln was nonplussed. Uncle John was rigidly honest, but had no sense beyond the doing of farm drudgery. How would it look for "honest old Abe" to bestow an office which required business training on a rustic simpleton, simply because he was a friend and kinsman? Besides, John Hanks could neither read nor write, but then Uncle John had proposed his son, who could do both, for his clerk. "How will it do?" asked the president of me, ruminatingly. "Just the thing," I answered, "an honest man as an Indian agent will be a good send-off for you." "But the trouble is his ignorance?" "Never mind, his honesty is better than knowledge," I said. Other advisers concurred in my opinion. However, at the cost of a bitter struggle, the president refused Uncle John's request, as he also did that of Dennis Hanks, who came on to Washington later, and asked that the president's foster sister, his wife, might be appointed postmistress of Charleston, Illinois. **Both requests were refused.** Would Abraham Lincoln have believed in the possibility of such a thing on the night of March 1, 1830, thirty-one years before, when he and Dennis and Matilda gathered about the humble board of old John in the Macon wilderness, and enjoyed the first square meal under a roof for two weeks? **I cannot approve of this neglect of John, Dennis, and Matilda Hanks. "Muzzle not the ox that treadeth out the corn,"**[13] **and it seems to me that the virtue of appointing the friends of congressmen to these insignificant offices over his own kith and kin, the companions of his youth and humility—one the daughter of his best friend on earth, Sarah Bush Lincoln, and one the man through whose**

13. "For the scripture saith, Thou shalt not muzzle the ox that treadeth out the corn. And, the labourer *is* worthy of his reward." 1 Timothy 5:18.

settlement in Illinois the humble clodhopper was attracted thither on his way to honor and patronage was so harsh a virtue as to have the appearance, if not the substance, of a vice.

A homely and happy family circle gathered around the blazing hearth of old John Hanks that evening. Conversation came in a broad, swift, raging torrent. The little ones toddled and clambered everywhere. The beds were brought in from the wagon and spread thick over the floor. The room was small, the company numerous, but love and friendship exorcised inconvenience, and the perfection of rustic happiness animated the scene. The equality was perfect—Abraham Lincoln and Dennis Hanks? How wide the gulf which separated their destinies—how perfect the amity which bound them together then! Alas! for the freaks and inequalities which Fate imposes on its creatures.

Not until the wee sma' hours did Tom and Abe and John and Dennis and Levi and their good host lie down to **secure a little needed** rest, for the newcomers were homeless, crops must be speedily planted, and a program of inspection and selection had to be made out for the succeeding day.

Six miles further down the stream, John Hanks had selected a place for the settlement of his kinfolks and had cut logs sufficient for a cabin. Thither all the men went the next morning; a site was selected for a field and the cabin, and the united energies of all were bent toward planting homes in the forest for the three families. **Exactly what Lincoln did toward this is *in nubibus* [unknown], but it is understood that somehow or other, the log hut was erected and** fifteen acres of river bottom were cleared for the use of Thomas Lincoln's family proper, it then consisting, theoretically, of his wife, Abraham, and John D. Johnston.

Those who observe and remember, can recall glorious nights during gibbous phases of the moon, when the sky was replete with masses of swift passing clouds afterward through whose fantastic rents appeared glimpses of pure dark azure, studded with glittering stars, but that with the flight of each recurring cloud that cast its opaque shadow across the glorious orb of night, another would fall into the solemn procession, producing an array of pronounced or funereal shadows, and arresting the brilliancy and glory which reigned serenely beyond the clouds.

This was typical and symbolical of the great president's life and career: afterward the solemn and somber procession of his life, lay shadows, sometimes baleful, always gloomy, which no moonlight glories or "sunshine sheen" ever rent asunder: and altho' he might behold glimpses of several, possibly ecstatic happiness, beyond the somber shade of his destiny, as in case of his engagement to Miss [Ann] Rutledge, his election to the presidency, or the dawn of peace, yet a cloud surcharged with black sorrow would intervene just as happiness seemed assured, and shut out the glorious vision from his sight, forever.

Yet even in his melancholy journey of life, there were three eras of unusual hardship and misery: one will be hereafter narrated—the premature death of Ann Rutledge. Another was the period between the death of his mother and the arrival of Sallie Bush Lincoln in the wretched house. Misery more abject, childish grief more poignant, privation more pronounced than presided over that rude Indiana home without a mother it would be difficult to conceive. Another era of more than normal misery was the first year in Illinois.

Abraham was now a legal *man*, having no claim for parental aid **or any reliance thereon**, and charged with all the responsibilities of budding and ambitious manhood. He was in a new State, **in a huge snowdrift**, surrounded by the most primitive society of the frontier—a mere adventurer, with nothing on earth but his right arm and uneducated brain as a capital with which to commence the journey of life. He was legally, but not morally, independent. His father had no financial ability, and, to put it plainly, was very liable to need the aid of his only son in the future as in the past. Faithful to all moral obligations then as thereafter, Abraham felt resting upon his shoulders, contingently, the burden of his father's and stepmother's support; and, all things considered, it would not be easy to find a more unenviable condition of American manhood than that which environed Abraham Lincoln when he cast off from the shores of dependent youth, and embarked on the uncertain voyage of independent and responsible life.

His home with his father thenceforth was but nominal; **his actual house was now at the humble cabin of John Hanks, although** he really lived with families for whom he worked, for most of the time as a hired laborer. All that is known of his career during the first year in Illinois is that he worked at odd-jobs when he could in the immediate neighborhood. He probably did not visit Decatur once during all that time. His residence in Macon County was apparently a simple bridging over from the irresponsible and reckless career of a fanciful youth of uncertain instincts to the incipient career of responsible life. His propensity to air his eloquence was not, however, in abeyance even then, for we learn that a candidate for the legislature, by the convenient and conventional name of "Posey" (that name standing as the John Doe of Lincolnian biography [actually John F. Posey]),[14] made a speech in the Hanks neighborhood on the then current political issue of the navigation of the Sangamo River. "Posey" seems to have been opposed to its improvement for navigation, and Lincoln in favor of it. Uncle John evidently knew his kinsman's views on the subject, for he at once took issue with "Posey," and avowed that "Abe" could beat it. So John brought out a box, which Abe mounted and made his oratorical bow to the sovereigns of his adopted State in the advocacy of a subject which never had anything but a fictitious political standing, and

14. Posey won election to the Illinois General Assembly in 1830.

60   *Chapter III*

which was soon overshadowed by the advent of the railway question, first as a political factor, and ultimately as a potential fact. It appears from Uncle John's statement that Abe beat "Posey" "to death" in the discussion, and that his discomfited antagonist, asking him where he had learned so much, encouraged him to assume the role of politician.

It will be recollected that Henry Clay, in addressing a class of students once, informed them that he had largely improved himself in the art of oratory by addressing imaginary audiences represented by hencoops, stumps, trees, etc. **It seems that** the future hero of the [1858] "joint debates" underwent a similar self-imposed discipline, and **that** alike in Spencer County, Indiana, and Macon County, Illinois, he was wont to convert the "deep, tangled wildwood" into an imaginary audience, and thus discipline his genius in the ways and graces of the effective orator.

It will be recollected that an especial reason why Thomas Lincoln removed from Indiana to Illinois was, as Dennis Hanks puts it, to get "where *'milk sick'* was not."[15] The new settlers did indeed escape the "milk sickness," but they encountered a disease which was nearly as bad. The fall of 1830 was an unusually severe season for chills and fever, and Thomas and his family were so sorely afflicted with it as to become thoroughly discouraged. Their little sorry cabin presented a melancholy sight, the father and mother both shaking at once, and the married daughter who came to minister to their sufferings not much better off. So terribly did they suffer that the father vowed a vow that as soon as he got able to travel he would *"git out o' thar."*

The winter season came on and was one of "ethereal mildness"[16] up to Christmas, when a terrible and persistent snowstorm set in and lasted without intermission for forty-eight hours, leaving between three and four feet on the ground on the level, a depth never attained before nor since, and remaining so for over two months. Its effect upon the rural districts was disastrous: the wheat crops were totally ruined; cattle, hogs, and even horses perished; all sorts of provisions gave out. There was no means of getting help from abroad. In some places, teams would bear up on the crust of the snow; in others, there was no road communication at all, and athletic men would be compelled to journey on foot to neighbors for food. Many perished on the prairie from cold; some even perished in their homes from hunger. Selfishness was exorcised by the common calamity; charity was universal. The whole interior districts of the State were made akin by that one touch of nature, the "big snow."

That awful event was made a chronological era ever afterwards. Many a fireside gathering has in the past generation of men been thrilled by a

15. Lamon, *Life of Lincoln*, 74n1.

16. "Come, gentle Spring! ethereal Mildness!" James Thomson, *The Four Seasons: Spring* (1730).

recounting of the **florid as well as sundry** incidents of that drear and awful "winter of the deep snow."

The "Hanks" neighborhood was unusually uninteresting, much more so than that which the emigrants had left behind in Indiana, and the twin calamities of "chills and fever" and the "deep snow," coming in succession, **and it was not long before** Thomas Lincoln emigrated in the succeeding spring to "Goose Nest" Prairie in the southern part of Coles County, about one hundred miles southeast of Decatur. Here he lived until his death in 1851.[17]

Flowing in a sinuous course, generally southwestwardly, through Champaign, Piatt, Macon, and between Christian and Sangamon Counties for a hundred miles, then turning abruptly to the northwest for about fifty miles, then pursuing a course due west until it finally reaches and mingles its turbid current with that of the Illinois is a river now known improperly as the "Sangamon." Its correct name, given by the Indians, "Sangamo," pronounced "Sangamaw," and it was so called in Lincoln's early manhood. The Hanks neighborhood is on the right bank of this river, at a point near to where its course is changed from a southwesterly to a northwesterly one. It was in the river bottoms of this stream, in this neighborhood, that Lincoln passed the first year of his manhood.

In February 1831, one Denton Offutt, a bibulous, "devil-may-care" sort of person, a combination of speculator and mountebank, drifted into this neighborhood and casually met John Hanks, who had somehow achieved a local fame as a flatboatman. Offutt proposed to Hanks to transport a flatboat load of country produce to New Orleans. Hanks was not unwilling to go, but deferred a definite answer till he could consult Lincoln and John D. Johnston and ascertain if they could be induced to accompany him.

Now I have heretofore stated that one of Lincoln's mental traits of character was a propensity for a diversion of employment, a hopping about from one thing to another, rather than consecutive, steady, and monotonous labor. He was, moreover, not disinclined to adventure, to seeing the world, to achieving knowledge in the school of experience and variety; and thus it was that he entered promptly into a business engagement with Offutt, by the terms of which Offutt was to provide a boat and cargo at the confluence of Sugar Creek and the south fork with the main Sangamo, a few miles east of the then obscure and ill-built village of Springfield. This boat Lincoln, John Hanks, and John D. Johnston were to navigate to New Orleans. The three argonauts met promptly at the appointed rendezvous, Lincoln and Hanks sailing down in a frail canoe, and their companion preferring the safer method of pedal locomotion. But they found neither boat nor cargo awaiting them. In point of fact, all that the energetic but erratic contractor had done was to engage to

17. Elsewhere, Whitney wrote that Thomas left "in search of a better chance to live an indolent life." *Life on the Circuit with Lincoln*, 19.

62 Chapter III

purchase sundry supplies of the few cross-road merchants. Thus the enterprise was, for the time being, suspended. However, the trio of prospective navigators, nothing daunted, but without a solitary cent, change of clothing, or anything corporeal except their bodies and the rude clothing which they wore, started on foot for Springfield, where they supposed some tidings of their employer might be obtained.

As I am not unfamiliar with the styles and modes of life of our frontier people in primitive days and conditions, I can see in my mind's eye this loutish crowd as they entered into the precincts of this uninviting village, then a sparsely settled community of five hundred people, poorly built, the streets almost totally impassable with deep "sticky" mud, **and presenting a cheerless, dismal, and inhospitable exterior, now the seat of opulent refinement and multitudes.**

It is not difficult for me to reproduce in fancy the supercilious stare which greeted these ragged searchers after light and knowledge as they prosecuted their inquiries at the few stores, for the whereabouts of "Denton Offutt." That their mission was supposed by those who took any interest in the matter to be a barren one was undoubted, for Offutt was generally known **in that little secluded community** to be an irresponsible projector. **Business formed the engrossing subjects of consideration, for Denton was a man for whom cause and effect had no connecting line, who took no note of the future, but lived wholly in and for the immediate present. His employment of these three denizens of the forest and the proposed trip was a passing fancy evoked by the casual concurrence of having in some loose way learned that John Hanks had run a flatboat down some of the same rivers of Kentucky. Meeting John soon after, and being led by the coincidence of hearing the story and meeting its subject at about the same time to the idea of trying a similar trip on the as yet unnavigated Sangamo.** Had not our adventurers followed the matter up, it is probable Denton would have done nothing further about it, but would have turned his attention to some other wild scheme. For this venture was not in the line of legitimate commerce or adventure; the Sangamo was not rated as a navigable stream; there was at least one mill-dam, and the river's availability for **purposes of** commerce and as a highway was then **widely** advocated, so far as was known, by only two individuals in the whole world, viz.: Abraham Lincoln in theory and Denton Offutt in practice.

It was at the Buckhorn Tavern, the leading place of its kind in town,[18] that Offutt was finally found. Although it was in the middle of the day, he was lying in a corner fast asleep, and most decidedly drunk.

---

18. Andrew Elliott of North Carolina owned that tavern. Paul M. Angle, *"Here I Have Lived": A History of Lincoln's Springfield, 1821–1865* (Springfield, IL: Abraham Lincoln Association, 1935), 15.

Lincoln as a Laborer

The presence of his boat's crew and the necessities of the occasion soon roused and stimulated the energies of the enterprising but erratic projector; and he gave *carte blanche* to his three employees to invade the government land and get out gunwales and to repair to a rude mill managed by one [William] Kirkpatrick (of whom more anon) and obtain the necessary lumber, at Offutt's expense, to construct the **indispensable** boat.

The three accordingly improvised a camp and adopted an organization to consummate the project in which to Lincoln was assigned the role of *"chief cook and bottle washer."* In thirty days hence the flatboat was completed and rode proudly on the bosom of the river, moored to the mud banks of the Sangamo—the pioneer of all water craft in that region.

I shall hereafter have occasion to note that Abraham Lincoln was always and ever ready to meet and master any of the real exigencies **of life** which lay in his pathway, and this incident furnished the first occasion for the exercise of his faculties in that line. He was the controlling spirit of the entire affair. It is even more than probable that Lincoln's advocacy of the practicability of navigating the Sangamo first induced Offutt to risk the venture, and it is also reasonably clear that his enthusiasm and spirit brought out of chaos and made practicable the carrying out of the enterprise. While **the three men were** engaged in building the boat, a peripatetic prestidigitator came along and gave an entertainment in a garret. This our boatbuilders attended, and it was Lincoln's hat that the magician used, in the manner of his craft, to cook eggs in, **after the style and manner of legerdemain cooking**. This was the first public entertainment **of** which we have any record that Lincoln attended. Throughout his subsequent career he was very fond of such amusements. That he was shot while gazing on a mimic scene has troubled many good folk who disapprove of theatres, and they have sought various excuses for his presence at the fatal play, such as his desire to honor General Grant, who was expected there, etc. The fact is, Lincoln had from the first a keen interest in any public performance, and in time developed a critical appreciation of the highest form of entertainment, the drama.

Offutt's adhesion to the flowing bowl retarded the enterprise, but during his spasms of sobriety, the load was engaged—the boat was loaded—the parting signal was given, and this argosy under command of Lincoln was, in the middle of April, set **afloat** on the raging tide.

At a distance of thirty-seven miles, as the river runs, a mill-dam was encountered on the 19th day of April, on which the rude craft, after passing one third of its length, stuck fast.

In the exigency thus presented, Lincoln was the directing and master mind. The forward end of the boat was tilted up, and the rear end submerged; a smaller boat was procured, and part of the load transferred. Lincoln then bored a hole in that part of the bottom of the boat which projected over the dam, and then rolled some heavy pork barrels forward, which gave a pitch to the boat and let the water run out, after which the hole was stopped up, and, by a skillful use of poles, the vessel was got over, reloaded, and sent forward on its course.

When the craft reached Beardstown, its odd appearance and wild-looking crew excited the derision of the inhabitants, who committed the undignified and inexcusable act of openly ridiculing them as they passed. The venture reached New Orleans at last, probably as rude a craft with as awkward a crew as ever floated out of the wild forest.

While at New Orleans, Lincoln saw the institution of slavery in one of its most revolting and reprehensible aspects. Nothing was more common in those days than the traffic in slaves, and New Orleans was the greatest slave market in the Union. One could not walk extensively in the streets without being an involuntary witness to the horror and infamy of the institution. Lincoln saw an octoroon girl offered for sale on the auction block. As the auctioneer dilated on her physical perfections to the lecherous crowd of tobacco chewers and whiskey-blossomed sots congregated in the market, and these passed **the coarse and** ribald jests on the subject **which attended the ceremony of transferring this young girl from an avaricious slaveholder to a lustful buyer,** the young Northerner was sickened by the scene and hastily withdrew from it, prophetically remarking to Hanks: "If I ever get a chance at that thing, I'll hit it hard."

In June, the venture having been concluded, the party returned up the river on the deck of a steamer as far as St. Louis, where the three companions left Denton, and started on foot for their several homes, so far as they had any. The companions followed the National Road as far as Edwardsville, where Hanks left them, taking a more direct road to his home in Macon County, and Lincoln and Johnston proceeded *via* the National Road, then extensively travelled, **as far as** a few miles beyond Ewington, where they made a detour north. Travel-stained and foot-sore, they finally presented themselves at the humble cabin door of Thomas and Sally Bush Lincoln. **They were two waifs on the great ocean of life, with no home or abiding place beyond the rude shelter of the loft of this humblest of human abodes.**

After seeing the world, the prospect of settling down in the Macon County cabin was not very inviting at best. The region was new, and the people all poor. Thomas Lincoln's hut was as rude and uncomfortable as was possible, and there was no incentive to exertion, nothing to stimulate the ambition. Yet Thomas was cheery and stout of heart. His squalor, so apparent to everyone else, was unobserved by him. In the dull surroundings of his rude abode, his spirits were jocund; and he was **blithe as a lark,** wholly unconscious that life held any greater happiness in its solution than that which animated his existence.

A few years after this time, William G. Greene was going to Kentucky on a visit, and as his way would lie near to where Thomas Lincoln lived, Abraham requested him to visit his father and deliver him a letter. Greene did so, and as he approached the cabin just before nightfall, his heart sank within him, for he beheld the most wretched hovel he had encountered in his journey. It was without a stable, outhouse of any kind, and not a shrub or tree was in sight. The proprietor appeared and, as soon as he learned the situation, exclaimed cheerily, "Get right down, Bill. You're welcome—heartily welcome. I'm right glad to see you. I'll make you and your beast so comfortable that you'll stay with me a week. Here's just the place to hitch your beast (indicating a log of the cabin with a projecting end). I use it to dress deer hides on: and I've got an iron kettle here, jest the thing for a feed-trough, and lots of shelled corn; so all you've got to do is to make yourself at hum as long as you like."

Greene said that Thomas was one of the shrewdest ignorant men he ever saw—that he took in, at a glance, the feelings of dismay which possessed the stranger as he rode up to the wretched abode, and that his task was to dispel that feeling; and he did it by making the guest feel that the host, at least, thought everything about to be of prime excellence. Seated before the rude hearth, Thomas Lincoln said, "I suppose that Abe is still fooling hisself with eddication. I tried to stop it, but he has got that fool idea in his head and it can't be got out. Now I hain't got no eddication, but I get along far better than ef I had. Take bookkeepin'—why, I'm the best bookkeeper in the world! Look up at that rafter thar. Thar's three straight lines made with a fire brand. Ef I sell a peck of meal I draw a black line across, and when they pay, I take the dishcloth and jest rub it out; and that thar's a heap better'n yer eddication," etc. (In point of fact, a part of his business was to superintend a small neighborhood mill). When Mr. Greene left his garrulous host the next morning, he said he felt as if he had gone out from the presence of an intellectually great, but entirely unpolished and uncultivated, man. Thomas Lincoln's rude methods of reasoning reminded him of the son, then likewise rude and unpolished.

After remaining at his father's home for four or five weeks, Abraham left it **finally and conclusively**, never again to enter it as an inmate. He had but a very light mortgage on the future, and that not based upon a very substantial title. Offutt, with all his recklessness and frivolity, had a considerable fund of sagacity and discernment, and he saw in Lincoln the making of a great man, and he was desirous to ally himself as closely to him as he could; hence, before parting at St. Louis, he entered into an arrangement with the young man by the terms of which Offutt was to tarry long enough there to gather up a stock of goods and open a store at the place where the boat had stuck on the dam, and Lincoln was to act as clerk. The first of August succeeding was designated as the period for the commencement of this business arrangement. With this slender hold upon fortune, Lincoln packed his entire worldly effects in a cotton handkerchief, and, slinging the bundle across his shoulder, and bidding a dutiful good bye to his father and a pathetic farewell to Sallie

Bush Johnston, he set his face **and directed his footsteps** westward in quest of a livelihood, with as **little advantageous aid, and as** cheerless a prospect, as ever attended a young man going out into the world.

The distance to the place where the boat stuck upon the dam was a hundred miles as the bird flies, but considerably more as he must travel it. He would probably consume four days in the journey, unless, as was probable, he deviated from a direct line and stopped at old John Hanks's *en route*. As he walked along that lonely way, what thoughts coursed through his busy brain as he contemplated that he was all alone in the broad ocean of life— that there was no visible outlook satisfying his craving ambition—that, to all appearances, he was a predestined "hewer of wood and drawer of water" forever! The dull monotony and dreary wretchedness of his past life cast its long baleful shadow over his future career. There seemed no visible mode to quiet that "vague unrest" which animated him was apparent. Hitherto he had sustained a bare existence by prosaic, muscular labor. Would it be always thus? Where was the harbinger of a better future? What had the vast future in store for this homeless wanderer who thus set out to baffle destiny and conquer fate?

IV

The Romance of New Salem

Sweet Auburn! Loveliest village of the plain,
Where peace and plenty cheer the laboring swain.[1]

૨૭

To griefs congenial prone,
More wounds than Nature gave, he knew;
While misery's form, his fancy drew
In dark ideal hues, and horrors, not its own.[2]

During the year 1824, James Rutledge,[3] Edward Rutledge, brothers, and John Miller Cameron,[4] their brother-in-law [actually nephew], settled in that portion of Sangamon County now known as Concord Township, in Menard County. Cameron was a Cumberland Presbyterian preacher;[5] the Rutledges belonged to the celebrated family of that name whose members were the

1. Oliver Goldsmith, "The Deserted Village" (1770). Unlike the 1892 manuscript version of the book, the material in this chapter is found in the published 1907 version as a continuation of chapter 3 rather than a separate unit. In the view of the present editor, to retain the chapter distribution of the 1892 version makes more sense. The poetry serving as the chapter's epigraph, unlike the text of most of the chapter, does not appear in the published book.

2. Thomas Warton (1728–1790), "The Suicide: An Ode" (1771).

3. In 1829, James Rutledge (1781–1835) and his nephew John M. Cameron founded New Salem. Two years later, he converted his house into a tavern and sold it the following year. He left the village in 1833 and died of typhoid fever in 1835, as did his daughter Ann, Lincoln's sweetheart.

4. The Rev. Mr. John Miller Cameron (1791–1878), husband of Mary Orendorff, left New Salem in 1832 for Fulton County, Illinois, then moved to Iowa, and finally to California.

5. The Cumberland Presbytery, formed in 1802 for Kentucky and Tennessee, became controversial when its leaders felt compelled to ordain underqualified ministers because so few educated men moved to the frontier.

68   *Chapter IV*

political leaders of South Carolina in the auroral days of the republic. **They had come originally from Henderson County, Kentucky. One of the families had settled in White County, Illinois; both brothers—along with their sister and her husband—were reunited at Concord Township.**

Two years thereafter, James Rutledge and his brother-in-law, Cameron, built a rude dam **and mill** across the Sangamon at a point ten miles distant from Concord, and established a very primitive saw- and grist-mill, known interchangeably as "Cameron's" or "Rutledge's" mill. It was upon this dam that the flatboat of Offutt's venture got fast.

Upon the brow of a rocky ridge, overlooking the dam, Mr. Rutledge and Mr. Cameron each built a log dwelling-house, and installed their families therein. **The ridge was fringed with timber, the black walnut, the sycamore, the ash, elm, locust, and jack oak. The unvexed prairie was gay and brilliant with the verbena, the violet, the primrose, the dandelion, the daisy. The solemn silence was unbroken save by the mellifluous and slumbrous falling of the waters over the dam, and the brilliant notes of the song birds, and as the eye portrayed to the fancy the scenes of arcadian beauty which created the vision on all sides, and the ear translated to the imagination the poetry of the feathered songsters' bird songs, a feeling of tranquility and of suppressed enthusiasm would steal over the senses; and one might exclaim with the poet**

> **"And if there is an Elysium to be found in this world,
> It is this: it is this!"**[6]

The neighbors **of the Rutledge bothers and Cameron** were Bowling Green,[7] who lived a half or three quarters of a mile north; Bennett Abell,[8] whose house was a mile further on; "Billy" Greene, who lived three miles southwest; and a considerable settlement a few miles southwestward in "Clary's Grove."

Business at the mill prospered, and the economical exigencies demanded more commercial facilities than the original enterprise furnished. So Rutledge and Cameron added to their enterprise by purchasing the ridge adjacent to the mill, and on October 13, 1829, laying out a town there. This they called New Salem, a name indicative of the religious turn of mind of its founders. Cameron

---

6. Thomas Moore, "Lalla Rookh," Part IX: *The Light of the Harem* (1817).

7. Shortly after his arrival in New Salem in 1831, Lincoln found a surrogate father/mentor in the farmer Bowling Green (1786–1842), a rotund, hospitable, easygoing, humorous, jovial "reading man" from North Carolina known as a gifted spinner of yarns.

8. Dr. Bennett Howard Abell (1796–1876) was a farmer at whose house near New Salem Lincoln lived for a time.

The Romance of New Salem

had already erected a log hotel of four rooms, and, immediately thereafter, two enterprising young men from the East, Samuel Hill[9] and John McNamar, alias John McNeil,[10] opened a small store there. A post office was established, and once a week the stagecoach, or "mud wagon" as it was termed, in its journey from Havana to Springfield, turned aside from the main road, ascended the ridge, and gladdened the few dwellers there with the weaving of a commercial and literary link between them and the outer world.

The hamlet took on a slow, plodding, irregular growth; people came from fifty miles to acquire anything exotic to their farms, and, in **the** natural course of trade, this supply soon came. **Henry Onstott brought a cooper's kit, erected a shed, and opened up;[11] Martin Waddell improvised a hatter's shop;[12] Joshua Miller started a blacksmith shop;[13] Jonathan Dunn, a millwright,[14] settled there; George Warburton established a store;[15] one [Henry] Sinco did the same;[16] Samuel Hill started a carding machine; several physicians were there at different times (Drs. Jason Duncan,[17] John Allen,[18] and [Francis] Regnier);[19] Rowan Herndon became a merchant**

9. The prosperous merchant Samuel Hill (1800–1857) owned not only a store but also a carding machine that turned raw wool into fiber for spinning.

10. The well-to-do John McNamar, alias McNeil (1801–1879), erected the first general store in New Salem and owned a farm seven miles northwest of town. He courted Ann Rutledge, who, after he had evidently abandoned her, chose Lincoln over him.

11. In 1830, Henry Onstott (1804–1876) moved to New Salem, where he worked as a cooper, did some farming, and opened a tavern.

12. In 1832, Martin Waddell moved to New Salem, where he made woolen and fur hats and enjoyed a reputation as an unusually good-natured fellow.

13. Kentuckian Joshua A. Miller (1795–1894), a wagon maker as well as blacksmith, was the brother-in-law of Lincoln's close friend in New Salem, Jack Kelso.

14. Jonathan Dunn (1801–1866) built the New Salem mill and in 1831 moved to nearby Athens, where he was a merchant.

15. George Warburton (d. 1840) was a merchant who helped found the town of Petersburg, near New Salem. He drowned in the Sangamon River, evidently after passing out while drunk.

16. Henry Sinco, constable of Sangamon County, operated a store/grocery in New Salem, which he left for Kentucky in 1834.

17. Vermont-born Dr. Jason Duncan (b. 1799), who wed Nancy Burner, was a physician who lived in New Salem (1831–1834) before moving to Knoxville, Illinois.

18. A devout Presbyterian and graduate of Dartmouth Medical School, John Allen (1801–1863) established a Sunday school and a temperance society in New Salem.

19. Dr. Francis Regnier (1808–1859) of Marietta, Ohio, bought Henry Sinco's cabin in 1831, then moved to Clary's Grove in 1834.

there;[20] **Edmund Greer became a schoolmaster and a justice of the peace;[21] Bowling Green a farmer, three quarters of a mile distant, was also a justice of the peace; and Mentor Graham, a pedagogue of ancient and high renown, kept school on a ridge east of town and on the yon side of Rock Creek;[22] and when Justice Greer got his commission, together with a copy of the old statutes and a stock of blanks, enlightenment was formally enthroned, and the goddess of justice lifted "aloft her scale."[23]**

20. In 1830, John Rowan Herndon (1807–1882) and James Herndon, cousins of Lincoln's law partner and biographer William Herndon, opened a store in New Salem that they later sold to William Berry.

21. Schoolteacher Edmund Greer was among the first candidates for whom Lincoln cast a vote. In 1831, Greer was soundly beaten in his bid to win election as a magistrate despite receiving Lincoln's support. He eventually became a justice of the peace.

22. Mentor Graham (1800–1886) could not fairly claim much credit for teaching grammar to Lincoln, who said that he "studied with nobody." Lincoln's sharpness in debate may have been honed by Graham, whose forte as a teacher was elocution.

23. "All crimes shall cease, and ancient fraud shall fail;
> Returning Justice lift aloft her scale;
> Peace o'er the world her olive wand extend,
> And white-robed Innocence from heaven descend."

Alexander Pope, "The Messiah: A Sacred Eclogue, in Imitation of Virgil's Pollio."

V

Lincoln as a Storekeeper

When Denton Offutt's boat stuck on the dam, New Salem was in the second year of its existence, and had then quite a population. So notable and unusual an occurrence as a flatboat, and especially one **stuck** fast on their mill dam, aroused the curiosity of the citizens, and brought the entire hamlet to the river banks, where Lincoln, in the role of commander, was the most conspicuous object. So he was not forgotten, when, in August thereafter, he walked into the town with a bundle in a handkerchief slung across his shoulder, and joined the little knot of idlers sitting on their haunches on the shady side of Hill's store. He opened out his Pandora's box of jokes, affiliated with the crowd at once, and, "as the setting sun cast his lengthened shadow athwart the little village, it showed no sign of his parting from them."[1]

Lincoln gave no intimation as to what brought him there, but soon endeared himself to all by exhibiting great muscular strength, *bonhomie,* and his propensity to entertain by anecdotes.

A local election coming on, and "scribes" being scarce, the village schoolmaster, Mentor Graham, asked him if he could write. He was cautious then as thereafter: "I can make a few rabbit tracks," was the answer, and he acted as clerk of elections, in company with a young Mr. [Thomas J.] Nance.[2] It should be noted that distrust did not prevail in those new regions in that early day. Decent-appearing strangers were taken into the hearts and homes of the people, without criticism or inspection; if work was pressing, they were invited

---

1. "As the sun declined to its setting, casting long shadows athwart the soil from every pebble, Jean Valjean sat down behind a bush upon a large ruddy plain, which was absolutely deserted." Victor Hugo, *Les Miserables.*

2. Born in Kentucky, Thomas Jefferson Nance (1811–1842) taught in subscription schools in the vicinity of New Salem, where he settled in 1832.

to buckle to; if they proved to be drones, they were stung from the hive. If work was slack, they were invited to join a fishing or a hunting party; to social life they must contribute their share. In that respect, Lincoln was a valuable acquisition; he knew no one when he came there except such persons as he had seen from his flatboat, yet in two days, he was no longer a stranger.

In a day or so after the election, a Dr. [David P.] Nelson, who had lived in the neighborhood, desired to migrate to Texas, and proposed to float with his family and effects, from below the dam at New Salem to Beardstown; thence to the Mississippi, and finally, down that majestic stream to the mouth of the Red River by means of a small flatboat. Being in need of a pilot to convoy the outfit to Beardstown, he employed Lincoln to fill that **(to him)** responsible role. At Beardstown, Lincoln encountered his employer, Offutt, who had just arrived with a part of his goods, the rest being due by the next steamer. Lincoln was left to await their arrival and to see to their proper storage, while Offutt should repair to New Salem in order to rent or build a store and engage teamsters to haul over the goods. Offutt employed one [John] Potter[3] and another man to transport the goods, and advised them that on the way they might meet Lincoln, from whom they should procure the necessary order for them. "How will we know him?" queried Potter. "You can't mistake him," replied Offutt. "He's as long as bean pole, and as awkward as he is long."

They met Lincoln on the highway, and he wrote an order for the goods on a blank leaf of a small memorandum book he had with him. Potter looked at it and observed; "you've spelt money, m-o-n-y." Lincoln glanced at it and replied, "Well, they can't make anything else out of it." The goods came in due season, and Lincoln took charge of unboxing and putting them in position, after which he commenced his new career as the most awkward and ungainly store clerk, probably, in the State of Illinois. Offutt, however, was perfectly satisfied with his clerk, and besides, was enthusiastic in his praise of him as a man. Having had occasion, during his flatboat trip, to witness his marvelous strength and to see his prowess satisfactorily tested, he admired Lincoln extravagantly, and there were in New Salem those who shared Offutt's admiration, though in a minor degree.

Offutt's unlimited admiration for Lincoln in the abstract was not satisfactory, but he must needs make concrete applications of it, by contrast and comparison; and, in effect, he threw down the gage of battle to all mankind, which, in that era of muscular development, was instantly taken up.

In point of fact, Bill Clary[4] challenged Offutt's proud boast that Lincoln could throw anybody who might offer. About three miles distant from New Salem was a large grove, termed Clary's Grove, which was inhabited by a wild

---

3. John Potter (1808–1900) was a farmer living near New Salem.
4. William Price Clary (1800–1870) operated a grocery/tavern in New Salem.

lot of pioneers from Kentucky and Tennessee. Their early education and proclivities induced the habits of drinking, fighting, wrestling, horse-racing, shooting at a mark &c., and their residence on the frontier with no attrition with any society or civilization except themselves, tended to foster and intensify the wild and uncivilized habits and tendencies of their youth. The Clary's Grove boys, as they were termed, when **massed together,** animated with bad whiskey, and decorated with shooting irons of the rude patterns incident to the time, were so thoroughly reckless and on mischief bent as to be a source of the utmost terror to all well-disposed people who lived in the track of their bacchanalian forays. Prior to the advent of Cameron's mill, they had had no stated rendezvous, but when that was founded, it provided a sort of common rallying point, which was made more definite and became more pronounced when Hill and McNeil started a store on the hill. In that era of the settlement of our frontier, all merchants kept cheap and bad whiskey as one of the chief and indispensable staples. This necessary article of merchandise was purchased in its fiery, untamed state and condition in Cincinnati and Saint Louis at the stated and constant price of eighteen and three-quarters cents per gallon. A thrifty merchant could easily, after he got started, by the aid of a pump, perform the benefaction of causing three barrels to flow in the place of two.

One Jack Armstrong was the leader **(or a leader)** of these rowdy pioneers.[5] Their mode of life was to waste the first five secular days of the week in farm or forest labor, then on Saturday to put on their best attire, mount their nags, **gather together in a wood**, and consume the day and night in various modes and manifestations of frontier rowdyism. When any issue was joined with any other segment of mankind, the trial was by wager of battle, in which Jack was their champion, **the Tancred of the Clary Grove boys, and to his credit, be it spoken, he never caused the whiskey-blossomed faces of his adherents to take on a more brilliant carnation hue, by reason of any failure or delinquency**.

The closest approach to organized opposition to the pretensions of the Clary's Grove boys was a loose band known as the "River Timber boys," who inhabited the timber belts which skirted the river bottoms. The several issues of supremacy—**such** as wrestling, fighting, scrub-racing &c—had been settled between these two sets of "back settlement" rowdies before the advent of Lincoln, **in the tented field, so to speak.**

"The cankers of a calm world and a long peace"[6] held place in the **stagnant** settlement. It was then that Bill Clary, one of the "Clary's Grove" boys,

---

5. John "Jack" Armstrong (1804–1857) was a blacksmith and a brother-in-law of Bill Clary.

6. Falstaff in Shakespeare, Henry IV, part I, act 4, scene 2.

74   *Chapter V*

sounded a blast on his bugle-horn by proposing a little bet, at the close of a heated dispute with Offutt, that Jack Armstrong could throw Lincoln, "the best two out of three." This very greatly annoyed Lincoln; **as** preeminently a man of peace, he abhorred personal conflict, or anything that savored of ill-feeling. He had gained the good will of everybody in that little community, and deprecated aught that would disturb the *entente cordiale*. Besides, it could lead to no good results. What matters it if Jack or Abe was the stronger? Lincoln could see no utility in the contest proposed, and his whole soul rebelled against it. Of course Offutt's intentions were good; he supposed that Abe would come off conqueror, and that it would bring zest, if not satiety, to a great ambition **and that it would be a brilliant feather in his cap. But the adage "save me from my friend" found an application here, and Offutt's well-intentioned designs were prolific of mischief to his friend's sensitive feelings.**

However, the edict had gone forth, and Lincoln must pose **as** a contestant or be branded as a coward in a community where such an accusation was the foulest and most damnatory conceivable—social death, in fact.

The combatants and their respective allies adjourned to the scene of the coming fray; bye bets of all conceivable kinds were made; dirk knives, horse pistols, "slick quarters," &c were staked galore on the contest. No such excitement ever reigned within the peaceful precincts of New Salem before or since. Many of Lincoln's biographers have enlarged upon the prolific theme of this contest, but for some reason they have generally allowed the wings of their imagination to exceed the tail feathers of their judgment, and have woven a brilliant fabrication out of a very commonplace incident.

The most zealous friend whom Lincoln had on the field of conflict, aside from Offutt, was William G. Greene. He narrated the incident to me in this wise: it does not attest the strength of Samson to be a part of his friend's equipment, as other biographers do, but it does in a characteristic manner show his moral force. The two wrestlers caught "*holts*" and the contest began.

Long time in even scale the battle hung.[7]

In point of fact, the men were so evenly balanced that not the slightest headway was made.

Lincoln took the sensible view of the case then, as always. "Let's quit" said he. "We are evenly matched, and we may as well quit even."

The Clary Grove crowd foolishly deemed this frank confession as an exhibition of the "white feather," and a huge yell of derision and defiance enforced the decree that the contest must go on.

Lincoln, now goaded to a sort of semi-desperation, profiting by his great strength, and roused to its highest pitch of achievement by the attendant

---

7. Milton, *Paradise Lost*, 2:628.

excitement, fairly lifted his burly antagonist off his feet, but the dexterous wrestler, by an adroit movement of his supple legs, landed squarely on his feet instead of on his back, as Lincoln had intended, and, in his turn, by what is termed in sporting vernacular, a *foul*, threw Lincoln. **It was an outrage and a moral felony; and** a victory thus achieved was only maintainable by the *ultima ratio regum*, in other words, by open war.

It was not legitimate wrestling, but contemptible trickery, which should forever have barred out its perpetrator from the society and companionship of legitimate rowdies. It is reported that, once, at a horse race, Andrew Jackson became conscious that a triad of gamblers had taken possession of the field, had secured large bets, had corrupted the jockeys, and by other nefarious practices had organized victory on their behalf. The great hero assembled the few honest men present, briefly stated the case, and proposed to compel the stakeholders, who also were in the gamblers' pool, to disgorge. Jackson then drew his pistols and advancing to where the felonious gang were quartered, with the look of an infuriated tiger, demanded the stakes and the sullen crowd saw in that determined look and emphatic demand, an imperious necessity that they should yield, which they did without parley, in abject fear and confusion.

In a similar manner Lincoln rose from the ground **"like Brutus Refulgent from the stroke of Caesar's fate"**[8] with **a countenance in** every feature indicative of vengeance. Said he, in a tone and manner which struck consternation to all present: "That won't do; and I'll show anyone who doubts it, that it won't do. You can't make that game work with me!" The crowd understood perfectly what Lincoln meant, **and they stated almost in chorus, "It was a joke, of course it was."** It was at once claimed that Jack took that mode of acceding to Lincoln's desire to end the contest by calling it a *draw*. So the *entente cordiale* was restored, and Lincoln and Jack Armstrong became thenceforth the closest of friends, which amity and concord bound and embraced the entire Armstrong family, **through which Lincoln found a welcome home at Armstrong's hearth ever thereafter.** In 1858, Lincoln saved a son of the family from the gallows, **which son he** discharged from service during the war.[9]

It need scarcely be added that Lincoln's prowess and manhood were put to no further test in that neighborhood, but I should add that at an election

---

8. Thomas De Quincy, "Sortilege on Behalf of the Glasgow Athenaeum" (1848).

9. In 1857, William "Duff" Armstrong (1833–1899) was accused of murder; the following year, Lincoln successfully defended him in what became known as the "almanac trial." During the Civil War, young Armstrong, serving as an enlisted man in the Union Army, became ill, and Lincoln approved his discharge at the request of his mother, Hannah. See George R. Dekle Sr., *Abraham Lincoln's Most Famous Case: The Almanac Trial* (Santa Barbara, CA: Praeger, 2014).

held one year thereafter at which Lincoln was a candidate, every vote was cast for him from Clary's Grove; it would have been social ostracism to anyone to do otherwise.[10]

Offutt's restless ambition demanded other worlds to conquer than a small store, so he added to his list of mercantile ventures a lease of the mill and then employed William G. Greene, a son of a neighboring farmer, aged eighteen or nineteen years, as an assistant. Between the two clerks, a friendship and cordiality sprang up which lasted as long as the life of the senior. In fact, Mr. Greene, still alive, and now a wealthy banker and capitalist, avers that even in those rude days he had a belief that Lincoln was the greatest man who ever lived, and it is a source of great satisfaction to him to find the opinion of the polite world of this enlightened day and generation rapidly crystalizing to his belief.

The course of business at New Salem, in Lincoln's day, was for the farmers to send their boys to mill at all times except Sunday, but they themselves reserved and set apart Saturday to visit town—do their little trading, give and receive gossip—indulge in scrub racing, cock fighting, rowdying—getting drunk &c. Consequently the little village would be replete with excitement, animation, bustle, and business during Saturday, but would be stagnant during the rest of the week; and, in consequence, Lincoln could devote most of his time at the mill receiving *grists*, taking tolls, loading up and tying up sacks &c while Greene attended to the humdrum business of the little store on the hill.

Each morning, the two clerks, and sometimes the proprietor, would wend their way down the slanting road which led to the bottom land northward, and proceed up the State road for three quarters of a mile to a primitive farmstead owned by one Bowling Green, where they would get their breakfast, generally of bread and milk. They would greet their motherly hostess as Aunt Nancy. At noon and evening they would repeat this custom, for their boarding place was at this farm, and they slept on a narrow cot in the loft of the store.

Although Lincoln was but an ordinary clerk and mill hand reared in the frontier, awkward and modest in the extreme, ill-favored to the superficial view, unkempt and badly attired, yet he had the respect and esteem of all. Lincoln's morals and manners were singularly chaste and pure for that day. Although the customs were well-nigh universal to drink, chew, smoke, and habitually swear, he indulged in none of these habits. Mr. Greene avers that he never saw him take a drink of liquor but once, and then he at once spat it out; that he never chewed or smoked, and that he never swore but once in his presence (which I shall refer to again).

10. Lincoln ran unsuccessfully for the Illinois state legislature in 1832.

Lincoln **was brought up in the midst of a wild crowd, yet he was not only strictly moral himself, but he** was also sedulous to impart moral instruction where it could be effectually done without improper intrusion upon the prejudices of the delinquent. William Greene was, like ordinary youth in those days, addicted to petty gambling, betting &c. Lincoln perceived it and one day said to his fellow clerk: "Billy, you ought to stop gambling with [Elijah] Estep."

Greene replied, "I'm ninety cents behind, and I can't quit till I've won it back."

Said Lincoln, "If I'll help you win that back, will you promise never to gamble again?"

Greene reflected a moment and made the promise.

Lincoln then said, "Here are hats which are on sale at seven dollars each, and you need one. Now when Estep comes, you draw him on by degrees, and finally bet him one of those hats that I can lift a full forty-gallon barrel of whiskey and take a drink out of the bung hole."

Accordingly, they fixed the barrel so the bung hole would be in the right place, and when the victim appeared, after a little parleying and bantering, the bet was made. Lincoln then squatted down and lifted one end of the barrel on one knee and then lifted the other end of the barrel on the other knee, and stooping over, actually succeeded in taking a drink out of the bung hole, which, however, he immediately spat out. Greene thus won the hat and never gambled again.

Offutt soon "busted up" and left his creditors in the lurch; and Lincoln did odd jobs when, and as, he could for a time. He had an assured home at Bowling Green's, and another at Jack Armstrong's, and when under the stress of difficulties, he wended his way to one or the other with perfect freedom, and was a welcome guest.

Ten years thereafter, Mr. William G. Greene encountered Offutt at Memphis, Tennessee, posing as a veterinary surgeon and also as a horse-tamer. He was fantastically arrayed and prone to garrulity but seemed to be eking out an existence by his calling.

Let us not disdain this wild product of frontier civilization, however, for we should cherish and honor any agency in the evolution of Abraham Lincoln. Offutt was his generous friend and gave him his first start in life. Through his agency, Lincoln was transplanted from the somber wilderness of Hanks's neighborhood to the more progressive conditions and more congenial surroundings of New Salem—his first living in an aggregate community. **But for Offutt his career would have been different; and it is certain that Offutt was a link in the chain of causation which linked Lincoln the fieldhand with Lincoln the emancipator; and as Offutt was a factor in his destiny, his name should be ever mentioned with respect.**

78   *Chapter V*

As a merchant's clerk in New Salem had an abundance of leisure, Lincoln spent much time in reading and studying. He was never without a book. From Billy Greene he borrowed Kirkham's grammar,[11] and from his brother, L. M. Greene,[12] he also borrowed Lindley Murray's grammar.[13] **At still another time,** Ann Rutledge used to lend him her grammar to study of nights; this same grammar is in possession of the Rutledge family with the name of the once-fair owner on a fly leaf, and that of the great emancipator printed under it, both names inscribed by himself.

Lincoln recited his lessons in grammar to Greene, and in three weeks knew as much of the subject as Greene **himself knew**. At Washington in after years, Greene was in the Executive Chamber, and Lincoln took pride and pleasure in introducing Greene to members of his Cabinet and others as his "grammar master."

New Salem was bounded on the south by a ravine, at the foot of which flowed a rugged, sprightly rivulet termed "Rock Creek" or "Greene's Rocky branch," which could be readily crossed by pedestrians. At the top of the ridge beyond this branch was a log school house in which one Mentor Graham, a professional pedagogue, kept school, and to which the children and youth of New Salem, and the adjacent country, repaired. Graham was devoted to his calling, for he taught in log school houses for fifty consecutive years, **two terms each year. His financial success, or the lack of it, is exemplified by the fact that, at the administrative sale of Bowling Green's effects in 1843, he made purchases to the extent of One Hundred Dollars and gave his note with two securities, and which note on default of payment was sued by Nancy Green**[14] **the widow and administratrix in the circuit court, Lincoln himself drawing the declaration.**

Mentor lived at New Salem during his term of service on the adjacent hill, and to him Lincoln applied for private tuition, with the result that he made rapid progress in mathematics, geography, grammar, and spelling. A favorite diversion of his was to visit the little rustic school at spelling time and sit on

11. Samuel Kirkham, *English Grammar in Familiar Lectures* (Cincinnati: N. & G. Guilford, 1828). At first, Lincoln needed help mastering this dry tome, for, as he said, Kirkham "was a puzzler at the start, with its four, five, and six headed rules, about as complicated to beginners as the Longer Catechism and the Thirty-nine Articles to young ministers." But he quickly acquired a sound knowledge of English grammar.

12. Lynn McNulty "Nult" Greene (1814–1882) attended Illinois College and helped Lincoln study grammar.

13. In 1795, Lindley Murray (1745–1826), published the bestselling English grammar book of all time, simply called *English Grammar*.

14. Nancy Potter (1793–1867) was married to Bowling Green. For a while, Lincoln lived with the Greens at their home half a mile north of the village.

Lincoln as a Storekeeper 79

the back bench and listen attentively as the lesson progressed. Occasionally he would make some comment, **such** as, "I could almost spell that myself," but his presence was always welcome, and his intrusion was never reprobated.

It was a marked characteristic of Lincoln that under all circumstances and in every condition, his mind was ever on the alert in pursuit of knowledge. Books were then very scarce, but he somehow obtained access to them. **While living in Indiana, he ardently sought and greedily possessed himself of all the information obtainable in the few books which were owned in that neighborhood; the same habit prevailed at New Salem. He borrowed schoolbooks, as we have said, and when he finally returned them, he had** possessed himself of their contents, assimilating the knowledge to himself and to his own needs. In reading his speeches and official documents, one can hardly conceive that their composer acquired his academical knowledge almost entirely out of school and without a teacher; his spelling was almost without flaw and his syntax practically accurate. His faculty of composition was not only faultless, but embellished with the grace and adornment of *belles lettres.*

After Lincoln had terminated his novitiate in mercantile life with the downfall of Offutt, his next mercantile venture and experience was achieved in a mode peculiar, and possibly only, to the business methods, or lack of any, of the frontier.

It occurred thus: Reuben Radford[15] brought a stock of goods to New Salem and opened a store. He was duly warned against the idiosyncrasies of the "Clary's Grove boys," but incorrectly reasoned that he could keep them under control if he limited their allowance of drinks to two each. It so happened, however, that, upon the occasion of their first visit to New Salem after his settlement there, he was on a visit in the country, three miles distant, and his young brother was in charge.

After the crowd had drunk twice around, the young clerk informed them that he had reached the limit of his orders, and that the faucet to the whiskey barrel was laid under an embargo till their next visit. That was an abnormal condition of affairs, and not in accordance with the theory of government and latitudinarianism of conduct for which their forefathers "fit," and they sought, but in vain, so to impress, by logical methods, the warden of the indispensable *spiritus frumenti.* But the youth was a rigid disciplinarian and declined to yield, whereupon the crowd whipped out their horse pistols and made targets of the various alluring show bottles of whiskey which adorned the shelves, and in a few minutes spread chaos and devastation throughout the whole interior. **Disorder was regnant for a while, and at the conclusion of the diversion, the floor of the store presented a scene of horror**

15. Reuben Radford was a Springfield businessman.

and disaster shameful to behold. The "boys" then made good use of the exhilaration which an unlimited supply of whiskey superinduced, and riot reigned supreme in that neighborhood extending into "the wee sma' hours" of the succeeding morning. Shortly before day, Radford's peaceful sleep was disturbed by the bacchanalian yelling of the rowdies *en route* for their homes, and fearing danger at his store, he mounted his horse and rode posthaste toward the little hamlet. Billy Greene, then still a boy, was on his pony going early to mill. Seeing Radford dash past him, his horse reeking with sweat, he followed at a breakneck pace to learn the cause of such excitement. Radford reached his store, and hastily alighting, stood on the platform and gazed in at the open door with dismay upon the broken bottles and other debris of the saturnalian debauch. Greene, reaching the store a minute later, rode up to the open window just as Radford in desperation exclaimed, "I'll sell out this whole 'shebang' at the first offer I get." Greene, at a venture, exclaimed, "I offer $400."

"Done," said Radford; "the concern's yours."

"But I've got no money," said Greene.

"Never mind about money," said the disgusted merchant. "Come right in and give me your note at six months," which Greene promptly and recklessly did.

Radford bestrode his steed, and left young Greene "monarch of all he surveyed."[16] The store was located immediately opposite to the hotel (so called) where Lincoln, at that time, abode, and just at this moment he appeared at the washstand out of doors, **to wash his face for the day.** Seeing the youthful speculator, and divining his embarrassment of riches, Lincoln said cheerily, "Hold on, Bill, till I get a bite of breakfast, an' we'll take an inventory and see what you've got."

"I doan' want any more inventory," was the reply. "The Clary Grovers have done all the inventoryin' I want."

But after breakfast Lincoln and Greene went through the stock and found that the stock was worth $750, at least. Lincoln was out of a job just then, and one William Berry[17] was then also out of employment, but the possessor, just at that juncture, of $250 in cash, and a good horse, saddle, and bridle. In less than an hour from the time the inventory was made, a trade had been made as follows: Berry and Lincoln formed a partnership and bought out Greene; Berry paid him $250 in cash and gave him the horse, saddle, and bridle estimated at $100, and assumed payment of his debt to Radford, and Greene was

16. "I am monarch of all I survey
　　My right there is none to dispute."
William Cowper, "Verses, Supposed to be Written by Alexander Selkirk" (1782).

17. William Franklin Berry (1811–1835) was the bibulous son of John M. Berry, a Cumberland Presbyterian minister.

to have the store receipts for that day. The new firm then went into possession and took in $15 and a Spanish shilling; and young Greene, highly elated by his first business venture, rode home that night with $265.12½ and a horse, saddle, and bridle as a result of his investment of a boy's pluck and enterprise.

The firm of Berry and Lincoln next absorbed the stock and business of a moribund firm entitled James and Rowan Herndon.[18] The new enterprise was, however, greatly handicapped, first by the lack of capital of the firm, and secondly by the devotion of the senior partner to the whiskey jug and of the junior partner to "star-eyed science."[19] **Lincoln did, indeed, attend perfunctorily to the wants of the customers, but he brought no enthusiasm or commercial talent to the work, and while engaged in waiting on customers he was quite apt to be diverted by something he "was put in mind of," or by some scientific or educational diversion, during the consideration of which business in the store would cease or languish. So when females would seek to trade at the counter of Berry & Lincoln, the junior partner would retire out of sight and leave them to be imperfectly ministered unto by the bibulous Berry, all to their detriment, and finally, extinction of their trade.**

While Lincoln does not seem to have been animated with any great ambition to achieve distinction as a clerk or miller, he yet was **entirely faithful to, and honest in performance of his duties; he was** rigidly honest **both** as to money matters and likewise **as** to representations made in course of trade. He would not dissemble, color the truth, or excite a customer's desire to buy unnecessarily or beyond his means; he frankly told good customers that the very whiskey which he drew for them would prove their ruin, and that the tobacco which he dealt out was nasty and unfit for use. If he knew nothing of the merits or quality of goods under review, he frankly said so. **He was in no case guilty of** *suppressio veri* **[suppression of the truth] or** *suggestio falsi* **[false statement] in his mercantile or other operations.** His propensity to entertain by stories attracted customers to some extent, but that same tendency, likewise, obstructed business, for it was no unusual spectacle of a Saturday to behold sales arrested while Lincoln was regaling a crowd in the store by incidents, "airy nothings," but to which he gave "a local habitation and a name."[20] Upon such occasions, **one might be sure that the whole crowd of outsiders would flock into Offutt's store or that of Berry & Lincoln, as**

---

18. In 1832, the bachelor James Herndon, wanting to move west, sold his half interest in the store he jointly owned with his brother Rowan to William Berry, while Rowan sold his interest in that store to Lincoln.

19. "O star-eyed Science! hast thou wandered there,
    To waft us home the message of despair?"
Thomas Campbell, "Pleasures of Hope: Part 2" (1799).

20. Shakespeare, A Midsummer Night's Dream, V:1.

the case might be, and that uproarious laughter was heard from one end of the little hamlet to the other. Mrs. Hill[21] says that she could always tell when Lincoln had let himself loose. She adds that his stories seemed never to **flag or** lose interest, **but** that his entertainments were apparently as fully appreciated in the fourth year of their run as during the first.

So far as appeared, Lincoln did not seem to have any exalted ambition or towering aspirations. His juvenile prophecies of attaining the presidency seem to have evanesced with his callow youth, and he seemed content to make both ends meet financially, to entertain his fellows with clownish antics and ludicrous stories, and to climb the hill of science in a usual way by aid of books and conversation with educated persons, **whether boys or men**. He was not a brilliant genius but a struggling, slow-plodding one.

21. Parthena Williams Nance Hill (1816–1898) married the successful New Salem merchant Samuel Hill.

VI

Soldier, Surveyor, and Postmaster

I have already stated that Lincoln's nature, disposition, and training indisposed him to stable and continuous business, and impelled him to change desultory employments. Hence it was that the episode of the Black Hawk War was the precise sort of adventure which harmonized with his nature **and disposition**. This brief but thrilling episode in the early Illinois history occurred thus: one Mucata Muhicatah, meaning Black Hawk, was principal chief of the Sacs-and-Foxes, a tribe which **has, from first to last, given the government so much trouble**, occupied the northwestern part of Illinois, including the teeming Rock River valley. As early as 1804, General [William Henry] Harrison, on behalf of the United States government, made a treaty at St. Louis with several of the minor chiefs for the cession of their country to the United States; which treaty, after lying dormant and only partially executed for some years, was confirmed by this tribe in 1815 and 1816. The last treaties distinctly embraced within the cession the great town of the Indians near the mouth of Rock **Run** (River). Black Hawk was a proud, independent chieftain of great valor and renown, having been one of Tecumseh's chief councilors and warriors. His word was law to the better order of his tribe. He despised the American pioneers but was enamored of the British. He always denied the validity of the treaty, averring that it was made only with some of the minor chiefs, and then by chicanery and compulsion. These chiefs were imprisoned for murder, and the whites had made them drunk and then extorted the treaty from them as the price of their liberty. So Black Hawk resisted removal from the land and had to be transported into Iowa by force.

One provision of the treaty was that none of the tribe should revisit Illinois without first obtaining leave of the president or of the governor of Illinois. This permission, it is needless to say, was not intended that they should ever obtain, although the whites led the Indians to suppose that they could

84   *Chapter VI*

get it for the asking. Not being able to **get leave, the matter-of-fact chief, disdaining conventional modes and tedious technicalities, proposed to nullify the decree by practical methods and the application of force, and accordingly** in the early spring of 1831, Black Hawk invaded the State with his tribe, avowing his intention to "plant corn" in the Rock River valley. **This was the Indian's writ of ouster, its moral basis being debatable perhaps, but its effective foundation being nil for lack of that virile argument under whose sway the receding and diminishing wave of savage autonomy has been slowly and relentlessly impelled westward—force: and to the acquisition of this indispensable factor of civilization.**

General [Edward] Gaines, then in command of the U.S. forces at Rock Island, called on the governor of Illinois[1] for 700 militia to expel the Indians. Fifteen hundred came in response to the governor's call. Abraham Lincoln was on his flatboat trip to New Orleans at the time, or he would probably have been among the volunteers. The troops marched against the Indians, who promptly ran away and recrossed into Iowa, abandoning their large town at the mouth of Rock River, which the troops burnt. Black Hawk himself then made a treaty, agreeing to remain west of the river. But with the advent of planting time the next season, the old chief gazed with covetous eyes upon the valley of so many bright reminiscences before the spoilers came; and allying Keokuk, another chief of renown with him, crossed the Mississippi again with all the warriors, braves, squaws, and papooses of the Sac-and-Fox nation. **The Mississippi was gay and animated with the keels of the Sac-and-Fox navy and transports, as they again embarked to rescue their farms and ancestral homes from the dominion of the invader.** Again, the United States commander called on the State authorities for a militia contingent.

One of the normal incidents of frontier life is the maintenance of possession by force. **The typical pioneer is never without his trusty rifle and skinning knife. The Pilgrims carried to church their Bible in one hand and supported their rifle with the other.** The early western pioneers attended their "logrollings" and "shindigs," gun on shoulder, and the animus of shooting Indians on their mind. Hence this call prognosticated a diversion to the frontiersmen of Illinois, and in response, 1800 men met together at Beardstown, their period of enlistment being a term of 30 days.

The spirit of mercantile adventure had "winked out"[2] in the mind of Lincoln by this time. He was one of the first volunteers in the county of Sangamon. The rendezvous of the Sangamon contingent was about seven miles west of New Salem, and at that point the adjutant general attended, in order

---

1. Democrat John Reynolds (1788–1865) served as governor of Illinois (1830–1834).
2. Basler, *Works of Lincoln*, 4:65.

Soldier, Surveyor, and Postmaster

to organize the company, the date being April 21, 1832. The chief candidate for captain was one William Kirkpatrick, a sawmiller.[3] Lincoln had also been mentioned in a loose way for the distinction, although, unlike Kirkpatrick, he had not actually canvassed for the honor. It so happened that Lincoln had worked for Kirkpatrick, who had treated him meanly. So Lincoln was moved by more than ambition to enter into the contest. The men being mustered in line, the adjutant requested all who were candidates for the office of captain to advance and face about at right angles to the line. Thereupon Lincoln and Kirkpatrick marched out, after which the order was given for the men to fall in line behind the candidate whose success they desired. The first man to move was Billy Greene, who planted himself squarely at Lincoln's back. **The entire sorting was thus accomplished in a few minutes, and** at the end of the voting Lincoln had double the number of Kirkpatrick's followers, and seven more. While the vote was in progress and its **certain** issue was palpable, Lincoln, casting an eye rearward, placed his brawny hand on Greene's shoulder and exclaimed excitedly **and joyously**: "I'll be damned, Bill, but I've beat him." Mr. Greene, sixty years thereafter, informed me that that was the only time he ever heard Lincoln utter an oath. Lincoln informed me in general terms of this, his first candidacy, and observed that no event of his life ever gave him such a thrill of happiness as this triumph.

This so-called war was replete with wild incidents and some massacres, although nowhere did it attain the dignity of genuine civilized warfare; in fact, it had more the substance of a grand frolic. Its noted features, so far as Lincoln was concerned, were in his being mustered into service by Robert Anderson, then a Lieutenant, and in 1861 Major in command at Charleston; and in the fact that Jefferson Davis, likewise a Lieutenant, was engaged in the same **spirit-stirring,** unheroic enterprise.

The reckless character of the recruits forbade any enforcement of discipline. Each man felt himself to be as good as any other, the officers included, and respect of the latter was only to be hoped for by force of character, and in no wise by virtue of dignity or conventional rank.

Lincoln was as closely environed by this condition of affairs as the others, but it was in no wise galling to him; he was always, in little or supreme greatness alike, quite willing to abnegate his rank and title and rely exclusively for "audience and attention" on his manhood and moral force.

To one of his earliest orders about an unimportant matter, it was suggested that he "go to hell," and when Lincoln interposed to save a captive Indian from unmerited and unauthorized death at the hands of his own men, he was branded as a coward, to which his sole and conclusive reply was: "Any

---

3. William Kirkpatrick owned a sawmill near New Salem. Lincoln reportedly had once hauled logs for him.

one who *raly* thinks I'm a coward, can soon be convinced of his mistake, if he so desires."

A trifling incident, however, exhibited the force of will and estimation in which Lincoln was held by his followers. There was in Capt. Henry L. Webb's company from Union County a very strong and athletic man named Nathan M. Thompson, nicknamed "Dow" Thompson. The question of comparative muscular strength arising between him and Lincoln, they resorted to a wrestling match in order to decide it. After struggling for a while with no advantage either way, Lincoln said, "This is the strongest man I ever met." Soon thereafter, amid great and growing excitement, Lincoln was fairly thrown. This was for the first time in his life. The wrestlers took hold again, and a second time, Lincoln was thrown. Instantly, **as if by magic**, a hundred men jerked off their coats, crying "*Foul!*" and an equal number on the other side followed suit, crying, "*We'll see if it was.*" A deadly fight seemed imminent, but Lincoln commanded attention, and said, "Boys, this man *can* throw me fairly, **even** if he didn't do it this time, so let's give up that I was beat fairly."

Peace reigned at once, for as my informant said, "His word was more than law and gospel" to his followers.

That Lincoln was fond of the tented field is palpable in this, that after his original term of service and his captaincy was at an end, he reenlisted as a private in Captain Elijah Iles's company, and served as such to the end of the service.[4]

For this service, besides his pay of eleven dollars per month and one ration a day from the general government, he likewise obtained under an act of Congress enacted in 1850 a land warrant, No. 52,076, for forty acres of government land which he caused to be located in his own name on July 21, 1854 on the northwest quarter of the southwest quarter of section 20, T. 84, North Range 39 West, in Iowa, and in the succeeding year, he obtained a patent therefor which is recorded in Vol. 280 page 21 of U.S. Patents. Also under the act of 1855, he received still another land warrant: No. 68,465 for 120 acres was issued to him on April 22, 1856 and located by him on December 27, 1859, on the east half of the northeast quarter and the northwest quarter of the northeast quarter of section 18, T. 84, North Range 39 West, in the State of Illinois; for this a patent was issued on September 10, 1860, and recorded in Volume 408, page 53, of Patents.

Lincoln returned from the war (so called) to New Salem in August 1832, and found the business of Berry & Lincoln in a hopeless tangle and pretty well played out. So he and his luckless partner sold out to some parties named Trent[5] wholly on *tick*. These soon "busted up," and left the town. Shortly

---

4. The successful merchant Elijah Iles (1796–1883) helped found the city of Springfield.

5. Alexander Trent (1797–1862) and his brother Martin took over the store.

thereafter Berry died insolvent, and Lincoln was left not only without employment but owing $800 to a prairie Shylock named [Peter] Van Bergen,[6] who had bought for a song the notes of Lincoln and Berry, given in payment for the **purchase of the** stores of Radford and the Herndons. Eight hundred dollars was then a far greater sum than it would be now, and Lincoln was accustomed to call his obligations *the national debt*. **(In all, it amounted to about eleven hundred dollars in payments, principal, and interest.)** Billy Greene was an endorser for two thirds of the amount, which he paid; and Lincoln ultimately repaid him; finally, however, Lincoln paid the entire debt, principal and interest, amounting to about $1100, the last payment being paid made about the year 1850.

While Lincoln was in the army, encouraged thereto by the flattering vote received by him for Captain, he avowed his purpose to run for the legislature in the fall. Accordingly he presented himself as a candidate to some of the voters at an executor's sale at Pappsville, a small hamlet, now extinct, located in the western part of the county. Before the political element of the gathering was brought into play, a fight occurred, in which Lincoln acted as peacemaker by hurling the ringleader up in the air so that when he lit, he was too much surprised to renew the fray, and it ended then and there.

Lincoln then made his first speech intended for a practical object; it was about thus: "Feller Citizens: I reckon you all know me; I'm Abe Lincoln. I am runnin' for the Legislature. I needn't take long to give you my principles. I am a National Bank man; I also am a high tariff man; and in favor of all internal improvements which may be needful. As I am runnin,' I of course want to be elected; and I hope all my friends, or the friends of the above principles, will vote for me. That is all. I thank you for your attention, and I will thank you still more if I git your votes."[7]

Lincoln himself, however, did not expect to be elected; he had no general acquaintance, and he held such radical views on the subject of the navigation of the Sangamo River that he was regarded by the matter-of-fact voters as *loony*. Some of the boys even deemed his candidacy as a joke; they supposed

6. Peter Van Bergen (1800–1879) was a horseman, landowner, and money lender in Springfield.

7. "Fellow citizens, I suppose you all know who I am. I am humble Abraham Lincoln. I have been solicited by many friends to become a candidate for the Legislature. My politics are short and sweet, like the old woman's dance. I am in favor of a national bank. I am in favor of the internal-improvement system and a high protective tariff. These are my sentiments and political principles. If elected I shall be thankful; if not it will be all the same." *Illinois State Journal* (Springfield), 5 November 1864. According to the *Journal*, Lincoln "cut his remarks short" because the sun had almost set. Several other speakers had preceded him. See James A. Herndon to William H. Herndon, Quincy, Illinois, 29 May 1865, Wilson and Davis, *Herndon's Informants*, 16–17.

they would garner a bountiful crop of fun and diversion and hence encouraged him in his ambition.[8] The responsible voters, however, could not seriously believe that so ill-dressed and *fresh* a spectacle could decently represent this important and populous county in the legislature, yet he received 657 votes, heading the list of five other defeated candidates. In his own precinct of New Salem he obtained 277 votes out of a total of 280 votes.

Lincoln was now entirely out of **his** business and quite uncertain of the future; he had among his close and intimate friends at New Salem one [Joshua] Miller, a blacksmith; and he consulted him as to the feasibility of his adopting that calling, but he took no practical steps in that direction. Destiny had a higher mission in store for him.

He did not, in point of fact, enter upon the performance of any stated or systematic labor; occasionally he would "clerk" for a day, help in the cornfield, chop logs, or build fences. He was fond of visiting Bowling Green or Jack Armstrong and staying for days at a time, during which visits he would indifferently aid the men in their out-of-doors work and help the women with their milking, rocking the cradle, or other feminine employments, **and thus it was, that by reason of his willingness to turn his hand to anything, and of his visibility, his ability to perform substantial or domestic labor—to amuse the children, chop the wood, gather the corn, or tell stories—that** he was exceedingly popular with every inmate of the households of his hosts.

While in the war, he became intimately acquainted with John T. Stuart, a Springfield lawyer, and having revealed his ultimate intention to become a lawyer, was invited to make use of his law library when he desired.

Accordingly, Lincoln started early one morning for Springfield, and returned the same evening with **the first** [of] *Blackstone's Commentaries*, then published in four volumes. During his walk back to New Salem he had managed to read a large number of the pages of the first volume. **He then became absorbed in the pursuit of this science, so far as he did anything systematically;** thereafter he might be seen either lying prone upon the ground, or seated upon the woodpile, or in any other place suitable for study, abstracted from the outer world and wholly occupied with the volume before him. Russell Godby, an emigrant from Logan County, Virginia, without a particle of education or ideality, once saw Lincoln sitting astride a woodpile

---

8. "Judge [James] Matheny informs me that when Lincoln first ran for the legislature it was regarded as a joke; the boys wanted some fun: he was so uncouth and awkward, and so illy dressed, that his candidacy afforded a pleasant diversion for them, but it was not expected that it would go any further. It was found, however, during the canvass, that Lincoln knew what he was about and that he had running qualities: so Matheny told him he was sowing seeds of success: and that next year he would win." Whitney, *Life on the Circuit with Lincoln*, 33.

with a book in his hand. Lincoln had worked for him, and he regarded him in no different light from that of any other field hand, **whose feet remained firmly planted in the circular track of unskilled and irresponsible labor which led nowhere,** doomed through life to the dreary treadmill round of paid farm labor **And so the anomalous spectacle of a common field hand, perched up on a wood pile with a book, where he should have been in the cornfield,** struck Godby with surprise, and he asked, "What's that you're readin' Abe?"

"I'm not readin'—I'm studyin'," was the reply.

"Studyin' what?"

"Law," replied Abe.

"Great God Almighty!!" exclaimed Godby, **an expression that he afterward recalled when yet Godby lived to see the fullness of Lincoln's fame. His law knowledge was achieved under great difficulties. Through the daytime, the friendly shade of a fir or of a cabin was his only protection from the elements, and a recumbent position on the ground, or a cellar door, or a puncheon bench, or a seat against a friendly wall constituted his seat, desk, and table. At night the glare of the hearth fire, or the illumination produced by some twigs or shavings from Constable's cooper shop,**[9] **constituted his only artificial light. He had no instruction at all, and was limited to one book at a time. He must, perforce, earn the small amount required to pay for his board and clothes by labor; and thus handicapped, no wonder he found it hard "to climb the steep where Fame's proud temple shines afar!"**[10]

At the same time that Lincoln was studying all the law books he could get his hands on, he read all the papers which he could borrow, and was fully advised as to the general facts of current and political history. He also gave some attention to current light literature and enjoyed with great relish, *funny* books. At that time Mrs. Caroline Lee Hentz was quite a prolific author of sensational novels, and Lincoln read many of her works,[11] **but he was an industrious student and seems to have embarked on the study of the law in dead earnest and gave to its study all his time except such as he needed to earn a sufficiency to sustain existence.**

---

9. Henry Sinco was the constable of New Salem and Henry Onstott was the cooper. Whitney seems to have confused the two Henrys.

10. James Beattie (1735–1803), "The Minstrel, or, The Progress of Genius" (1771).

11. Caroline Lee Hentz (1800–1856) was noted for her opposition to abolitionism, which would hardly have endeared her to Lincoln, who hated slavery from the time he was young. In *Life on the Circuit with Lincoln*, p. 110, Whitney stated that Lincoln "once said to me that he had never read a novel clear through." To New York Senator Ira Harris, Lincoln similarly confessed: "I never read an entire novel in my life. . . . I once commenced '*Ivanhoe*,' but never finished it."

In the spring of 1833, John Calhoun, then surveyor of Sangamon County,[12] designated him as deputy surveyor **and assigned him to the considerable duties of that position in that part of the county**. Lincoln procured somehow an outfit, secured needed instruction from the pedagogue, Mentor Graham, and entered upon the duties of his office with zeal. **And in their performance**, he gave universal satisfaction, and was continued in office by Calhoun's successor; in fact, he held the office until his removal to Springfield.

Many examples of his work are still extant in Menard County, where he was principally employed, and are shown with proud satisfaction by their owners.

Russell Godby employed him to do some surveying and paid him two deerskins and one dollar for the job; Jack Armstrong's wife Hannah used the skins to repair Lincoln's ragged pantaloons.[13]

The city of Petersburg, the present county seat of Menard County, is one of the most prettily situated and pretentious of the third-rate towns of Illinois. Lincoln laid it out, setting the first monument at the southwest corner of the public square, where it still remains. He then turned his compass southward, but found in the line of vision a storehouse belonging to a friend, **so, in order to save it from destruction, he directed his bearing one degree. Although no surveyor had ever ventured to call it in question since, it is an obvious blemish in the survey. What moral can one draw from this? It illustrates character. His official oath and duty bound him to an accurate survey; his friendship decreed that he should spare his friend's house.**

Here was a dilemma of a kind that frequently arose in his subsequent career. The conflict [was] between sympathy and official duty, **and personal friendship won the day. Many and many a time afterward did similar conflicts agitate his bosom; and great disquietude arose in his feelings, by reason thereof.** Friends applied to him for offices they were unfit to fill, and tearful wives and mothers, on bended knees, implored him to save their husbands and sons from merited punishment. **His life was a stern and relentless conflict between duty and sympathy. He was too just to be a philanthropist, and too merciful to be a servitor of rigid duty.** So here, official duty required an accurate survey, and consideration for the householder a deviation from it. He solved it in characteristic fashion by an adjustment: he contrived to divert his bearings enough to save the storehouse from removal but so slightly that no succeeding surveyor has called the survey into question.

12. John Calhoun (1806–1859) had known Lincoln in the Black Hawk War, when they both served in the same regiment.

13. Hannah Armstrong (1811–1890) was a kind of surrogate mother to Lincoln in New Salem. He represented her son Duff in the famous "almanac trial" of 1858.

Soldier, Surveyor, and Postmaster 91

Lincoln was quite busy as a surveyor for three years, and a great many lines are still extant which were established by him; no one who has such a line in his domain, but mentions it in terms of pride. As a surveyor, Lincoln was not without honor, even in his own county. But the founding of Petersburg was the downfall of New Salem; in a year from the date of Lincoln's survey, the place began to grow, and its site was so far superior to that of New Salem that it at once gained all accretions of population, and the latter place yielded to the inevitable and was very soon a thoroughly deserted village. Not a structure now remains, and even the sites of many of the former buildings are in dispute.

John Hill [1839–1898, son of Samuel and Parthena Hill] relates that when he was a young lad, Lincoln came to his father's house to return something, and that the youngsters were much interested in the compass, and that Lincoln took great pains to show the whole thing to them.

At the same time that he was a surveyor, Lincoln received from Andrew Jackson, President of the United States, the appointment of postmaster of New Salem, *vice* John McNamar, who had gone east for a year, and consequently had resigned the office. Both duties and emoluments were slight. The mail came once a week by stage, and the bulk of it was distributed within an hour after its arrival. When Lincoln quit the office, he owed the government a small balance which some obstacle prevented his placing to the credit of the post office department, so he wrapped it up in a scrap of paper, indicated its ownership by a memorandum, and laid it by. When years thereafter, an agent of the department called on him for settlement, Lincoln withdrew from a safe place this identical parcel and paid it over.

Lincoln had many residences at New Salem—in fact there were many homes always eager to welcome him as an inmate. He lived at Bowling Green's, Jack Armstrong's, Rowan Herndon's, and at the tavern kept by James Rutledge. Part of the time he slept in the loft over a store; indeed for a time he slept on the store counter of Offutt's store.

Billy Greene paid off that part of Lincoln's debt for which he stood as security, but Van Bergen brought suit on the other part, and getting judgment, sold on execution everything that Lincoln had on earth except the clothes on his back, **and they had no commercial value.**

But Lincoln's friends came to the rescue and by general agreement suppressed competitive bidding. James Short, **one of Lincoln's staunch friends,** bid on all the goods and presented them to Lincoln; his horse, compass and chain, and saddlebags were among the effects.

It was while living at this place that Lincoln first acquired the sobriquet of "Honest" Abe. As a judge of scrub races, or wrestling bouts, or of bets, his services were sought by all sides and always acquiesced in, with no heartburnings. **His character was above the least reproach, and he was esteemed by everyone.**

He was then, as thereafter, extremely bashful. **He avoided the society of females with the greatest particularity**; he avoided waiting on women at the stores or meeting them casually. Once a family of ladies stopped at the hotel while he was a boarder there, and he failed to appear at the public table while they were there, **but to women with whom he was placed in social contact he was very gracious and extremely popular.** He **likewise** was very popular with the men, and also with the women such as Nancy Green and Hannah Armstrong, by whom he was made to feel "at home."

His story-telling, mimicry, *bonhomie,* and overflowing goodness were all felt and appreciated. Whenever he chose to let himself out on pleasantries, he drew a crowd; and if he chanced to shift his seat **from one locality to another**, the crowd followed him. His drolleries were repeated at every gathering and at every fireside, and he was universally commended in terms of unstinted praise.

Another legislature was to be chosen in the fall of 1834, and Lincoln was elected by a handsome majority. Duly impressed with the importance of his representative character, he borrowed $200 of one Coleman Smoot[14] in order to buy his first decent outfit in which to respectably appear at Vandalia, in a legislature which was a mosaic of Federalist aristocracy and backwoods democracy. **And this was the stepping stone to a most illustrious day.** He made his "touch" in characteristic fashion: "Smoot, you voted for me to represent you at Vandalia, and so made yourself responsible that I should do so creditably."

While Lincoln was not admitted to the bar till March 1837, he yet practiced, informally, at New Salem while he was still a student. His friend Bowling Green was a justice of the peace, and Edmund Greer, the schoolmaster, officiated also as a justice **of the peace**. Lincoln not only "pettifogged" cases before them but did sundry office work, such as drafting deeds, wills, contracts, &c. In everything he undertook, he gave satisfaction **and did well**. Lincoln failed nowhere and in nothing; he was a genius of affairs, and, commencing at the lowest round of the ladder, he reached the top round without a misstep or misadventure of any kind.

Lincoln's religious views were not very clear or well settled at this time; he believed in fatalism, and that we were impelled along on the journey of life with no freedom of the moral will. Owing to a line of remark he was once indulging in, Mrs. Samuel Hill said, "You surely don't mean that there's not to be an hereafter?"

14. Coleman Smoot (1794–1876) was a successful farmer and moneylender.

Soldier, Surveyor, and Postmaster

93

"I'm affeered there ain't," was the reply, "but it's an awful thing to think that when we die, that's the end of us."

He wrote a small monograph on his religious views which he read to several people, including Samuel Hill. Hill urged him to abandon such extreme heterodoxy, assuring him that he had a brilliant and useful public career before him, which an indulgence in such views would tend to cloud. Finally, taking the book, Hill thrust it into the fire, where it was consumed. Lincoln lived to radically change his religious views, as I shall show, but being brought up on the frontier, with little religious training, and the uninspiring example of Thomas Lincoln as a church member constantly before him, and having no ingrained element of inspiring faith in his nature, it is little wonder that in his callow youth his views on religion were loose **and irresponsible** and superficial, **but were corrected by the experiences, contemplation, and maturity of later years.**

VII

Lincoln's Early Love Romance

It goes without saying that all men, however great, are susceptible to the blandishments and endearments of the tender passion.[1] Bulwer says that "love, like death, levels all ranks, and lays the shepherd's crook beside the sceptre."[2]

Since the days when the liaison of Helen and Paris engaged the world in mortal combat, and brought sorrow and bereavement to every hearthstone in the civilized world, or the Egyptian queen took captive the otherwise unvanquished Antony, history is replete with instances of fair women smiting destruction upon brave men.

Abraham Lincoln had his share of natural human passion, if not of religious sentiment. One of the great psychic crises of his career was his tragic love affair with Miss Ann Mays Rutledge. This young lady was one of the children of James Rutledge, one of the founders of New Salem. **Her family came from Henderson County, Kentucky, and settled at first, about ten miles north of the site of New Salem on a government claim, the land not yet being in market, where they resided for one year.** Ann was in her sixteenth year when the Rutledges came to New Salem in 1828 or 1829. She was very handsome: tall, symmetrical, inclined to plumpnesss, with a fair

---

1. This version of the Ann Rutledge story contains much that does not appear in "Romance of Ann Rutledge," Whitney, *Life on the Circuit with Lincoln*, 162–170.

2. "Old gossips tell how maidens sprung from Kings
    Have stoop'd from their high sphere; how
    Love, like Death,
    Levels all ranks, and lays the shepherd's crook
    Beside the sceptre."
Edward Bulwer Lytton, "The Lady of Lyons, or Love and Pride," III.2.

complexion, rosy cheeks, and dark auburn hair. Her manners were graceful, and she was self-possessed, had an excellent address, was courteous and dignified, and, though raised chiefly on the frontier, had the ambition, deportment, and bearing of a well-bred lady. She was **also** a **bold,** dashing, and fearless rider, making a striking appearance on horseback, which was her favorite mode of locomotion in her journeys throughout the neighborhood. Her beautiful character and winning ways endeared her to young and old. As may be inferred, she smote the hearts and engaged the susceptibilities of all the marriageable youth of the settlement, among whom were Samuel Hill and John McNeil, partners in trade, and the leading merchants of New Salem. She capitulated to McNeil's attentions, and they became betrothed in 1833. This young man had migrated from New York State in 1829 and by good management and shrewd business methods had acquired a farm and a handsome sum of money for those primitive days.

Just after his betrothal, however, his father died, making it necessary that he should return to his childhood's home and settle the estate. This, he supposed, would consume a year, and promising to return at the expiration of this period, he took leave of his *fiancée* and went, after the manner of those days, on horseback to New York. A sad domestic calamity befalling his family, one incident of which was a lawsuit which was greatly delayed, extended his eastern sojourn. The time elapsed for his return, and he still remained absent, and, moreover, gave no satisfactory excuse for his prolonged absence. This, of itself, caused uneasiness on the part of Ann and her family, which reached a climax when a report became current in the neighborhood that a local blight had fallen upon the family at home, and that the object of her affection himself had lived at New Salem and pledged himself in betrothal under an assumed name.

Now pride of name was a characteristic of the Rutledges. They were descended from the renowned family of that name in South Carolina which had included a signer of the Declaration of Independence, a nominated Chief Justice of the United States, Congressmen, &c. **and Cameron was a descendant of the Scottish Covenanters and he himself was a man of austere morals and habits, being also a "Cumberland" Presbyterian preacher.** The existence of these rumors filled the souls of the Rutledges **and Camerons** with **dismay and** consternation, for it seemed apparent to them that the *alias* was employed as a shield for some dark and indelible disgrace **and to no one of the family was the report more unwelcome and provocative of anguish than to the party most interested herself. Yet she refused to credit it and** avowed that she never would give the report credence till she received it from the inculpated party himself. This opportunity was not long wanting, for it had happened that McNeil had bought a tract of land of her uncle Cameron just before he left, and had himself signed the deed **which**

96 *Chapter VII*

evidenced the transactions, and which had been signed by the granter, after hearing a hasty reading of it by the grantee. It was supposed, and, as the sequel proved, properly, that McNeil would insert his correct name in the deed, inasmuch as he desired to trade off this land at his eastern home.

The matter was discussed at a family council, and it was proposed to ascertain from the records at Springfield in what name McNeil had taken the title to this land. Ann insisted on forming one of the party of inspection, averring with firmness and emphasis, that she would not believe the perfidy and disgrace of her affianced lover upon any less indubitable evidence than that of her own senses. **And so, at a most eventful moment of her life, she mounted her horse, armed with a resolute, undaunted and determined air and purpose, and** accompanied by her brother David (then a law student) and her uncle Cameron, **the investigating party started.** She rode on horseback to Springfield, **on what to them was a very momentous errand, for they felt that the issue at stake was the honor or dishonor of the family.**

The courthouse wherein the records were kept stands yet—now used as a cheap second-hand furniture store, a few doors north of the northwest corner of the public square. In front of this unpretending building the three equestrians alighted and went in. The record book was readily found, and the page eagerly scanned by the male members of the trio, eagerly watched by the third member. How often has the fate of a family been dependent upon the single word which the jury are just ready to pronounce? As David Rutledge pointed out to his sister, the fatal word which was to be the well-spring of happiness or the precursor of despair, the resolute girl was as impassive as a marble statue; the blood had receded from her face, which was as colorless as death, and reading in the pained look of her brother and her uncle no lesson but one of disaster, she gazed impassively at the one word, cabalistic to her, and in that simple solitary word read alike her disgrace and her fate. The word was *McNamar* and it avowed that by its portrayal, her affianced love himself proclaimed that he had wooed, won, and plighted his troth to her under the felon's artifice of an *alias.*

Arrived at home, Miss Rutledge promptly wrote her recreant lover an account of his apparent infamy and demanded an instant explanation. In due time an answer came, stating nonchalantly that he would explain fully when he saw her. She then wrote a curt note, abruptly dismissing him.

McNamar, however, affected to believe that she spoke in a Pickwickian sense, for he continued to regard himself as her affianced and started west with his mother, brother, and sisters. For some reason, not plainly apparent, he stopped in Ohio, rented a farm, and remained for a year. Then in 1835 he wrote to Ann that he should buy furniture in Cincinnati and be there soon after his letter arrived, to claim her in marriage, and settle down to housekeeping. This letter, however, was never read by her for whom it was intended, for the eyes which should have read it were by this time sealed in death. Sure enough, in November 1835, McNamar, his family and furniture reached New Salem, there to learn the startling news that his misconduct had hastened the death of her with whose virgin affections he had cruelly and inexcusably trifled. The wagon was unladen and the bedroom set, which was to have graced the nuptials of the young couple, stood out of doors in the weather, **homeless and apparently friendless**, through the rigors of the early winter.

The disgrace of betrothal to a man who posed under the baleful shadow of an *alias*, and declined to explain to her, who had a right to demand it, had told upon the proud and super-sensitive nature of this ambitious and spirited girl, and a settled melancholy took possession of her nature. **She was ill-at-ease, and in a false position. McNamar had given abundant cause for detraction, and it was not long in sullying his theretofore good name and this 'name' was coupled with his in commiseration with his misfortunes.**

Lincoln, like the rest, was not insensible to the beauty, charms, and merit of this most estimable girl whom, of course, he had seen often and whose relations to McNamar he had known and respected; and when she had dismissed her **quondam and** recreant lover, Lincoln mustered up the courage to address her in terms of sympathy and endearment, and finally to propose marriage to her. His proposal the young lady was certainly free to accept if she chose, yet she desired first to receive a ratification of her dismissal of McNamar before she made any new engagement. This ratification, however, never came; McNamar had her promise and meant to hold her to it. She finally, however, on the advice of her friends, disdained longer to be technically bound to a man who had deceived her, and she became the affianced of Lincoln. Her family had meanwhile left New Salem and then resided at Concord, several miles north, and it was arranged between them that Lincoln should study law during the succeeding fall and winter at Springfield, while Ann should attend the seminary at Jacksonville for the same time, and that in the spring, the marriage should take place, and the twain should reside at Springfield. But on the 12th day of August, she took to her bed with a raging brain fever, largely induced by the mental anguish of engaging herself to a polynomial lover, who had so sullied his real name as to render a disguise necessary, and then, while not yet released by him from her engagement, of affiancing herself to another. Her illness caused serious alarm to her physician and the members of her family. Lincoln and her brother David, who was attending school at Jacksonville, were at once sent for.

When Lincoln entered her room she urgently requested to be left alone with him for a short time, which request was allowed. **When Lincoln terminated the sad interview** after the lapse of half an hour, he came out of that bedchamber, betraying signs of the most extreme and pitiable grief, **which**

could not be allayed. Her brother came later, but she did not recognize him and she died on August 25, 1835, of brain fever.

The remains of this unfortunate girl were consigned to their mother earth in Concord burial ground and should have been suffered to remain there till aroused and animated by the Angel of the Resurrection but it was not to be so. Recently, an enterprising undertaker who desired to advertise his cemetery at Petersburg, invaded the sanctity of the grave with the assent of the scattered and few members of the family then living, and, gathering together the moldering bones, the buttons of her shroud, and a few rusty nails of her coffin, carted them off in triumph to Oakland Cemetery, near Petersburg, and there reinterred them, where it is to be hoped that no dime museum proprietor or other enterprising ghoul will bid high enough to have them again exhumed for further speculation.

Lincoln was completely prostrated and unnerved by the death of his *fiancée*; he took it so deeply to heart that the universal pity which had animated all breasts for the "loved and lost" was transferred to him. His friends condoled with him and tried, by every mode, to mitigate his sorrow.

"Bear it like a man," said one.

"I'll try," said he, "but I must first feel it like a man."

His grief did not abate, and it was feared that he would be bereft of his reason. When storms would come, he would grow nervous and almost frantic. "The rains *shan't* beat on my darling's grave," said he, passionately and piteously. He would steal away to the little graveyard and sit and commune with the dead for hours; his friends **feared for his reason. He mourned for his lost love as a proud husband for his wife or a father for a beloved daughter. [They]** deemed it unsafe to leave him alone **longer**, and **hence,** by strategy, induced him to stay at his old friend Bowling Green's **for a while**, till time and reflection should assuage his grief. The device measurably succeeded; he grew less excitable and less passionate in his grief, and settled down to a chronic condition of apparently hopeless despair. **He grew sadder, abstracted, melancholy.** He would sit by himself in solitude, apparently dominated by his grief, a habit he exhibited at intervals through life. He would wander off alone, with no apparent aim or object, and would occasionally break out in meaningless soliloquy, a habit which never left him, and of which I furnish examples, in "Life on the Circuit with Lincoln."[3]

Dr. [Jason] Duncan of New Salem came across a poem in an almanac, which he repeated to Lincoln by way of solace to his wounded spirit, and the latter by his adoption **and advocacy** of it as his favorite poem, conferred upon it the spirit and essence, as it had before the name of "Mortality."[4]

3. Whitney, *Life on the Circuit with Lincoln*, 162–70.
4. This poem, by William Knox of Scotland, is also known by its first line,

O why should the spirit of mortal be proud!
Like a fast flitting meteor, a fast flying cloud,
A flash of the lightning, a break of the wave—
He passes from life to his rest in the grave.

The leaves of the oak and the willow shall fade,
Be scattered around and together be laid;
As the young and the old, and the low and the high,
Shall moulder to dust, and together shall lie.

The child that a mother attended and loved,
The mother that infant's affection that proved,
The husband that mother and infant that blest,
Each—all are away to their dwelling of rest.

The maid on whose cheek, on whose brow, in whose eye,
Shone beauty and pleasure—her triumphs are by:
And the memory of those that loved her and praised,
And alike from the minds of the living erased.

The hand of the king that the sceptre hath borne,
The brow of the priest that the mitre hath worn,
The eye of the sage, and the heart of the brave,
Are hidden and lost in the depths of the grave.

The peasant whose lot was to sow and to reap,
The herdsman who climbed with his goats to the steep,
The beggar that wandered in search of his bread,
Have faded away like the grass that we tread.

The saint that enjoyed the communion of Heaven,
The sinner that dared to remain unforgiven,
The wise and the foolish, the guilty and just,
Have quietly mingled their bones in the dust.

So the multitude goes—like the flower and the weed
That wither away to let others succeed;
So the multitude comes—even those we behold,
To repeat every tale that hath often been told.

For we are the same things that our fathers have been,
We see the same sights that our fathers have seen,
We drink the same stream, and we feel the same sun,
And we run the same course that our fathers have run.

The thoughts we are thinking our fathers would think,
From the death we are shrinking from they too would shrink,

"O, why should the spirit of mortal be proud?" It sometimes is misidentified as
"Immortality."

Chapter VII

To the life we are clinging to, they too would cling—
But it speeds from the earth like a bird on the wing.

They loved—but their story we cannot unfold;
They scorned—but the heart of the haughty is cold;
They grieved—but no wail from their slumbers may come;
They joyed—but the voice of their gladness is dumb.

They died—ay, they died! and we, things that are now,
Who walk on the turf that lies over their brow,
Who make in their dwellings a transient abode,
Meet the changes they met on their pilgrimage road.

Yea, hope and despondence, and pleasure and pain,
Are mingled together like sunshine and rain:
And the smile and the tear, and the song and the dirge,
Still follow each other like surge upon surge.

'Tis the twink of an eye, 'tis the draught of a breath,
From the blossom of health to the paleness of death,
From the gilded saloon to the bier and the shroud—
O why should the spirit of mortal be proud!

Lincoln frequently tried to ascertain the name of its author, but he never succeeded. It was William Knox, a Scotchman. Lincoln was wont to repeat these verses upon all occasions, and especially by himself when he supposed no ear but his own heard him; and on the occasion of the death of President [Zachary] Taylor, he, being at Chicago, made a speech at the celebration of the obsequies, in the course of which he repeated **the twelve stanzas which he was acquainted with entirely**.[5]

James Buchanan, when a young lawyer, was engaged in marriage to a Miss Anne C. Coleman. Since trifling circumstance caused an estrangement, he sealed up his affections hermetically and never ventured to address a young lady again. It is doubtless well that his great successor adopted a different practical view of the matter, and that his somber spirits rebounded from the deep and dark depression into which they had fallen, and sought a solace from impeded love in a kindred manner. He indeed once exclaimed in times of heart-rending sorrow, referring to Miss Rutledge: "My heart is buried in the grave with her," and this is probably as true as could be averred of a practical, prosaic man whose whole energies were engrossed in a stern and relentless conflict with Fate for existence, establishment, and supremacy.

5. While in Chicago to represent Charles Hoyt in federal court in a copyright infringement case, Lincoln delivered the eulogy for Zachary Taylor on July 25, 1850. Basler, *Collected Works of Lincoln*, 2:83–90.

Lincoln's Early Love Romance

Lincoln was never the same man after the death of Ann Rutledge that he was before; he never ceased to mourn and bewail her loss, but he lived a man's life thereafter and carried out the plan devised for him by destiny, as he best could.

About a mile below New Salem, on the crest of a hill overlooking the broad river bottom, and on a farm adjacent to that of Bowling Green, lived Bennett Abell and family, who had emigrated there from Green County, Kentucky. Mrs. [Elizabeth] Abell had been an Owens from Green County, but had incurred the displeasure of her father by espousing a man not of his choice; and, in point of fact, she was superior in education and refinement to her husband.[6] Lincoln was a welcome visitor at the Abell household, and Mrs. Abell had often remarked that she was going to bring about a match between him and her sister Mary,[7] and, in point of fact, Mary had visited her sister in 1833 and remained a month, leaving an excellent impression upon the minds of all, as to her person and character. She returned again in November 1836, some fifteen months after the death of Ann Rutledge. She was about four and a half months older than Lincoln.

While she was not so lovely a character and did not possess so sweet a disposition as Miss Rutledge, she yet was a very handsome and brilliant girl, gifted with rare talents that had been cultivated and polished with a high and liberal education. So far as she was concerned, her visit to her sister had no significance beyond the naked fact itself, but it is not unlikely that Mrs. Abell had loftier aims, mainly **the scheme or project of** bringing about a match with a man-already entered upon a promising political career.

Mrs. Abell was incautious enough to promulgate her design so publicly that her sister heard of it, and also heard that Lincoln had said that if Mrs. Abell's sister Mary ever came to New Salem again, he would have to marry her. "We'll see," soliloquized the Bluegrass beauty. "It takes two to make such a bargain."

Other beaux stood back, however (if there were any), and Lincoln had full swing, and the courtship, such as it was, progressed at cross purposes. In the first place, despite Lincoln's public career, he was a timid and bashful man, especially as regards the gentler sex; then he was conscious of the wide disparity of culture and style between Miss Owens and himself, likewise of the extreme contrasts between her beauty and grace and his plainness and angularity. His wealth of talent he gave no credit to in the comparison; he merely took a superficial glance at the account in which everything was *plus*

6. According to a good friend of Lincoln, it was from Elizabeth Owens Abell (1804–1869) that he "first got his ideas of a higher plane of life." She "gave him the notion that he might improve himself by reading."

7. Lincoln courted Mary Owens Vineyard (1808–1877) for a time.

on the lady's side and *minus* on his side, with the always inevitable result, that what was embarrassment and bashfulness on his part, she accepted and considered as indifference and disdain. On the other hand, what was playful reproof on her part for his social delinquencies was construed by him into pride and arrogance.

It appears to me conclusive that if Lincoln had dealt with this estimable and refined young lady in a spirit of his usual candor and naturalness, and had properly wooed her, there would have been no difficulty in the way of a match; **but** Lincoln felt a sense of inferiority, for which the fair charmer gave no occasion **in her conduct**, and he only played at courting, not pressing his suit in the manly and dignified way so characteristic of him in other roles.

For instance, Nancy Green was carrying a heavy child from her house up a steep hill to Abell's house and was accompanied by Miss Owens. It was evident that Mrs. Green was very much exhausted, yet Lincoln, who joined and accompanied them, made no offer of assistance. Miss Owens could not fail to take note of her gallant's delinquency and told her sister, who repeated it to Lincoln, that she did not think Lincoln would make a good husband. Yet his reason was, as he informed [William] Greene, who informed me, that he was ashamed to be seen by a lady of Miss Owens' culture carrying a baby.

At another time, **a party of equestrians was out riding. Among them were** Miss Owens and Lincoln, **who was acting** as her escort. In crossing a deep stream, Lincoln forged on ahead, leaving his **fair** partner to get on as **best** she could. Being reproved for this, he told her she was smart enough to get over alone, but the probabilities are that he had embarked upon and was in the midst of some **moral** reflections, or else felt that his awkwardness in attempting to be gallant to a cultured lady would be worse than neglect. However that may be, Miss Owens, while holding Lincoln in high esteem, as everyone **else** did, felt, as she said years later, that "he was deficient in the minor attentions and little civilities which constitute **and make up** the chain of a woman's happiness."[8]

Lincoln wrote her some letters after he settled in Springfield as a lawyer, but they were of a decidedly repelling character, and the lady took him at his word. As I have said, he felt himself **way** beneath her in a social sense, and the mistakes, misunderstandings, and *contretemps* which arose from this anomalous condition of affairs prevented, in my judgment, a matrimonial union which would have been congenial and prosperous, for Miss Owens was polished, brilliant, and amiable, and Lincoln had nearly every element to make a good husband.

8. Mary Owens Vineyard to Herndon, Weston, Missouri, 23 May 1866, Wilson and Davis, *Herndon's Informants*, 256.

In 1839, Lincoln said to Mrs. Abell, who was returning to her childhood's home, "Tell your sister Mary, that I think she was a great fool that she didn't remain here and marry me." [Whitney footnote: I cannot refrain from saying that the letter to Mrs. (Orville H.) Browning by Mr. Lincoln about this estimable and refined lady should never have strayed beyond Mrs. Browning's desk. It was an unworthy thing for her to give it to Mr. Herndon, and equally unworthy for him and Lamon to give it to the world.][9]

While Mr. Lincoln's exploits in his callow youth are of minor interest and of less utility, and certainly not worth the serious efforts employed in their development, it should also not be forgotten that the communities amid which he was reared were extremely primitive and uncouth, and that the elements of wonder, mystery, and hyperbole were conspicuous, involving marked inaccuracies in portraying the idiosyncrasies of conduct in an original or otherwise remarkable character. Hence the frontier narratives of the embryonic president's characteristics should not be too implicitly relied on. The stories which ascribe to him **the strength of an ox**, the persiflage of a fool, or the vulgarity of a boor have no force of authority to me. From the simplicity of his origin and surroundings and the environments of his condition, he was of necessity rustic, uncouth, and unassimilated, but this crudity was only as the rock-crystal holding in place the pure metal of his *character*, which shone so resplendently in later years. All that is needful to be said of his career during his life in Indiana is that if the diary of the modern [Samuel] Pepys is correct, the mind of the coming man in its impressionable state, as it developed, was a rank, luxuriant garden of thought, but that for lack of proper culture it yielded only weeds in which satire, sarcasm, coarse wit, irony, and eccentric pasquinades were ill assorted with moral apothegms, sage but immature reflections, and an ostentatious exhibit of rustic philosophy; that even then he had an exuberant *cacoethes loquendi* [way with words], and was a leader of men in embryo; that he was restless, uneasy, and prone to adventure; and that kindness, humanity, and philanthropy were essential elements of his nature.

His five years' residence at New Salem was passed under more favorable external conditions, and his mental and moral horizon had been largely widened **in circumference** by two trips to New Orleans. In consequence, his character in this time begins to assume a semblance of harmony and logical consistency and to afford a glimpse of the psychical superstructure whose **sound** moral architecture was destined in after years to dazzle, astonish, and bless mankind. His insatiable thirst for knowledge and its wide range

9. On April 1, 1837, Lincoln wrote a quasi-satirical letter to Eliza Browning describing his courtship of Mary Owens in terms flattering neither to her nor to himself. Basler, *Collected Works of Lincoln*, 1:117–119.

and desultory character are shown in many ways; his superlative honesty is exhibited in the utmost sincerity, although his unswerving loyalty to friendship trenches upon its border lines. His exploits in the Black Hawk War and his political diplomacy **in the legislature** attest that he was a natural leader of men. **His ardent advocacy of an elaborate system of internal improvements shows his catholicity of enterprise and negligence of details and furnishes evidence of the wide scope and generality of his aims, plans, and pursuits.**

The time had come at last when he must leave the place where he had lived for nearly six years, where he had carried on two several courtships, and where he had been evolved from a mere adventurer to a lawyer and a legislator. He had served two terms in the legislature, and had acquired considerable distinction. He had seen the rise, growth, development, and decay of New Salem, and he probably foresaw its speedy downfall, for Petersburg had been established and was growing at the expense of the earlier settlement. Indeed, the latter was already moribund **even now**. And so, immediately after the adjournment of the legislature in March 1837, Lincoln sold his compass, chain, marking pins, and Jacob's staff, packed his little clothing and few effects into his saddle bags, borrowed a horse of his friend Bowling Green, and bade a final adieu to the scene of so much of life and so much of sorrow to him. In less than a year from that time New Salem ceased to exist. Its mission had been fulfilled: it was the Nazareth of the nineteenth century.

Not a stone or a log is left on top of another now to attest that a settlement ever existed at New Salem. Upon the site of Offutt's and Clary's stores, respectively, are depressions in the surface, indicating the former existence of cellars; from the side of the former has sprung a sycamore and an elm in such fraternal union that though separated in midair, at their bases, they clasp and envelop each other in a rigid and tenacious embrace. At the locality of the hotel is a small collection of small decaying logs and from the interstices, polk stalks emanate. The mill where Lincoln first saw Ann Rutledge still exists, but no longer emits water—it is a mere barren depression. That is all.

The Clary's Grove boys that made the welkin ring with sounds of "wine and wassail"; Dunn the millwright; Onstott the cooper; Mentor Graham the pedagogue; Greer the justice: Waddell the hatter; **Miller the blacksmith**; **Duncan and** Allen the physicians; Radford; Berry; Hill; McNamar; [James] Richardson[10]; Sinco; Warburton; the Herndons; [Matthew] Rogers;[11] Offutt;

10. James Richardson operated a ferry at New Salem.

11. Col. Matthew Rogers (1770–1847) of nearby Athens lent Lincoln books from his extensive library during Lincoln's New Salem sojourn.

Lincoln's Early Love Romance

and [Jack] Kelso[12] are gone, all dead. Bowling Green died in 1842. Lincoln was invited by the Masons, under whose auspices Green was buried, to make a funeral address; he manfully made the attempt and ignominiously failed. His feelings overpowered him as the past rose in his fancy and the disinterested affection of his departed friend passed in review; his sobs choked his utterance, and he withdrew from the mournful scene to accompany Mrs. Green to her desolate home.

George Warburton drowned himself in the river. Rowan Herndon accidentally shot his wife in their little cabin. Jack Armstrong died long since, and Lincoln's excellent friend Hannah Armstrong died one year since, and is buried in the same cemetery with Ann Rutledge. The rise and development of Petersburg was a synonym for the decline and fall of New Salem; the citizens left one at a time, Samuel Hill being the last to go. The mill held its lease on life a while longer, but the advent of railways made the little water mill seem effete, and naught now remains to mark its site or certify to its former existence except a slight ripple at the site of its former dam. Mrs. Samuel Hill, William G. Greene, McGrady Rutledge,[13] Thomas Watkins,[14] and one or two more remain to give personal demonstration that New Salem once existed, and now

> **Sweet smiling village, loveliest of the lawn,**
> **Thy sports are fled, and all thy charms withdrawn;**
> **Now the sounds of population fail,**
> **No cheerful murmurs fluctuate in the gale**
> **No busy steps the grass-grown foot way tread,**
> **But all the blooming flush of life has fled.[15]**

12. John "Jack" Kelso, brother-in-law of New Salem's blacksmith, William Miller, was a close friend of Lincoln, to whom he introduced the works of Shakespeare and Robert Burns.

13. James McGrady Rutledge (1814–1899), cousin of Lincoln's sweetheart Ann Rutledge, was a farmer who lived in Sand Ridge, near New Salem.

14. Thomas Watkins was a stock raiser who lived in Clary's Grove, near New Salem.

15. Oliver Goldsmith, "The Deserted Village" (1770).

VIII

State Legislator

Mr. Lincoln's political career proper may be said to have commenced on March 9, 1832, when he issued an address "To the people of Sangamon County."[1] As he was not as well versed in grammar then as by experience he afterwards became, he procured John McNamar to correct its grammar—otherwise the production is entirely his own.

The election took place about two weeks after his return to New Salem from the Black Hawk War, and he was defeated, as has been stated.

In 1834, Lincoln again decided to run for the legislature. The highly complimentary vote he had received before, the oratorical reputation he acquired in the prior canvass, his local popularity in the northern end of the county, and his creditable record in the Black Hawk War constituted his political stock in trade. There were no conventions in those days; the field was a "free for all," and, while there were some combinations among the candidates themselves, the fact was that each candidate stood or fell upon his own merits. Lincoln was classed as a Whig, although he held the office of postmaster under President Jackson and that of deputy surveyor under Calhoun, a most ardent Democrat. The canvass was unusually tame and spiritless for some reason. It resulted in the election of John Dawson,[2] Lincoln, William Carpenter,[3] and John T. Stuart. **He now was launched upon his tortuous, but ultimately brilliant, political career; his feet took hold upon the paths of glory which led him to his premature grave.**

It should not be forgotten that the legislature was a much more dignified, consequential, and important body then than it later became, and that it was

1. Basler, *Collected Works of Lincoln*, 1:5–9.

2. John Dawson (1797–1850), a former Democrat, led the ticket.

3. William Carpenter (1787–1859) was a Springfield merchant who served as the town's postmaster (1837–1841).

State Legislator

invested with much greater political power and social consequence. The granting of corporate charters, and other special legislation had not then been withheld from it, and it elected judicial and other officers.

Vandalia, the capital, put on its best holiday attire when the legislature met, and the beauty and fashion of the Illinois communities congregated there to a large extent. Lobbyists of the sleekest order hied thither on schemes of plunder bent; town belles flocked in with their pantalettes, flounces, and ruffles to enjoy the novelty and excitement; and "Becky Sharps" repaired thither with matrimonial schemes.

The legislature was the culminating point of all effort and all diversion **alike**. The interest in the sessions was so great and abiding as to last and to endure without diminution throughout the whole session. The brilliant modes of the *elite* of Kentucky society were imitated, and young lady graduates from the Kentucky seminaries were introduced into Illinois society here. Local statesmen affected the lofty airs of Kentucky politics, and Vandalia, during a legislative session, was a reflex of Frankfort during a similar period. **In fact, in many particulars, Illinois was assimilated to a province of Kentucky.**

The Yankees had made no perceptible impression as yet; Chicago was *in nubibus* [not in actual existence]—even Cook County had no existence. **The chief northern settlement near the Fever River lead mines had not as yet acquired a political standing. It was not till 1840 that Galena had a member.**

The legislature met on the first day of December, 1834. James Semple,[4] afterwards United States senator, was elected speaker: Lincoln's first political act was to vote for the losing competitor, Charles Dunn.[5] Transportation was the great subject of political discussion at the time. The acting governor, in his message, said: "Of the different modes proposed of effecting this communication [intercommunication] the general sentiment of the community as well as the report of an able engineer and the experience of other states seems to be in favor of a railroad. . . . A railroad commencing at the intersecting point of the Indiana canal on the Illinois River and terminating at an eligible situation on the western extremity of the state would pervade a country of great fertility and unequalled adaptation to its construction."

The governor-elect (Joseph Duncan), who was inaugurated soon thereafter, took a different view.[6] In his inaugural address he said: "Of the different

---

4. Kentucky-born James Semple (1798–1866) of Elsah represented Illinois in the U.S. Senate (1843–1847).

5. In 1836, Charles Dunn (1799–1872) was appointed the first chief justice of the Wisconsin Supreme Court.

6. Joseph Duncan (1794–1844) served as governor of Illinois (1834–1838), the only Whig to hold that office.

plans proposed for intercommunication I find that the Board of Canal Commissioners and my worthy predecessors have recommended a railroad, in which I regret that I am compelled to differ with them in opinion. In my judgment, experience has shown canals to be much more useful, and generally cheaper of construction than railroads."

This was the dawn of the era of premature internal improvements which brought fruits meet for repentance then, and whose glorious fulfillment was postponed for two decades. The political preponderance in the legislature was against Lincoln's party, yet, somehow, he was placed second on the important standing committee on public accounts and expenditures, quite an honor, since in those days there were not nearly so many standing committees as now. On the fifth day of the session, he performed his first legislative work by giving notice that on a subsequent day, he would ask leave to introduce a bill to limit the jurisdiction of justices of the peace; and later, he offered this bill. Soon thereafter he gave notice that he would present a bill "to authorize Samuel Musick to build a toll bridge across Salt Creek."

What became of his first bill seems to be unknown, but it never became a law; contrariwise, a law was passed at that session to enlarge (rather than limit) the powers of a justice of the peace, so **it is probable that** his first attempt at practical legislation proved to be a failure. His second bill, being rather in the nature of a private act, was more successful, for it matured into a law; and "Musick's bridge" was long one of the institutions of Illinois.[7]

Lincoln generally voted with his party but his early independence appears in his being one of three to resist the small petit larceny of hiring a suitable place for the use of the Committee on Revision. An election for U.S. Senator to succeed John M. Robinson[8] resulted in his reelection, Lincoln voting for Richard M. Young;[9] and five judges were elected by the legislature, viz.: Stephen T. Logan, Sidney Breese,[10] Henry Eddy,[11] Justin Harlan,[12] and Thomas Ford.[13]

7. Basler, *Collected Works of Lincoln*, 1:29–30.

8. Democrat John M. Robinson (1794–1843) represented Illinois in the U.S. Senate (1832–1840).

9. Richard M. Young (1798–1861) represented Illinois in the U.S. Senate (1837–1843).

10. Jurist Sidney Breese (1800–1878) represented Illinois in the U.S. Senate (1843–1849).

11. Attorney Henry Eddy (1798–1849) of Shawneetown, Illinois, published a newspaper and represented his district in the Illinois General Assembly.

12. Attorney Justin Harlan (1800–1879) of Marshall, Illinois, was a friend of Lincoln, who in 1862 appointed him superintendent of an Indian agency.

13. Democrat Thomas Ford (1800–1850) served as governor of Illinois (1842–1846).

At the election for State's Attorney, Stephen A. Douglas made his first appearance in politics, coming from Jacksonville, where he was temporarily domiciled, to Vandalia, to press his claims for that position in the First Circuit against John J. Hardin,[14] an eminent lawyer who was thought to be sure of an election. The appearance of Douglas, who was then five feet and one inch high and weighed about one hundred pounds, greatly amused Lincoln. Douglas was active, adroit, and insinuating, then and thereafter; Lincoln pronounced him to be "the *least* man he ever saw," little dreaming of the time to come when this same dwarf was to **become the Aeneas who should** bear him on his shoulders to the Executive Mansion of the nation. To the surprise of all, the then pigmy Douglas was elected over the then giant Hardin by 38 against 34 votes, and this was the commencement of an illustrious though clouded political career. It is singular that in the competition for this office for the Quincy district, Lincoln supported [William A.] Richardson, a Democrat,[15] against [Orville H.] Browning, a Whig,[16] the former afterward becoming a chief ally of Douglas and enemy of Lincoln, and the latter one of Lincoln's greatest political friends.

Lincoln's name is not very conspicuous in the proceedings of this session, which adjourned on February 13, 1835, after lasting two and a half months; but his career was satisfactory alike to his colleagues and constituents. In the succeeding year, he again became a candidate and constructed his political platform, upon which he proposed to stand.

There were seven members to elect to the lower house and two to the Senate. While no one was debarred from becoming a candidate, yet there was a sort of tacit understanding that each section should be considered in the list and that the support of the candidates of each party should be homogenous and compact. This canvass was as exciting **and trenchant** as the other had been tame. It was a presidential year, and the spirit of Jackson animated it. Then there was a sentiment that the capital was too far south and that it should be removed; and as Springfield was one of the competing places, it was discerned that a wealth of political glory awaited the delegates if they could succeed in scooping the capital into the Sangamon net.

14. Kentucky-born attorney John J. Hardin (1810–1847) of Jacksonville represented his district in the U.S. House of Representatives (1843–1845).

15. Kentucky-born attorney and close ally of Stephen A. Douglas, William A. Richardson (1811–1875) represented the Quincy district in the U.S. House of Representatives (1849–1856).

16. Attorney Orville H. Browning (1806–1881) of Quincy, Illinois, was an active Whig/Republican and a close friend and ally of Lincoln. He served as a U.S. senator (1861–1863).

A stirring and vigorous campaign followed; not only did political spirit run high, but muscular force was **more often** brought into requisition **than now**. It was an age of rudeness; **manners were not gracious, and** fights were an inevitable and ordinary incident of a political canvass in the Jacksonian era; insults were often given, and usually resented.

During the canvass, one Colonel Robert Allen, a **bloviating** Democrat,[17] perpetrated some petty slander about Lincoln and Ninian W. Edwards, to which Lincoln made a bold reply in which he said: "If I have done anything, either by design or misadventure, which if known would subject me to a forfeiture of that confidence (placed in me by my constituents), he that knows of that thing and conceals it is a traitor to his country's interest."[18]

In addition to the usual speeches, the several candidates indulged in joint debates, in which several would join. Not infrequently, bad blood would be engendered. Robert L. Wilson,[19] one of the candidates, **was one of my best friends years afterwards** (whom, **along** with Ninian W. Edwards and myself, Lincoln appointed paymasters in the Army) told me many incidents of this celebrated campaign. Among other things, he said that Lincoln was by common consent looked up to and relied on as the Whigs' leading exponent; that he was the best versed and most captivating and trenchant speaker on their side; that he preserved his temper nearly always, and when extremely provoked, he did not respond with the illogical proposal to fight about it but used the weapons of sarcasm and ridicule, and always prevailed. Ninian W. Edwards and Lincoln seemed to hunt in couples, although the former was a scion of wealth and aristocracy, while the latter was of the poorest of his class. When Lincoln would combat his friend's ridicule with its kind, and give "railing for railing," Edwards would get mad and propose to fight it out, then and there.

George Forquer was a lawyer of wealth and ability who had been a Whig, but had turned his coat and received the appointment of register of the land office, **which office he then held**.[20] He had recently erected a new house and had protected it with a lightning rod. This rod was then a new device, being the first one that Lincoln had seen, **and its novelty** engrossed his attention. Forquer attended a meeting at which Lincoln spoke, and thinking to ingratiate himself with his new allies, jumped up and asked to be heard. This a crowd

17. Colonel Robert Allen, a leading Springfield Democrat, presided over the 1840 Democratic Sangamon County convention.

18. Basler, *Collected Works of Lincoln,* 1:489.

19. Pennsylvania-born attorney Robert L. Wilson (1805–1880) of Athens served with Lincoln in the state legislature.

20. George Forquer (1794–1837) of Springfield served at various times as a state legislator, as secretary of state, and as state attorney general.

in those days was always ready to accord, and he replied in a very supercilious and insulting vein, whose haughty prelude was that "this young man" (alluding to Lincoln) "would have to be taken down."

Lincoln was thoroughly roused by the insolent and domineering style employed. The minute Forquer had concluded, he arose, animated with an excitement unusual to him, and replied in a strain that surpassed all his previous oratorical efforts. **He was indeed thoroughly aroused and angry. Forquer had spoken in a vein of irony and disdain that attuned his combativeness to its highest tension, and he was unsparing in his satire as well as forcible in his argument.** After **not only fully and** effectually replying to all of the arguments advanced, he concluded with this flagellation of the intruder: "This anomalous Forquer, if he has taken me *down,* as he calls it, I reckon you know it, and if he is satisfied, I am. He seems to be thoroughly up to political tricks—something I am not familiar with, and I never intend to be. If I can't get office honestly, I am content to live as I am, and I hope I never may be so thoroughly steeped in political trickery as to change my political coat for a big office, and then feel so guilty about it as to run up a lightning rod to protect my house from the vengeance of an offended God."[21]

In no element of political controversy did Lincoln fail during this canvass. He was, as thereafter, clear and skillful in statement and logical in discussion; he generally preserved his equanimity and good humor, and discomfited his enemies, but when it was apparent that forbearance had ceased to be a virtue, Lincoln made points and gained friends by the force, spirit, and defiance of his replies. In his first and second canvass he was bashful and timid, and confined himself to the strictly rural districts; this time, he put away his maidenly reserve, and spoke as unrestrainedly at Springfield as at New Salem. He gained the approval and applause of his friends and the respect and fear of his enemies, and became by that very canvass, a leader of his party in Sangamon County, which distinction he never lost.

The results of this noted canvass were very great, and of prime importance to Sangamon County. Whereas it had theretofore leaned strongly to the Democracy, it now gravitated towards the Whigs, who never thereafter lost their prestige. The entire Whig ticket was elected, Lincoln receiving the largest vote, and the Whig party, which had been below *par* theretofore, was on the mountain heights of rejoicing then and thereafter in that county.

This celebrated legislature assembled at Vandalia on the fifth day of December, 1836. Among its members were Stephen A. Douglas and John J. Hardin from the same county—one a leading Democrat and the other a

21. Joshua F. Speed, *Reminiscences of Abraham Lincoln and Notes of a Visit to California: Two Lectures* (Louisville, KY: John P. Morton, 1884), 17–18.

112   *Chapter VIII*

leading Whig—General John A. McClernand,[22] Augustus C. French (afterwards governor),[23] and Usher F. Linder, then the greatest orator in the state.[24]

The delegation from Sangamon first engaged the attention of the legislature on account of their size, **being nine in number**. They were denominated as "the Long Nine," their average length being over six feet, and their average weight being over 200 pounds. They received the appellation of the Long Nine from their size and number. Their political force was soon felt to be as strong and impressive as their physical force, for the people of Sangamon had been generous in the conferring of political power, and their reputations were pledges not to be disobedient to the trust so confided to them.

The father of Lincoln's thereafter law partner, Archer G. Herndon[25], and Job Fletcher[26] were the senators, and Lincoln, Ninian W. Edwards, John Dawson,[27] Andrew McCormick,[28] Dan Stone,[29] William F. Elkin, and Robert L. Wilson were the members of the lower house. Lincoln was made a member of the important committee on finance, and both he and Douglas were on the committee on the penitentiary.

Douglas led off that session by offering a sweeping resolution in favor of a broad and catholic system of internal improvements which was adopted,

22. Democrat John A. McClernand (1812–1900) represented the Shawneetown district in the U.S. House of Representatives (1843–1851) and the Springfield district (1859–1861).

23. Democrat Augustus C. French (1808–1864) of Palestine, Illinois, served as governor of the Prairie State (1846–1853).

24. Attorney Usher F. Linder (1809–1876) of Coles County served in the Illinois state legislature and participated in several legal cases with Lincoln, with whom he was quite friendly.

25. Democrat Archer G. Herndon (1795–1867), father of Lincoln's law partner and biographer William H. Herndon, served in the Illinois General Assembly (1834–1842) and was one of the "Long Nine" who managed to have Springfield chosen as the state capital.

26. Job Fletcher (1783–1872), a farmer in Sangamon County, represented his district as a Whig in the Illinois State Senate (1835–1840).

27. A justice of the peace in Sangamon County, John Dawson (1791–1850) settled in Clear Lake township, near Springfield, in 1827 and represented his district in the Illinois state legislature throughout the 1830s.

28. Stonecutter Andrew J. McCormick (b. 1801) won election as mayor of Springfield in 1843, after having served in the Illinois State House of Representatives for two terms in the 1830s.

29. Born in Vergennes, Vermont, attorney Dan C. Stone (1800–1880) served in the Illinois State House of Representatives (1836–1838) and as a judge of the circuit court of Illinois (1837–1843). In 1837, he signed a protest drafted by Lincoln condemning slavery as "based on injustice and bad policy."

inasmuch as the demand therefor was as great at the hands of the Whigs as of the Democrats.

At the election for United States senator which was had at that session, Lincoln abandoned Richard M. Young, whom he had voted for before (and who was elected this time) and voted with a few others for Archibald Williams, the same whom he appointed district judge of Kansas as his first appointment after that of his cabinet in 1861.[30]

The most important measure to the Sangamon delegation was the removal of the capital. There were several competitors for it, of which Springfield was really one of the least meritorious. Peoria, Jacksonville, and Alton were places of sufficient consequence to properly aspire to this great honor. Decatur and Springfield, the other two aspirants, had no merit save that of centrality; they were inconsequential villages, approachable during the legislative season by roads almost impassible by reason of mud. The geographical center of the state, called Illiopolis, a place between Springfield and Decatur, was a competitor. [Whitney note: Illiopolis was in the extreme eastern part of Sangamon County, but considerably nearer to Decatur than to Springfield. It had no buildings then. It was only a geographical point on the map.] On account of its consequence and accessibility, Peoria should have been selected. In this contest, Lincoln was the leader and advocate, and the Long Nine surrendered the scheme to his management almost entirely. Their power and efficiency of management soon drew all attention, and concentrated all the opposition against them; it was *the field* against Springfield. [Robert] Wilson and Henry L. Webb[31] have narrated to me many incidents of that apparently hopeless and unequal struggle.

30. Attorney and judge Archibald Williams (1801–1863) served in the Illinois General Assembly in the 1830s and as U.S. district attorney for the Southern District of Illinois (1849–1853).

31. In the manuscript, Whitney inserted this italicized passage within parentheses: *Webb was a member of this legislature. He was a younger brother of J. Watson Webb, proprietor of the Courier and Enquirer of New York and uncle of General A. S. Webb, and Seward Webb, who married a Vanderbilt. In 1817, at the age of 22, he left his home in New York and settled at Unity on the Cache River near Cairo and became a celebrated local politician—was clerk of the court of Alexander County, repeatedly served in the legislature in both branches, and was a captain in the Black Hawk War and a major in the Mexican War. In 1852 he removed to Cahill County, Virginia, where I knew him; and he was full of border anecdotes, and dwelt especially on the removal of the state capital, which he deemed to be the master stroke of diplomacy of the Western hemisphere. He avowed then that Lincoln was a Napoleon of astuteness and political finesse. He voted for the measure because of his admiration of Lincoln and the inability to resist his importunities. His policy was to leave the capital at Vandalia, but yielded to Lincoln. He returned to Makanda in Illinois and died in 1876.*

Upon several occasions their opponents deemed that they had circumvented the movement, and incautious ones *crowed* lustily over the supposed defeat and discomfiture of Lincoln and his colleagues. **Even** the pessimists of the Sangamon delegation supposed that the measure was lost, but Lincoln was tenacious and resolute. He would make a flank and unexpected movement which would revive their chances. The final result was that, under his adroit leadership, the bill was carried, although the only political strength in its favor at the start was seven votes in one house and two in the other, with no natural allies, and several delegations of active enemies. This was felt to be one of the greatest of political triumphs, and its credit was freely ascribed to Lincoln. Wilson, one of the delegation, assured me that had Lincoln not been there, it would have failed.

In one sense, it may be said to have been a triumph over his later adversary on a larger field, Douglas, for his town, Jacksonville, was one of the leading competitors.

The most important general matter which engrossed the attention of the legislature was a broad and extended system of internal improvements, and in this, Lincoln was as enthusiastic as in the removal of the capital.

The railroad had become an institution in New England, and it was even then prefigured as the great highway of intercommunication; the canal had been, and then was, the Appian Way[32] of commerce, but its construction was limited to level plains and hampered by sundry other conditions which barred it out as the common carrier of civilization.

The magnificent system of internal improvements which this legislature evolved from the *nebulae* [clouds] of desire and necessity would have been all right if the state could have afforded it, or if the hoped-for development had been a well-founded pledge and promise of enough taxes to pay the interest on bonds promptly and surely, but, unfortunately, no such conditions existed, and this really able legislature was in the condition of a visionary but hopeful man, entering into enlarged business enterprises, with roseate hopes and brilliant anticipations for his sole capital. However, then as always in a farming community, the ordinary tax list was the greatest burden to be borne, and to have carried into effect the grand schemes which were here proposed by law and on paper, would have bankrupted nine men out of ten in the whole state, so the inevitable and necessary result was that, after expending millions, the whole scheme was hopelessly abandoned, with very little substantial benefit. In point of fact, I happen to remember that as late as 1884, a railway was built in the southern part of the state partly upon a grade made at the expense of the state nearly a half a century before. That no voice should have been raised in condemnation of such extravagant legislation, whose evil effects were so

32. This long ancient Italian superhighway connected Rome with Bari.

palpable in a few years thereafter, seems now strange to us; but so it was, that the general acclaim of the people was vocal for intercommunication, and legislators could not resist it if they would. **In point of fact, the entire state was agricultural and nothing else; there were no large places, no manufacturing, but little capital and no men who understood the peculiar and recondite science and art of finance—of ways and means, to get and use money. But the people did know their minds, and methods of personal and freight transit were sadly needed.**

The soil of Illinois was of that character of rich loam that, while of the very best to yield luxurious crops, it yet was a bar to good, or even tolerable, roads in the fall, winter, and spring times of the year. In the southeastern, western, and southwestern parts of the state were navigable rivers. The Illinois was available as far as La Salle, the Wabash as far as Lafayette in Indiana, and Lake Michigan touched the northwest; there was likewise a waterway for lead ore in the Fever [or Galena, or Fevre] River to the Mississippi; and the canal from Lafayette to Covington in Indiana furnished an outlet for a small scope of country on the eastern border; but most of the state was without any means of communication save the "mud wagon" [stagecoach] for passengers and the ordinary farm team for produce. Many communities had to go a hundred miles to haul farm produce: corn, oats, wheat, and hay. So the necessity for internal improvements was imperious, and the people, discarding those practical and businesslike considerations which guided them in ordinary business affairs, somehow deemed legislation as a magical mode of bringing things to pass which could not be achieved by ordinary business processes. They seemed to think that when the legislative body solemnly proclaimed "Be it enacted," **that it was, in fact, *enacted*, that** the improvement was already made, and in this flimsy delusion the legislators affected to share. The "Long Nine" were instructed on the subject by their constituents; they were ordered to advocate a general system of internal improvements; and to brace up the lawmakers, a mass convention was held at the capital, which resolved that the legislature should provide for a system which should be commensurate with the desires of the people.

Every locality had its scheme. Chicago desired then, as constantly thereafter, and properly, a canal to connect the waters of her lake with those of the Illinois River; all possibly available rivers were to be improved as "highways of commerce," and in this branch of internal improvement, Lincoln was an enthusiast, for always since his flatboat experience with Offutt, he had ardently believed even in the adaptation of the Sangamon to purposes of navigation as far up as Springfield.

Wherever waterways were theoretically possible, a demand arose for the necessary appropriation to make them available, and when there was no potentially navigable stream, railways were demanded; that there was no

116   *Chapter VIII*

money in the treasury, or surplus wealth in the state, or proper bases for taxation, did not seem to disturb or check these rustic Solons in the least. They developed and matured their schemes of traffic conquest as if they had the means in hand to enforce their legislation, and the only attempt to provide the sinews of war lay in a bill which passed, with no considerable opposition, to provide a loan of twelve millions (an enormous sum for those days) to carry their schemes into effect. In the enforcement of these measures of legislation, Abraham Lincoln and Stephen A. Douglas, the two greatest men of Illinois, worked in perfect amity, accord, and enthusiasm.

It is a singular idiosyncrasy of dialectics that statesmen of broad gauge, as well as dolts therein, alike consider themselves to be capable of constructing correct financial theories and enforcing them in practice; while the fact is, that the science of finance is single, distinct, and recondite, and its correct study and proper practice are inharmonious with the study of general and enlarged statesmanship. In proof of this adage is to be noted the fact that many of our greatest statesmen have not exhibited sufficient ability to manage even their own private finances with success or skill, while the masters of finance are most generally the most narrow gauge order of men elsewhere.

Daniel Webster and Henry Clay were always the necessary recipients of financial assistance at the hands of their friends; Stephen A. Douglas was a bold investor and, though living in an era of great rises in values, was always hopelessly in debt. Lincoln was prudent, and yet when elected president at fifty-two years of age had but ten thousand dollars; and similar conditions may be attributed to many others—indeed, our millionaire statesmen, as a rule, have little else but their millions and successes acquired by the construction of piles of gold to save them from utter and abject scorn.

While Illinois Solons in 1836 and 1837 were voting millions for internal improvements, every year thousands of farms were being sold and being forfeited for delinquent taxes. Finally, retribution came, and the whole airy fabric collapsed and brought immediate, though reparable, disaster, and came near causing repudiation, which would have been an irreparable calamity.

But while the measures were being matured, the sword of Damocles was not visible, nor yet did the shadow of an avenging Nemesis darken the legislative halls. All was bright and beautiful **in their legislative fancy**. Capitalists were rushing in with money to buy the bonds, and immigrants were swelling the roll of taxpayers, and Illinois promised to supplant New York as the Empire State.

Never was Lincoln more earnest, enthusiastic, or hopeful than in the advocacy of these measures; as he had never seen more than a hundred dollars or so in one lot, and had no financial negotiation of greater magnitude than his partnership transactions with Berry **involved, he could not expect to be an accomplished financier; in fact, so far as experience went,** he knew

State Legislator

comparatively nothing of finance. While he could formulate schemes for expending the public money, he had no idea of the conservative qualities needed to complete the process and secure a logical balancing of accounts at the end. His ambition, in view of the future of history, took a strange direction, and had no legitimate basis; he had read of the glorious Erie Canal system and the luster conferred upon its founder, and he confidentially avowed to his friend [Joshua] Speed his ambition to become the "DeWitt Clinton"[33] of Illinois. Instead, he came nearer to being its John Law;[34] at least the enterprises in which he courted distinction ended almost as disastrously as the "Mississippi bubble." **Among other "wildcat" schemes was one to incorporate the Spoon River Navigation Company, another to improve the navigation of the Big Vermilion River, another to incorporate the Western, Ottawa, and Kishwaukee Rail Road Company, and many others equally obscure, whose terminal points are not now known, even to the oldest settlers.**

Lincoln was on the important committee on finance, in which were matured these magnificent schemes of internal improvement; and both Lincoln and Douglas were brought, in a legislative sense, face to face by service on the committee on the penitentiary. In pursuance of their official duties, it was necessary for them to visit the institution at Alton, then about sixty miles distant, and one can imagine this committee, one of whose members was six foot four inches in height and the other five feet and one inch, *en route* in the stage thither and return, entertaining each other to while away the tedium of the journey. **It certainly is a unique experience among presidential candidates that such a jaunt as that across the mud-beleaguered prairies of Illinois should be made by the two leading candidates in the most important canvass of our history.**

During the session, a motion was made to express the thanks of the legislature to President Jackson for the firm, consistent, independent, and able manner in which he had performed his duties, and to tender its best wishes to him on his retirement from office. Jesse K. Dubois moved to amend it by inserting the prefix "in" before consistent. This was rejected. Lincoln moved to divide the proposition, which was done; and he himself voted "nay" to the first branch and "aye" to the second branch. Both branches of the motion were carried.

It is noticeable that an election took place at this session for a judge at Chicago (I suppose of the Common Pleas Court), at which Thomas Ford was elected, and Browning and Lincoln were the tellers.

33. DeWitt Clinton (1769–1828), governor of New York (1825–1828), was regarded as the man most responsible for the construction of the Erie Canal.

34. John Law (1671–1729) was the Scottish financier responsible for the "Mississippi Bubble," a financial disaster that ruined many investors (1718–1720).

The session ended on March 6, 1837, and the "Long Nine" mounted their horses and started for home, except Lincoln, who had no horse to mount, and hence went by means of "Shanks' mare," [i.e., walking] as he termed it. Being long-legged and an excellent walker, he was enabled to pick his way through comparatively dry fields and by the roadside, thus avoiding the mud which his favored companions must contend with, and so he managed to keep up with them for the whole journey, which consumed four days. It is quite probable that, in order to have the benefit of Lincoln's humor, they suited their gait to his, and it is manifest to such as were familiar with the methods of the "wild and wooly west" in those days, that the literary entertainment of the journey was highly spiced, if not classical. The poorest scintillation of wit of the journey reveals a border of sadness. The future Emancipator, thinly clad for the season, shivered as a cold northeaster struck him, and said, "Boys, I'm cold." "No wonder," was the unfeeling reply, animadverting on the size of his feet, "There's so much of you on the ground."

However, the "Long Nine" were received with great *eclat* at Springfield. The keys and freedom of the little mud-begirt city were accorded them, and free dinners *galore* were spread. At one of these the following toast was proposed to Mr. Lincoln: "Abraham Lincoln; he has fulfilled the expectations of his friends, and disappointed the hopes of his enemies." And Lincoln proposed this toast: "All our friends; they are too numerous to mention now individually, while there is no one of them who is not too dear to be forgotten or neglected." And Douglas, who was also there, having been appointed register of the land office, offered this toast: "The last winter's legislation. May its results prove no less beneficial to the whole state, than they have to our town."

But the novelty wore off in a day or two, and the usual humdrum of existence prevailed. Lincoln had had the lead in the honors accorded, and although his name was as sonorous and more applauded than any, he was the sole one of the "Long Nine" who had no local habitation or home, and the necessity for achieving one pressed remorselessly upon him.

Soon after leaving Springfield at this time, he visited Athens, where his colleague, Robert L. Wilson, of the "Long Nine" resided, and that community extended to Mr. Lincoln the compliment of a banquet, at which he was accorded the toast, "Abraham Lincoln: one of nature's noblemen."

One can scarcely credit the extreme rusticity which then prevailed. These extremely raw "toasts" **are in harmony and** sound very like a crossroads debating club. In fact, Lincoln and his surroundings smacked of the justice of the peace order of law business, and the "log cabin and hard cider" style of social life. From Mr. Wilson, whom I knew intimately in after life, I learned much of the career of the great president in those early days. Wilson said, "Lincoln was a natural debater; he was always ready and always got right down to the merits of his case, without any nonsense or circumlocution. He was quite as much at home in the legislature as at New Salem; he had a quaint and peculiar way, all his own, of treating a subject, and he frequently startled us by his modes—but he was always right. He seemed to be a born politician. We followed his lead, but he followed nobody's lead; he hewed the way for us to follow, and we gladly did so. He could grasp and concentrate the matters under discussion, and his clear statement of an intricate or obscure subject was better than an ordinary argument. It may almost be said that he did our thinking for us, but he had no arrogance, nothing of the dictatorial; it seemed the right thing to do as he did. He excited no envy or jealousy. He was felt to be so much greater than the rest of us that we were glad to abridge our **intellectual** labors **of causation** by letting him do the general thinking for the crowd. He **always** inspired respect although he was utterly careless and negligent. We would ride while he would walk, but we recognized him as a master in logic; he was poverty itself when I knew him, but still perfectly independent. He would borrow nothing and never ask favors. He seemed to glide along in life without any friction or effort."

Soon after the termination of this session, Jackson's relentless war on the National Bank bore fruit, and that institution closed its doors, followed by a suspension of the banks in the large cities of the Union. The danger was imminent, and the conservative governor convened the legislature in special session at Vandalia on July 10, 1837, when a practical message calling attention to the financial perils which environed the state and advising the legislature to reef sails and throw out ballast awaited them.

The optimistic legislature paid no heed to these monitory and temperate suggestions but, on the other hand, with an astonishing recklessness, persisted in their mad schemes of inflation, and not only so, but added to them.

The Sangamon delegation was strengthened by the addition of Edward D. Baker, afterwards known to a great fame, and a fervent and thrilling orator;[35] and the pyrotechnics of oratory held sway over prudence, and the approaching and inevitable pay-day. So ultimate financial ruin was accelerated, in which Lincoln was more enthusiastic than his fellows, although at that time, he probably did not pay one cent of taxes, for he not only owned nothing, but was twelve hundred dollars, or such matter, in debt. However, this was one branch of Lincoln's training school by which, in process of time, he became the wisest of our public men.

At the ensuing session of the legislature, which convened on December 9, 1837, Lincoln was again a member, and so conspicuous that he received the

35. Attorney Edward Dickinson Baker (1811–1861) of Springfield, a close friend of Lincoln, represented his district in the U.S. House of Representatives (1845–1847, 1849–1851) and served as a U.S. senator from Oregon (1860–1861).

votes of his Whig colleagues for speaker—thirty-eight votes to forty-three for his Democratic colleague. He was reappointed to the important committee on finance and was likewise made a member of the committee on counties. Edward D. Baker, afterward U.S. senator from Oregon, and Isaac P. Walker, afterwards U.S. senator from Wisconsin,[36] were members. But little of public importance was done, except to bemoan the sad condition of the finances and make tentative efforts to retrieve the errors and profligacy of past legislation. Lincoln started in the session with a heroic resolve to maintain this ground, but finance was not his *forte*, and he succumbed to the inevitable, as the others did. Repudiation in disguise was boldly mentioned. It was not deemed possible that the state could pay its entire debt, and discussions were entered into as to which parts were more, and which less, meritorious. Lincoln candidly admitted "his share of the responsibility in the present crisis"—admitted that he was no financier, and did not have the least idea how the state would be extricated from its embarrassment. The legislature could do nothing effective; work was suspended on the public improvements, and Lincoln's roseate hopes of becoming the "DeWitt Clinton" of Illinois faded away like the mists of morning.

He returned home from this session very deeply chagrined at the anticlimactic ending of his brilliant schemes and had to endure the taunts and gibes of the Democrats, to whom his career had afforded so excellent an opportunity for the display of ridicule and envy. In order to restore, if possible, his lost prestige, and to retrieve his political character, he offered himself again as a candidate and put all the vigor he knew into the campaign.

The campaign was a vituperative one. Among the Democratic orators was Edmund D. Taylor, a professional politician, having held office for most of his life;[37] in fact, both he and his brother had a weakness for land office appointments, and one or the other, and sometimes both, were constantly feeding in some way at the public crib.

So Taylor, in one of his speeches, took occasion to appeal to the prejudices of the people by calling the Whigs "English aristocrats," and speaking of them as bankers, capitalists, *toadies* to the English, etc., and to laud his party as the lover of the poor man, plain manners, honest workmen, &c. In point of fact, Taylor himself, with a strange inconsistency of conduct, was a consummate fop. He never appeared in public without a ruffled shirt, a blue coat with brass buttons, and a gold-headed cane. This habit he persisted in to his ninetieth

36. Isaac Pigeon Walker (1815–1872) of Springfield represented his district in the Illinois House of Representatives (1838–1840) and later served as a U.S. senator from Wisconsin (1848–1853).

37. Edmund Dick Taylor (1804–1891) served in the Illinois state legislature (1830–1835) and eventually became known as "the father of the greenback."

year, when, with his oiled and glossy locks and erect deportment, he would easily pass for a youth of sixty. **Well, Lincoln listened to this bucolic demagogic speech which he was to answer, and** when Taylor had concluded this demagogic appeal, Lincoln caught the lower edge of his vest and suddenly jerked it open, exhibiting a huge ruffled shirt and a ponderous gold watch-chain with a lot of ornamental appendages, which Taylor had designed to conceal for the occasion, to the dire confusion of Taylor and the infinite merriment of the crowd. Then Lincoln "sailed into" the pretensions launched forth by Taylor, in this style: "And here's Dick Taylor, charging us with aristocracy and gilt manners, and claiming to be an exponent of the farmers and cattle raisers; and while he's doing this, he stands in a hundred-dollar suit of clothes in a dancing master's pomp and parade, with a ruffled shirt just such as his master, General Jackson, wears, and a gold log-chain around his neck to keep his watch from being stole by some of us, and with a big gold-headed cane. And while he was raised in this style, I was a-steering a flatboat down the river for eight dollars a month, with a torn shirt, one pair of buckskin breeches, and a *warmus* as my only suit. The Bible says, 'By your fruits ye shall know them;' now I have got on my best today and Taylor has got on his shabbiest. You can judge which one of us is the aristocrat by our appearance."

This same Taylor, after Mr. Lincoln's lamented death, used to aver that it was he that induced Lincoln to study law and also that it was on his advice that the administration of Lincoln adopted the "greenback," propositions about as veracious as his claim of pure and undefiled democracy.

The canvass was full of bitterness. Baker was once making a Whig speech in the courthouse, in the course of which he dealt the Democracy some pretty severe blows, and inciting the wrath of the Democrats so **much** that they cried: "Hustle him down!" and began to move toward him to carry out the threat. The room had a very low ceiling, and there was a hole in the floor just above the judge's stand (which was in the center of the building) to let in light and air. Lincoln's office was in the second story, and he was lying **down** right by this hole, to hear Baker's speech. When he saw this attempt to mob Baker, he at once let himself down through this hole, and, appearing at the side of Baker, shouted in a voice of authority that was at once respected: "Stop this. Baker has a right to speak as he pleases, and if you take him off of the stand, you'll have to take me too!" Baker then finished his speech just as he desired, and Lincoln went out in the street, and stayed with him as long as he was menaced with danger.

Jesse B. Thomas,[38] a leader of the Democracy, in the absence of Lincoln, made a good deal of sport of him, which some friends of the latter reported

---

38. Jesse B. Thomas (1777–1853) represented Illinois in the U.S. Senate (1818–1829).

Chapter VIII

in time for him to reach the meeting before it broke up. As soon as Thomas had concluded, there were vociferous shouts for Lincoln from all over the house. The latter was "on tap." Having heard of Thomas' line of remark, he was wrought up to his extremest tension and abused Thomas in a merciless way. **The latter had thrown down the gage of warfare, and his antagonist showed him no mercy. He exhibited his power as a controversialist if he chose to exert it**. He mimicked Thomas perfectly, showed off all his peculiarities and weaknesses, and kept the audience in a roar of derision at poor Thomas, who was in full view of the audience during the whole scene and could not escape. It was a long time before this incident, called the "skinning of Thomas," was forgotten in Springfield, but Lincoln himself, to whose nature the attack was entirely foreign, after it was over felt very sorry for it and even went so far as to apologize to Thomas.

Lincoln himself told me of an incident that happened at the election. Baker was born on the sea when his parents were emigrating to this country from England, and it used to be occasionally said that he was not a qualified voter. So on this election day a prominent Democrat said to Baker, "I'm going to challenge your vote." This was a tender point with Baker, as well as a deadly insult, and he quickly said, "If you do, I'll lick you." Baker tendered his vote, which the man challenged, and Baker took the oath and voted. Then in quicker time than he could comprehend that anything had occurred, the man lay in the street, his face covered with blood, the worst whipped man that Lincoln said that he had ever seen.

No event prior to the repeal of the Missouri Compromise ever happened in Illinois which created so much excitement as the removal of the state capital. The first measure was a joint resolution to relocate it by a joint convention of the two houses on a day named. That day was a red-letter day in the history of Vandalia, for all the politicians in the state met there, each one advocating his favorite location. There were a dozen competing places, six actively so, and the rest hoping that an emergency would arise that would bring one of them to the front. The leading places were Springfield, Jacksonville, Vandalia, Peoria, Alton, and Illiopolis (the center of the state). When the first ballot was taken, intense excitement prevailed. Lincoln's adroit tactics were felt and acknowledged throughout, and Springfield secured more votes than any two of its competitors combined on the first ballot and continued to grow on every ballot, securing the coveted prize on the fourth.

An appropriation of $50,000 was made toward providing a capitol building, and Springfield was required to obligate itself to pay $50,000 toward the same object. It took herculean efforts to raise this amount, and Douglas proposed a measure to release the city from its obligation, but Lincoln opposed it. Said he: "We have the benefit; let us stand to an obligation like men." The sum was divided into three installments; the first two were raised, but they had to borrow the last installment from the State Bank. To secure this a joint note was made, signed by every citizen of the place.

The first legislature to convene in Springfield used temporary quarters; the lower house sat in the Second Presbyterian Church on Fourth Street; the senate in the Methodist Church; and the Supreme Court in the Episcopal Church.

Of this legislature which sat at Springfield, Lyman Trumbull,[39] William H. Bissell,[40] Thomas Drummond,[41] and Ebenezer Peck[42]—all greatly distinguished thereafter—were members, and John Calhoun, of "candle-box" notoriety afterwards, was clerk.[43] Lincoln was again the Whig candidate for Speaker, receiving thirty-six votes, but was defeated by W. L. D. Ewing,[44] who received forty-six votes. On account of the financial distress and incidents growing out of the same, the governor convened the legislature two weeks earlier than its regular session. The banks all over the nation had been forced by the panic of 1837 to suspend specie payments, and at the previous session, the legislature of Illinois had authorized its State Bank to suspend specie payments till the end of the next General Assembly. The Democratic party got into a quarrel with the bank, and, in consequence, conceived a plan to force it to resume specie payments, by adjourning *sine die* at the end of the first fortnight of the regular session, which would have been ruinous for this reason, that the banks of all other states being suspended, if the state bank of this **one** state was alone compelled to redeem its bills, an attempt would be made to run every one of them home at once, which of course would very soon exhaust their small stock of specie. The Whigs, having heard of this scheme on the morning of the day it was to be attempted, resolved to counteract it in this way: it needed several of the Whig members to constitute a quorum for

39. Connecticut-born Lyman Trumbull (1813–1896) of Belleville was a lawyer, judge, and U.S. senator (1855–1873). He married Julia Jayne, a sometime friend of Mary Todd Lincoln.

40. William H. Bissell (1811–1860) of Belleville represented his district in the U.S. House of Representatives (1849–1855) and served as governor of Illinois (1857–1860).

41. Judge Thomas Drummond (1809–1890) of Chicago presided over the federal circuit court for the district of northern Illinois (1855–1869).

42. Canadian-born Ebenezer Peck (1805–1881) of Chicago helped found the Republican party of Illinois.

43. In 1857 and 1858, Calhoun was serving as surveyor general of the Kansas Territory, where he presided over a constitutional convention. In the latter capacity he facilitated a voting fraud scheme that involved the burial of election returns in a box that had once held candles.

44. William Lee Davidson Ewing (1795–1846) of Shawneetown served as speaker of the Illinois State House of Representatives (1830–1832, 1838–1842).

the transaction of business, but in an attempt to take a vote, a quorum would be assumed as present, if unchallenged, and so all Whig members stayed out of the chamber except Lincoln and Joseph Gillespie,[45] who remained to call for the *ayes* and *noes* when an attempt should be made to adjourn *sine die*. The Democrats, seeing the ruse, made a call of the house, and sent the sergeant-at-arms out to hunt up the absentees. Lincoln and Gillespie, seeing Whigs brought in, agreed with two of them that *they* should move for the *ayes* and *noes*, **and then** attempted to withdraw; but finding the doors locked by order of the Speaker, they raised a window and, joined by Asahel Gridley of Bloomington,[46] jumped out and secreted themselves.

I have ventured to talk with Mr. Lincoln about the "Shields" duel,[47] but never about this episode, although judged by the canons of political morality, this was a justifiable act, **yet** Lincoln ever thereafter regretted it, and would always have some little inapposite story to narrate whenever the story came up, in order to divert the subject. A most rancorous partisan spirit prevailed throughout the entire session, and the Democrats, having the power, carried measures with a high hand, one of their schemes being a total overthrow of the judicial system of the state, and the substitution therefor of a strictly partisan bench, for partisan objects.

The law as it then stood provided that all white male *inhabitants* should vote, etc. This, the Democrats contended, included *aliens*, but the Galena judge, in a test case, decided that it did *not* include aliens, whereupon Judge Douglas drafted a bill vacating the seats of the nine circuit judges and providing for the appointment, by the legislature, of nine additional Supreme Judges, who also should perform "circuit" duty. Of course, the legislature appointed Democrats, who decided the law as the party wished; and thus, by one of the most high-handed outrages upon the judiciary and usurpations of

45. Attorney Joseph Gillespie (1809–1885) of Edwardsville served in the Illinois General Assembly and was a close friend of Lincoln's.

46. Asahel Gridley (1810–1881), law partner of John M. Scott, served in the Illinois state legislature (1840–1842, 1850–1854).

47. In 1842, Lincoln accepted James Shields's challenge to a duel, which was called off at the last minute. In *Life on the Circuit with Lincoln* (p. 36), Whitney wrote: "Apropos of this duel: I tried, on one or two occasions, to draw him out on it: but he always parried the subject, as if he was ashamed of it, but [Usher] Linder, one of our contemporaries, was more fortunate: being with Lincoln at Danville court the latter picked up a lath and was going through the broadsword manual, when Linder asked why he chose broadswords in his proposed duel with Shields, to which Lincoln replied: 'To tell you the truth, Linder, I didn't want to kill Shields, and felt sure I could disarm him, having had about a month to learn the broadsword exercise: and furthermore, I didn't want that damned fellow to kill me, which I rather think he would have done if we had selected pistols.'"

political and constitutional power, the law was subverted, the independence of the judicial power invaded, and a general degradation of the law and public morality enforced. Douglas, the author of the law, became one of the new judges. But the odious system did not last long. Public opinion everywhere condemned it, and the new constitution made it impossible for the legislature thereafter to punish the judiciary for trying to administer the law honestly. This example indicates the rabid and vicious character of local politics in Illinois in the days of Lincoln's novitiate in that field, where he was destined to garner such colossal fame in the days to come. Lincoln subsequently in the debates with Douglas made good use of this episode in his opponent's early career, showing that the advocate of the Dred Scott decision had not always upheld the sanctity of the judiciary.

Mr. Lincoln was absent for a considerable part of the regular session on account of nervous irritation and general ill-health. He visited his friend Joshua F. Speed, who had removed to the Speed plantation, near Louisville. While there, he was wont to visit James Speed's law office in Louisville and amuse himself with the law library, neither one then thinking that one of them would become president of the United States and the other his cabinet law adviser.[48]

This was Lincoln's last legislative service. During its existence he gained much experience, became acquainted with the genius of Illinois laws and politics, and the laws themselves, and the politicians, and was enabled to gauge, to some extent, his own merits and abilities as a politician and public man. **That he was a natural politician and leader of men was clearly exhibited; the two greatest measures which he advocated were the removal of the capital and the internal improvement system. The means employed to secure the former would not abide the test of ideal morality, hardly of political morality; the enactment of the latter was indefensible on any correct business principles**.

Mr. Lincoln's statesmanship was in a chrysalis state. His evolution from a backwoods youth to a man of affairs was not yet complete. His training for his true mission in life had just begun. *A. Lincoln* was not made in a day.

In 1854, his political friends brought him and Judge Logan out as candidates for the legislature, and although both Lincoln and his wife tried to prohibit it, yet both he and Logan were kept in the field and both were elected. Lincoln was a candidate for the U.S. senate and declined the position. The Democrats took advantage of the opportunity and elected one of their number to fill the vacancy. Had Lincoln remained in the position, the result of the senatorial election might have been otherwise.

---

48. James Speed (1812–1887) of Kentucky, brother of Lincoln's good friend Joshua Speed, served as attorney general of the United States (1864–1866).

William Jayne, a brother-in-law of Senator [Lyman] Trumbull, was one of the most active and persistent of the Springfield local politicians.[49] He attended all conventions, great and small, and was a man of inflexible integrity to his friends and principles. Jayne went to Lincoln to get his consent to run and thus reports the occurrence: "I went to see him in order to get his consent to run. This was at his home. He was then the saddest man I ever saw—the gloomiest. He walked up and down the floor almost crying, and to all my persuasions to let his name stand in the paper, he said, 'No, I can't; you don't know all. I say you don't begin to know one-half, and that's enough.' I did go, however, and have his name reinstated."[50]

It is scarcely necessary to say that it was Mrs. Lincoln's opposition which so much disturbed him. She insisted in her imperious way that he must now go to the United States Senate, and that it was a degradation to run him for the legislature.

49. Dr. William A. Jayne (1826–1916), brother of Julia Jayne Trumbull, served as mayor of Springfield (1859–60) and as one of the Lincoln family's physicians. In 1861, Lincoln appointed him governor of the Dakota Territory.

50. Lamon, *Life of Lincoln*, 359; Wilson and Davis, *Herndon's Informants*, 266.

IX

Congressman

Mr. Lincoln's first law partner, John T. Stuart, ran for and was defeated for the 25th Congress, which sat in December 1837, but he was successful for the 26th and 27th Congresses. For the next Congress in course, the 28th, which was to meet on December 4, 1843, the city of Springfield presented three several Whig competitors for the nomination, viz.: Judge Logan, E. D. Baker, and Mr. Lincoln. Logan withdrew, leaving the field to Baker and Lincoln. Baker secured the delegation, one of whom was Lincoln, who humorously wrote that he felt, in attending the convention, like attending as the "best man" at a successful rival's wedding. However, Baker lost the nomination, it going to John J. Hardin of Jacksonville, who was elected. At the next convention, held in 1844, Baker was nominated and thereafter elected. He resigned on December 30, 1846, in order to return to the Mexican War, he having participated in it the previous summer, and one John Henry[1] was elected to fill the vacancy of nearly a month.

Lincoln and Logan were both candidates for the succession, but the latter withdrew, in consequence, probably, of an agreement that he should run next time. He presented Lincoln's name to the convention, which met at Petersburg in May, 1846; and the latter was unanimously nominated.

The Democrats nominated Rev. Peter Cartwright, the most eminent and widely known Methodist preacher in the State.[2] Cartwright was an untiring worker **of great endurance** and personally very popular, owing to his force of character. The canvass on both sides was made with great vigor and spirit,

1. Illinois state Senator John Henry (1800–1882) briefly represented the Springfield district in the U.S. House of Representatives (February 5–March 4, 1847).

2. Peter Cartwright (1785–1872) was a popular Methodist circuit-riding minister.

128   *Chapter IX*

not to say acrimony. Cartwright appealed to the prejudices of the religious community against Lincoln, branding him as an infidel, which was a more terrible accusation then than now. That the reverend gentleman took no pride in this canvass is patent in this, that in an autobiography published by him afterwards, the circumstance is not alluded to at all. Lincoln was elected by an unprecedented majority—1511 votes—the usual majority in the district being about 500. This was a great honor, **especially** in view **of the opposition and** of the kind of canvass which was made against him.

The principal subject for political consideration was the Mexican War, which was then raging. In Illinois the war was popular, even among the Whigs. Hardin and Baker, both Whigs, fought in it, and Hardin was killed at Buena Vista. Lincoln partook of the spirit of the time, and made a fervent war speech to his constituents on May 29, 1847. In December 1847, he appeared in Congress, the only Whig from Illinois, his Democratic colleagues from Illinois being Robert Smith from Alton;[3] John A. McClernand from Shawneetown; Orlando B. Ficklin from Charleston;[4] William A. Richardson from Rushville; Thomas J. Turner from Freeport;[5] and John Wentworth from Chicago.[6]

This was a very talented and eventful Congress, **the Mexican War being in progress and** questions relating to the accessions and government of new territory were being considered. In the senate were [John] Bell,[7] [John C.] Calhoun, [Thomas] Corwin,[8] [John J.] Crittenden,[9] [Jefferson] Davis, [William] Dayton,[10] [Daniel S.] Dickinson,[11] [John A.] Dix,[12] [Stephen A.] Douglas,

3. Robert Smith (1802–1867) represented an Illinois district in the U.S. House of Representatives (1843–1849, 1853–1859).

4. Orlando B. Ficklin (1808–1886) of Charleston represented his Illinois district in the U.S. House of Representatives (1843–1849, 1851–1853).

5. Thomas J. Turner (1815–1874) of Freeport represented his Illinois district in the U.S. House of Representatives (1847–1849).

6. John "Long John" Wentworth (1815–1888) represented his district in the U.S. House of Representatives (1843–1851, 1853–1855) and served as mayor of Chicago (1857–1858, 1860–1861).

7. John Bell (1796–1869) represented Tennessee in the U.S. Senate (1847–1859) and ran unsuccessfully for president in 1860.

8. Thomas Corwin (1794–1865) represented Ohio in the U.S. Senate (1845–1850).

9. John J. Crittenden (1787–1863) represented Kentucky in the U.S. Senate (1855–1861).

10. William L. Dayton (1807–1864) represented New Jersey in the U.S. Senate (1842–1851).

11. Democrat Daniel S. Dickinson (1800–1866) represented New York in the U.S. Senate (1844–1851).

12. John A. Dix (1798–1879) represented New York in the U.S. Senate (1845–1849).

[John P.] Hale,[13] [R. M. T.] Hunter[14] and Webster; in the lower house, [John D.] Ashmore,[15] Andy Johnson, [Robert] Toombs,[16] [Joshua R.] Giddings,[17] [David] Wilmot,[18] [Jacob] Collamer,[19] [Robert Barnwell] Rhett,[20] [Alexander H.] Stephens, and [Thomas] Clingman.[21] Robert C. Winthrop of Massachusetts was speaker.[22]

On December 20, 1847, the following resolutions came up for action on a motion to lay on the table, and Lincoln voted with his party against the motion, and in favor of the measure:

Resolved, That if in the judgment of Congress it be necessary to improve the navigation of a river to expedite and render secure the movements of our Army, and save from delay and loss, our arms and munitions of war, the Congress has the power to improve such river.

Resolved, That if it be necessary for the preservation of the lives of our seamen, repairs, safety, or maintenance of our vessels of war, to improve a harbor or inlet, either on our Atlantic or lake coast, Congress has the power to make such improvement.

On December 21, 1847, Joshua R. Giddings presented a petition from certain citizens of Washington City for the repeal of the slave trade in the District of Columbia (there then being a slave market within earshot of the Capitol). Mr. Giddings attempted to have it referred to the Judiciary Committee, with

13. John Parker Hale (1806–1873) represented New Hampshire in the U.S. Senate (1855–1865).

14. Robert Mercer Taliaferro Hunter (1809–1887) represented Virginia in the U.S. Senate (1847–1861).

15. John D. Ashmore (1819–1871) represented a South Carolina district in the U.S. House of Representatives (1848–1852, 1859–1860).

16. Robert Toombs (1810–1885) represented a Georgia district in the U.S. House of Representatives (1845–1853).

17. Joshua R. Giddings (1795–1864) of Jefferson, Ohio, represented his district in the U.S. House of Representatives (1838–1859).

18. David Wilmot (1814–1868) represented a Pennsylvania district in the U.S. House of Representatives (1845–1861) and represented Pennsylvania in the U.S. Senate (1861–1863).

19. Jacob Collamer (1791–1865) represented a Vermont district in the U.S. House of Representatives (1843–1849) and represented Vermont in the U.S. Senate (1855–1865).

20. Robert Barnwell Rhett (1800–1876) represented a South Carolina district in the U.S. House of Representatives (1837–1849).

21. Thomas Clingman (1812–1897) represented a North Carolina district in the U.S. House of Representatives (1843–1858).

22. Robert C. Winthrop (1809–1894) of Massachusetts served as speaker of the U.S. House of Representatives (1847–1849).

Chapter IX

instructions to inquire into the constitutionality of all laws by which slaves are held as property in the District of Columbia. The pro-slavery hordes tried to lay the measure on the table but failed. Mr. Lincoln voted with Giddings not to lay it on the table.

On December 22, [John] Wentworth from Chicago, moved as follows:

Resolved, That the General Government has the power to construct such harbors and improve such rivers as are necessary and proper for the protection of our navy and commerce, and also for the defences of our country.

It passed, after an animated debate, by 138 to 54, Mr. Lincoln voting aye.

On December 22, Mr. Lincoln attempted a political *coup de main*, if not indeed a *coup d'etat*, which he took great pride in at the time, but which proved to be a *coup de grace* to his immediate political aspirations. He made a motion which was ever afterwards called in derision the "*spot*" resolutions, and brought upon their author unmerited obloquy. The reception and fate of this proposed measure show the political folly of attempting to impede or cavil at a national war, whether just or unjust.

In point of fact, these resolutions were, in the highest degree, proper. It was the administration which inaugurated the war, and yet President Polk, at the behest of the slavocracy, took especial pains to set forth, in all ways, and whenever he could, that the Mexicans had done so. The Whig party in Congress denounced this lie, as was proper, but Mr. Lincoln seriously crippled his political career by (**perhaps I may say**) being too *fresh* and furnishing a basis for slander. Thomas Corwin dug his political grave even deeper by exclaiming in the senate: "Were I a Mexican, as I am an American, I would say to the invader: We will welcome you with bloody hands to hospitable graves."

Always thereafter the Democratic press and orators charged Mr. Lincoln with voting against the supplies for **our soldiers in** the Mexican War, and in the [1858] joint debates, Douglas charged that Lincoln took the side of the enemy against his own country.

As late as June 1858, the Chicago *Times* charged Lincoln with voting against the supplies to our soldiers in the Mexican War, the "spot resolutions" being its only basis. I sent the paper to Mr. Lincoln and he replied **to me**: "Give yourself no uneasiness about my having voted against the supplies, unless you are without faith that a lie can be successfully contradicted."[23] He further stated that he was then considering as to the best way to contradict it, but he deemed it best to do nothing about it.

On the 17th of February, 1848, the question of supplies for the army in Mexico came to a test vote on a loan bill to raise $16,000,000 to pay government debts, chiefly incurred in carrying on the Mexican War. Recollect that the House of Representatives was a Whig one with a Whig Speaker, yet this

23. Basler, *Collected Works of Lincoln*, 2:472.

measure passed by a vote of 192 to 14, Mr. Lincoln voting with the majority, thus giving the direct lie to the brood of maligners and liars who pursued him with their venom constantly thereafter.

On December 28, 1847, sundry citizens of Indiana sent in a petition for the abolition of slavery in the District of Columbia, and it was laid on the table, although Mr. Lincoln voted against thus summarily disposing of it.

And on the 30th of December, a memorial against the slave trade in the District was presented, and Lincoln sustained its respectful consideration by his vote.

On January 17, 1848, Giddings introduced a resolution reporting alleged outrages against a colored man in Washington, and asking for a special committee to determine on the expediency of prohibiting the slave trade in the District. Many test votes were taken on the resolution, and Lincoln sustained Giddings each time.

On February 28 a resolution was offered in the House which read thus:

> *Whereas*, in the settlement of the difficulties prevailing between this country and Mexico, territory may be acquired in which slavery does not exist; and whereas Congress, in the organization of a territorial government at an early period of our political history, established a principle worthy of imitation in all future time, forbidding the existence of slavery in free territory:
>
> Therefore be it *Resolved*, That in any territory which may be acquired from Mexico, on which shall be established territorial governments, slavery or involuntary servitude, except as a punishment for crimes whereof the party shall have been duly convicted, should be forever prohibited, and that, in any act or resolution establishing such government, a fundamental provision ought to be inserted to that effect.

It was laid on the table by 105 to 92, Mr. Lincoln voting with the mover and Giddings in the negative.

On April 3, and also on the 18th, Mr. Lincoln moved to suspend the rules so as to take up for action the "Ten Regiment" bill.

On June 19, 1848, [Andrew] Stewart of Pennsylvania[24] offered a resolution favoring a protective tariff:

> *Resolved*, That the Committee of Ways and Means be instructed to enquire into the expediency of reporting a bill increasing the duties on foreign luxuries of all kinds and on such foreign manufacturers as are now coming into ruinous competition with American labor.

Mr. Lincoln voted in favor of the resolution.

---

24. Andrew Stewart (1791–1872) represented a Pennsylvania district in the U.S. House of Representatives (off and on from 1821 to 1849).

132   *Chapter IX*

An important bill came down from the Senate on July 28 to establish territorial governments for the territories of California, Oregon, and New Mexico. It authorized slavery in California and New Mexico, and was very obnoxious to the Whigs, even to those from the South. This measure was of especial importance, as showing the change of base executed by Mr. Webster between that day and March 7, 1850, for in the speech of the latter date he took grounds entirely antagonistic to those exhibited by him on this occasion.

He closed his speech with these words: "Under no circumstances would I consent to the further extension of the area of slavery in the United States, or to the further increase of slave representation in the House of Representatives."

Thomas Corwin made a forcible speech in opposition likewise, ending as follows:

"I must consider it bad policy to plant slavery in any soil where I do not find it already growing. I look upon it as an exotic that blights with its shade the soil in which you plant it, and therefore, as I am satisfied of our constitutional power to prohibit it, so I am equally certain it is our duty to do so."

Stephens of Georgia, afterwards vice president of the Confederacy, moved to lay the bill on the table and voted "aye." Lincoln did the same.

On August 2, the House bill for organizing the Territory of Oregon came up, and a motion was made to repeal the Ordinance of 1787 prohibiting slavery there. Mr. Lincoln voted against it. From first to last he was consistently on the side of freedom in the Territories.

During this session, Mr. Lincoln showed his sterling qualities as a debater in the delivery of several speeches, all **noteworthy for their** clearness of statement and vigor of reasoning characteristic of him during the slavery discussions. On January 12, 1848, he made a notable speech on the war with Mexico.[25]

I do not believe that anybody could have crowded more matter in the same amount of space.

On June 20, he spoke on the subject of internal improvements.[26]

On July 27, he made a speech[27] in derision of General [Lewis] Cass's claim to be a military hero[28] which, though sadly lacking in dignity, entertained the House and the nation, and formed an admirable campaign document.

At the second, or short, session, on December 12, 1848, the following resolution was submitted:

25. Basler, *Collected Works of Lincoln,* 1:431–442.

26. Basler, 1:480–490.

27. Basler, 1:501–516.

28. Lewis Cass (1782–1866) fought in the War of 1812 and served as a U.S. senator from Michigan (1845–1848) and presidential candidate of the Democratic party in 1848.

Resolved: That the Committee of Ways and Means be instructed to inquire into the expediency of reporting a Tariff Bill based upon the principles of the Tariff of 1842.

And Mr. Lincoln voted for it.

As showing Mr. Lincoln's love of perfect justice is this incident: [John Gorham] Palfrey of Massachusetts[29] proposed a bill to abolish slavery in the District of Columbia without any compensation to owners, and Mr. Lincoln voted *No*, because no provision for compensation was included. On the same day, however, a resolution was offered as follows:

Resolved: That the Committee on Territories be instructed to report to this House with as little delay as practicable, a bill or bills providing a territorial government for each of the territories of New Mexico and California, and excluding slavery therefrom.

Mr. Lincoln supported this measure heartily.

On December 21, Mr. Gott[30] proposed the following resolution:

Whereas, the traffic now prosecuted in this metropolis of the Republic in human beings as chattels is contrary to natural justice and the fundamental principles of our political system, and is notoriously a reproach to our country throughout Christendom, and a serious hindrance to the progress of republican liberty among the nations of the earth:

Therefore, be it *Resolved*, that the Committee for the District of Columbia be instructed to report a bill as soon as practicable prohibiting the slave trade in said district.

Because Lincoln did not like the meager provisions of the bill, he voted to lay it on the table; and that having failed, on the passage of the resolution, Mr. Lincoln voted, "nay."

On December 21, the following resolution was proposed in the House:

Resolved: That the present traffic in the public lands should cease, and that they should be disposed of to occupants and cultivators on proper conditions, at such a price as will nearly indemnify the cost of their purchase, management, and sale.

This measure received Lincoln's support.

An important principle was deduced from a very small matter which arose in the lower House on January 6, 1849: the case of Antonio Pacheco, who had hired out a male slave as a servant to a U.S. officer, and the slave

29. John Gorham Palfrey (1796–1881) represented a Massachusetts district in the U.S. House of Representatives (1847–1849).

30. Daniel Gott (1794–1864) represented a New York district in the U.S. House of Representatives (1847–1851).

134 Chapter IX

escaped to the Seminoles and fought with them against the government. A very heated and interesting discussion took place. Much parliamentary skill and acumen was displayed in disposing of this simple case, which was finally carried by a small margin, and Mr. Lincoln voted in the negative.[31]

The "Gott resolution," heretofore mentioned, to prohibit the slave trade in the District of Columbia having again come before the House on a reconsideration, Mr. Lincoln offered an elaborate measure **abolishing slavery in the District** as a substitute.[32]

On January 31, a bill was reported from the District of Columbia to prohibit the bringing of slaves into the District, either as merchandise or for hire. Mr. Lincoln sustained it.

On February 21, Mr. Lincoln sustained a bill to abolish the franking privilege. His congressional career came to an end on March 4 ensuing.

While Mr. Lincoln's congressional career gave no sign of the tremendous possibilities afterwards developed, it nevertheless, if tested by principle, is a very creditable career, although it was deficient in matters of policy.

It was not Mr. Lincoln's style, however, to let policy govern principle or stand in its way. He knew that the Mexican War was founded on a lie, and he felt that it was his duty to contribute to the unmasking of the fallacies and deceit of an administration given over completely to the behests of the slave power.

On the subject of slavery, he was consistent then, as always. He believed that Congress had the right to abolish slavery in the District of Columbia, and he so stated as early as 1837 in his protest in the Illinois legislature; but he also believed that the rights of the white people of the District, and of the slave owners, should be respected.

He believed in the perfect right of Congress to prohibit slavery in the territories, and that no right at all existed in Congress to interfere with it in the slave states, and to the observance of these principles he was, throughout, consistent.

The "spot" resolutions, however, formed a basis for misrepresentation and vilification, which rendered Mr. Lincoln's career unsavory on the whole, ruled him out of politics for the time being, and turned his district over to the embraces of the enemy. In point of fact, it has always had a Democratic representation since, although it must be said that a redistricting took place in 1851, by a Democratic legislature.

---

31. Pacheco's heirs sued the government for compensation. Lincoln and other Northerners thought the issue involved the question whether there could be property in man. A bill to authorize compensation passed the House narrowly but died in the Senate.

32. Basler, *Collected Works of Lincoln*, 2:20–22.

X

Citizen and Neighbor

Springfield is now a city of many numbers—some manufactures, rank politics, and much aristocracy. In Lincoln's day, **it rejoiced in the aristocracy and reveled in the politics, but possessed neither the numbers nor yet the manufacturers.** The seminal principle of the *haut ton* of his home town was derived from the Kentucky "bluegrass" region. Two sons of Governor [Ninian] Edwards, who had been chief justice of Kentucky, territorial governor of Illinois, and minister to Mexico;[1] three daughters and a nephew of Hon. Robert S. Todd, who had been a leader of the political and social aristocracy of Kentucky;[2] the Mathers, Ridgeleys, Opdykes, Forquers, Fords, Lambs, and Herndons formed the Springfield aristocracy. **At different times it has furnished seven or eight United States senators for Illinois and other states, and rejoices in possession of the incumbents now. It has had five or more citizen judges at different times, enrolled among its citizens, and has nearly always since 1837 had a congressman within its corporate limits. Of Presidential aspirants it has had no lack; it rejoices in two now [1892].** Mr. Lincoln gained an excellent social as well as political standing at Springfield by his successful efforts about the capital removal, and also by his partnership with John T. Stuart. Consequently, when he married Miss Mary Todd, who was a member of the Kentucky aristocracy, it was not considered to be a *mésalliance*; its only social consequence was to engender an envious feeling among the plebian fraternity who had theretofore claimed him. Throughout his social life, he was always plain and unassuming; he

---

1. Ninian Edwards (1775–1823) served as governor of the Illinois Territory (1809–1818) and governor of the state of Illinois (1818–1824).
2. Robert Smith Todd (1791–1849), Lincoln's father-in-law, was a Kentucky banker, businessman, and politician.

lived in a very moderate condition, had no man servant or errand boy, and attended to his horse, cow, woodpile, and stable himself. He chopped wood, went to market, and did the chores and odd jobs about the place. This round of duties did not cease till a week after his nomination **at Chicago** for the presidency. His nearest neighbor was a working carpenter, and Lincoln used frequently **and habitually** to go into his yard on neighborly errands, to do which he would straddle a low fence, **but which was not an arduous task for the whilom ox driver and flatboat man and emancipator** *in posse* **[in potential but not yet in actuality]; however,** his neighborly association extended no further. This geographical neighbor was never in Mr. Lincoln's house except to **do errands [and] to** make repairs, and the great president was never in his neighbor's house, except on small errands. I recollect that one of Lincoln's queerest stories includes a visit to his neighbor's kitchen to borrow spoons one evening, when he had company to tea.

To reconcile some otherwise irreconcilable incidents of Mr. Lincoln's biography, an understanding of the political and social bias of his neighbors and neighborhood is necessary. In 1856, we are advised by local history that although Herndon took extra pains to get up an enthusiastic reception to his illustrious partner upon a distinguished occasion, yet that no one came except one obscure man, and the discomfited partners turned off the gas, and went home, very meek and chopfallen.[3] Yet Lincoln had been his townsmen's congressman eight years previously, had been five several times elected by this same people to the legislature—the last time only two years before, **and at a banquet given by the ruling classes less than twenty years before, Lincoln was the especially honored guest, and this very statehouse in which he found himself without an audience would have housed another community had it not been for his almost superhuman efforts—besides, this general tendency of Lincoln was to be one of the most popular of men; and he was allied by marriage with the** *crème de la crème* **of the Springfield aristocracy.**

This inharmony between cause and effect had its basis in social and political prejudice; the early settlers of southern Illinois were from the slave States, and they were wedged in between either slaveholding communities or those having such affiliations, so that the Yankees and abolitionists were as much *below par* in southern and central Illinois as they were in Kentucky or Missouri. This prejudice invaded the sanctuary, and even when there was abounding grace and universal brotherhood, it still was not temporarily laid aside. The virtue of fraternal love could not be assumed, even in the fervor of religious zeal. A Chadband [preacher][4] of the "hardshell" order there

3. This story is untrue; no such failed meeting was called.
4. Chadband is a character in Charles Dickens's *Bleak House*.

exclaimed in a sermon, "The overwhelming torrent of free grace *tuk in* the *mountings* of *Ashy*, the isles of the sea, and the uttermost ends of the *yearth*. It *tuk in* the Eskimo and the *Hottingtots*; and some, my dear *brethring*, go so *fur* as to suppose it *tuk in* them *air* poor, benighted *Yangkeys*: but I don't go that *fur*!"

Of course, when the Nebraska bill was passed [in 1854],[5] this feeling became all the more rancorous, in view of the fact that the adherents of the "Anti-Nebraska" party came from the ranks of the hitherto pure and undefiled Democracy, as well as from the moribund Whig party, and the line of cleavage which had theretofore separated the Whigs and Democrats now divided the proslavery Democrats from the anti-extension-of-slavery element, and the prejudices became more intense and unyielding than before. An exception may be given in the case of Governor [William] Bissell who, as a member of Congress from Illinois, had electrified all classes of the State by his prompt defense of the Illinois brigade in Mexico when assailed by [Albert Gallatin] Brown of Mississippi; and by his equally prompt and eager acceptance of a challenge from Jefferson Davis growing out of the same. Every Illinoisan felt a thrill of pride and exultation at this episode, and especially as Bissell abjured any mock-fighting, by naming rifles at short range. Yet when this same gallant soldier was elected as governor by the Anti-Nebraska party, and being paralyzed, so that he had to take the official oath in the Executive Mansion, the pro-slavery Democrats, from pure spleen, put forth Hon. Elijah Pogram[6] [John A. Logan][7] to insult and vilify this brave soldier because he had taken the official oath in the Executive Mansion instead of in public, the fact being that he was too disabled by his wounds to do otherwise. **Pogram [Logan] occupied two days, January 13th and 14th, and his entire twelve hours was but an amplification in bad rhetoric and worse grammar, of stuff like the following: "If corruption enters into high places, it is my duty, as a faithful public servant, to drag it from its *polluted den* and expose its *hideous deformity* to public criticism and contempt. I will demonstrate to the world, a degree of *moral turpitude without parallel* in the history of the state. No Governor of Illinois has ever sought retirement to take**

---

5. Senator Stephen A. Douglas of Illinois introduced "An Act to Organize the Territories of Nebraska and Kansas," which repealed the 1820 Missouri Compromise prohibiting slavery above the latitude of 36°30' in the Louisiana Purchase area, thus reopening the political struggle over slavery in the territories.

6. Elijah Pogram is a fictional American congressman satirized in Charles Dickens's *Martin Chuzzlewit*.

7. For the speech by John A. Logan (1826–1886), American soldier and political leader, see Alexander Davidson, *A Complete History of Illinois from 1673 to 1873* (Springfield: Illinois Journal, 1874), 661.

138   *Chapter X*

the oath of office. . . . we might infer from this that a *guilty and bleeding conscience* had sought seclusion, rather than *stand erect* upon this floor and pass the *fiery ordeal*. The secluded and unusual place at which it was taken may afford grounds for an inference as to the workings of a mind *goaded to desperation* by a mighty conviction of *moral turpitude*. . . . I am *lost* in *amazement*. . . . avowing his own guilt of a reckless disregard of all that can inspire confidence in man. . . . the moral sense of a million and a half of people has been *shocked* by that fearful *oath*. Truth (sir) has been crushed to Earth. The votaries of virtue and honesty have been extinguished and one *universal wail* from Chicago to Cairo has been heard in consequence of the prostration of the executive chair by the hands of a man whose lips are *quivering* with *falsehood*. The Constitution of my beloved state lies *prostrate* in the *dust, bleeding* and *mangled*. . . . I pray God that we may never again witness such an occasion; virtue and truth bereft of all their charms which the hideous and *hateful gods of vice* hold dominant on the people."

And so on till Pogram [Logan] ran down.

The acerbity and illiberality of politics, of which this is a fair example, were more pronounced in Springfield than in other parts of the State because the politicians from the whole State gathered there and made a public exhibition of party rancor and animosity, **as shown above,** and the citizens could not fail to imbibe it in its intensity. Even before 1854, the political contentions wherein the Whigs and Democrats had been violent and rowdy and led to occasional physical collisions, but the Nebraska bill increased the rancor and changed the combatants. In Springfield, Lincoln, Logan, Herndon, Milton Hay,[8] William Jayne, William Butler,[9] and [Shelby] Cullom[10] adhered to the Republicans, while [John Todd] Stuart, [Norman] Broadwell,[11] [Francis] Springer,[12] and [Joel] Matteson[13] allied themselves to the Democrats, while the Edwardses [Ninian and Cyrus] were sometimes on one side and sometimes on the other.

8. Attorney Milton Hay (1817–1893) of Springfield studied law with the firm of Lincoln & Stuart and later had an office adjacent to Lincoln's.

9. A long-time friend of Lincoln, William Butler (1797–1876) of Springfield served as Illinois State Treasurer (1859–1863).

10. Attorney Shelby M. Cullom (1829–1914) was elected to the Illinois General Assembly in 1856 and later served as governor of Illinois and in both houses of the U.S. Congress.

11. Attorney Norman Broadwell (1825–1893) of Springfield studied law in the Lincoln-Herndon office and served as a county judge starting in 1861.

12. The Lutheran pastor Francis Springer (1810–1892) was a near neighbor of Lincoln in Springfield.

13. Joel Matteson (1808–1873) served as governor of Illinois (1853–1857).

The cast and structure of Mr. Lincoln's mind and ambition forbade him from having regard for politics having less **area than a state, having a lesser reward than a national office, having less** than a national principle; hence city or town politics had no charm for him.

In his own family circle, Mr. Lincoln was the most affectionate and gentle of men; no man thought more of his wife and children than he, and he ofttimes was seen fondly carrying one of his children in his arms up and down on the sidewalk before the house, or drawing one in a little rude cart.

Mr. Lincoln was an excellent citizen in the sense of being a citizen of the whole State, and ultimately of the whole nation. Although at the outset of his career, his affiliations were local, and quadrated with Sangamon County alone. However, with expanded experience, his social and political horizon expanded and enlarged, and he was no more intimately in touch or accord with the people of Springfield or Sangamon County than with those in Logan or McLean [Counties]. He considered himself as much obligated to the people of Danville as to those at his home. In his appointments to office, he wholly ignored geographical lines—even the local appointments for his judicial district were not from Springfield. In his administration at Washington, it was in principle the same. He wanted a cabinet minister, [Norman B.] Judd,[14] from Illinois, but he considered that that State had enough consideration in his election; he had no more regard, in the matter of executive favors for Illinois than Maine; geographical propinquity and social propinquity had no alliance in his mind. His social area covered the whole nation; his field was the world. He dealt in *principles* and *institutions*. To him, men were but agents or *media* to enforce, promulgate, or originate principles, and a man's locality had naught to do with his efficiency in that regard. Lincoln's highest social pastime was achieved on the circuit with the "boys" (as we were termed) at court time.

This catholicity of association and consequent failure to localize his attachments explain in some degree the lack of that ardent sympathy for him at home which sometimes cropped out. The bitterness of partisan politics, especially on the part of those who deemed his anti-slavery sentiments recusant to the land of his fathers, aided this feeling, and his failure to recognize his fellow citizens properly in the distributions of federal offices, all combined to produce a somewhat social alienation, and prevented him from being, as abstractly, and on his individual merits, he would be, an ideally popular citizen. Not that he was unpopular, but he should have been popular to the verge of enthusiasm as he was when news of the location of the capital at Springfield reached that small village.

14. Norman Buel Judd (1815–1878) was a Chicago railroad lawyer and Republican leader.

That Mr. Lincoln, aside from the prejudices appurtenant to the slavery question, was a very popular citizen, as was frequently attested. His four several consecutive elections to the legislature attest it; his immense majority for Congress on his ticket exhibits it; his being elected to the legislature in 1854 against his earnest protest confirms it.

He was a scrupulous observer of the laws, local and otherwise; he paid his debts and taxes promptly; did not let his little real estate get on the delinquent list, and his daily walk and conversation among men were circumspect. He neither attended church himself, nor sought to influence others from so doing; his example in all the minor morals was excellent. Politicians were accustomed to drop in at saloons, of which there were plenty at Springfield and elsewhere on the circuit, but no one knowing Lincoln would have dreamed of seeing him in a saloon on any pretense. Yet he did not obtrude a temperance lecture on anyone.

In the joint debate at Ottawa, Douglas, in his reckless way, averred that Lincoln "could ruin more liquor than all the boys of the town put together," while the unembellished fact was that Lincoln never at any time drank any liquor at all, and when he was younger, it was the custom for all to drink. He told Swett that he absolutely never drank a drop of liquor in his life,[15] and William G. Greene's testimony I give elsewhere. A life on the frontier is not conducive to the reign of ascetic habits, yet Mr. Lincoln did not even embrace the vice of tobacco. Like all men on the frontier with whom intellect and its exercise is the engrossing quality, and especially one whose business on the circuit kept him absent half the year, his domestic habits were irregular. He had a habit of being out with the "boys," and might be found frequently at [Jacob] Bunn's grocery[16] at the southwest corner of the public square entertaining the crowd, such being the custom of the place at this time, and Bunn's was a general loafing place for all the local wits of the place and was in the strict sense of the word a *grocery*—not a groggery.

Mr. Lincoln shone resplendently in an association, in a social sense, with men, but not in a general company, which likewise included the fair sex. Occasionally on the circuit, we would be invited out to some social gatherings, and sometimes we would force Lincoln along, for he never would gravitate to such a place of his own accord. But he would be ill at ease. Judge Davis would be perfectly *au fait* [well versed] in the little trivialities and *"smorl tork"* demanded, but Lincoln could make no effort to shine. In my own home, with my little family, when he was a visitor, he was at ease, and would hold

15. Swett, "Lincoln's Story of His Own Life," in Rice, *Reminiscences of Lincoln*, 462–63.

16. Jacob Bunn (1814–1897) established a wholesale grocery in Springfield, an enterprise that expanded when his brother John joined the firm. They were both staunch friends and allies of Lincoln.

my children as fondly as one of coarser mold; but the presence of females he was not familiar with abashed him extraordinarily, especially if they had on extra frills or tuckers. He was not a polite or polished man outwardly; his graces and amenities were of the heart and affections. Several of us once were stopping at Judge Davis's by invitation; in his absence, Lincoln was quite familiar with us all and likewise with our hostess, who was a lady of rare attainments and of extreme simplicity of style and character. There was no margin for restraint there, but as we came to the dining room for our first meal, Lincoln adroitly and suddenly sat down at a side of the table. "Why, Mr. Lincoln," said the lady of the house, "I expected you to occupy Mr. Davis's place at the foot of the table."

"I thought so," was the reply with a chuckle of satisfaction, "and that's why I hurried up and got here. Let Whitney run the carving."

But when a real exigency was presented, then Mr. Lincoln could be relied on as thus: "When I was a lad, I was coming from Pekin to Springfield on horseback in muddy times. I met and passed a countryman, whose wagon was mired down and his team unable to extract itself from the difficulty. A little further on, I met Lincoln and [Stephen T.] Logan on horseback *en route* to Pekin. When they reached the town, they hitched their horses to the fence and each got a rail from the fence, and by dint of hard straining, got the wagon so it could be moved, and then carefully replaced the rails, and resumed their journey." The above story was communicated to me by Judge [Joseph] Cunningham, who got it direct from the witness, who is a reputable citizen and that is so characteristic and lifelike as to be recognizable at once as the truth that Lincoln would act in just that way is inevitable and true.

On the circuit, Swett, [Asahel] Gridley, Oliver Davis, [Ward Hill] Lamon and others seemed to consider that the dignity of the profession required that they should erect some sort of a social fence or barrier between themselves and the masses that we would meet, but there was none of this attempt at exclusiveness with Lincoln. It was not infrequent to see him, while court was engaged in something which did not concern him, sitting on a store box on the sidewalk either entertaining, or being entertained by, some of our villagers, nor was there any affectation or demagogical art in this; it was in accordance with his plain, unaffected, undramatic style. **I recollect that once, that he was passing a photograph gallery in an outskirt of our town [Urbana] which had no reputation at all and was generally unknown; but the proprietor happened to be at the door, and invited him in. Lincoln went in and sat, and in the course of a day or two, a daguerreotype appeared which was a travesty as the "human face divine" but it was labeled "Lincoln."**[17]

17. German-born Samuel G. Alschuler (1826–1882) of Urbana took Lincoln's photo in April 1858 and again in November 1860.

Chapter X

Judge Cunningham narrates that at our mass meeting in 1858, he had charge of arrangements on the ground and placed Mr. Lincoln at the post of honor at the guests' table; when Lincoln saw an old lady whom we called "Granny" Hutchinson without a seat, he insisted that she take his seat while he stood up and munched from his hand something he had procured from the table, **and ate his dinner in that rude way**.

I suppose we could not sanely imagine Daniel Webster or Rufus Choate appearing before a justice of the peace and trying a case involving a few dollars for a $5.00 fee, yet Mr. Lincoln did not disdain to do that on our circuit. "All was fish that came into his net," and I have in my mind's eye at this moment, a rudimentary lawyer who then was merely an aspirant to the bar, and whose chief pride and boast has been for thirty-five years, and is yet, that he tried a case against Lincoln before a justice in our county in 1856 and beat him. And I may remark here, that "the justice of the peace" style of trying cases was more agreeable to Mr. Lincoln than any other. The ancient style of pleading was *"ore tenus,"* [presented orally] and written pleading came later. A simple verbal statement of the issues in a case was suited to Lincoln's simplicity of style and manner, and the simplicity attendant upon a justice court was much more in harmony with his wishes than the elaboration and red tape of a court of record.

Mr. Lincoln did not meddle with or obtrude himself upon his neighbors, or their local matters, nor did he after 1840 personally ask them to support him for office. When he ran for Congress his largely increased vote over the ticket at a previous election indicated his local popularity, and I have already said somewhere that at his first candidacy in 1832, he secured every vote in his own precinct, but three. Mr. Lincoln personally was a very popular man; aside from political animosities, I don't think he did have, or could have, an enemy.

While he was careless, indifferent, and "slouchy" about his attire, no note was taken of it by acquaintances; his companionship was so interesting and desirable that his attire was not regarded. The same principle inhered in his personal appearance. An **English** dude or a snob might deem him "homely"; no man or woman of sensibility would think of that subject in any way on acquaintance.

Aside from all politics, Lincoln was one of the most interesting men I ever saw; he had no envy, malice, or spite—no ill-feeling of any kind toward anybody; he was deferential but not obsequious; he made no sarcastic remarks **and made no one a butt for an ill-natured joke**. He employed no social tyranny to one in his power; he had no angularity except physically; was not inquisitive about the affairs of others; was disinterested and magnanimous, not supercilious or discourteous; was generous and forgiving to a fault. He was not only sincere and candid, but he assured you by his conduct that he

Citizen and Neighbor

was so; his actions towards men symbolized his belief that the greatest of the social virtues was charity.

Every social element was agreeable; no true man ever had cause to repent his acquaintance; in the extremely rare cases of those who disliked him on other than political grounds, the party offended was of a narrow, illiberal order. The fault certainly could not be laid at the door of generous Abraham Lincoln. Of him the classic eulogium may in sober truth be said without hyperbole:

> Justim et tenacem propositi virum
> Non civium ardor prava iubentium
> Non vultus instantis tyranni,
> Mentel quatit solida.

Neither the ardor of citizens ordering base things, nor the face of the threatening tyrant, shakes a man just and tenacious of principle, from his firm intentions.[18]

18. Horace, *Odes*, iii. 3. 1.

XI

Lawyer

Mr. Lincoln was not well grounded in the principles of law, nor was he a well-read lawyer.[1] He had an intuitive sense of abstract justice, but he had no conception of rules, technicalities, or limitations; he knew nothing of decisions, except such as came with his own experience; he did not approve of being hampered by precedents.[2] To him, estoppels were unjust; he had no patience with technicalities as such, desiring to consider every case as disconnected with all else, and to be tried on its abstract and unincumbered merits alone.

While lawyers of small abilities would array a list of authorities to support their contention, Lincoln would try to establish his by logic. His strength as a lawyer lay in his analytical and reasoning faculties, i.e., he could apperceive the matter at issue and deduce the true conclusion from it with as much facility and strength as he could achieve the same results from moral questions.

A lawyer has a right—in fact it is the present mode of law practice—to use the labors of the profession, and appropriate former decisions, to enforce his views. Lincoln did this, of course, but only subordinate to his own logical consideration of the case; hence the labors of those who preceded him were not of nearly the same value to him as to his adversary. However, when it

1. Compare this chapter to Whitney, Chapter X, "Lincoln as a Lawyer," *Life on the Circuit with Lincoln,* 250–66.

2. Though this chapter contains much useful information, it is marred by some questionable assertions, like this one. Readers interested in Lincoln's legal career should consult the writings of knowledgeable veterans of the Lincoln Legal Papers project, most especially John A. Lupton, executive director of the Illinois Supreme Court Historic Preservation Commission, and Professor Mark Steiner, South Texas College of Law Houston.

Lawyer 145

came to cases with no well-defined precedent, then it was that Lincoln had a powerful advantage, for he had no superior, certainly, and but very few equals, at our bar in original reasoning. Take it all in all, he had probably only one superior as a lawyer in our circuit, viz.: Stephen T. Logan.

In a rough-and-tumble practice on the circuit, where advocacy was relied on rather than **an** exact knowledge or application of legal principles, he was especially effective. He had a frank and cordial way of dealing with witnesses, and his memory was of a methodical **and orderly** cast; he recollected the evidence as it accrued, and assigned each element thereof to its proper room, hall, or vestibule in his memory, to be withdrawn, when needful, for use.

He was courteous, yet skillful in cross examination, and had a faculty of so cajoling a witness as to make him (as my father once put it) say just what he wanted him *to* say.

His candor and honesty were very effective weapons for success; a statement made by Lincoln was almost invariably accepted as correct. I have on more than one occasion known of a case with intricate details being made to appear so clear on both sides, by Lincoln's lucid and comprehensive statement, as to be very much simplified, if not indeed, as was sometimes the case, made ready on both sides for the decision without argument.

Mr. Lincoln contemned useless or irrelevant litigation; he had little patience with *tort* cases or with technical defenses. He was much annoyed at dilatory tactics or preliminary skirmishing for advantage; he disliked long drawn-out trials and desired quickly obtained results; he was fond of settlements and compromises when the parties themselves would move in the matter, but if the litigation was wholly useless, he would move in the matter himself. **In the celebrated slander case of [Peter] Spink vs. [Charles] Chiniquy,[3] brought by change of venue from Kankakee to Champaign County, he betrayed more anxiety and expended as much effort to achieve a settlement, after two unsuccessful trials, as he did in trying the case.**

He would always give a perfectly fair and candid opinion as to the merits of a case and the probability of success, and would not enter into a case he knew to be dishonest. In a case, however, where the dishonesty was developed during the trial, he would simply do what he honestly could for success, and no more. I have known him to injure a case when he became convinced during the trial that he was on the dishonest or unjust side of it.

His view of morals was broad and catholic; his integrity was not confined to any special line or particular mode; to him, there should be a *quid pro quo* in all social attrition or mercantile dealing. To charge too much for a thing was, to his view, dishonest; to gain a lawsuit by sophistry or chicanery, equally

---

3. This libel case was tried in Champaign and resulted in a hung jury. Whitney described it in *Life on the Circuit with Lincoln*, 54–55.

so. The basis of his hostility to slavery was **by reason** his consciousness of its *dishonesty* in exacting service for nothing, and of its *injustice* in coercing and enslaving men. Although he was philanthropic toward his own race, he had no feelings of philanthropy toward the black race, but only the feeling that injustice should not be visited upon them.[4]

He had this marked peculiarity, that although he was one of the most amiable and courteous of associates in a case, yet he pursued his own independent course in his share, whatever it was, of its management, nor would he reveal his designs, in the least degree, to his colleagues. I have, on many occasions, held consultations with him in which I would get no hint from him as to his views or designs about the case. On one occasion **that I well recollect**, Swett and I sat on a bench in the extreme rear of the courtroom while Lincoln closed to the jury on our side, and we were utterly astonished at the cruel mode in which he applied the knife to all of the fine-spun theories we had crammed the jury with.

He was extremely accommodating and courteous to his adversary, and likewise to the adverse witnesses, provided they told the truth; but woe to them if they falsified! for he had no charity for falsehood anywhere, least of all for exhibitions of it on the witness stand, and the logical structure of his mind afforded him the means to detect falsehood almost inevitably. He would brook no insult or sarcasm from an opponent, but he never unfairly or uncharitably presumed that an insult was intended. He waived all mere technicalities and minor and inconsequential matters; conceded in advance all that he knew could be well proved, gathered up the *essential* matters in a bunch, and rested his case upon *them*.

The consideration and trial of cases was to him matter-of-fact, responsible labor; he introduced no pleasantry or quips therein, but soberly and discreetly arrayed all advantages for his side of the case. He studied both sides of his case, and considered the course of tactics which his opponent would probably pursue quite as thoroughly as he considered his own. Nothing moved or excited him in the course of a trial; he presented the same calm, placid, and imperturbable exterior when disaster frowned as when good fortune smiled upon the career of a case.

We had a client once who took occasion to complain to me about **an** alleged unsatisfactory management of a case. I asked Lincoln to placate him, as I could not. "Let him howl," was the only reply I got, after a moment's deliberation.

---

4. In fact, abundant evidence shows that Lincoln was instinctively a racial egalitarian. See Michael Burlingame, *The Black Man's President: Abraham Lincoln, African-Americans, and the Pursuit of Racial Equality* (New York: Pegasus Books, 2021).

He minded his own business better than any lawyer I ever saw; he stuck to his case, or to his part of it, and rendered no advice to anyone else about his or their duties; but he performed *his* functions independently and *sui generis*, and let the responsibility of others' actions rest upon themselves. Considering the magnitude of my early business at the bar, I was **an extremely poor and** careless lawyer, and often drew **down** upon myself the reproofs of older colleagues, but never from Lincoln. In our joint cases, of which there were many, he did the best he could for the case in hand, *plus* the difficulty caused by my affirmatively bad management, or *minus* the advantage that proper management on my part would have secured.

To the "mint, anise, and cumin"[5] [i.e., minor details] of a case, he was indifferent. Whether the pleadings were artistic or inartistic; whether the formal facts had been sufficiently established, etc., he cared nothing and attempted no advantage thereby; he wanted no less a fight than on the merits.

No matter how eventful or exciting a trial was, he remained entirely calm, unexcited, imperturbable; you could not discern by his manner that he had the slightest tinge either of trepidation or enthusiasm, but he remained inflexible and stoical to the last. Once I had an important railroad suit that I secured his aid in, and as the able counsel on the other side was dealing out heavy "wisdom licks" at us, I got alarmed and spoke to Lincoln about it. He sat inflexibly calm and serene, and merely remarked, "All that is *very* easily answered," and when his time came, he blew away what seemed to me an almost unanswerable argument as easily as a beer-drinker blows off the froth from his foaming tankard.

Through his accurate perceptions, he would discern what was genuine and what was sophistical; many a time have I seen him tear the mask off from a fallacy and shame both the fallacy and its author. In a railway case we were trying, the opposing lawyer tried to score a point by stating that the plaintiff was a flesh-and-blood man, with a soul like the jurymen had, while our client was a soulless corporation. Lincoln replied thus: "Counsel avers that his client has a *soul*. This is possible, **of course**; but from the way he has testified under oath in this case, to gain, or hope to gain, a few paltry dollars, he would sell, nay, has already sold, his little soul very low. But our client is but a conventional name for thousands of widows and orphans whose husbands' and parents' hard earnings are represented by this defendant, and who possess souls which they would not swear away as the plaintiff has done for ten million times as much as is at stake here."

He did not, as a rule, "play to the pit" in his addresses to the jury, but simply confined himself closely to his case. However, I recollect once in the evening at Urbana, Lincoln was arguing a case, when some ladies came in,

5. Matthew 23:23.

148 Chapter XI

and we made room for them within the bar, which caused a little commotion, and Lincoln said: "I perceive, gentlemen, that you are like all the rest of the *fellers* in your admiration of the fair sex—in fact, I think, from appearances, that you are a little worse than the common run," and he added something else that provoked laughter; and he waited a minute and then said patronizingly: "Now, boys, behave yourselves," and went on with his argument.

I have heretofore adverted to his intellectual honesty, and, of course, by that I do not mean his acumen or intellectual grasp and vigor of mind. It is common to have intellectual power. [Daniel] Webster had that in a marked degree, but he was not intellectually honest, and hence we find him in history advocating free trade in 1816 and a high tariff in 1836. He is seen working hand in hand with the friends of freedom anterior to 1850 and abnegating his record on the 7th of March, **and under pretext of defending the Christian faith is found attacking and aiding to minify and dissipate the most munificent Christian charity ever established in this nation.** That "honesty is the best policy" was well established in the career and empty results of the life of this man so great intellectually and so essentially feeble morally; and in the career and fruitful results of the life of Abraham Lincoln, as seen in his greatest mission, its faithful performance and his immortal fame. A man of the former class, of which, alas! there are too many in our history, is equally at home in arguing either in unison with, or contrary to, his convictions; it is simply a little more difficult to argue dishonestly than honestly—that is all with him. But it was morally impossible for Lincoln to argue dishonestly; he could no more do it than he could steal; it was the same thing to him, in essence, to despoil a man of his property by larceny or by illogical or flagitious reasoning. Even to defeat a suitor by technicalities or by merely arbitrary law savored strongly of dishonesty to him. **He tolerated it sometimes, but always with a grimace.**

Truth is polygynous, and the average mind can see only the nearest side perfectly, the nearest oblique sides imperfectly, and the rear not at all. But Lincoln possessed that kind of mental eyesight (if I may use that expression) that saw all sides and angles of every moral proposition inherent in his law or politics and hence knew both sides; and if he acted at all, must state his convictions to all whom it might concern, even if it brought disaster to his side of the case.

He instinctively knew that "on every subject on which difference of opinion is possible, the truth depends on a balance to be struck between two sets of conflicting reasons. Even in natural philosophy, there is always some other explanation possible of the same facts, some geocentric theory, instead of heliocentric, some phlogiston instead of oxygen; and it has to be shown why that other theory cannot be the true one; and until this is shown, and until we know how it is shown, we do not understand

Lawyer **149**

the grounds of our opinion. But when we turn to subjects infinitely more complicated, to morals, religion, politics, social regulations, and the business of life, three-fourths of the arguments for every disputed opinion consist in dispelling the appearances which favor some opinion different from it. The greatest orator, save one, of antiquity has left it on record that he always studied his adversary's case with as great, if not with still greater, intensity than even his own. What Cicero practiced as the means of forensic success requires to be imitated by all who study any subject, in order to arrive at the truth. He who knows only his own side of the case knows little of that. His reasons may have been good and no one may have been able to refute them. But if he is equally unable to refute the reasons on the opposite side, if he does not so much as know what they are, he has no ground for preferring either opinion."[6]

Lincoln was usually very mild, benign, and accommodating in his practice on the circuit, but occasionally he would get pugnacious. "Oh! No! No!! No!!!" said **Amzi** McWilliams[7] once in a trial to a witness who was straying beyond the domain of legitimate evidence, as he thought. "*Oh!* yes! Yes!! YES!!!" shouted Lincoln, looking daggers at McWilliams, who quailed under Lincoln's determined look.

He gave but the slightest attention to rules of evidence and rarely objected to the admission of anything at all allowable; he could not endure those illiberal practices required at the hands of the complete lawyer; he could not practice or countenance that selfishness which the requirements of good practice demanded. All the generalizations of his mind tended to frankness, fairness, and the attainment of substantial justice, and the simplest mode was to him the best. In entering upon a trial, he stated the whole case on both sides, as he understood it, with fairness and frankness, not attempting to gloss over the faults and imperfections of his own case or to improperly disparage the adverse side.

But when the *strain* came, Lincoln was very apt to bear down heavily on his adversary's case, and a novice who presumed much on Lincoln's graces and amenities as the case was being developed frequently found himself in the lurch when the crisis was reached.

I once brought suit on a Kentucky judgment, and Lincoln, with others, was employed to defend. Oliver L. Davis, who was with Lincoln, taunted me before trial that they not only would defeat me but would make me ridiculous. I appealed to Lincoln, who comforted me by saying: "Don't you mind Oliver;

6. John Stuart Mill, *On Liberty* (London: Longman, Roberts, & Green, 1859), 66–67.

7. Amzi McWilliams (1824–1862) of Bloomington, Illinois, served as the McLean County prosecuting attorney (1854–1856).

it is merely like any other case, and I'll see, at least, that there is no ridicule about it." But when we went into trial, and the thermometer of the case got up to 96 degrees in the shade, Lincoln went for me and my case as vigorously as the others, and I was entirely alone against all the talent of that end of the circuit. It is needless to say that I was gloriously beaten.

Lincoln's guileless exterior concealed a great fund of shrewdness and common sense about ordinary matters, as well as genius in the higher realms.

I remember once, that while several of us lawyers were together, including Judge Davis, Lincoln suddenly asked a novel question of court practice, addressed to no one particularly, to which the Judge, who was in the habit certainly of appropriating his full share of any conversation, replied, stating what he understood the practice should be.

Lincoln thereat laughed and said: "I **have** asked that question, hoping that you would answer. I have that very question to present to the court in the morning, and I am glad to find out that the court is on my side."

When Lincoln desired to make an extra good effort, or when he had a difficult case, he would be missing—he would hide somewhere and by self-introspection mature his plans. He did not have any particular place to hide—the unused back room of a law office, or an obscure corner of the clerk's office, or a lonely bedroom **of some of** the traveling bar, **or** the streets of the village, or the woods, were alike serviceable and equally put in requisition by him. He had a talent for embracing the whole scope and plan and all essential details of a case within the area of his mind, in an orderly and systematic manner. He took no notes and made no memoranda, and rarely, if ever, made any mistake in referring to the evidence in his argument.

The petty advantages on his side in a case he did not urge with any force or pertinacity, but arrayed his strongest points and relied exclusively on them. His ability to separate important and controlling matters from those which were secondary was marked and showed great analytical skill; he abhorred that style of practice which attributed unworthy motives to an adversary or enforced technicalities to the exclusion of justice or progress, **or which were just sufficient to win, with no margin**. He allowed to adverse evidence or arguments their fullest value and importance, never sought to disparage or "damn with faint praise" an opponent or his arguments, and in minor and inconsequential points would help his adversary along, and this especially if he was a young practitioner. In trying a case before the court, without a jury, he would summarize the case as impartially on both sides as the impartial judge could do it himself. No matter what the case was, he would get possession of the facts and form his own conclusions upon them without any extraneous aid or suggestions. In formulating his mode of treatment, he gave little attention to technicalities or any advantage to be derived therefrom. His guiding star was not expediency but principle, not coigns of vantage but justice; **not technicalities but right and equity.**

He made no pretensions to anything beyond circuit court ability, yet he was occasionally employed in important cases outside and not infrequently went to Chicago and once or twice to Cincinnati on business connected with a patent suit. [Whitney note: The suit was *McCormick vs. Manny*. William H. Seward, Reverdy Johnson, Edward M. Dickinson, and Isaac N. Arnold[8] were for complainant; and Edwin M. Stanton, George F. Harding, and Abraham Lincoln were for defendant.]

The last case he ever tried was an important case involving the question of *accretion*, in which he took the lead on our side and argued the question, so far as he was concerned, on original principles and with great ability. This case was tried in March **1860** and decided early in April, somewhat less than two months before the assembling of the "Wigwam" convention. It is somewhat singular that the senior opposing counsel to Mr. Lincoln was Hon. Buckner S. Morris,[9] who had been a leading lawyer in Chicago and who was afterwards treasurer of the "Sons of Liberty" and who was tried by a court martial at Cincinnati during the war on a charge of being involved in the Camp Douglas conspiracy,[10] of which he was acquitted. In point of fact, Mr. Morris read law with Henry Clay at Lexington at the same time that Mary Todd, who became Mr. Lincoln's wife, was a schoolgirl there.

I may, however, say that Mr. Lincoln was an uneven lawyer, that his best results were achieved as a result of long and continuous reflection. The various elements of a case did not group themselves in apt and proper position and order in his mind on first impression; hence he was not so self-reliant in a new case as in one he had fully discussed and decided in his own mind, and his first impressions in a case were not his best ones.

He did not disdain any association, and listened to all suggestions from those associated with him with patience and deference and gave as much weight to a good suggestion from a novice as from a veteran. In a hard case, however, he was eager for good auxiliary connections, and Leonard Swett was his favorite in a difficult jury case. Lincoln was preeminently a man of peace, and discountenanced all litigation whose origin, vital principle, or main auxiliary was vengeance **or** ill feeling. He promoted and favored all compromises, as I have said, but asked no quarter or favors, and fought to the bitter end all contested cases not susceptible of accommodation.

His imperturbability was one of his strong points; the only excitement he ever betrayed in court was when he got righteously indignant at the actions

---

8. Attorney Isaac N. Arnold of Chicago (1815–1884) represented his district in the U.S. House of Representatives (1861–1865) and wrote two biographies of his friend Lincoln.

9. In 1838, Buckner S. Morris (1800–1879) was elected mayor of Chicago.

10. Confederates plotted unsuccessfully to liberate the prisoners of war confined in Chicago's Camp Douglas, one of the largest Union Civil War prison camps.

of someone in a case. Then he was terrible in his wrath. He has been known (though rarely) to transcend the bounds of decorum on such occasions. While as a lawyer he was not great, yet he admired a great lawyer and despised a charlatan with a high reputation. He once told me that John McLean, U.S. Supreme Court Judge,[11] had considerable vigor of mind but no acuteness of discernment at all. He also said to me of Archibald Williams, whom he made U.S. judge in Kansas, that he had more ability to discuss law questions to learned lawyers than any lawyer he knew. Of Judge T. Lyle Dickey[12] he said, "He can draw such fine distinctions where I can't see any distinction, yet I have no doubt a distinction does exist."

He studied the character and ability of Lord Bacon and was greatly charmed with it.[13] "But how about his taking bribes?" I asked him. "He did take bribes, but never made any changes in his decision" was the reply. It struck me as strange. Bacon's transcendent ability seemed **to me** to condone, in Lincoln's estimation, his flagitious conduct.

I do not think Mr. Lincoln would be overshadowed at any bar by any lawyer, but in a purely law case dependent on precedents, technicalities, and routine, and especially when before a technical judge, I think he would not shine. He was a profound thinker and logician but not a thorough student, and, as I have said, was not only not well grounded, but also not thoroughly well versed in the current and practical law of the given period. But in a case involving original research, and where time and opportunity were allowed him to master the case, he would match any.

He charged insignificant fees. The first really adequate fee I ever knew him to charge was $5000 for trying the case of the Illinois Central Rail Road Company v. McLean and Champaign Counties.[14] The railway claimed that the land comprised within its land grant was not taxable till a patent issued, while the counties claimed that they were taxable as soon as they were allotted. A formal decision was rendered by the lower court, and the case argued before the supreme court at Springfield. There were three several counsel:

---

11. John McLean (1785–1861) of Ohio served as an associate justice on the U.S. Supreme Court (1829–1861).

12. Theophilus Lyle Dickey (1811–1885) of Ottawa was an Illinois jurist and military leader.

13. Francis Bacon (1561–1626) was an English philosopher and statesman who championed empiricism and the scientific method.

14. *Illinois Central Rail Road Company v. McLean and Parke* (1853–1857), Daniel W. Stowell et al., eds., *The Papers of Abraham Lincoln: Legal Documents and Cases* (4 vols.; Charlottesville: University of Virginia Press, 2008), 2:373–415.

Lawyer 153

Lincoln and Herndon, James F. Joy of Detroit,[15] and Mason Brayman.[16] Joy was an influential railway lawyer with a great influence and an exalted opinion of himself, and, although it is probable that Lincoln did the most effective service, it was quite natural for Joy to disparage Lincoln's efforts, and he did in fact do so. Accordingly, when his bill came in and Joy had to audit it, he not only disallowed it but spoke contemptuously of its author as "a common country lawyer." Lincoln then sued in the McLean circuit court, and somehow, no defense being made, a default was taken. Lincoln, however, allowed the default to be set aside and the case set down for trial. John M. Douglass, then our [i.e., the Illinois Central's] solicitor,[17] consulted with me about the matter; I said that even if the amount was too large, we could not afford to have Lincoln as our enemy, instead of an ally on the circuit, and I insisted further and with greater force that he would beat us anyhow both in the circuit and supreme courts. Douglass paid the fee. (Somehow, plain as this case is, it has never been correctly stated by any historian.)

Mr. Lincoln never let his diversion obtrude upon the serious business of his law practice, but he felt the responsibility and gravity of his position, and entered into all trials with the attention, dignity, and decorum demanded; he would sometimes score a point by fun in some way, but he did not resort to pleasantry to the detriment of his case.

In the long run, his honesty and, more particularly, his reputation therefor, was a great and potent factor for success. When he made a statement for judicial or forensic action, it carried weight and authority. He stated nothing morally impossible; his demeanor was that of personified honesty; and his reputation was a letter of recommendation, convincing if not conclusive.

After his **lamented** death, the Nestors[18] of the Illinois bench and bar, and lawyers and judges of high and low degree, grave and sedate men with no imagination or fancy, spoke in eulogy of him. There was not the slightest diversity of opinion on either his honesty or ability, and the apparent disparagement of Judge Davis—that Lincoln had no managing faculty nor organizing power in a case and that a child could conform to simple and technical rules better than he—was not literally true. The whole truth is that Lincoln did not grovel amid the minor trivialities of the technical but reigned amid the stars of the immutable and eternal principles of justice.

15. James Frederick Joy (1810–1896) served as counsel general for the Illinois Central Railroad (1852–1857).

16. Mason Brayman (1813–1895) of Springfield was a friend of Lincoln and a railroad attorney.

17. John M. Douglass (1819–1891) became president of the Illinois Central in 1865.

18. In Greek mythology, Nestor was a wise old counselor.

154   *Chapter XI*

The styles and methods of present law practice [1892] depend so far as is possible on *authority*, but when Lincoln was a practicing lawyer it depended chiefly upon *principles*—upon original reasoning, and that was the method which approved itself to Lincoln. He came nearer to being discomfited by having a fabric of argument which he had laboriously built up demolished by a *case* than in any other way.

In the days of Demosthenes and Cicero, he would have been a great advocate. To construct a case wholly on principle, with no authority to fall back on for support, was the sort of law practice in which he would have excelled, and in that sort of advocacy, he would have been a match for any of the brilliant names which have adorned the judicial history of the United States.

While I cannot think with any idea of propriety of Lincoln sitting as a judge, it yet seems to me that if he had been made a successor of John Marshall, he would, by his moral and logical acquirements, have achieved as great renown in spite of his lack of the judicial temperament.

Isaac N. Arnold, one of the leaders of the Chicago bar, delivered a lecture before the Illinois Bar Association on January 7, 1881, in course of which he said of Mr. Lincoln: "In any courtroom in the United States, he would have been instantly picked out as a Western man. His stature, figure, dress, manner, voice, and accent indicated that he was of the Northwest. In manner, he was always cordial and frank, and although not without dignity, he made every person feel quite at his ease. I think the first impression a stranger would get of him, whether in conversation or by hearing him speak, was that here was a kind, frank, sincere, genuine man of transparent truthfulness and integrity; and before Lincoln had uttered many words, he would be impressed with his clear good sense, his remarkably simple, homely, but expressive Saxon language, and next by his wonderful wit and humor. Lincoln was more familiar with the Bible than any other book in the language, and this was apparent both from his style and illustrations, so often taken from that book. He verified the maxim that it is better to know thoroughly a few good books than to read many."[19]

Career and Methods on the Circuit

Lincoln's partnership with John T. Stuart commenced in March 1837 and ended on April 14, 1841, when he formed a partnership with Judge Stephen T. Logan, who had previously been the circuit judge and was then the best lawyer in the state. The firm of Logan & Lincoln lasted till the early spring

19. Isaac N. Arnold, *Reminiscences of the Illinois Bar, Forty Years Ago* (Chicago: Fergus, 1881), 19.

of 1843, when Lincoln withdrew on account of some little feeling, growing out of the political canvass for Congress, both partners then being aspirants. William H. Herndon had just commenced to practice, and he was not only a young man of promise, but his family was very extensive, of great respectability, and highly influential.

Lincoln therefore proposed a partnership, which Herndon gladly accepted. It lasted eighteen years, and during the entire term no accounts were kept and not a word of dispute ever occurred between the partners **but their fees were divided offhand as they were earned and received. Thus, when Lincoln received a fee on the circuit, he wrapped one half of it up in a scrap of paper, entitled the case it was in, and delivered it to Herndon when he next saw him. And similarly in their home practice, Herndon did the same, and throughout eighteen years, the business was all transacted in this way without any difficulty or disagreement of any kind.**

At the time when Lincoln formed his partnership with Stuart, Judge Logan was judge, and the circuit embraced nine courts, Stuart practicing in Tazewell, McLean, Logan, and Christian; and inasmuch as he was just then, and in fact throughout the whole term of this association, deeply immersed in politics, Lincoln was obliged to venture out into the circuit and give the partnership business such attention as he could. An amusing instance of his experience in this line is recorded in my work "Life on the Circuit with Lincoln," being a case in which one John W. Baddeley[20] had employed Stuart in a case and the latter had sent Lincoln to attend to it. The story sounds like the many apocryphal tales afloat regarding Lincoln, but Baddeley himself was my informant in 1855, he then being a citizen of my own county and one of my best clients.

After Lincoln became Logan's partner, he did not venture far from home to practice; he did, however, attend Menard County, thus embracing the region of country which had been the theater of his surveying and early political operations, and where, therefore, he had a large and favorable acquaintance. After his partnership commenced with Herndon, he extended his circuit business somewhat, but still did not attempt to achieve a general practice on the circuit. Entering into politics in 1846 and being absent in Washington for a considerable part of two years, his practice was very much broken in upon—in fact was largely dissipated and lost.

His comparative failure in Congress induced in him a belief that he was not adapted to politics, and besides, his finances had become somewhat attenuated by its pursuit. The result **all around** was **to lead to** a more general and

---

20. Whitney, *Life on the Circuit with Lincoln*, 33–35. Born in Cheshire, England, John W. Baddeley immigrated to Champaign, Illinois, where he operated a general store. The case was probably *Moran v. Baddeley,* a slander suit filed in 1837.

156   Chapter XI

systematic application to the practice of law, and accordingly, he commenced **to not only attend to such business as came along spontaneously, but** to travel the entire circuit with Judge Davis, the circuit then being denominated the Eighth, and embracing the counties of Sangamon, Logan, Tazewell, Woodford, McLean, Champaign, Vermilion, Edgar, Coles, Piatt, Macon, DeWitt, Shelby, Moultrie, and Christian.

In those early days, it should not be forgotten, the law business was not only very meagre but quite informal; cases were not then decided upon *authority,* as I have said, so much as upon logical consideration. Lincoln gained friends at once; politics and law were closely entwined, and political prejudice was quite as intense then as it ever was. Lincoln had been the only Whig from Illinois in the Congress of 1847–1849, and partisans of his faith on the circuit were likely to cleave to him both as parties and jurors. His story-telling propensities stood him in good stead and yielded a large following of admirers. He was more thoroughly advertised on the circuit through the media of his anecdotes than by either his congressional experience or his law practice. Law practice was more difficult then than now by reason of the dearth of authority, and of the method then in vogue of reasoning out cases upon primordial and original principles. As a consequence, young men counted for little in law practice in contested cases, and the habit was general to employ leaders on the circuit in anything which savored of a contested case. There was not, at that time, any lawyer who travelled over the entire circuit. Logan rarely left his own county; Stuart attended only Tazewell, Logan, and McLean; the Macon lawyers went only to Piatt; Swett and Gridley attended McLean, DeWitt, Champaign, and Vermilion; [John M.] Scott of McLean[21] went only to the northern counties; and [Clifton] Moore of DeWitt[22] limited his practice to his own county and McLean.

Courts lasted nearly six months in the year, and the judge and lawyers generally contrived to spend as many Sabbaths at home as they could, but Lincoln did not join in this effort, but contrariwise, when he set out on a tour of the circuit, **he** generally continued until the end. Nothing could be duller than remaining on the Sabbath, in a country inn of that time after adjournment of court. Good cheer **and conviviality** had expended their force during court week, and blank dullness succeeded, but Lincoln would entertain the few lingering roustabouts of the barroom with as great zest, apparently, as he had previously entertained the court and bar, and then would hitch up his horse, "Old Tom," as he was called, and, solitary and alone, ride off to the next

21. In 1862 attorney John M. Scott of Bloomington (1824–1898) replaced David Davis as judge of the Illinois Eighth Circuit Court.

22. Attorney Clifton H. Moore (1817–1901) of Clinton was a business partner of David Davis.

town in course. One would naturally suppose that the leading lawyer of the circuit, in a pursuit which occupied nearly half his time, would make himself comfortable, but he did not. His horse was as rawboned and weird-looking as himself, and his buggy, an open one, as rude as either; his attire was that of an ordinary farmer or stock-raiser, **and he might very easily have been taken for one or the other,** while the sum total of his baggage consisted of a very attenuated carpetbag, an old weather-beaten umbrella, and a short blue cloak reaching to his hips—a style which was prevalent during the Mexican War. This he had procured at Washington while a congressman and carried about with him as a winter covering for years thereafter. He read no law on the circuit, except when needed for a special case, nor did he read general literature. Instead he would **occasionally** read and study a pocket geometry which he **not infrequently** carried about with him. After the year 1854, he gave especial attention to the newspapers and watched the growth and drift of political sentiment in that way more assiduously than any one whom I ever knew.

He was utterly indifferent as to the appearance or merits of any tavern or place he stopped at; it was a matter of no consequence to him whether a caravansary was good, bad, or indifferent. The chief solicitude with him was the magnitude of the bill, for from necessity he was very prudent in his expenditures; **and if he could do so as well as not, he preferably stopped** at the cheapest taverns. He did not, however, violate good policy in that regard, and whenever it was convenient roomed with the judge while out on the circuit, the general knowledge of this fact being helpful in the way of securing business from people who augured therefrom that advantage accrued to him in consequence. This inference was entirely erroneous for social "chaff" made no impression on the judge on the bench. Frequently on the circuit we were accustomed to stop at farmhouses for dinner and sometimes overnight. Upon such occasions Lincoln would not be long in entertaining the whole household with his drolleries. He readily assimilated himself to any position or circumstances, and was **quite** as thoroughly at home **and at perfect ease** in an unhewed log cabin as at the Pike House, an elegant hotel in Bloomington, where he stopped when in that city.

In civilized society, it is a fact well known that there is a necessary restraint on the part of anyone in making their first acquaintance with, or advances to, a stranger, especially if he is invested with the glamour of celebrity. No such restraint, however, existed in case of Lincoln; no formal introduction was needed, or if accorded, was scarcely heeded in his case, but he entered into conversation in a frank, genial, unconstrained manner as if the stranger was on perfect terms of familiarity and mutual concord, and had been so for years. He never condemned, disparaged, or spoke ill of any, but did frequently praise or commend; he had the

utmost magnanimity and the least envy of any man I ever saw; and he went through the trial of the most important cases on the circuit, year after year, without the slightest asperity or friction.

While Mr. Lincoln was more guarded and less unrestrained in his narration of anecdotes to a crowd in a public place than to a select few in the privacy of one room, yet he was not particular as to the character of his auditory. In fact, I have known of his regaling a miscellaneous crowd of farmers, stable boys, and general roustabouts in the common waiting room of a country inn with as much apparent zest as to our coterie, embracing the *elite* of the bench and bar. Probably, however, his story-telling adjuncts were more completely attained in our morning and evening walks than at any other time, and if the ghosts of the departed trees in the "big grove" at Urbana or the *manes* [souls] of the stumps east of Danville could speak, they might unfold some startling revelations.

I can easily recall in fancy the crowd of roisterers, all of whom save myself have departed for the land of shadows, and especially the Abraham Lincoln of my early days as we thronged these primitive ways. Imagine a loose-jointed, carelessly attired, homely man, with a vacant, mischievous look and mien, awkwardly halting along in the suburbs of the little prairie village, in the midst of a crowd of wild, western lawyers, he towering above the rest, taking in the whole landscape, with an apparent vacuity of stare, but with deep penetration and occult vision. Something would remind him of "the feller in Indiana" or the "man down in Florida" and all would crane their necks to hear the story. At its conclusion, the whole crowd would explode with laughter—Lincoln himself more emphatically than the rest.

Or anon, wrapped up in a short blue cloak, alone with a care-stricken face, oblivious of all external things, making rapid strides toward the unromantic, one story, unpainted courthouse, mayhap to try or listen to a fifty dollar law suit, as unromantic and undramatic a figure as one could conceive. The reflection that this uncouth and clumsy joker **of the broad prairies and crude courthouses** should have been designated by Providence and destiny to be "the greatest leader of men that the world ever saw" could never have occurred in fiction, and is almost too improbable for belief as a practical fact.

I was once complaining, while attending court at Danville, that I had no business in that court, having but two or three cases, when Lincoln said: "You have as much business here as I used to have; I listened to a French street peddler's antics **outside** here a half a day once, simply because I had not one particle of business."

Just think of the afterward great president standing on the sidewalk with a crowd of boys and countrymen, listening with interest to the cheap wit of a street fakir!

The only remark savoring of sarcasm or rebuke which Mr. Lincoln ever bestowed on me at the bar or elsewhere (except one incident while he was president) occurred **once** while a small case in which we were interested was being closed by a speech on the other side, to which Lincoln was languidly listening, the next case for trial being an important one in which we also were together. Said I, "I am afraid the old war horse ain't stirred up to the importance of the next case." He looked at me listlessly and said: "Do you want the old war horse to haul two loads at once?" That and one other time I refer to in my "Life on the Circuit" (page 474) are the only times Lincoln ever said anything to me to cause me to feel *cheap*.[23]

I think it would be impossible to imagine a more paternal and considerate judge or man than our judge [David Davis].[24] He knew and remembered all about the kinships and characteristics of every conspicuous man on the circuit. A sum of money was to be invested for a child under direction of the court. The judge being about to take a trip to Cincinnati, took the Masters in Chancery along, hunted out some safe and profitable security, and invested the child's money as responsibly and profitably as if doing it for himself. I brought a suit for divorce for a "California" widow whose husband [in faraway California] was currently sending her all his earnings; when the case came on for hearing, the judge saw that no case existed for a divorce, but that night, I informed him *sotto voce*

23. "I once [in 1861] went to him to procure a very small favor for me at the War Department, while I was in the army. He had not yet come from breakfast, and I sat in his office to wait. In a few minutes he came in, in the best of humor, and I made known my errand, which he could perfectly fulfill by a line on a card; but upon hearing me, he said: 'I reckon we can do that better if I go straight to the Department with you. I reckon Col. Larned will be there by this time,' and we started together, he being in the best of humor. But I, unfortunately, had seen an applicant for office, waiting in an ante-room, whom I knew, and he implored me to help him: so I immediately commenced to say: 'William Houston is here, waiting to see you, and I think,' but Lincoln stopped me from advocating Houston's claims, by as dark a frown and as severe a burst of anger as I ever knew him to display. I desisted at once, and we did our errand, his good humor being immediately restored. The fact was that William Houston was a brother of the celebrated Sam Houston, and much resembled him. He had come from Memphis, Tennessee, where he had been a lumber merchant, and was now an applicant for a clerkship, I thought he should have had it, but Lincoln seemed very inimical to the appointment, for some reason which he did not disclose to me; but I never saw Lincoln, or any one else, change from good-humor to rage, and back to good-humor again, so quick as on that occasion," *Life on the Circuit with Lincoln,* 473–74.

24. Whitney has much more to say about Davis in *Life on the Circuit with Lincoln,* 55–67.

of the facts of the case, and he surprised the community by granting a divorce, simply placing morality and beneficence above technicalities; and it was well, for the woman married her paramour, and has already thus far lived a blameless life for thirty-five years and more thereafter. In any such case, he had a proclivity of digging out the extrajudicial facts of the case out of court, and when he had got them all, would say deprecatingly, "You mustn't talk to the Court about it outside." He had a faculty of being sneeringly polite in a mock dignified style to such as he abhorred, and talked of them in the loftiest style. A Mr. Quigg,[25] a gentleman of extreme dignity and exalted character, but of no sense of humor or adaptability to a wild western crowd, was travelling the circuit with one of the lawyers, his kinsman, just to see the country and people, but he committed the unpardonable sin of non-assimilation and non-affiliation. "He's a d___d old fool! D___d old fool! Eh! Don't know nothing. Don't know nothing," said the judge, a dozen times a day out of hearing of the parties involved. John Pearson[26] had been an old judge at one time; his circuit embraced the county that Chicago is in and some five other counties, but he fell into disfavor and settled in Danville, where he had no general practice, and but one or two special and intricate cases. The judge despised him, and when he commenced to make a long argument once to the jury, the judge called me up and said, "I'm going to Culburtsons to stay while old Pearson is talking, and when you set here and keep order, and when you see he is nearly through, send the bailiff for me." Judge Davis was bound somehow to share his contempt for everyone he did not like and often delegated his judicial functions to others. I have known of his getting [Clifton] Moore of Clinton to hold court for him in Bloomington for whole days, Lincoln to hold an entire term, and frequently to sit for short times, and I even know of Colonel [James R. M.] Bryant of Indiana[27] to hold court for him at Danville. All judgments rendered by these lawyers were voidable. Time has probably now cured them. It was a hazardous business for them and the plaintiff and suitors in their cases.

During the greater part of the time that Lincoln rode the circuit, railways did not form the usual means of travel, and our methods of locomotion and accommodation on the circuit were of the era of the stagecoach and country

25. David A. Quigg of Bloomington, brother-in-law of Leonard Swett, began his legal practice in McLean County in 1857.

26. John Pearson (1802–1875) served as judge of the Seventh Illinois Circuit Court (1837–1840) and represented the Chicago district in the Illinois State Senate (1840–1844).

27. Attorney and law professor James R. M. Bryant (1802–1865) of Williamsport, Indiana, served as lieutenant colonel of the 10th Indiana Infantry in the Civil War.

Lawyer 161

taverns. Those who are without experience cannot know to how great an extent the advent of the locomotive is the exodus of sentiment and a destruction of homely simplicity.

In those sober and prosaic days, the public-house was called a tavern, and at mealtimes the guests were placed at a long table, with the most distinguished guest at the foot of the table, and the sum total of the victuals arrayed all along the table. During court week, the choice places at the foot of the table were reserved for the court and bar, and witnesses, jurymen, and prisoners out on bail were ranged along the same table. Peddlers and traveling mountebanks took advantage of the throngs which court week usually brought, to ply their vocations, and the outlying farmers embraced those occasions to pay their taxes and debts, swap horses and jackknives, do their trading, and listen to the exchange of professional compliments, clashing of wits, sallies of sarcasm, and flights of eloquence in the courthouse. As the court and bar were necessarily together, sleeping or waking, throughout the circuit, in business or at rest, there must needs be social attrition and intimacy, more or less pronounced, all around, and Judge Davis's "best hold" was as a host, entertainer, and head of the social organization of the circuit. The judge greatly loved attention, **to shine in society, to be attended to, and** to be paid court to; he was extremely fond of prudent and proper conviviality, and was wont to put every newcomer on the circuit on a period of probation, giving him **an** opportunity to prove himself a proper member of our coterie, where, if he succeeded, he was admitted into full membership; from which, if he failed, he was informally excluded, and made to thoroughly understand that he was so.

A method of social entertainment more in practice then than now was story-telling, and it was somehow one of the greatest of accomplishments to be able to narrate stories in an entertaining way.[28] Exactly why lawyers should be addicted to this species of entertainment more than votaries of other callings, I cannot see, but the fact is nevertheless so, and it seems to have been assumed in Lincoln's time that the eighth circuit was the locality *par excellence* when entertainment by story-telling was to be looked for, **and no disappointments to occur**.

It is probable that Lincoln was never exceeded, on the whole, as a story-teller, but he had no ambition or pride in this art, nor the slightest envy towards anyone who vied with him in that respect; indeed, he preferred to listen to another good story-teller **rather than** entertaining in that way himself. And there were other humorists on our circuit besides Lincoln; indeed, fun was the chief staple of our leisure hours.

28. Cf. "Lincoln as a 'Merry Andrew,'" chapter IX of Whitney, *Life on the Circuit with Lincoln*, 171–99.

162   *Chapter XI*

In some of the courts, the terms occupied two or three weeks; in others, as in Piatt and Champaign prior to 1854, they occupied but a day or two. There was as little formality in these courts as in any other proper ones, and most of the civil cases were tried by the court, without the intervention of a jury. The first business was to charge the grand jury; the next to call through the dockets, grant defaults, continuances, or orders; then followed the disposition of criminal cases; then civil law cases; and finally the disposition of the chancery docket. Davis was a very prompt and energetic judge, and despatched business with great celerity. In the evening we would all assemble in the judge's room and listen to stories or talk sense till bedtime; and I will venture to say that no coterie of men, thrown accidentally together as we were, was more harmonious or engendered more sincere and generous friendships than ours. Lincoln was the most noted of our circle; Swett scarcely less so; then Oliver L. Davis, Oscar F. Harmon,[29] and Judge [Elias S.] Terry of Danville;[30] **Clifton H. Moore and** Lawrence Weldon[31] and James B. McKinley[32] of Clinton; Amzi McWilliams, William W. Orme,[33] John M. Scott, Asahel Gridley, and Ward H. Lamon of Bloomington; and General [Usher] Linder and O[rlando] B. Ficklin of Charleston, **among others**. From Indiana there used to come, partly on business but chiefly for pleasure, Dan Mace[34] and Jim Wilson[35] from Lafayette; Ned Hannegan,[36] Dan Voorhees,[37] and Joe Ristine[38] from Covington; and John P. Usher[39] and Dick Thompson[40] from Terre Haute.

29. Oscar F. Harmon (1827–1864) served as the colonel of 125th Illinois regiment in the Civil War.

30. Judge Elias S. Terry (1807–1891) lived in Indiana from 1836 until 1859, when he moved to Danville, Illinois.

31. In 1861, Lincoln appointed Lawrence Weldon (1829–1905) U.S. attorney for the Southern District of Illinois.

32. James B. McKinley (1821–1903) moved from Clinton to Champaign in 1857.

33. William W. Orme (1832–1866) was the law partner of Lincoln's close friend, Leonard Swett.

34. Daniel Mace (1811–1867) represented his Indiana district in the U.S. House of Representatives (1851–1857).

35. James Wilson (1825–1867) represented his Indiana district in the U.S. House of Representatives (1857–1861).

36. Edward Allen "Ned" Hannegan (1807–1859) represented Indiana in the U.S. Senate (1843–1849).

37. Daniel W. Voorhees (1827–1897) represented his Indiana district in the U.S. House of Representatives (1861–1866, 1869–1873).

38. Judge Joseph Ristine was clerk of the court in Fountain County, Indiana, and served as the state's auditor (1862–1863).

39. John Palmer Usher (1816–1889) served as secretary of the interior in Lincoln's cabinet (1863–1865).

40. Richard W. Thompson (1809–1900) represented his district in the U.S. House of Representatives (1841–1843, 1847–1849).

Lawyer 163

The main characteristic of Lincoln's practice was to achieve justice, equity, and fair dealing by the shortest and least embarrassed mode. I think he would rather be right than victorious. I think he would prefer to encounter defeat by honest methods than to achieve victory by dishonesty. He would disfavor and discountenance all dishonest and unfair litigation, but if he found himself involved in such, he was more likely to be an injury than a benefit to the case. He was an effective and a great lawyer by virtue of his honesty, which assured strength to his cause by virtue of the prestige which it brought with it; and he was also a great lawyer by reason of his great reasoning and logical finesse. Indeed in the matter of original thinking and analytical power he was without a peer or an equal in Illinois.

The primitive condition of affairs on our circuit was adhered to faithfully till 1850. Prior to that time it was the Pleistocene age of the tavern, "Mud wagon," [stagecoach] and tallow drip, but it suddenly changed to the post-Pleistocene age of the steam car, hotel, and kerosene lamps.

The eighth circuit was radically changed soon after, and Lincoln's county left out, and he then divorced from all his old circuit associations. In addition, he had got so deep into politics by that time as to trench on his industries in his profession. I do not recollect ever to have used the telegraph or to have known of its being used in our circuit practice in any way prior to that year, and the only counties reached theretofore by rail were Sangamon, McLean, and Dewitt. Our county [Champaign] was on a railroad but there was no cross line. The first term of court that was held at Danville, which was [initially] reached by rail in the fall of 1856. The county seat of Logan remained at Mt. Pulaski till that year.

We got assimilated gradually. Judge Davis once had need to go to Peoria to hold court for Judge [Elihu N.] Powell,[41] and in order to be there on Monday morning, he had to take the train for El Paso, a city of one house, the tavern (on Saturday afternoon) then to change cars for Peoria, but he missed the train, and had to lie at El Paso till hours on Monday. He tried to hunt up some literature, and the only book in the house was "The Arabian Nights." This book he read through four times while he was waiting. The means of locomotion prior to the locomotive were primitive but sure. The Judge generally used a two-horse covered buggy but he figured down close the difference in the expense paying for the feed *en route* and trusting to the haphazard modes.

I have known of ten of us riding all day in one vehicle and singing over half the way and listening to jokes from our clowns, of whom we had several, the other half of the journey. "When I lived way down in Ole Virginny" was our favorite song for two or three terms. We only knew a verse and a half

41. Elihu N. Powell (d. 1871) was the law partner of William F. Bryan of Peoria.

but we sang them over and over again. Lincoln made no attempt to sing. He would do nothing and attempt nothing he could not do well. I never knew Lincoln to make "a fool of himself" at anything; never knew of him making a *fiasco* in telling a story, or anything else. If anyone wanted to quarrel with him in court or out, which was rare, Lincoln never backed down. Swett used to "log roll" (as he called it) for business on the circuit; Lincoln never. And there was this peculiarity about his practice, that, although he was a poor lawyer in the sense of knowing the technical and concrete law, yet I never saw him discomfited or disgraced in court. He was a genius of affairs in the courthouse as well as on the circuit. His tenderness and humanity cropped out on the circuit as it did at the White House. An old farmer named Van Atta (as I remember it) took a lot of sheep to winter on shares, fed his entire spare crop to them, and they all died in the spring, when the sheep owner sued for the loss of the sheep. Lincoln and I defended. The first trial was a mistrial, and we had a second; the costs amounted to $700. **Our client knew that if he was defeated, it would sweep away his farm, and he was seventy years old.** We were defeated, and our client had large judgment to pay, which took nearly all he had. He started west where he could find cheap land and found a new home. When he bade us goodbye, Mr. Lincoln was affected almost to the point of tears; **doubtless he thought of his father, making three several migrations before he could find a home where he could die in peace.**

Whenever Mr. Lincoln took up a **new** case on the circuit of any intricacy, if there was time to make research, he would counsel sufficiently with his client and joint counsel to ascertain all that could be learned; then would examine to see if the statute was likely to contain anything bearing on the subject; then he would seclude himself and formulate the whole case, in all its details, into concrete plan and harmony, and unless it was essential that we should know his conclusions, we would first learn his views when the trial came on. When I was new to the bar, I was trying to keep some evidence out, and was getting along very well with the court, when Lincoln sang out, "I reckin it would be fair to let that in." It sounded treasonable, but I had to get used to this eccentricity. He made no attempt to gain **friendship or** favor by cajolery. He made no apologies. If anyone got mad at him, they must get pleased again in their own way; Lincoln would never seek a reconciliation. The judge told me he never saw Lincoln angry at poor accommodations on the circuit but once. They arrived at Charleston on a cold, wet afternoon, chilled through and uncomfortable; the landlord was away; there were no fires nor wood. Lincoln was thoroughly incensed; he threw off his coat, went to the wood pile, and cut wood with an axe for an hour. Davis built a fire, and when the landlord made his appearance later, Lincoln gave him a good scoring.

His favorite attitude in the room while telling stories was standing up with his back to the fire; it gave him a good chance to gesticulate. If the weather would admit, his favorite place for consultation with a client was at the foot of a tree. I have seen him seated on his haunches, counseling with one or more clients. Unless the case was very intricate, he would master all the facts without a note or reference. If a case was on hand for more than one term, he would recollect the details from term to term, without omitting one. The first chancery case I had was a *boy's* case, for I filed a bill for a mortgagee to compel the mortgagor to insure the mortgaged property. I applied to Lincoln for neighborly help, and he puzzled over it but couldn't **quite** decide at first whether the bill was good or not, finally **thought it *was* good.** [William] Somers,[42] however, cut the Gordian knot in a minute by handing the bill to the judge, saying: "Jedge, won't you look over this bill and see if there is any equity in it?" The judge was prompt if Lincoln was not; he held the bill to be worthless.

In the early days on the circuit, nearly all things were as primitive as was consonant with the reign and rule of civilization; the taverns were of the old-fashioned, "high post" bedstead order; **the dining room had one long table at which all guests ate upon terms of perfect equality**. The best rooms were assigned to the judge and his coterie of lawyers; and these, except in case of **Judge** Davis, who tipped the scale at three hundred **pounds**, slept two in a bed, and sometimes he had to take a lean bedfellow. At each semi-annual session of court, a general housecleaning and turning over was had; the sheriff, clerk, and local attorneys reported to the semi-annual drawer or closet, and arrayed themselves in the disguise of clean, "biled" shirts, and good clothes, the creases of the store shelf yet patent. The rude courthouse benches were dusted and the floor swept and doused with many buckets of water; fires were lit; the neglected water pitcher was replenished, and quires of foolscap and quill pens were placed upon the jackknife-indented tables. Little knots of country statesmen, attired in their best jeans suits, met in the courtroom, yard, or sidewalks, and in the county offices, and discussed everything from the Crimean War or the California gold diggings to the newest seed wheat or Lincoln's latest joke.

Veteran lawyers met their constituents with a lofty and condescending air of mock or strained dignity, which the latter appreciated at more than its value, and young lawyers, resplendent in ill-fitting suits of creased store clothes and stand-up collars that chafed their ears at every turn of the head, affected a courage not well based, and made ostentatious display of judicial paper which had no office except to exhibit the mock substance of business hoped for, the evidence of retainers not yet seen. When the court would actually arrive, there would be a *hurryin'* and a *scurryin'* in the courthouse and vicinity.

42. Attorney William D. Somers (1812–1900) held office in various local and county governments.

166   *Chapter XI*

The judge would march in pomp from the tavern, attended by such of the court loungers as had sufficient "gall" to obtrude themselves upon him; the lawyers would gather with their little dockets and, mayhap, their lawbooks too; the clerk would carry up the court archives in a little hair trunk; the bailiff would bring up the stone water jug, full, cool, and flowing, unless he should forget it, as he seems to have done at Piatt one term. "If the Court please," said State's Attorney [David] Campbell,[43] holding up a partly filled pitcher suggestive of antiquity and neglect, "is this the same water left over from last term?"

The sovereigns would gather in, each ready and proud to perform his allotted mission as juror, witness, party, or looker-on. "Mr. Sheriff, open court" was ordered perfunctorily: "O Yes! O Yes!! The **Champaign** Circuit Court is now open for the dispatch of business," the sheriff would ejaculate in a quavering voice.

"Mr. Sheriff, send outdoors and move that peddler away from the square," might be the next order. "Mr. Clerk, call up the grand jury." And from that time, it might be said *"opus fervet."* [the work is in full swing] The grand jury would be charged and sent to their room, the docket would be called through, and many cases disposed of in some summary way; and by the time of adjournment, the work of the session would be well outlined.

The charm which invested the life on the Eighth Circuit in the mind and fancy of Mr. Lincoln, yet lingered there, even in the most responsible and glorious days of his administration. Over and over again, has the great president stolen an hour or a few minutes from his life of anxious care to live over again those bygone exhilarating and halcyon days in brief epitome, with Swett or me as the purveyor or historian of the bright reminiscences. **The great president, in the midst of the pomp, power and luxury of the American court, laid aside his business, listened with rapt awe to recitation of the homely joys of our rustic practice, reveled for the moment in these calm, peaceful, and joyous reminiscences of his happiest time.** Lincoln could not resist the influence of association, as was demonstrated when he cast policy, statecraft, and proper administration to the winds in behalf of sentiment, and appointed David Davis to the high office of Supreme Court Justice simply because he was the exponent of that period of bright and auroral reminiscences, his life on the Eighth Judicial Circuit.

The courthouse benches are [now] bare; the prosy technical lawyer stupidly reading from Slam v. Bang 149 Illinois, or Pudge vs. Mudge 38 Buzfuz, exhibits no interest at all, whereas forty years ago [i.e., 1852], no talk in the streets, in the stores, in the family circle, or elsewhere was

---

43. David B. Campbell (1814–1855), who had a reputation as a so-so lawyer but a good prosecutor, served as Illinois's state attorney (1846–1848).

morally possible except of the court in session or some of its incidents. Now, one might be in town during court week throughout the whole term session and yet not know that it was in session.

[The following passage is a loose fragment in the manuscript, inserted in this chapter by the current editor.] **But if society would spurn a dishonest lawyer, he would cease to exist. A dishonest lawyer seeks present success, and risks the future; an honest one casts his bread upon the water to be gathered after many days. An upright and meek man, will ultimately become a corrupt lawyer; to have an extended career as an honest lawyer, he must have firmness as well as integrity.**

Again, there are many classes and degrees of ability at the bar, and legal ability may be ascribed to many lawyers of widely different cultures, intellects, and business methods, while inefficiency may be found among men of intellect and force of character, at the bar. The quality "good," as applied to a lawyer, is well-nigh meaningless: any lawyer who acquires a sufficient standing to be criticized is, of necessity, good, in a certain sense and degree, but good, how? And how good? One lawyer may be a good advocate—another a good councilor—a third a repository of the law. The strong fruits of the former may be an excellent *bonhomie* and an exuberant imagination; that of the second good judgment, a fine sense of propriety and sound common sense; while the third may have great industry and a retentive memory; they may all be good lawyers, but each be distinctly different; one follows approved methods and precedents; another resorts to original and untried modes; one is strictly a "case" or precedent lawyer; the other reasons from original principles; occasionally a man is intuitively a lawyer—another must become so by induction.

XII

Lincoln's Religion

However completely hidden, there is a proper relation alike between the things unseen and the things seen, as complete logic and harmony between the apparently fortuitous events of life as in the fall of an avalanche as abundant reason for the appointment of apparently incongruous agents to effect the Divine Will, as for the snowfall and rainfall clouds and sunshine to bring forth the harvests.[1]

"Physical science is one and indivisible . . . and the ultimate object of the physical enquirer . . . is the discovery of the rational order which pervades the universe," and the object of the investigation into the secrets of the moral world should be the same.[2]

> "God moves in a mysterious way,
> His wonders to perform"[3]

Alike in the moral and the material world, and even as physical progress is obtained as well by the desolating storm as the summer zephyr, thus also moral advancements are achieved equally by the worth, and the love, of man.

The Savior employed the last supreme moments of his agony and dissolution, not in proclaiming sublime matters, and his last will and testament to the entire race, but in issuing to a convicted thief a passport to immortality. Paul and Peter were chosen to rear the superstructure of

---

1. Compare this chapter to "Lincoln as a Christian," Chapter XI of Whitney, *Life on the Circuit with Lincoln*, 267–95.

2. Thomas Henry Huxley, *The Advance of Science in the Last Half-Century* (New York: D. Appleton, 1887), 30–31.

3. William Cowper, "Light Shining Out of Darkness" (1774).

Lincoln's Religion

His church; the former had breathed out threatenings and slaughter to the Christians and consented to their death, and the latter had denied his master thrice. And Abraham Lincoln who, in the years of his adolescence, was extremely latitudinarian in his religious beliefs, when entrusted with the mission of greatest import to humanity ever confided to man since Moses the Lawgiver, became fully reconciled to the essential truths of Christianity.

Joshua Fry Speed, the most intimate and unselfish friend that Mr. Lincoln ever had, said: "When I knew him (Lincoln) in early life, he was a skeptic. He had tried hard to be a believer, but his reason could not grasp and solve the great problem of redemption as taught. He was very cautious never to give expression to any thought or sentiment that would grate harshly upon a Christian's ear. For a sincere Christian, he had a great respect. He often said that the most ambitious man might live to see every hope fail, but no Christian could live to see his **hope** fail because fulfilment could only come when life ended. But this was a subject we never discussed. The only evidence I have of any change was in the summer before he was killed. I was invited out to the Soldiers' Home to spend the night. As I entered the room, near night, he was sitting near a window, intently reading his Bible. Approaching him, I said, 'I'm glad to see you so profitably engaged.' 'Yes,' said he, 'I am profitably engaged.' 'Well,' said I, 'if you have recovered from your skepticism, I am sorry to say that I have not.' Looking me earnestly in the face, and placing his hand upon my shoulder, he said, 'You are wrong, Speed, take all of this Book upon reason that you can, and the balance on faith, and you will live and die a happier and better man.'"[4]

Judge Gillespie of Edwardsville, Illinois (the same who jumped out of the window of the legislature with Lincoln) says: "I asked him (Lincoln) once what was to be done with the South after the Rebellion was put down. He said some thought their heads ought to come off, 'but,' said he, 'if it was left to me, I could not tell where to draw the line between those whose heads should come off and those whose heads should stay on.' He said that he had been recently reading the history of the rebellion of Absalom and that he inclined to adopt the view of David: 'When David was fleeing from Jerusalem, Shimei cursed him. After the rebellion was put down, Shimei craved a pardon. Abishai, David's nephew, the son of Zeruiah, David's sister, said: 'This man ought not to be pardoned, because he cursed the Lord's anointed.' David said, 'What have I to do with you, ye sons of Zeruiah, that you should this day be adversaries unto me? Know ye that not a man shall be put to death in Israel.'"[5]

Mr. Lincoln's early religious views conformed not to dogmas and creeds but to the religion of humanity. Of Sabbaths, when his parents would be at

4. Speed, *Reminiscences of Lincoln*, 32–33.
5. Speed, 33; 2 Samuel 19:22.

church, he would hold a simple religious service at home, and would enforce upon his small auditory the duty of kindness toward all animate objects. As he grew to manhood, his practical mind discarded all conventional matters appertaining to religion and boldly took issue with every artificial barrier, mediator, or approach which lay between his maker and man. Whether he kept his protest within the strict realms of ideal propriety it is needless to inquire; what the great martyr believed in the years of his adolescence can have none but speculative interest. The theories of the untutored mind are prone to fallacies, alike in sacred and secular things. What he believed as the result of maturity of intellect, inquiry, suffering, and experience, is all that is valuable as example.

While all men are agents of the Deity to enforce His will, Mr. Lincoln was the especial nuncio and viceregent of the Deity, to execute a supernatural mission. So Mr. Lincoln believed, and he humbly and reverently accepted the mission and performed it with zeal and fidelity.

Logically and inevitably, therefore, he believed in God, in His superintending Providence, in His intervention in mundane affairs for the weal of the race. To Him he made report; from Him he took counsel; at His hands he implored current aid; he ascribed glory and thanks to Him; he recognized Him as the Supreme Good. God came to him monitorially; with succor; with good cheer; with victory. He confounded the counsels of his accusers; He made the wrath of his enemies to minister to his good; His direct intervention the president experienced in many ways. Lincoln acknowledged all with a grateful heart; he ordered national thanksgivings and praises on every suitable occasion, and for some reason clear to Omniscience but inscrutable to us, he was stricken down as his great prototype was at Mount Pisgah when he came in sight of the promised land. Therefore, he had more proofs to warrant his belief and believed more implicitly in God, and approached nearer to Him, than any man of the race since Moses the Lawgiver.

In my "Life on the Circuit with Lincoln," in an elaborate chapter,[6] I make, as I believe, a conclusive argument in favor of Mr. Lincoln's claims to be called a Christian, but the proofs are so ample and conclusive, unless Mr. Lincoln be a trickster in speech, as to leave no excuse for any contrary opinion.

In a brief letter of acceptance of the first Presidential nomination, Mr. Lincoln implores "the assistance of Divine Providence."[7] Again, in his farewell address to his neighbors, he also gratefully and reverently placed his reliance on Providence, and invoked the prayers of his neighbors upon his mission, and in several of his speeches *en route* to the Capitol, he recognized the power and mercy of God.

6. Whitney, *Life on the Circuit with Lincoln*, 267–95.
7. Basler, *Collected Works of Lincoln*, 4:52.

In his Inaugural Address, he says: "Intelligence, patriotism, Christianity, and a firm reliance on Him who has never yet forsaken this favored land, are still competent to adjust, in the best way, all our present difficulty."[8] The closing sentence of his first Message to Congress was thus: "And . . . without guile and with pure purpose, let us renew our trust in God, and go forward without fear, and with manly hearts."[9]

He opens his first regular message to Congress by expressing gratitude to God, and closes by expressing reliance on Him. And in a special message to Congress on March 6, 1862, he says: "In view of my great responsibility to my God and my country" etc.[10] His fourth and last regular Message bestows the profoundest gratitude to Almighty God.

The second Inaugural is an almost unbroken invocation to God for His assistance and succor in behalf of our bleeding nation. It contains passages (I say it without irreverence) which approach the Divine Sermon on the Mount for moral sublimity and supreme elevation of thought as closely as a merely human document can do it. It is, in my judgment, the most sublime of Mr. Lincoln's utterances. I think it exceeds even the Gettysburg speech. It is, and will ever remain, a sacred classic.

In the general exultation which followed the surrender of Lee, the President said: "He from whom all blessings flow must not be forgotten."[11]

And a call for a National Thanksgiving was being prepared when he was stricken down.

I have thus presented but a small part of the documents and sayings in which Mr. Lincoln recognized, praised, and relied on the Almighty. He seemed to act as if He was present, exercising a personal supervision over our affairs. In every way, and upon all proper occasions, he recognizes and attests his gratitude to Him for mercies and providences, and humbly receives blows from His chastening hand.

The proper Christianity of such a man cannot be questioned. The President once said: "When any church will inscribe over its altar as its sole qualification for membership, the Saviour's condensed statement of the substance of both law and gospel, 'Thou shalt love the Lord with all thy heart and with all thy soul and with all thy mind and thy neighbor as thyself,' that church will I join with all my heart and all my soul."[12]

8. Basler, 4:271.
9. Basler, 4:441.
10. Basler, 5:146.
11. Basler, 8:399.
12. Henry Champion Deming, *Eulogy of Abraham Lincoln before the General Assembly of Connecticut, at Allyn Hall, Hartford, Thursday, June 8th, 1865* (Hartford, CT: Clark, 1865), 42.

His absolute morality, purity of life, beneficence of conduct, abounding charity, and the catholicity of his love of his kind, must inure to his infinite credit. No ruler of a republic ever had so much power; none ever employed it so tenderly, so benevolently, so mercifully. No man ever saved so many human lives by the pulsations of his kindly heart; no power save the Almighty ever used the power of pardon so graciously and benignly; no man ever dried the mourners' tears, assuaged **the** grief of stricken ones, restored the condemned to life and hope to such an extent, and with such a sympathetic soul, as he. His succor was almost Divine in essence, and gracious and gentle as the dews of Heaven in manner.

More than any other man in modern life, he completely fulfilled the requirement, and justified the asseveration of James, the brother of our Lord, that "pure religion and undefiled before God and the Father is this, To visit the fatherless and widows in their affliction, and to keep himself unspotted from the world."[13]

Mr. Lincoln was an extremely sad and melancholy man; at times this sadness was laid aside for an hour, and he felt really blithe and jocund; but his feelings gravitated and tended to be somber, mystical, and melancholy. In the realms of his diseased fancy, the heavens were always hung in funereal black. **"Gorgons, hydras and chimeras dire"[14] were his familiars. The sword of Damocles was always suspended over his head**. He was prone to fits of weird abstraction, and enveloped in an atmosphere of morbid reverie; he lived largely in unseen realms, communed oftimes with invisible spirits, and talked with a personal God; **withdrew often from mundane existence, and wandered in the world of the unhuman. He might have said,**

> **Take Oh! Boatman, thrice thy fee,**
> **For I pay it willingly:**
> **Spirits twain have crossed with me.**[15]

I have known of his indulgences in the most vacant and absurd monologue; and immediately lapse into a spell of mystical abstraction when his face would assume phases of melancholy as black and awful as that of a lost soul:

> **To griefs congenial prone**
> **More wounds than Nature gave, he knew**

13. James 1:27.

14. "Paradise Lost" in *The Poetical Works of John Milton*, ed. Henry John Todd (London: Bye and Law, 1801), 136.

15. Johann Ludwig Uhland, "The Passage" (1823) as translated by Sarah Austin in Henry Wadsworth Longfellow, ed., *Poems of Places: An Anthology in 31 Volumes* (1876–1879), https://www.bartleby.com/lit-hub/poems-of-places-an -anthology-in-31-volumes/the-passage-2.

> **While Misery's form his Fancy drew**
> **In dark ideal hues, and horrors, not its own.**[16]

He lived alternately on the prosaic Earth and in the realms of Fancy; like the hashish eater, he was frequently in a huge pavilion whose curtains were cumulus clouds adorned with fretted purple edges. Although in apparent opposition to his tendencies to fatalism, he yet believed in the direct intervention of God in our national affairs, and he frequently used to ask Him, in a direct, manly way to grant this boon, avert that disaster, or advise him what to do in a given contingency.

"The Mystics," says Murdock "profess a pure, sublime, and perfect devotion, wholly disinterested, and maintain that in calm and holy contemplation, they have direct intelligence with the Divine Spirit, and acquire a knowledge of Divine things which is unattainable by the reasoning faculty."[17] In religion, Lincoln was in essence a mystic, and all his adoration was in accordance with the tenets of that order.

16. Thomas Warton (1728–1790), "The Suicide: An Ode" (1771).

17. The first part of this definition is found in several standard dictionaries, including Noah Webster's 1828 version.

XIII

Lincoln's Mental and Moral Natures

There are but the merest few great men.[1] Many men are called great in their own day, but History strips off the lion's skin and reveals the donkey. No man can be called great from possession of the attitude of insipid goodness. Goodness alone never moved the world. "Goodness must have some edge to it, else it is none."[2] Moses was a good man, but he had great self-reliance and great organizing capacity as well. The basis of Mahomet's greatness was a superstitious idea enforced by great self-reliance and decorum of character. [Philip] Melanchthon was the brains and Luther the mensch of the Reformation; and the former is unknown. The courage and obstinacy of Luther was of greater merit than the ideality and logic of Melanchthon. Caesar and Napoleon were great in spite of their lack of virtue. Cromwell, Wellington, and Washington were great, although devoid of exalted intellectual qualifications. Webster, physically and mentally, was great; in private and political morality he was a dwarf. Calhoun was great in his mind and pure in his private morals, but diminutive in his political ideals. Mr. Clay's brilliant record seems to have successfully put in abeyance his extremely flagitious morals.

Charlatanry and demagoguism may dazzle for a time, but time will make all things even; and as water will find its level, so will the froth of reputation be dissipated; and all individual character will find an uniform standard. "All things real are so, by so much virtue as they contain."[3]

---

1. A fuller, rambling version of this chapter appears in Whitney's *Life on the Circuit with Lincoln*, 103–61.

2. Ralph Waldo Emerson, "Self-Reliance" (1841).

3. Emerson, "Self-Reliance."

The intellectual capabilities of some are handicapped and frequently vilified by impracticable morality, as witness M. Neckar[4] or Horace Greeley, and very much oftener high moral qualities are nil for want of an intellectual driving wheel.

No such incongruity was found in Mr. Lincoln's intellectual and moral natures were blended and harmonious, nor could any line of cleavage be discerned between the two. His moral honesty and intellectual honesty were one and the same; and I defy the ages to discover the ratio in which the moral and intellectual elements commingled in his daring deeds of statesmanship. The greatest trophies were indeed moral achievements, but they had an intellectual framework and fiber. But he was not born great; contrariwise, he was defective, inharmonious, and unassimilated; anatomically, he was disproportioned and unsymmetrical; physiologically, he was both organically and pathologically deficient; phrenologically, he was without emphasis on the region consecrated to the logical and reasoning faculties. Only the deep and earnest reflection indicated by his sad eyes is in harmony with his intellectual trophies.

These views are confirmed alike by his youthful tendencies and by what—for want of a more appropriate name—I may call his literary productions between the ages of fourteen and twenty eight; for there is no embryonic or assured greatness there apparent. Nor was greatness ever thrust upon him, as is obvious, upon the most superficial view.

By sheer force of political enterprise and intellectual energy, he conquered an honored place in the political forum, and by the display of wisdom, ethics, and strength, he achieved a venerated name in the gallery of the immortals. Therefore, I think he achieved greatness; but in the mystery of his being, can its genesis be portrayed?

His scholastic education, as he distinctly told Swett, was limited to four months' tuition of unlettered masters in log schoolhouses, yet his literary performances have the technique of a rhetorician; and while his modes of expression are original, bizarre, and inverted, they are never extravagant or meretricious but frequently glisten with the sublime and beautiful and attain to the heights of the classical.

His coarse texture and homely exterior style and address betray his primitive and wilderness extraction, but the absence of the petty vices and gross habits incident to the frontier gives assurance of psychological refinement; and the wide compass, intense energy, and deep profundity of his mind are attested by the range and diversity of his achievements, of which the wild

---

4. Jacques Neckar (1732–1804) served as finance minister to Louis XVI.

"Chronicles of Reuben"[5] and the second Inaugural are extremes of the chronological and intellectual span.

This marvelous, if not indeed, miraculous, progress could not, according to human experience, have been wholly achieved by orderly evolution; it would seem as if he underwent a mental metamorphosis. In the coarse "Chronicles of Reuben" or even the more dignified products of the obscure *nebulae* of his youthful aspirations, one found no promise of the "Cooper Institute" speech or germ of his inaugurals; but his speeches and state papers, commencing in 1854 and continuing until the end, each and all attest the master workman, and not the apprentice, in politics and statesmanship. After he was fully invested with the responsibilities of state, charged with the awful burden and heart-rending sorrows of an internecine war, and was encompassed by "the fierce light that beat about a throne," the contrasts between the apparent man as a man, and the undisguised ruler, were emphasized. So far as *method* was concerned, he exhibited no ostentation, but so far as *principles* and official policy were concerned—the chart, so to speak, by which he sailed—he was as unyielding and implacable as Fate, whose agent he was, and none could mistake the fundamental ideas which he enforced.

In these matters he "wore his heart upon his sleeve," and the historian and biographer has no biographical or ethical surprises to record, for certainly nothing in history could be more simple than his ethics and philosophy.[6]

[Some of the following quoted passages are inaccurate and followed by corrected versions enclosed within square brackets.]

"Slavery is founded in the selfishness of man's nature; opposition to it in his love of justice."[7]

"Much as I hate slavery, I would consent to its extension, rather than see the Union dissolved."[8]

"I would save the Union; I would save it in the shortest way under the Constitution; . . . if I could save the Union without freeing any slave I would do it; if I could do it by freeing all the slaves, I would do it; if I could save it by freeing some and leaving others alone, I would also do that."[9]

"The question whether slavery is *wrong* depends upon whether or not the negro is a *man*." ["The doctrine of self government is right—absolutely and eternally right—but it has no just application, as here attempted. Or perhaps

---

5. See Howard M. Feinstein, "The Chronicles of Reuben: A Psychological Test of Authenticity," *American Quarterly* 18 (1966): 637–54.

6. Cf. Chapter XIII, "Lincoln and Slavery," in Whitney, *Life on the Circuit with Lincoln*, 317–67.

7. Basler, *Collected Works of Lincoln*, 2:271.

8. Basler, 2:270.

9. Basler, 5:388.

Lincoln's Mental and Moral Natures

I should rather say that whether it has such just application depends upon whether a negro is *not* or *is* a man. If he is *not* a man, why in that case, he who *is* a man may, as a matter of self-government, do just as he pleases with him. But if the negro *is* a man, is it not to that extent, a total destruction of self-government, to say that he too shall not govern *himself*? When the white man governs himself that is self-government; but when he governs himself, and also governs *another* man, that is *more* than self-government—that is despotism. If the negro is a *man*, why then my ancient faith teaches me that 'all men are created equal;' and that there can be no moral right in connection with one man's making a slave of another."][10]

"The negress is not my equal in color, and perhaps in other respects, but in the right to eat the bread which her own hand has earned, she is my equal, and the equal of everybody else." ["In some respects she (a Black woman) certainly is not my equal; but in her natural right to eat the bread she earns with her own hands without asking leave of any one else, she is my equal, and the equal of all others."][11]

"If slavery is not wrong, nothing is wrong."[12]

"He who would be no slave, must have no slave." ["He who would be no slave, must consent to have no slave."][13]

"They who deny freedom to others, deserve it not for themselves." ["Those who deny freedom to others, deserve it not for themselves."][14]

"Labor is prior to, and independent of, capital, and deserves the higher consideration." ["Labor is the superior of capital, and deserves much the higher consideration."][15]

"The soldier risks his life, and frequently yields it up, for his country; to the soldier, therefore, belongs the highest honor," etc.

["The soldier puts his life at stake, and often yields it up in his country's cause. The highest merit, then, is due to the soldier."][16]

And because his philosophy and modes of expressing it are so simple and unadorned, superficial minds are apt to consider that his character may be readily analyzed. Such, however, is not the fact. The twenty-six alphabetical letters, the nine numerical digits, and the algebraic and geometrical symbols are indeed simple, like Lincoln's apothegms; but from the former are formed

10. Basler, 2:265–66.
11. Basler, 2:405.
12. Basler, 7:281.
13. Basler, 3:376.
14. Basler, 3:376.
15. Basler, 5:52.
16. Basler, 7:254.

theorems and problems in mathematics, philosophy, and metaphysics, which task and confound genius, and from the latter were deduced concrete political principles which millions of men in arms assailed, and other millions with shot, shell, and gleaming steel defended.

In the practical application of principles to actual administration, Lincoln was handicapped by the inharmony and conflict of opposing interests, and, although not impervious to the charge of affirmative dissimulation, he, nevertheless, beneath the mask and disguise of listlessness, humor, simplicity, and guilelessness, concealed the wiles and artifice of *finesse* and sagacity. He observed frankness, candor, and ingenuousness in his dealings with men, and when honor and integrity were involved, conformed rigidly to their monitions, but he was conventionally, practically, and by stress of circumstances a politician. He believed in drawing *party* lines and in enforcing *party* discipline. When Buchanan was removing Douglas' friends from office, Lincoln told me the former was right in putting in office those who conformed to his views, and that he would have done the same in Buchanan's place.

His awkwardness of manner, heartiness of welcome, promises, and direct statements were genuine, his dissimulation was never express or affirmative but always negative, implied, and utilitarian. He would listen to matters and not agree with the narrator, but with no symptoms of impatience or displeasure. He would frequently launch out or lapse into inappropriate and fatuous themes in order to evade or neutralize those which were *malapropos* or mischievous, and so interpose the president's jester as a shield or foil to an inapposite or undesired interview with the responsible president himself. These by-plays of diplomacy served a needed purpose, and met a current emergency, but did not add to the fame or dignity of its possessor. Superficial men who met him on these terms, judged him by the ostensible act, and not by its occult force or ultimate results, and either ascribed to him the tame attributes of the commonplace and prosaic, or disparaged his great qualities and exploitations by ascribing to them no higher qualities than a cheap attribute of vapid and insipid goodness. **And though it may be said that even in its best estate, and under the most favorable conditions, as Emerson said, "To be great is to be misunderstood."**[17]

A recent astute critic says that "the preeminently striking feature in Lincoln's nature was the extraordinary degree in which he always seemed to be in close and sympathetic touch with the people—that is to say, the people in the mass wherein he was imbedded, the social body amid which he dwelt, which pressed upon him on all sides, which for him formed the public. First, this group or body was only the population of the frontier settlement, then

17. Basler, 3:376.

it widened to include the State of Illinois, then it expanded to include the entire North."[18] This propensity has been noted by many observers, and is thus stated by [George] Bancroft:[19] "As a child in a dark night, on a rugged way, catches hold of the hand of its father for guidance and support, he clung fast to the hand of the people, and moved calmly through the gloom."[20]

In contemplating the methods by which he kept *en rapport* with the people there are a logic and harmony, a consistency of aim and an adaptation of means to ends that it would be an abuse of common sense to call fortuitous.

In the childhood of the race, and in primitive conditions, muscular force is dominant, examples of which may be noted in the hunter of the javelin or the wielder of the huge battle axe, the Roman gladiator, the Grecian athlete, the Spartan wrestler, the strong arm of the cradler in the harvest field, but as society and civilization make progress, muscular labor and supremacy give way to intellectual prowess in the inventor's art, capitalist's combination, or statesman's finesse; and steam, electricity, wind, and gunpowder rule. But as the refinements of physics, manners, and morals come in apace, moral force becomes the motor and life blood of progress and reigns supreme over both mind and matter.

No fact of biography is clearer than the evolution of Mr. Lincoln under and in pursuance of the laws of progress and development. Amid his primitive surroundings in Indiana, on the flatboat, and at New Salem, physical strength was the key and talisman to popularity; by its agency he became leader of the Spencer County [Indiana] rustics, the New Salem coterie, and the Clary's Grove gang. It gained for him the respect and esteem of his conventional enemies so completely that on election day they who naturally should have been opposed to him became his allies and were riotous in his support. All elements attest that his first triumphs were muscular. As Donn Piatt[21] says, "Among his rough associates when young, he was a leader, looked up to and obeyed, because they felt of his muscle and his readiness in its use."[22] As he climbed

> **the steep**
> **Where Fame's proud temple shines afar**[23]

18. John T. Morse Jr., *Abraham Lincoln* (Boston: Houghton, Mifflin, 1893), 31.

19. Democrat George Bancroft (1800–1891) of Massachusetts, a leading American historian and diplomat, was chosen by Congress to deliver a eulogy on Lincoln.

20. George Bancroft, *Memorial Address on the Life and Character of Abraham Lincoln* (1866).

21. Donn Piatt (1819–1891) of Ohio was a prominent journalist.

22. Donn Piatt, "Lincoln the Man," in Rice, *Reminiscences of Lincoln,* 359.

23. James Beattie, "The Minstrel, or, The Progress of Genius" (1771).

180   *Chapter XIII*

the popularity which he had acquired by muscular acts he retained and extended over a wider and more highly cultivated area by intellectual prowess, and his force of dialectics had sufficient momentum to reach all peoples who prized liberty as a jewel. At a later period, when the fate of democracy depended on his correct and heroic performance of high moral exploitations, he rose to the dignity and demands of the occasion, and, however exalted his mental achievements, they were outclassed by trophies of moral exploitation, albeit there was an intellectual fiber running through the series. **In this respect, he is in harmony with universal history, for the great deeds of the world—the Exodus of the Jews—the advent of the Savior—the mission of Paul—the founding of Rome—the Reformation—the discovery of America—the French and American Revolutions—the development and fall of Napoleon—and the extirpation of American slavery—were all alike moral achievements. It thus appears as clearly as any historical fact can appear that Mr. Lincoln was logical and consistent in his strength and had form and force apposite to the exigency in hand—muscular strength when and as required; mental power when needed; and moral force, according to the demands of any occasion.**

The first specific tendency to illustrate and enforce this idea is indicated by an occurrence given by me on the strength of Major [Alexander] Sympson, and it illustrates alike his prodigious strength, sturdy independence, pronounced courage, and impermeability to insult.[24]

24. Whitney, *Life on the Circuit with Lincoln*, 111–12: "Major Alexander Sympson, of Hancock County, Illinois, now deceased, informed me that he was just about Lincoln's own age, and that he was raised in the same general neighborhood with him, on Nolin Creek, in Kentucky. He states that Lincoln himself, and all the other small neighborhood boys, were accustomed to meet at the mill, within a couple of miles or so of Lincoln's residence, and he well recollects of his attire and general appearance. He was the shyest, most reticent, most uncouth and awkward-appearing, homeliest, and worse dressed of any in the entire crowd. For some time he was suffered to look on in silence and take no part in the games, local contests or pugilistic encounters incident to these gatherings. But his turn to be ground up in the conventional mill of social routine came at last, and as it had been so long delayed, it was proposed to grind him into impalpable powder, socially, as it were. Sympson saw it all. Lincoln was standing at a huge tree when he was attacked, without either provocation or warning, by a boy larger than himself, and who, metaphorically, wore the belt, with the reserves thick and close at his back; but the very acme of astonishment was experienced by the eagerly expectant crowd, for Lincoln soundly thrashed the first, second and third boy in succession, and then placed his back against the tree, defied the whole crowd and taunted them with cowardice. But he was disturbed no more, then or thereafter. His prowess and mettle secured him immunity for the future. But he left that country soon afterward." Born in Green County, Kentucky, in 1807, Sympson migrated to Illinois

Lincoln's Mental and Moral Natures

This unlovely and harsh but serviceable gift of pugilistic proficiency, and the more laudable quality of resolute courage, was his chief paternal inheritance and bequest. Insofar as the somewhat untrustworthy chronicles of those rude days afford light, it does not appear that he abused the gift, being always wary of entering into a quarrel, but being in, he bore it so that the opposer would beware of him ever thereafter.

But exterior, logical, and visible agencies defined only the starting point of his matchless career; the film of sorrow and bereavement which glazed his eyes at the deathbed of Nancy Hanks Lincoln was never effaced, and the mystic chords of memory and sympathy which stretched from the neglected grave in the unkempt furze and deep-tangled wildwood to the sad heart of the bereaved boy were constant in their tension, impelling him in all efforts that were noble and heroic toward all results that were good and true.

Shortly thereafter, a marked transformation was wrought in his nature, so radical and obvious as to be visible to all. To the superficial view this sudden change, while out of all harmony with the ordinary laws of evolution and not a growth or progress, yet seemed no more than a metamorphosis and an exotic sort of psychological meteor falling into his orbit and assimilating somewhat imperfectly with his system. But might not an intelligence sufficiently occult discern in his life of psychomancy a communion with the "loved and lost" in a sense differing from, and deeper than we know, even he could tell, but imparting a cabalistic meaning to his oft-repeated and fervent exclamation: "God Bless my Angel Mother! All that I am or hope to be I owe to her."[25]

---

in 1836 and settled in Carthage eight years later. Lincoln called him a "confidential friend." Basler, *Collected Works of Lincoln*, 4:43. "With few exceptions, Mr. Lincoln, while upon his frequent visits to Carthage, was the guest of Mr. Sympson. . . . Mr. Lincoln was very comfortable at the Sympson home. He found there a chair that just suited him. He occupied it so regularly and with such evident satisfaction that it is known to the present generation in Carthage as 'the Lincoln chair.' Mr. Lincoln was very fond of a lounging attitude. Those long legs were not at ease always when their owner was sitting. Only when he stood up did Mr. Lincoln tower above other men. His excess of stature was in his legs. Hence when Mr. Lincoln found a chair or settee so constructed as to meet his odd proportions he enjoyed it thoroughly." Reminiscences of Joseph B. Messick, in Walter B. Stevens, *A Reporter's Lincoln*, ed. Michael Burlingame (Lincoln: University of Nebraska Press, 1998), 194–95.

25. Whitney's source was probably Lamon, *Life of Lincoln*, 32: "When, in after years, Mr. Lincoln spoke of his 'saintly mother,' and of his 'angel of a mother,' he referred to this noble woman," Sarah Bush Johnston Lincoln. But William Herndon contended that although Lincoln was ashamed of his birth mother and other Hankses, he did, as noted above, praise her (not his stepmother) one day around 1850.

182   *Chapter XIII*

Mr. Lincoln's character might be defined as a combination of many *antitheses*, some obvious, some perplexing, others occult. The extreme simplicity and profound secrecy of his methods of administration, and the daring of his enterprises and magnitude of his achievements, presented the widest contrasts and provoked illiberal criticism. **In any event, contemporaries view and judge historical characters by their methods, but posterity and history estimate them by the results achieved; detraction swings the pendulum of reputation towards condemnation during life—adulation swings it toward commendation after death.**

It is singular to reflect that the "Conway Cabal" was organized by some of the best men of the nation to destroy Washington in the heyday of his usefulness, and that the "Wade and Davis" intrigue[26] was inaugurated to relegate the great emancipator to private life just after he had "proclaimed liberty throughout the land, to all the inhabitants thereof."[27] It is instructive to the historical student to trace the serpentine line which defined the formative public opinion of Mr. Lincoln during his administration. The pro-slavery coteries would alternate with the radical abolitionists in praise and censure, while the several personal followings would do the same. In pursuing a just, constant, and necessary course, he at one era trenched upon, and at another ministered to, the prejudices of all.

Intimately connected with the disparity between methods and results was Mr. Lincoln's profound and impenetrable reticence. With almost prophetic vision, he foresaw crises in our national affairs in advance of the general view and bore the woes of the nation vicariously in advance, but shared the burden with none. Of the many sad scenes presented by the unholy rebellion, none was more melancholy than the spectacle of this august victim, **blasted by the fruition of a noble ambition, and** expiating in silence and without complaint, the great national sin of which he was guiltless.

While a majority of his supporters were quick to discern in emancipation a righteous act and one essential to the autonomy of the administration, the border States were equally clear that its adoption would be the knell of the cause. Mr. Lincoln was the first to discern its portentous shadow advancing

---

26. A bill written in 1864 by Congressman Henry Winter Davis of Maryland and Senator Benjamin F. Wade of Ohio that sought to replace Lincoln's Reconstruction plan with a more stringent one. Lincoln vetoed it, prompting its authors to denounce the president in a blistering manifesto.

27. "And ye shall hallow the fiftieth year, and *proclaim liberty throughout all the land unto all the inhabitants thereof*: it shall be a jubilee unto you; and ye shall return every man unto his possession, and ye shall return every man unto his family." Leviticus 25:10. The passage in italics is inscribed on the Liberty Bell in Independence Hall, Philadelphia.

as an imperious necessity to national salvation. In the solitude of self-intro-spection, he formulated plans of emancipation and wrought out the details, carefully avoiding offence in all places and modes where it might prove fatal to the cause of the Union. His policy about provisioning Fort Sumter was similar; while giving no sign and apparently bestowing none but perfunctory thought upon this momentous matter, he was in fact secretly but most anx-iously devising proper means to do it at the apposite time. Other instances will readily occur, as the surrender of [John] Slidell and [James M.] Mason,[28] the reinstatement of [George B.] McClellan, his veto of the [Second] Confiscation Act, refusal to arm negroes, etc. For all these and other matters, he gave no premonition or sign of a parturition of mighty events, but proclaimed them in the least startling and most undramatic mode practicable to efficiency.

His modes of thought, speech, and action were *sui generis*; he imitated nobody; his manners were hearty, honest and sincere, and no one had any distrust of affirmative deceit or latent treachery. In social and personal democracy he was like Jefferson or Jackson, but unlike those great leaders, he possessed the crowning virtue of magnanimity, and he administered his great trust "with malice toward none, with charity for all."

His companions on the circuit were as prone to be the unconventional and the unpolished as the polite and genteel. To his apprehension that part of the man composed of wool, fur, leather, and bear's grease was unnoted; the soul and ethical tendencies alone made the man. He practiced himself, and appreciated in others, cordial, homely, and unrestrained manhood and disdained the vacuity of mock gentility and the inanity and hypocrisy of vain and empty deportment. Benevolence and conscientiousness, causality, order, and association of ideas abounded in his character, and his concrete ethics, political philosophy, and responsible administration were drawn from these.

Abstractly, he desired to be thoroughly logical and consistent in his hon-esty; concretely, he was as effectively so as propriety and expediency autho-rized. He would as lieve break into a man's house and despoil the owner of his goods as to secure the same result through the medium of an unjust lawsuit. To acquire values by malpractice or by unjust and inequitable action in court, **by a lawsuit**, by flat perjury, or by larceny were alike in essence to him. The form of the mal-appropriation was of no consequence, nor was he deluded by ornate names or euphemistic, **misleading** titles. Dishonesty was dishonesty to him, whether it was concealed in the burglar's kit, the "dicer's

---

28. Confederate diplomats John Slidell (1793–1871), who had represented Louisi-ana in the U.S. Senate (1853–1861), and James Murray Mason (1798–1871), who had represented Virginia in the U.S. Senate (1847–1861), were captured by the Union Navy in 1861 while on the high seas aboard a neutral vessel. Lincoln released them after the British threated war over that illegal act.

oath," [i.e., false promise], or the lawyer's sophistical speech. But his honesty was more essential and abstruse than this, for it was equally an attribute of his intellect and conscience, and he was, with equal intensity, materially, morally, and mentally honest. But he was not fanatical, bigoted, or dominated with one idea; he strove for the most wholesome and utilitarian results, even in the observance of honesty. Thus he believed it was radically dishonest to hold slaves in bondage, but he also knew that our national life was founded and vouchsafed by a contract to hold them thus; and by the latter contract he abided, even to the extent of restoring fugitive slaves, as embracing the higher ethics and utility.

He believed that nature was as logical and harmonious in the moral as in the material world, and that the interrelation between cause and effect was as unerring in one case as in the other. "Whatsoever a man soweth, that shall he also reap,"[29] was, to him, alike a practical truth and a divine law.

He said to Herndon: "There are no accidents in my philosophy; the past is the cause of the present, and the present is the cause of the future; all these are links in the endless chain, stretching from the finite to the infinite."[30]

Lincoln's logical tendencies were indigenous **to the man**. He had no tutor **and needed none**. He learned nothing from schools, academies, or professors. His inductive methods came wholly by self-introspection; and like an acorn, which comprises within itself not only the oak in embryo but also the form of structure and development, his mind comprised within itself not only the potential president and emancipator, but equally the mechanism and motor of growth and development to that sublime destiny.

In physics and mathematics, poise is required. The architect reproduces his patron's idea on paper; the builder reproduces the architect's plans in brick, mortar, lumber, paint, and glass, forming a structure of which the original idea was the germ. From the blotter, the bookkeeper evolves the ledger and the balance sheet; the artisan constructs the engine from the drawings and pasteboard plans. In this achievement of these results, empiricism will not answer; the specifications, plans, and elevations of the architect must harmonize; the builder's work must conform to the architect's plans; the bookkeeper's balance sheet must prove itself, and the engine must have the prescribed traction.

According to Lincoln's philosophy, affairs in the moral world should approximate to the certainty of affairs in the material world. If clients had good sense and perfect integrity, and lawyers complete knowledge and sterling honesty, there would be no lawsuits; if people led orderly and well-appointed lives, sorrow would be reduced to the inevitable; if philosophers,

---

29. Galatians 6:7–9.

30. William H. Herndon and Jesse W. Weik, *The Life of Abraham Lincoln, President of the United States* (3 vols.; Chicago: Belford-Clarke, 1889), 3:438.

statesmen, and rulers were wise and upright, the history of mankind would not be a melancholy retrospect of wars, violence, and passion. As a political casuist or law advocate, he deemed it to be his duty to bring to his subject the force of demonstration as completely as the environments of moral questions would allow.

To Mr. Lincoln's senses, a moral proposition was as essential an entity as a stone wall; moral conduct as evident to primordial law as physical objects; a mental object as absolutely ruled by the square, plumb, and line, as a material one. In his conception, the first steam engine was constructed in the brain of [James] Watt; the first railway train spun its journey in [George] Stevenson's thought; the first steamboat was propelled in the fancy of [Robert] Fulton; the first telegraph clicked its monotone in the lurid imagination of [Samuel F. B.] Morse; and to his view, those sublime inventions were as perfect in their mental phases as they thereafter were in their attention with utility; nor could he believe that a principle in human conduct was less perfect.

Sound principle to him was like a man in perfect health; a proposition in which fallacies were inherent was like a body full of tumors or a man with a broken leg. He introduced no fallacy in his own creations; he suffered none to go without detection in his opponents; he was a practical and in no sense a speculative philosopher. **With him,**

> "Old thrones were worn and grey
> Green was life's golden hue."

He contemned the historical argument about slavery, either as a sword or shield. His abstract argument was like this: "Whether slavery is or is not wrong, depends upon whether the negro is or is not a *man*; to admit that the negro is a *man* is also to concede that *his* slavery is *wrong*."[31] His concrete argument was like this: "While a negress may not be my equal in everything, in the right to eat the bread which her own hand has earned, she is my equal, and the equal of everyone else."[32]

31. Basler, *Collected Works of Lincoln,* 2:239: "If we admit that a negro is not a man, then it is right for the Government to own him and trade in the race, and it is right to allow the South to take their peculiar institution with them and plant it upon the virgin soil of Kansas and Nebraska. If the negro is not a man, it is consistent to apply the sacred right of popular sovereignty to the question as to whether the people of the territories shall or shall not have slavery; but if the negro, upon soil where slavery is not legalized by law and sanctioned by custom, *is* a man, then there is not even the shadow of popular sovereignty in allowing the first settlers upon such soil to decide whether it shall be right in all future time to hold men in bondage there."

32. Basler, 2:405: "Now I protest against that counterfeit logic which concludes that, because I do not want a black woman for a *slave* I must necessarily want her

186   *Chapter XIII*

A moment's reflection will render conclusive his view that these arguments are based on a solid foundation, and that the only ways to confound those arguments would be in the first case to establish the proposition that the negro is one of the lower animals, as the horse or the hog, and in the second place that the strong has a right to steal from the weak.

Thus it is apparent that the springs of his honesty and integrity of purpose welled up from his intellect, and that his conscience was not a derivation from either the fear of retribution or **even** from pride of character but was rather a product of logical perception and the eternal fitness of things. He knew that if he introduced alcohol or tobacco into the fine tissues of his system, evil consequences would ensue; he equally knew that if he harbored a fallacy in his meditations or practices, a disconnected and fallacious conclusion would be inevitable. As early as 1849, at least, he realized (though he did not act in unison with the belief) that the retributive justice of God awaited this nation for the awful sin of chattel slavery.

It is equally certain, and well attested from many statements made in his state papers and elsewhere, that he also recognized a consecutive order and method in the intervention of Deity in the affairs of men, and that it was the duty of the moralist to grope deep and search for the ultimate solution of all moral problems. One of his favorite expressions was

> There's a divinity that shapes our ends,
> Rough-hew them how we may.[33]

And this seems to have conveyed to him a deeper meaning than a merely trite proverb. He believed that all human actions were the result of motives, and that the basis of motive was selfishness. Utility was his crucial test; he had no faith in disinterestedness, not even in his charities.

A peculiar antithesis, and one that has provoked no end of speculation among his friends, was the apparent conjunction of Thalia [the muse of comedy] and Melpomene [the muse of tragedy] in his nature. I say *apparent*, altho' the appearance was *real*; but my view has always been that the exhibitions of pleasantry were assumed, mere exotic, and not ingrained, and forming no part of the real man. Indeed, within the limits of even my observation, such cases are not unknown. Real character is like the legitimate tree with its trunk, branches, and twigs, while assumed character is like the fungi which attach themselves thereto. The real character of Mr.

---

for a *wife*. I need not have her for either, I can just leave her alone. In some respects she certainly is not my equal; but in her natural right to eat the bread she earns with her own hands without asking leave of any one else, she is my equal, and the equal of all others."

33. Shakespeare, *Hamlet*, 5.2.10–11.

Lincoln, that which comprised his own proper individuality, was clear to the critical student. It was composed of the elements of gravity, responsibility, propriety, and melancholy, all in an intense degree, and the jocose element was altogether inharmonious with such sober characteristics; it was, in short, a *fungus*, and that may seem to explain, in some sort, the reason why men view his character with awe and reverence in which is no semblance of that masked contempt which exists for the ingrained humorist; still his wonderful faculty as an humorist, and the ill-adaptation of his nature to that role, must always enhance the mystery of his composition.

Lincoln had a remarkable faculty of *abstraction* from the cares and ills of life; ofttimes he had an absent, "far-away" look, the same, I infer, that **likewise** was attributed to his mother. **He would look straight into the eye of an intimate friend, he would take the proffered hand mechanically, the vision impressed upon his retina of vision must, by all optical law and moral necessity, have been of the person who confronted him, but the image stamped upon his consciousness and mental lens appertained to extra-mundane realms.**

When he was running for the presidency in 1860, I attended the great mass-meeting at Springfield, and going directly to his house, found him in the front yard watching the procession, which was then already passing, shook hands with him, and spoke briefly.

An hour later I returned and introduced a friend. After speaking to the newcomer, he seized me by the hand, gazed at me peculiarly, and said, "Whitney, I've not had hold of your hand before." I corrected him, and he gazed at me with a dazed look, and said, hesitatingly, "No! I've not seen you before today." His *mind* was absent at our former greeting.

In his social conversation on serious matters, and in his forensic and political speeches, he never made use of anecdotes. Biographers state it otherwise. It results from lack of familiarity with their subject; knowing of his anecdotal propensity in his hours of ease, they erroneously reason that the propensity must be universal in his practices, and that

> His mouth he could not ope
> But out there flew a trope[34]

and so it was in his *pastime*, but not in his *business*. The sober, practical, business Lincoln and the "mad-cap" wag Lincoln were two totally different and widely contrasted persons. In what political speech of his, **and there are many extant,** of his later career as an opponent of slavery [i.e., 1854–1865] can a single anecdote be found?

---

34. Samuel Butler, "Hudibras" (1663–78).

In his business matters, he was the incarnation of logic and adaptation; in his life in *dishabille*, he was the incarnation of humor.

He thought as a sage, though he felt as a man.[35]

Although Mr. Lincoln was ofttimes frivolous in *expression*, he always was dignified in *character*. And there was this peculiarity about Mr. Lincoln's pleasantry, that it involved no idea of contempt or degradation. A sense of superiority and dignity always attended him; the humorist in his nature was evanescent and temporary; the man of power, dignity, and responsibility was in abeyance for limited occasions. While he excelled all men as a humorist, this preeminence gratified no ambition **and satisfied nothing beyond a passing desire, and** that his humor ofttimes was forced and simulated, was palpable. **While not in form and manner so stately and imposing as Washington, in substance and reality, he was equally so, and there was in his being, beneath the mask of Momus [the personification of satire and mockery], an indefinable something that enforced respect. While he was approachable by all, he was respected by all likewise, nor did familiarity breed contempt in his case.**

Herodotus narrates that when Amasis, an early Egyptian king, was rebuked by his wisemen for the levity of his conduct, he thus justified himself: "They who have a bow, bend it only at the time they want it. When not in use, they suffer it to be relaxed; it would otherwise break, and be of no service when exigence required. It is practically the same with a man; if without some intervals of amusement he applied himself constantly to serious pursuits, he would imperceptibly lose his vigor, both of mind and of body. It is the conviction of this truth which influences me in the division of my time."[36] And Mr. Lincoln embodied the same idea.

Replying to an impatient exclamation of George Ashmun [James M. Ashley][37] over one of Lincoln's jokes, the president said, **sadly,** "I know you to be an earnest, true man, but if I could not find a vent for my feelings in this way, I should die."[38]

I have ofttimes been asked by scholarly and intellectual men who had never seen Mr. Lincoln, such questions as these: "How did Mr. Lincoln strike

---

35. James Beattie, "The Hermit" (1766).

36. William Beloe, translator, *Herodotus' History* (1830), 300.

37. James M. Ashley (1824–1896) of Toledo, Ohio, represented his district in the U.S. House of Representatives (1859–1869).

38. "Ashley, I have great confidence in you and great respect for you, and I know how sincere you are. But if I couldn't tell these stories. I would die." *Recollected Words of Abraham Lincoln*, ed. Don E. Fehrenbacher and Virginia Fehrenbacher (Stanford, CA: Stanford University Press, 1996), 19.

you at first view?" or "How did he impress you?" "What was his bearing?" &c. &c. My general reply to all such queries is that he always impressed me as commonplace and informal in all externals, but noble and dignified in all the essentials of conduct and affairs; that nothing in intercourse of any sort with him savored of **or had any smack or flavor of** meanness, insincerity, a craven or timid spirit, irresolution, "backing down," littleness, vulgarity, or any unmanly thing or quality. He never obtruded advice, aid, or sympathy, but was ready with either if requested, to those he approved, but not to such as he did not approve. His sympathy was not exuberant or demonstrative, nor yet active except when he must act as in the case of signing death warrants; **and it made a great difference whether it was the express act of commanding a man to die by approval or issuing a pardon.** He was not mawkish **or sentimental** in his sympathy, but manly and robust. The woman who kneeled to him in the exuberance of gratitude for an official favor, it will be remembered, was savagely rebuked. He was not cynical, sardonic, or sarcastic in company. Although he was frequently annoyed, he did not betray his feelings, nor did any outward manifestation at the time escape him unless it bore a relation to business or some substantial thing. In such cases he could cut the Gordian knot with facility, either by a humorous anecdote, an adroit evasion, or downright denunciation if needful.

I have known leaders in society in whose presence one felt always uncomfortable for fear of committing some *faux pas*, but no such restraint need be or was in fact felt when Lincoln was the social censor, for he required a great social license himself, and accorded it as freely to others.

Judge Davis may be said to have had a school of manners and deportment on the circuit, but Lincoln was the court jester with the most abundant license. It was difficult to tell by exterior appearances whom Lincoln really liked and whom he did not, except in extreme cases. **Oliver L. Davis**, a leading lawyer of Danville, told me that Lincoln thoroughly despised him. And I will venture to say that of the hundred or more lawyers whom Lincoln was thoroughly acquainted with on our circuit, not ten **of these** could show a single social letter from him, while the letters to the few whom he did honor by correspondence might be counted by hundreds. Lincoln really had but few close friends, and those few he cherished in his heart of hearts.

Master of Springfield

Lincoln made the promise, but did not fulfill it. But this does not exhaust the case. Stephen T. Logan was nearly as closely allied to Lincoln as Herndon was and was thoroughly fitted to be a Supreme Court Justice, a position to which he most earnestly aspired. Mr. Lincoln really was under no special obligations to the people of Springfield in general; they rather

were under a heavy load of obligation to him. They had treated his great political career with contempt and as a community deserved nothing at his hands. But this did not apply to Logan or Herndon—they at least had been faithful and sincere in their friendship, political and personal. Soon after the president was installed in office, a deputation of Springfield citizens waited on him with a request proposed by the leading citizens with no dissent, and requested the appointment of Logan as Supreme Court Justice and of Herndon as minister to Rome, and the request was repeated but without the least result. I will not say that this is inexplicable, for it is not, but it shows a combination of moral strength and moral weakness combined that is rare to be seen. Of the same nature was the treatment of Ninian W. Edwards which I give in my "Life on the Circuit with Lincoln" and other similar cases.[39] Now there would have been complete appositeness in these appointments—Logan was the greatest lawyer in Illinois and was one of the architects of the victorious party in its dark days. Herndon was a *great* man in all but style and pretension. Edwards had pedigree and high abilities as well as social and political standing. The true reason, however, why Lincoln failed to make these appointments was because of his close intimacy with the applicants and the fear of vilification. This is weak but not illogical, but it is completely illogical that he should with the same hand appoint [Ward Hill] Lamon, a man of not the slightest political or moral merit in force, to be marshal of the District

39. "Lincoln's brother-in-law, Ninian W. Edwards, at whose house Lincoln was married, applied for a similar position. One would suppose that he had the inside track; for he and his wife were domiciled at the White House, and met the President at breakfast, dinner and supper, as well as at the family hearthstone. He, also, was thoroughly qualified for the position, as Lincoln well knew. When the list of paymasters was announced; both [Robert L.] Wilson's and Edwards's names appeared, together with my own, to my great surprise, as I had not been an applicant. I sought out these two men to ascertain the nature of the office, etc., and all three of us visited the Paymaster-General's office and procured books and blanks, blank bonds, etc.: the latter of which Edwards, more fortunate than the rest of us, was enabled to perfect in Washington, and reported speedily for duty. He was then, however, informed, (several days having meanwhile elapsed) that he was not a paymaster; that such a name had indeed been on the original list, but that the President had gone to the Adjutant-General's office and expunged it. The discomfited party was told by the President, to whom he at once went, in high dudgeon, that he had changed the appointment to that of commissary of subsistence, to escape the imputation of appointing all his brothers-in-law to the higher office and the one in the greatest demand—having previously appointed Dr. [William] Wallace, another brother-in-law, [husband of Ann Todd] as paymaster." Whitney, *Life on the Circuit with Lincoln*, 471–72.

of Columbia and maintain him there in spite of the protest of his constitutional advisors (the United States Senate), and this fact does cast upon his dereliction toward his sincere friends the assurance of irreconcilable solecism of human conduct.

In point of fact, no effort of casuistry is so crucial as to define an involved issue. "Nothing," said Dean Trench, "is harder than a definition. While on the one hand, there is, for the most part, no easier task than to detect a fault or a flaw in the definition of those who have gone before us; nothing, on the other hand, is more difficult than to propose one of our own which shall not also present a vulnerable side."[40] Lord Lyndhurst said, "A definition, in order to satisfy the requisites of a good logical definition, ought not only to be sufficiently precise so that it should take in nothing except what was intended to be specified, but also sufficiently comprehensive to omit nothing which ought to be included."[41] Finally, Dr. Lieber, in his *Civil Liberty*, says that "The greatest portion of all law business arises from the impossibility of giving an absolute definition of things not absolute in themselves."[42] That portion of law practice most subtly metaphysical and affording the strictest test of a good lawyer is in special pleading, in the science of defining the issue in the controversy, and while there are many good lawyers, as the world goes, there are few lawyers who have the transcendent ability to become good pleaders.

It is at this exact point that Mr. Lincoln's preeminent greatness—in part discernible, and that in a twofold exhibition, first of criticism, second of creation, of destroying and of building up—lay in his combination of the powers of analysis and synthesis. He could discover and unmask a fallacy more completely than any other living man; and he could define a moral, political, or legal issue more perspicaciously than any statesman in American history.

In the debates between Lincoln and Douglas on the issue of the extension of slavery into free territory, the latter made vain attempts to divert or obscure the true issue. Because Mr. Lincoln deprecated the repeal of the time-honored Missouri Compromise, Douglas sophistically assumed that he wanted, and that the above implied, an abolition of slavery; social and political equality with negroes; and a making of, and enforcing by law of a uniformity of pursuits, practices, and social life throughout the Union.

40. Richard Cenevix Trench, *On the Lessons in Proverbs* (New York: Redfield, 1856), 15–16.

41. Baron John Singleton Copley quoted in Appleton Morgan, *The Law of Literature* (New York: J. Cockcroft, 1875), 296.

42. Francis Lieber, *Instructions for the Government of Armies of the United States in the Field* (1863).

Those who read Mr. Lincoln's speeches will find some of the most brilliant exhibitions of dialectics in political literature in his untangling of the knotted threads of Douglas's fallacious and involved statements, made with a view and animus to embarrass and confuse.

Here is shown one of Lincoln's salient points of intellectual character: his **own** clear and unimpeded view of a controversial subject and his lucid and terse manner and terms of statement. And this involves as a corollary his genius for unmasking and exposing all fallacies and involved statements and dissevering them from the real issue.

In such matters he was without a peer or a rival in all recorded history. Strong as the statement is, equally characteristic and pronounced were his powers, both of analysis and of synthesis. He could dissect a general and complex proposition into its simplest elements, or he could gather together a series of cognate propositions and weld them together into a mass with more skill than any debater in our political history.

In clearness and felicity of statement Lincoln was like Webster or Jefferson; in remorseless logic like John C. Calhoun or John Quincy Adams; in fiery and impetuous denunciation like Henry Clay or James G. Blaine; yet he equalled all in simplicity and terseness, and exceeded all in cogency and vigor, **and was quite as impressive and convincing as any named.**

Nothing within the wide range and compass of his mental view passed unchallenged; to all events, acts, incidents, accidents, phenomena, objects of vision, and moral propositions, he made the highwayman's demand, "stand and deliver." Every object presented to his physical or mental vision conveyed to him an object lesson. From everything actual or phantasmagorial he extracted a moral. His apparently indifferent gaze comprehended and included every element of the object in review; he was an eager student; under the mask and disguise of *nonchalance* and dissimulation; moral objects, which were chaotic and heterogeneous to the common view were homogeneous, orderly, and sequent to him. He had a most comprehensive association of ideas; while excluding all irrelevant subjects from the one under discussion, he included every element that was pertinent, and educed cognate, allied, and related matters that none but he would have discerned. Therefore, he strengthened every subject of consideration by including incidents which none but himself could have thought of, and equally by eviscerating those which, though passing the ordinary view unchallenged, would be halted, arrested, unmasked, and rejected as irrelevant by his critical gaze. **It was as if an otherwise opaque or translucent object had shed upon and through it the strong beams of a calcium light, as objects were, in that way, developed which were not revealed by the ordinary vision. Lincoln's mental vision was, in an extreme degree, much more intense than the average mental view.**

Lincoln's Mental and Moral Natures

Such was the strength of Mr. Lincoln's perceptive faculties, but he was equally pronounced, as I have foreshadowed, in his reflective ones. Having himself perceived an object clearly in all its parts, he joined these parts together by causation and comparison, with the result that his argument was a composite, logical, and symmetrical whole.

Mr. Lincoln never went to the extreme limits of his mental or fortuitous opportunities, never exhausted his subject, always and in all considerations suggested and pointed to more than he developed, invariably leaving much unsaid. His speeches of 1854 on the restoration of the Missouri Compromise apparently exhausted the "anti-extension of slavery" argument, but his speeches of 1856 on the same subject presented the same question concretely, according to the demands of current history; and his speeches of 1858 and 1859 demonstrated, by the trend of actual events, the correctness of his prior logical divination. His last studied and elaborate speech, the "Cooper Institute" speech, was his most ornate and most comprehensive historical speech. His first inaugural was still a new presentation of the subject, affording many texts for illustration and paraphrase.

He did not contest with opponents on principles on or near the borders of debate, took no advantage of technicalities or his adversaries' mistakes or weakness, ascribed no malign moral motives to flagitious political conduct. Considering the individual morality of wicked political offenders to be none of his concern, he impaled such offenders on the spear of political casuistry alone, and with the trenchant blade of debate clove in twain pernicious political principles, and not their mischievous advocate.

Thus, from an intellectual standpoint, Mr. Lincoln's *forte* was as a dialectical architect or builder, **and he was quite as efficient in demolishing an illogical structure as in erecting a logical one.**

As an architect projects in his mind the nave, transept, apse, and chancel of a cathedral, or an artist idealizes a landscape in his "fancy," or a sculptor develops a statue in his imagination, each and all of which when wrought out, are ideally perfect in harmony with the mental perception, or conversely, from an involved proposition. "Genius has privileges of its own; it selects an orbit for itself and, be this never so eccentric, if it is indeed, a celestial orbit. We star-gazers must at last begin to observe it and calculate its laws."[43]

A singular fact connected with Mr. Lincoln is that with no clearly apparent logical reason for it, he should have conceived a passionate fondness for the study of geometry. There was nothing within his ordinary experience to lead or even point to this; he was, it is true, a surveyor, but only in a practical application of right angles, according to the land office system of Mansfield.

43. Thomas Carlyle, "Jean Paul Friedrich Richter" (1827).

194 *Chapter XIII*

Evidently his *penchant* for the study of geometry had no correlation with any practical experiences or speculative fancy, but was a mere interlude, with no apparent association or interrelation with his life-drama; yet, singular to say, Bolingbroke says: "Mr. Locke . . . recommends the study of geometry, even to those who have no design of being geometricians, and he gives a reason for it . . . that although such persons may forget every problem that has been proposed, and every solution that they or others have given, but the habit of pursuing long trains of ideas will remain with them, and they will pierce through the mazes of sophism and discern a latent truth, where persons who have not this habit will never find it."[44] It may also, in this connection, be remarked that Quintilian says, "No man, assuredly, can become a perfect orator without a knowledge of geometry. It is not without reason that the greatest men have bestowed extreme attention on this science."[45] The ultimate basis of Lincoln's **colossal** greatness was his marvelous capacity for logical deduction, the exhibition of which was by his effective and fervid oratory and it would thus appear that Mr. Lincoln pursued the monitions of both Locke and Quintilian, though probably without knowing of either.

To Mr. [John P.] Gulliver,[46] he said that the term "demonstrate" puzzled him while he was a student, and that he investigated till he ascertained its meaning. Whether he sought to acquire the art of demonstration by the study of Euclid, or pursued that study as an idle fancy or congenial pastime, cannot be known, but it is fair to suppose that in his evolution from a corn-field logician and log cabin orator to the ratiocination of the joint debates, his study of the six books of Euclid held place.

His honesty was not of negative ethical obligation merely, as "Thou shalt not steal," "Thou shalt not bear false witness" &c., but was an active vital law of his being, which prompted affirmative performance of duty. He would not misstate or conceal a mental conviction or a conscientious scruple when he believed it was his duty to make disclosures, or even passively acquiesce in error, **even** though policy forbade, any more than he would misstate a fact.

44. Henry St. John, Viscount Bolingbroke, "Letters on the Study and Use of History" in *The Works of Lord Bolingbroke* (Philadelphia: Carey and Hart, 1841).

45. The Roman educator and rhetorician Marcus Fabius Quintilianus (35–96) wrote a treatise in which this quote appears. James J. Murphy, ed., *Quintilian on the Teaching of Speaking and Writing: Translations from Books One, Two, and Ten of the Institutio Oratoria* (Carbondale: Southern Illinois University Press, 1987), 77.

46. The Rev. Dr. John Putnam Gulliver (1819–1894) was a Congregational minister who founded the Free Academy of Norwich, Connecticut, a town where he heard Lincoln speak in March 1860. His reminiscences of a conversation with Lincoln appear in Francis Fisher Browne, *The Every-Day Life of Abraham Lincoln* (New York: N. D. Thompson, 1886), 319–21.

To his apprehension, one form of falsehood was as nefarious as the other, and the fact that one form might be kept concealed while the other was disclosed, was not taken into consideration. The *form* of the falsehood made no difference to him, whether it was a literal lie, an evasion or suppression of the truth, or a mental reservation, when he was bound by ideal honor to speak. Thus, in his earlier anti-slavery speeches, he deemed it to be his duty to avow certain conservative sentiments, as his adhesion to the fugitive slave law, &c., and he did it with emphasis, although it was grossly against the most relentless prejudices of his disciples and seriously injured his political standing. The incident of the "house-divided-against-itself" speech illustrates this tendency, as well as his moral courage and the good policy of honesty, in its ultimate effects.

The result was, as was clearly foreshadowed, that the voters in that State who had emigrated from Kentucky and Tennessee, and who would have sustained Lincoln as a Whig, were frightened off, and voted for the "Douglas" candidates [for the state legislature], and thus defeated Lincoln for the Senate.

This tendency is exhibited in another manner. On January 14, 1862, Simon Cameron was forced out of the cabinet by popular odium, and in the succeeding April, the House of Representatives by a large majority passed a resolution of censure of some of his official acts. Mr. Lincoln was under no especial obligation to shield Cameron, but he sent a special message to Congress saying: "I should be wanting in candor and in justice if I should leave the censure . . . to rest . . . upon Mr. Cameron . . . not only the President, but all the other heads of departments . . . were at least, equally responsible with him."[47] And it took an heroic man to defend anything that Cameron did.

This same trait was exhibited, in a minor way, in a letter dated July 13, 1863 addressed to General Grant in which he says: "When you turned northward . . . I feared it was a mistake. I now wish to make the personal acknowledgment that you were right, and I was wrong."[48] To Sherman, on December 26, 1864, he writes: "The undertaking (Savannah campaign) being a success, the honor is all yours; for I believe none of us went further than to acquiesce."[49]

And this quality is shown in a much more heroic exhibition by his letter to Joseph Hooker of January 26, 1863, from which I make these extracts:

"I have placed you at the head of the Army . . . but I think that during (your predecessor's) command . . . you have . . . thwarted him as much as you could, in which you did a great wrong to the Country . . . I have heard of your recently saying that both the Army and the Government needed a Dictator

47. Basler, *Collected Works of Lincoln*, 5:243.
48. Basler, 6:326.
49. Basler, 8:181.

196 Chapter XIII

. . . What I now ask of you is military success and I will risk the Dictatorship . . . I much fear that the spirit you have aided in infusing into the Army . . . will now turn upon you."[50]

And his contempt for falsehood was as pronounced as his reverence for the truth, as the following extract from the joint debate at Jonesboro will show. [Whitney then reproduces the same passage he quotes in Chapter XV below.]

The term "honest," so generally applied to Mr. Lincoln was not technical but comprehensive, and included candor, sincerity, single-mindedness, incorruptibility, kindness, morality, and purity, but **was** not mawkish sentimentality or impracticability. If he was as harmless as a dove, he also was as wise as a serpent, and he employed his wisdom as effectively as any wise and strictly honorable man would; but the only instances that I ever heard raised against him **of** any sort of criticism of personal conduct were in cases when the concrete claims of friendship and humanity were in conflict with abstract duty, for it was a practiced belief with him that if he could remove mountains and had not *charity* he was nothing; and that the greatest of all virtues was charity.

In ordinary life, Mr. Lincoln was to the end inartificial, unsophisticated, and unassimilated. No man of his experience ever wore his rusticity in its newest gloss and virgin freshness so persistently. Although his progress in life was not devoid of enterprise, yet he could not personate or imitate any behavior which was strained or artificial. There was candor and honesty even in his manners and habits. **He deluded no one with false hopes—never violated a promise—never paltered with his conscience—took no advantage of technicalities or "coigns of vantage"—took nothing but friendship on trust—asked no favors except in the inner circle of his friends which had but a small diameter, and was self-poised, self-reliant, and independent.** Style and pretensions made no impression on him. To him,

> The rank is but the guinea's stamp
> The man's the gowd for a' that.[51]

He wanted no attendance nor restraint, loved the largest liberty of all kinds, waited on himself, even to the performance of the most petty errands. He never had a clerk, errand boy, or student of his own will; he wrote his own law pleadings and made them brief; he never used a printed blank in his life; he respectfully listened to all advice and rarely if ever followed it; he kept his own counsels; and asked the fewest favors of all kinds of any man of his station.

50. Basler, 6:78–79.
51. Robert Burns, "A Man's a Man For a' That."

Imagine a lawyer and politician of his rank going out on the "commons" every evening, searching for, driving up, and milking his cow, cleaning out his stable, grooming his horse, chopping and carrying in wood for the kitchen! Yet Lincoln did all of these things, not from ostentation or eccentricity, but from motives of the strictest utility, even on the evening of May 18, 1860, when the telegraph from Maine to California, and from Minnesota to Texas was vocal with his name.

His disinclination to employ a clerk, errand boy, or servant arose from **his ignorance of petty enterprise, and** from his self-reliance, secretiveness, and absolute desire to be wholly independent. After he was elected [nominated], Mrs. Lincoln procured the services of an excellent colored man [William H. Johnson],[52] but Lincoln dispensed with his services whenever he could. At one time [in early February 1861], Lincoln and I were going on a short railway trip, when the servant tried to carry our hand baggage, but Lincoln could not relish the idea of a servant following him with a slender satchel, so he devised a pretext to get rid of him.[53]

The only account books he ever kept were those he found in the law offices of Judge Logan and John T. Stuart; he and Herndon kept none in their partnership. After coming to Springfield he never went in debt but twice, once when he bought his residence from Mr. Dresser,[54] he gave his note for the deferred payment with a mortgage on the property as security, again when he started to Washington on February 11, 1861, he borrowed enough to last for [the] necessary expenses of his family till he could acquire a month's payment for services. His simplicity in financial matters was almost childish. In 1856, when he was a "Fremont" elector at large, knowing that he paid his own bills on the canvass, I raised the sum of $35.00 in our county when he attended our mass meeting, and waited on him at the hotel, where I gave it to him. I recollect his embarrassment; he looked at the money and then at

52. William H. Johnson (d. 1864) was described by a journalist aboard the inaugural train as "a very useful member" of the entourage; his "untiring vigilance" as "he took care of the Presidential party" was "entitled to high credit." On Johnson, see Michael Burlingame, "Reflections on the Gravestone of William H. Johnson," in Jonathan W. White, ed., *Final Resting Places: Reflections on the Meaning of Civil War Graves* (Athens: University of Georgia Press, 2023), 239–47.

53. "A well-worn carpet-bag, quite collapsed, comprised his baggage. After we had started to the depot, across lots, his servant came running after us and took the carpet-bag, but he was soon sent back after some forgotten thing, and we trudged on alone." Whitney, *Life on the Circuit with Lincoln*, 495. In the present volume he refers to that piece of luggage as a "slender satchel."

54. The Rev. Dr. Charles Dresser (1800–1865), rector of the Protestant Episcopal Church in Springfield (1838–1855), officiated at Lincoln's 1842 wedding and sold to him the house at Eighth and Jackson Streets in 1844.

the committee sheepishly: "What will I do with it?" said he. "Put it in your pocket and keep it there," was the reply. He did so, but deemed it necessary to make a protest. "Don't you fellows do that again," said he humorously.

On a similar subject my old and valued friend, William D. Somers, Esq., for many years the leading lawyer of Champaign County, has sent me this anecdote, which illustrates the same trait and which I reproduce in his own words: "In 1855, George High was confined in the Urbana jail under two indictments for horse stealing. He sent for me to call and see him with reference to assisting in his defense, some time before the sitting of the court, and intimated his desire that I should associate Lincoln with me in his behalf. When Lincoln came, as was his custom, to attend court, I went with him to consult our client. We found his wife with him in the jail. After consulting about the matter of the defense, the subject of our fee came up, when High said he had but $10.00, which he handed to Lincoln. Lincoln, seeing from the condition of the wife that she would soon need pecuniary assistance, asked High, 'How about your wife, will she not need this?' He was answered that she would get along somehow. Lincoln then gave her $5.00 of the money, and divided the balance between himself and me, $2.50 to each."

That probably was all he received for defending the most noted horse thief in Illinois.

Lincoln was unexceptionable in his personal habits but careless of his outer dress as to style, being sedulous merely to make it go as far as it would. His appearance on the circuit was that of an Illinois farmer visiting town, adorned with his second-best suit. He wore this same suit till it was threadbare, and the same hat till its nap existed no longer, save as a **grateful** reminiscence. A short blue cloak, quite the style during the Mexican War, and which he had acquired when in Congress, and extremely unbecoming to one of his length of legs, he wore as long as in 1856 **to my recollection; for I well recollect of how very careful of it he was at our fall mass meeting of that year.** An umbrella, originally olive green, but faded to a dingy brown, he carried around the circuit for ten years. He had the letters comprising his name cut out of domestic and sewed on the inside. The knob was gone when I first knew him. His night-dress was a coarse, homemade yellow woolen flannel gown. His attire cost less than that of any man in the State **who** associated with others. He had not only no talent to dress well, but equally no physique to display dress. He put on no style anywhere; he did not defy or contemn fashion or custom, but was oblivious of it. He could not have been

A glass of fashion and a [the] mold of form,[55]

55. Shakespeare, *Hamlet*, 3.1.153.

had he tried; tailors could do little for him. In all things he was unique, and not susceptible to conventionality or to polish.

The "River and Harbor" convention which met at Chicago in July 5th 6th and 7th 1847 was the most important convention which had ever, prior to the time, occurred in Illinois.[56] **All men with pride of character attending put their best foot forward. Many got new suits to shine in as brilliantly as they could. But the greatest man there appeared, attired in a pathetic straw hat, a blue coat, vest, and pants akin to nankeen, if not indeed of that fragile material, and all being too short in every way. The coat was of the "bob tail" and "claw hammer" style then fashionable, the pants too short as usual, coarse yarn stockings, and unblacked brogans. He was the worst dressed man at that august assembly.**

The antithetical character of Mr. Lincoln is again illustrated by the wide contrast between his exterior and formal guilelessness and simplicity of nature, and the depth of *finesse*, sagacity, and diplomacy which that exterior simplicity masked and concealed. He was instinctively a politician as well as a statesman; these several roles are not diverse, but the latter is an amplification of the former.[57] A politician is a statesman in embryo, and a statesman is an enlarged politician. The campaign of 1858 illustrates this subject. While ostensibly it was a contest for a senatorship, in reality it was the vestibule to the White House. That this was so, as far as Douglas was concerned, was not disguised, but Lincoln's equal design was masked by speech, which, like that of Talleyrand, was employed to conceal his thoughts.

That Lincoln understood the occult trend of this discussion is clear by many tests. Douglas was so incautious as to interrogate Lincoln publicly. Lincoln seized the golden opportunity thus presented to impale his antagonist on one horn or the other of a political dilemma, by which he must lose either the senatorship or the presidency, and Douglas, in saving his standing at home, lost that which he had acquired in the entire nation. Contrariwise, Lincoln not only preserved his local reputation, but gained a national one. He also not only held his party allegiance to the Whigs but gained the allegiance of the abolitionists. He played a consummate political game and played it like a master of the art. He consciously and designedly baited his political hook with, and lost, the senatorship, and drew in the presidency.

Mr. Lincoln was peculiar in his social attachments, nor were they controlled at all by geodetic propinquity. His adhesion to men was the result of

56. The Harbor and River Convention of 1847, held to express support for federal funding of infrastructure projects, was attended by more than 2,000 delegates.

57. Cf. Chapter XIV, "Lincoln as a Politician," in Whitney, *Life on the Circuit with Lincoln*, 368–89.

congenial **cognate** qualities, regardless of mathematical or external considerations of any sort. His geographical neighbors could not define what he was, except outwardly, simply because he did not disclose himself to them. His most cherished friends did not live in Springfield at all, and with the exceptions of Herndon, Logan, Stuart, Dubois, and [James] Matheny,[58] the Springfield people knew nothing of him especially, beyond what they gleaned by seeing him pass through their streets and hearing him, sometimes in a cheery, and sometimes in an absentminded way, say, *"Howdye! Howdye!"* as a passing salute. Jesse K. Dubois served with Lincoln in the early legislature and became very intimate then, which intimacy was increased when Dubois was elected State Auditor in 1856 and lived there till 1861 within sight of Lincoln's house. Five days before the assassination, Dubois wrote me: "I have been intimately associated with Lincoln for twenty-five years, but I now find out that I never knew him."

At Washington, Lincoln was brought in close relations with many men of illustrious talents, but how few had any mental insight into the man? Yet he was not a Machiavelli or a Talleyrand; he had no duplicity, deceit, or affirmative dissimulation; but he had a peculiar ability to mind his own business and keep his own counsels without being offensive, which amounted to genius. To the limited few who possessed his confidence he was as unreserved in most particulars as men in ordinary, but to what I may term the exterior world—that portion outside his confidence—he was impenetrable. While to outward appearance he was brought face to face, and was *en rapport* with the whole nation for four years, **he was in fact during that sad era "grand, gloomy, and peculiar"**[59] **and** he occupied the chair of state "a sceptered hermit, wrapped in the solitude of his own originality."[60]

Although not magnetic or adhesive, like Clay, Jackson, or [James G.] Blaine, yet he had a "mystery of commanding"[61] **which yields to no logical deduction. I have known him when obscure to sit down alike in the**

---

58. Attorney James Matheny (1818–1890), a strong political ally and friend of Lincoln, served as a groomsman at his wedding.

59. Stephen Bishop, a slave, described the Mammoth Cave system in Kentucky as "a grand, gloomy and peculiar place." He acted as its first guide for tourists.

60. Charles Phillips, *An Historical Character of Napoleon* (London: Swan, 1816), 3.

61. "The monarch mind—the mystery of commanding,
    The godlike power, the art Napoleon,
    Of winning, fettering, moulding, wielding, banding
    The hearts of millions till they move as one;
    Thou hast it."
Henry Wadsworth Longfellow, "Red Jacket: A Chief of the Indian Tribes, the Tuscaroras."

common room of the village inn and in the gentleman's parlor of the Tremont House in Chicago and in a few moments, the whole assemblage present would be gathered around, listening to him, and when adjournment would come, all would be in a glow of enthusiasm or admiration of some sort.

For some men, Lincoln had special uses, and the social ligature was limited to that narrow utility; for others the affinity was catholic. To an intimate who had mistakenly supposed that he placed much reliance on the counsels of David Davis, judge of our circuit, he explained away the error by this illustration: "They had side judges down in New Hampshire, and to show the folly of the system, one who had been a side judge for twenty years said the only time the chief judge ever consulted him was at the close of a long day's session, when he turned to the side judge and whispered, 'Don't your back ache?'" Davis himself narrates that Lincoln never consulted him but once or twice. **In the winter of 1860–1, he wanted to get rid of Davis' officiousness and he did it then, as told by Thurlow Weed.**[62]

On the other hand, he had some general and genuine friendships which ranged throughout the entire gamut of correlative social amenities, and to such friendships his loyalty and constancy were inflexible. He never sacrificed a friend at the behest of personal policy or menace, but he has, over and over again, sacrificed policy and safety by reason of his loyalty and devotion to friendship. This trait I know in circumstance and detail, and I therefore affirm that Mr. Lincoln was the most firm, sincere, and unyielding devotee to the sacred cause of friendship that I ever saw, and whenever his sense of obligation to duty prevented his allowance of the claims of friendship, it gave him more pain than it did the disappointed one.

However coarse Mr. Lincoln was in physical texture and inharmonious with bodily refinement, he was "of structure in the mind which renders it capable of the most delicate sympathies, one may say simply, fineness of nature. This is, of course, compatible with heroic bodily strength and mental fineness, and in fact, heroic strength is not conceivable without such fineness and delicacy . . . the white skin of Homer's Atrides would have felt a bent rose leaf, yet subdue its feeling in the glow of battle, and behave itself like iron."[63]

An excellent test of Mr. Lincoln's high nobility of character and nature was his kindness and mercy. I never knew a brave and courageous man to be so abnormally sensitive about his own acts; he touched the world with

62. Newspaper publisher and political insider Thurlow Weed (1797–1882) of Albany was William Henry Seward's main advisor and alter ego.

63. John Ruskin, "Of Vulgarity," in *Modern Painters* (5 vols.; New York: J. Wiley, 1878–79), 5:263.

bare nerves, and suffered in secret more than was ever known or ever will be revealed about matters which, within the orbit of his great responsibilities, should be deemed to be extremely trivial. Once, on the steps of the War Department, he confided one of his minor sorrows to me to secure my sympathy apparently. I tried to make him relinquish it; he listened assentingly to my casuistry, but dismissed the subject with the conclusion, "I know all that as well as you do, but I can't get over it." And he turned sadly away.

Confidence was not only a very slow growth with Mr. Lincoln but was an extremely rare growth as well, nor was it withdrawn for any but extreme reasons; and when Lincoln's confidence was betrayed or forfeited for social misdemeanors, he took it to heart and brooded over it in general agony of mind. I recollect of finding him on the train at midnight at Champaign, *en route* to Chicago, and I accompanied him; and T. Lyle Dickey having just before announced to me his political recusancy, I told the news to Lincoln. The latter had not expected it, and I shall never forget the tremulous tones in which he lamented the loss of this, one of his thitherto most cherished friends. It touched his innermost soul; he almost groaned in spirit at the reflection.

By reference to the literature to be found in Mr. Lincoln's letters, messages, and speeches, it will appear that he had an exquisite taste for the ideal, and a wealth of imagery and metaphor almost miraculous for an uneducated man. His poetical taste attested alike his refinement of mind and mental gravitation toward the weird, somber, and mystical. In his normal and tranquil state of mind, "The Last Leaf" by Oliver Wendell Holmes was his favorite in the whole wide expanse of reflective literature; and over and over again I have heard him repeat

> The mossy marbles rest
> On the lips that he has prest
> In their bloom;
> And the names he loved to hear
> Have been carved for many a year
> On the tomb!

Tears would come unbidden to his eyes, probably at the thought of the grave [of his mother] at Gentryville or of that [of Ann Rutledge] in the bend of the Sangamo.

Herndon wrote to me of this poem, "I have heard Lincoln recite it—praise it—laud it, and swear by it; it took him in all moods and fastened itself on him as never poem on man. This I know." **During the war, if he had time to indulge in a sentimental seance, this gem of poetry was the golden thread which bound together the real and the ideal.**

His other favorite poetry was for particular moods: "The Inquiry," by Charles Mackay;[64] "Oh! Why should the spirit of mortal be proud?" by William Knox; and a passage from "Childe Harold"[65] were attuned to single phases of his existence. His feelings tended to the mystical, the weird, and the melancholy, and when his sympathies were steeped in the bitter waters of Marah,[66] he would break out in the dirge-like lamentation, "Oh! Why should the spirit of mortal be proud?"

In no mode of diplomacy was his sagacity employed to better advantage than in his urbanity and **insouciance of manner, his universal *bonhomie*, and** his close affiliation with the people. By a figure of thought, as it were, the ruler of any nation in arms stands as the exponent of the stake contested for. The patriotism of the nation rallied to the slogan of

"We are coming, Father Abraham 300,000 more"[67]

while the detestation of the "lost cause" found vent in the threat

"We'll hang Jeff. Davis on a sour apple tree."

The **beneficence and** mercy of the great-hearted president, though it weakened the army discipline directly, yet it strengthened it in its ultimate sources of support by identifying the wishes, welfare, and earnest desires of the loved and revered president with the vigorous prosecution of the war. If Mr. Lincoln had been animated with the unbending and imperious spirit of discipline of Jefferson Davis, no spirit of enthusiasm would have animated the "three hundred thousand," if indeed, they had come at all at his call. That philanthropy and mercy were the dominant motives of his frequent exercise of mercy and of his many acts of beneficence, is undoubted, but his administration is replete with instances of his courting, cultivating, cajoling, and soliciting the favor of the people, of his identifying himself with them, of his making the people and himself homogeneous.

64. Charles Mackay (1814–1889) was a British essayist and poet, best known for *Life and Liberty in America: or, Sketches of a Tour in the United States and Canada, in 1857–58* and *Memoirs of Extraordinary Popular Delusions and the Madness of Crowds* (1852). "The Inquiry" (1840) was published in *The Collected Songs of Charles Mackay* in 1859 and widely reprinted in American newspapers.

65. "Childe Harold's Pilgrimage" was an extended narrative poem by George Gordon, Lord Byron.

66. The waters of a fountain in the oasis of Marah were reportedly so bitter as to be unpotable. Exodus 15:22–27.

67. This poem, written in 1862 by General James Sloan Gibbons, was set to music by L. O. Emerson and several others.

Volumes are expressed in one sentence of Fred Douglass: "He is the only man I ever talked to for ten minutes, who didn't, in some way, give me to understand that I was a *nigger*,"[68] and yet he told the deputation of colored men who came to consult him about the future of their race, and without offence, that their race was different from his, and could not exist in the same nation **together** in harmony with it.[69]

The extreme Republican simplicity with which Mr. Lincoln performed his duties reminds me of Cincinnatus, Solon, William the Silent, or Jefferson.

68. The country's leading African American abolitionist, Frederick Douglass (ca. 1817–1895) made statements like this but not in this form. An example: in 1865 he called Lincoln "the only white man who could talk to a colored man without assuming an air of condescension." Douglass, eulogy on Lincoln, 1 June 1865, New York, Cooper Institute, manuscript, Douglass Papers, Library of Congress.

69. Basler, *Collected Works of Lincoln,* 5:371–75. Because he thought that anti-Black prejudice was so deeply rooted and widespread, Lincoln in 1862 was pessimistic about the chances that African Americans would ever achieve full-fledged citizenship in the United States and believed that they therefore deserved to have some refuge overseas where they could enjoy social and legal equality.

XIV

Free-Soil Advocate

The gold-seekers of 1849 and later years who journeyed overland as they crossed the brilliantly-bedecked prairies, or filed through the rich alluvial bottoms of *Kansas*, published widely, with all the exuberance and enthusiasm of panegyric, its merits, picturesqueness, and potential wealth; prior thereto, it had been a *terra incognita* to the world in ordinary, and its definition on the map as "the American Desert" caused it to remain an unsettled and almost unexplored wilderness.

Now, however, the advent of that "sapper and miner" of civilization—the pioneer—began, and the river courses and native groves resounded to the ringing sounds of the axe—the sharp crack of the rifles—the glad sounds of the human voice. The edict of the sovereign people went forth to our congressional halls that the star of empire must now make its way westward.

It so happened in the year 1853 that Stephen A. Douglas of Illinois and William A. Richardson, also of Illinois, were chairmen, respectively, of the "Committees on Territories" in their respective houses, one of the senate and the other of the lower house, and to those committees would belong the duty of reporting, or considering, any measure for the legal organization of the territory of Kansas, or of Nebraska, as it was then called.

Judge Douglas was an aggressive and progressive statesman, and, as quickly as anyone, saw the growing necessity of the case, to meet which, during the short session of 1852–3, he drew up and reported from his committee a bill to organize the territory of Nebraska, **it then** embracing the region which is now the states of Nebraska, Kansas, and part of Colorado, but it failed to become a law, simply for want of necessary time.

This bill merely embodied the technical and ordinary features of a territorial bill, and contained no elements of disputation. There was apparently no opportunity for objection or criticism; the necessity for organization was apparent in this, that emigrants were already occupying the country, and the land should be surveyed, so as to assure titles to them, and courts and legislature and an executive should be established, in order to guarantee to the settlers "life, liberty, and the pursuit of happiness."

A political bargain [the Missouri Compromise of 1820] had been entered into thirty-two years before, between the slave power and the exponents of freedom, by the terms and observance of which slavery had gained a large State north of the true dividing line between slavery and freedom, and the advocates of freedom had simply the unfulfilled assurance that the advocates of slavery would make no further attempts to introduce it north of that line.

Judge Douglas had publicly avowed that this bargain was sacred—"was canonized in the hearts of the people"—and that no "ruthless hand" would disturb it. David R. Atchison,[1] then a U.S. senator living on the border line of Missouri, and at that time president of the senate, had publicly announced that this compromise was a finality and no thought existed in any responsible mind that this compromise could be abrogated. Still, there was even then a little ground for misgiving; irresponsible newspapers in the South began to carp at the compromise; fault was found that the Illinois farmer could go to Nebraska with all of his property, while the Missouri planter must either keep out or leave his most valuable property, viz., his negroes, behind. The Southerners generally, in speaking of the compromise, berated it, and avowed that it was wrung from their necessities. The Southern statesmen who had enacted it pretty well satisfied their constituents at the time, but they had generally passed away, and the then existing delegations must meet the exigencies, necessities, and prejudices of that time. Some outside discussion had taken place at the time when, in 1853, the bill had been first offered, which disclosed a possibility that at least the displeasure of the Southerners would be expressed at their exclusion from this territory with their slaves.

This prejudice was not appeased, nor these objurgations stilled, by efflux of time, and seeming to fear that some effort would be made to expressly take some note of the compromise, and thus produce friction, Senator Douglas, on January 4, 1854, proposed an entirely new bill similar to the preceding one, but accompanied the same by a special report in which he expressly recommended that the Missouri Compromise be neither affirmed nor repealed—the idea being, probably, that the Supreme Court, then having a *proslavery* cast, might be invoked to pass on its constitutionality. Mutterings were heard on the Southern side of the chamber, as of parties who deemed themselves unfairly treated, but being without redress; but no well-defined fears of any

1. David Rice Atchison (1807–1886) represented Missouri in the U.S. Senate (1843–1855).

Free-Soil Advocate

sort were anticipated. On the 16th of January, however, Senator [Archibald] Dixon of Kentucky,[2] his prejudice in favor of the institution of slavery and against the Missouri Compromise being more intense than any other, arose in his place and gave notice that in due and proper time, he would offer an amendment to the territorial bill repealing the Missouri Compromise in express terms. On the succeeding day, Senator [Charles] Sumner[3] gave notice that he would propose an amendment expressly recognizing the vital force and authority of the compromise.

Thus the gage of battle was thrown down by the South and taken up promptly by the North. There could be no middle ground; that the South would stand united to repeal the Missouri Compromise was apparent and probable; that the powerful political faction would disinherit any Northern ally who should desert them in this crisis was equally sure; and that the free States would constitute a clear-cut and relentless opposition was quite as well foreseen.

Douglas had been the favorite candidate of the young and progressive Democracy for the presidency as early as 1851, immediately after the settlement of the slavery question then, and had not his friends treated the veteran statesmen of the party, like [Lewis] Cass, [Daniel S.] Dickinson, [William] Marcy,[4] [Isaac] Toucey,[5] and that class with superciliousness and disdain, he would have been nominated and elected in 1852. He had not, however, seriously damaged his political standing at this time, but it was clear that the time was now come when he could no longer hope to serve two masters; he must either pander to the views of the South or he must abandon the political heresies urged by that intemperate section. This necessity was immediately pressed home upon him by David R. Atchison, who informed him that unless he was prepared to incorporate into the committee bill a clause expressly repealing the Missouri Compromise, the party expected him to resign his place as chairman of the committee on territories, in which event he, Atchison, was to resign the presidency of the senate and take Douglas's place. Let it be recollected that at this time there was but one political party of any vitality in the field; at the prior presidential election [Franklin] Pierce had carried

2. Archibald Dixon (1802–1876) represented Kentucky in the U.S. Senate (1852–1855).

3. Abolitionist Charles Sumner (1811–1874) represented Massachusetts in the U.S. Senate (1851–1874).

4. Democrat William L. Marcy (1786–1857) represented New York in the U.S. Senate (1831–1833) and also served as governor of New York (1833–1838) and U.S. Secretary of State (1853–1857).

5. Democrat Isaac Toucey (1792–1869) served as governor of Connecticut (1846–1847), as a U.S. senator (1852–1857), and as U.S. Secretary of the Navy (1857–1860).

208   *Chapter XIV*

every State but four. Clay and Webster, the great leaders of the Whig party, had died in that same year; [William Henry] Seward[6] had hardly attained a national leadership, and the strong men of the Whig party—[Thomas] Clayton,[7] [George] Badger,[8] [Judah] Benjamin,[9] [Robert] Toombs, [Alexander] Stephens,[10] [John] Bell, and [James C.] Jones[11]—were Southerners, and on the test question of the repeal of the Missouri Compromise would doubtless affiliate with the Southern Democrats. The Abolitionists had no healthy political organization. To **all appearances, viewed with** a politician's eye, the alternative appeared to be offered to Douglas either to quit politics or consent to the repeal of the time-honored compromise.

Douglas could not deliberate long. The implacable Dixon was ready and anxious to take the "laboring oar," and even if he should fail, Atchison and others were quite as eager. So Douglas thus, at the point of divergence, took the wide gate and broad road which led to political damnation, **and abandoned the straight gate and narrow road which would have led him to political life everlasting.** That he knew the measure he was about to espouse was morally and politically wrong can scarcely admit of doubt. He had denounced in advance any possible violation of this compromise; he had introduced two different bills without proposing its repeal; and he had vainly remonstrated with Dixon on that subject. Still, waiving the moral question, it would appear that in the stress of circumstances in which Douglas was placed, his decision was the expedient one; he was, on the whole, the most conspicuous leader of the only political party in the nation of any courage. With his aid, the measure would certainly pass, and he would as certainly attain the presidency in 1856, after which, the deluge might come.

He took no account of the reserved force of the people. In addition, even if things should go awry, he had five years yet in the senate before he must render an account of his stewardship, and as he had succeeded, only two years before, in placating the people's wrath for his vote on the compromise measures, he deemed it reasonably clear that he could do so again, if needs

6. William Henry Seward (1801–1872) served as governor of New York (1839–1842), as a U.S. senator (1849–1861), and as U.S. Secretary of State (1861–1869).

7. Thomas Clayton (1777–1854) represented Delaware in the U.S. Senate (1824–1827, 1837–1847).

8. George Badger (1795–1866) represented North Carolina in the U.S. Senate (1846–1855).

9. Judah P. Benjamin (1811–1884) represented Louisiana in the U.S. Senate (1853–1861).

10. Alexander H. Stephens (1812–1883) represented a Georgia district in the U.S. House of Representatives (1843–1859).

11. James C. Jones (1809–1859) represented Tennessee in the U.S. Senate (1851–1857).

were, in 1858. Upon a balancing of chances, he decided to commit the bark which carried him and his fortunes to the political tide which flowed toward the Gulf of Mexico, and having decided to enter into a quarrel with Fate, he resolved to bear it so that Fate should beware of him for the future.

Having thus decided, he visited Senator Dixon (who was temporarily ill) at his lodgings and invited him to take a ride, during which he solicited the honor and danger of being the champion of the repeal of the compromise—a distinction which was generously accorded. So on January 23 he reported a substitute for his original bill, making two territories instead of one, and he incorporated a clause repealing the Missouri Compromise on the alleged ground that it had been "superseded by" the compromise measures of 1850—as flimsy and fallacious a pretext as could be conceived of. When this substitute was presented, there was great excitement all over the nation. Had the substitution of a king for our constitutional executive been suggested, the alarm could scarcely have been greater, for the public mind recalled the relentless advance of slavery toward imperial power, and saw in this moment a longer stride toward **political supremacy and** national slavery than had ever before been dared.

The bill came up for consideration on the next day, but was, by common consent, made a special order for the 30th instant, and immediately an address was drafted by Senator [Salmon P.] Chase[12] and issued to the people of the North, showing the flagitious character of the measure and urging that the political power of the people be exerted in opposition. It received the signatures of Senators Chase, [John P.] Hale, and [Charles] Sumner, and Representatives Gerrit Smith,[13] [Senator] Benjamin F. Wade,[14] Alexander R. De Witt,[15] and Joshua R. Giddings. The country responded to the excitement in Congress, and no political event—neither the deadlock between Jefferson and Burr, nor the War of 1812, nor Jackson's onslaught on the National Bank—so profoundly stirred the feelings of the people.

Debate on the bill commenced by an exhaustive speech from Senator Douglas in its support and was participated in by the leading debaters in the senate on the Democratic side, and by Messrs. Seward, Hale, Sumner,

---

12. Salmon P. Chase (1808–1873) represented Ohio in the U.S. Senate (1849–1855) and served as Lincoln's secretary of the treasury (1861–1864) and chief justice of the U.S. Supreme Court (1864–1873).

13. Wealthy abolitionist Gerrit Smith (1797–1874) represented a New York district in the U.S. House of Representatives (1853–1854).

14. Benjamin Franklin "Bluff Ben" Wade (1800–1878) represented Ohio in the U.S. Senate (1851–1869).

15. Alexander De Witt (1798–1879) represented a Massachusetts district in the U.S. House of Representatives (1853–1857).

210 *Chapter XIV*

Chase, Bell, and [Samuel] Houston[16] in opposition. The last session at which its consideration was had extended till daylight on March 3, when the bill passed the senate by a majority of twenty-three. **Thus, as theretofore and since, did the senate exhibit itself as the ally of oppression, as a handmaid of aristocracy and caste. Sam Houston of Texas then warned the senate that the passage of the bill would lead inevitably to disunion.**

Four days later, the bill reached the lower house and was referred to the committee on territories, whose chairman was Richardson of Illinois, the same whom Lincoln had aided in the legislature to elect states attorney over [Orville] Browning. Meanwhile, the power of the people was beginning to be felt in Congress, which rendered the ultimate decision somewhat doubtful, and the active opponents of the measure determined to make as gallant a stand in opposition as they could. Accordingly, on March 21 they moved to refer the bill to the Committee of the Whole House on the State of the Union, which, if accomplished and maintained, would probably dispose of the measure for that session, and it was so accomplished by a vote of 110 to 96, **and the bill was then tied up.**

However, on the 8th of May a resolution was adopted by a bare majority to take up the bill, which was done and the bill discussed for two days, after which Richardson moved the previous question, or gave notice of his immediate design to do so, and thus force a vote without further parley. The Democrats felt assured of a sufficient majority to carry it through, it having been made an administration measure at the White House, as it also was a party measure at the Capitol, besides having the support of the pro-slavery Whigs. On the 11th the previous question was attempted, and "filibustering," as it was called, was resorted to, and prolonged all through that day, the succeeding night, and the whole of the next day till midnight, when the legislative iconoclasts, fagged out with bad whiskey, yelling, shaking of fists, and discomfiture, raised the siege and went home, cursing their unlucky stars.

But the stake was too great to be yielded up, and in a couple of days Richardson moved, and, after a severe struggle, carried through a motion to take a vote after a discussion of four days. Discussion was then had, and while there was a majority in favor of the bill, under proper and authorized practice as then allowed by the rules of the House, the minority could have long retarded, and probably have ultimately defeated, the bill.

One hundred and nineteen was the number requisite to constitute a quorum of the Committee of the Whole. Unless there was a quorum, nothing could be done except rise and report *no quorum*. The anti-bill men refused to vote on the measure to rise and report the bill for passage, in consequence of

16. Samuel Houston (1793–1863) represented Texas in the U.S. Senate (1846–1859).

Free-Soil Advocate

which but one hundred and three members voted. Under fair ruling, as the practice then was, no progress could be made, but Edson B. Olds of Ohio,[17] the chairman of the committee, falsely declared the vote carried, and leaving the chair, made his false report, that the committee had recommended that the measure do pass. The friends and opponents of the measure then commenced the "life and death" struggle; the party lash was applied without stint to the Northern Democrats, who were inclined to be recalcitrant, and the Southern Whigs, of whom Alexander H. Stephens was the most conspicuous, were bound to vote according to the apparent interests of their section; and so, on May 22, 1854, this, the most important bill ever before Congress, was passed by a vote of 113 to 100, and the pro-slavery advocates of both political parties supposed that they had now entrenched slavery behind adamantine bulwarks.

It should be noted that Franklin Pierce, a native of New Hampshire, then president of the United States, was as zealous an advocate of slavery as ever his war minister, Jefferson Davis, was, and that he was likewise a rigid observer of the sabbath. When Douglas decided to espouse the championship of this bill, it was late on Saturday, and reflecting on the matter Saturday night, he concluded that the executive should be committed to its support before any step was taken. He rightly prognosticated that the power of the administration would be required to force the bill through Congress, and the sequel showed that he was right. Accordingly, he sought out Secretary of War Jefferson Davis, informed him of his desire to report the substitute repealing the Missouri Compromise, for the pending bill, on the ensuing Monday, and of the assumed necessity to commit the executive to the measure, gained an interview, explained the bill to the president, who gave his cordial assent to it and concurred in making it an administrative measure. And thus, while the Christian world was engaged in worshiping the Prince of Peace, the executive and social head of this great Christian nation was engaged in a conspiracy against humanity, whose immediate object was to consecrate a vast scope of free territory forever to slavery but whose ultimate design was to make slavery universal in the land of the Declaration of Independence.

The last act in this national drama bore the date May 30, 1854, when the president approved the bill and impressed upon it the *imprimatur* and sanction of law. **Douglas, out of abundant caution, got the president to write the words which repealed the Missouri Compromise in his own handwriting so as to commit him in writing to the measure.**

---

17. Democrat Edson B. Olds (1802–1869) represented his Ohio district in the U.S. House of Representatives (1849–1855).

The sanctity and prime importance of an observance of good faith in contracts so impressed itself upon the fathers of our Constitution that they forbade any state from passing a law to impair the obligations of a contract, and under the operation of that law, commencing with the "Dartmouth College" case, all courts since have held all men and institutions to a faithful observance of all contracts which they should make. In this case. the institution of slavery sought to achieve for its uses and aggrandizement a large state of unparalleled native wealth, resources, and intercommunication, located along the latitudes of the region whose habitat was slavery, and in return for this great boon, solemnly agreed that all other territory north of a line indicated, should be forever free, and having secured all advantages which could be secured on its side, deliberately retakes the consideration it gave.

The innate selfishness of man would justify the act on the part of those who came from south of Mason's and Dixon's line, but it ought to have consigned every politician north of it to the limbo of the politically damned, and it, in fact, did do so, except a few adroit cases who hedged their infamy. It was an atrocious political measure, and will be included in the same catalog of political perfidy as the dismemberment of Poland, the massacre of the Incas by Pizzaro, or the Mississippi repudiation.[18]

Thus, already dominated with the belief that, in some way, slavery was to be made general, as freedom had been, and that the slave power was rapidly striding on in the line of political conquest, Lincoln contemplated the introduction by Douglas of his bill repealing the Missouri Compromise with extraordinary interest, and just at the time when I first saw him, to wit on June 3, 1854—the "Nebraska bill" having become a law four days before—made up his mind, from a deep sense of patriotic duty, to contend actively and earnestly for a restoration of the Missouri Compromise, for in the repeal of this statute, the fell purpose of the slave power to impose its shackles of slavery upon soil which, thirty-four years before, had been purchased for freedom at a fearful price was apparent.

Senator Dixon of Kentucky, who was the pioneer in the repeal of the Missouri Compromise, served in the senate only two and one third years to fill out the uncompleted term of Henry Clay, who had always enjoyed the credit of being the father of that compromise. He relates **that** when Douglas came to him and solicited the privilege of bringing in a substitute for his previous bill and in that substitute including a repeal of the Compromise, Douglas then prophesied that he would be reviled, mobbed, burned in effigy,

---

18. In 1840, the State of Mississippi defaulted on $2,000,000 of Planters Bank bonds and $5,000,000 of Union Bank bonds.

&c. at his own home, but that he was prepared to accept all such ungracious consequences, etc.

The sequel justified his predictions. Douglas' home really was at Washington—but he hailed from Chicago, and when casually there stopped at the Tremont House, like any other transient; and having none but political business in Illinois, it being to secure the reelection of his colleague, General [James] Shields, who had voted to repeal the Compromise, he deferred his visit to Illinois till fall, and accordingly, in September, he put in an appearance at Chicago, only to find Judd, Wentworth, Peck, all the newspapers, and the entire responsible public sentiment arrayed in deadly and implacable hostility against him. To attempt to stem such a current was a defiance of Fate itself; but Douglas was one of the most audacious of men, and he announced himself for a speech, and made an attempt to gain a hearing but was hooted down. However, on a second trial, he was listened to disdainfully but created no converts, and did not aid his cause.

The State fair was to sit in October, and in view of the excited condition of politics, and of the fact that the fair was to be held at the capital, there was a tremendous outpouring of public men congregated there. In point of fact, Douglas, Shields, and the members of Congress who had voted for the repeal of the Compromise had used their efforts to secure as large an attendance of their supporters as they could, while the opponents of the repeal had been, with less desperation, perhaps, also active in gathering at the scene of action. The political situation was peculiar; there was no national election on hand, and no general ticket to be elected, except for State Treasurer and Superintendent of Public Instruction, and yet no election ever had taken place in Illinois before which aroused such intense interest and created such widespread excitement, for a legislature was to be chosen to select a successor to Shields, and congressmen to replace those who had voted for and against the Nebraska Bill, and thus to sit in judgment upon the repeal of the Missouri Compromise. Shields was, of necessity, a candidate, but there was no organized move to designate an opposition candidate, since one of the congressmen who had opposed the measure might have been selected, but none was. So when Douglas announced his purpose to speak on October 3 in the hall of the House of Representatives at the Capitol, it was simply to render an account of his stewardship in form, but in substance to advocate the re-election of Shields and such members of the lower house as had aided his political tergiversation.

There was no formal or stated reason why Lincoln should reply, except from a general recognition of his superior ability to do so. No one else was mentioned in that connection, **for** everybody seemed instinctively to indicate Lincoln as the champion, although he was a private citizen merely, with no political strand to bind him to the debate.

John T. Stuart relates that in 1850, he and Lincoln had a conversation about the Kentucky convention in which he remarked to Lincoln that the time was coming when all "must be proslavery or abolitionists," to which Lincoln responded: "when that time comes, my mind is made up," meaning to oppose slavery.[19]

Lincoln was not even present at the commencement of Douglas's speech but came in during its delivery, and at its conclusion, an announcement was made that Lincoln would reply to it on the succeeding day. Accordingly, on the next day, he spoke for three hours, and made one of the greatest efforts of his life. It was a terrible philippic against the Nebraska Bill. Douglas himself declared that he had heard nothing like it in the senate. Lincoln had not only thoroughly prepared himself on all matters of fact and of record, but his feelings were thoroughly aroused. He was not only indignant, but alarmed; he then believed that it was indispensable that the Missouri Compromise should be restored; **such was his specific object then**. In the repeal of the Missouri Compromise, he fancied that the moral sluiceway had been opened which would flood the entire Union with slavery, and that unless the dam was restored by the might of public opinion, a radical change would be wrought in the genius of our institutions. Freedom would be dethroned, and slavery made lawful alike in Massachusetts and South Carolina, Illinois and Texas, New York and Kentucky.

In that fall, Lincoln made a speech in reply to Douglas at Peoria on October 16, and another, independently of Douglas, at Urbana, on October 24; the former being of the same tenor and import, substantially, as the Springfield speech. While the Urbana speech, having no political critics present, was more unguarded and less diplomatic. Lincoln then took a rest in a political sense (having been defeated for the senate in January, 1855) till 1856, when he attended the Bloomington Convention as a delegate, said convention having been called to represent all who opposed the repeal of the Missouri Compromise.

His views on the subject of slavery, as the question was then presented for practical consideration, were fully expressed in a letter to his friend Joshua F. Speed in the succeeding August, from which we extract as follows: "You know I dislike slavery, and you fully admit the abstract wrong of it. . . . I do oppose the extension of slavery because my judgment and feelings so prompt me. . . . If Kansas fairly votes herself a slave State, she must be admitted, or the Union must be dissolved. But how if she votes herself a slave state unfairly, must she still be admitted, or the Union dissolved? *That will be the phase of the question when it first becomes a practical one.*"[20]

19. Wilson and Davis, *Herndon's Informants*, 64.
20. Basler, *Collected Works of Lincoln*, 2:320–21.

Free-Soil Advocate 215

In 1856 he was placed at the head of the electoral ticket and canvassed the State, his general arguments being in antagonism to allowing slavery to be established in territory which had theretofore been consecrated to freedom, but with no practical specific method of preventing it.

His antislavery record from thence to the war, including the joint debate and the Ohio, New York, and New England speeches are part of the history of the nation, and need no repetition here.

XV

Attainment of the Presidency

The choosing from forty to sixty millions of people, embracing hundreds of men of known and recognized ability and fitness for the place, one of their number to be the conventional head of the Army and Navy and Civil and Executive departments of government, as well as the social head of the nation, is controlled by destiny. **The most fit men cannot be discerned; the ablest men cannot be known.** The will of the individual **man** alone is powerless to bring him to the exalted station.

He cannot ascend or gravitate to his exalted station by accident, nor can craft and *finesse* achieve it for him.

Those who are apparently the most proper and suitable candidates for the position fail to attain it. Sometimes they lose it by an apparently trivial accident of mischance; sometimes a candidate achieves it also by a mere or haphazard chance. Thomas Jefferson, the greatest statesman of his era, was elected by the bare preponderance of our representatives vote in the lower house of Congress. James Monroe, a very inferior man, and not attaining to the dignity of a statesman, received every electoral vote but one.

Henry Clay would have been elected to this exalted position in 1844 had he not written his disastrous letter in disparagement of the annexation of Texas. James G. Blaine would have been elected had he not have taken New York City in his canvass on the eve of election with his smart pasquinade or had [Samuel D.] Burchard[1] been honest. Greeley, the statesmen Clay, Webster, Calhoun, Seward, Chase, [William H.] Crawford, [Hugh] White, and Blaine made prodigious, but vain, efforts to grasp the sovereign

---

1. Samuel D. Burchard (1812–1891), a Presbyterian minister in New York City, denounced the Democratic party's devotion to "rum, Romanism, and rebellion."

Attainment of the Presidency

prize. It gravitated without effort to the mediocre Van Buren, Polk, Pierce, Taylor, Buchanan, [Rutherford B.] Hayes, [Ulysses S.] Grant, and [Grover] Cleveland.

As I have said, Destiny controls the choice, but a statesman, sufficiently astute, may place himself in the road of Destiny. Had Mr. Lincoln not entered the political arena in 1854 or at some later period, he would have been unknown even to Destiny; that goddess does not make a president out of **an unimproved rail-splitter, or** a simple country lawyer, or a local politician; **he must achieve something for himself.** The candidate for this high office must align himself with the national spirit and movement of the time. Even Zachary Taylor won some comparatively petty victories at Palo Alto and Buena Vista. Had political merit and logical deduction decided the question in 1860, Seward would have been president in 1861. Indeed, guided by that test, there were several who would have been preferred to Lincoln, for, tested by business methods, he certainly should not, and would not, have been chosen. And even after he was chosen, the heart of the loyal American people sank in dismay, as his vapid and vacuous speeches *en route* to the inauguration revealed an apparent feebleness incompatible with the giant task then on his hands.

The task proved much greater than was dreamed of, but no single disinterested authority will now condemn the selections. It was an indispensable one. It was above human control. I doubt if any **single** man on earth thought seriously of Lincoln as a possible president on the morning of May 29, 1856. The only position he had **ever** held, which is deemed a stepping stone to that unique place, was that of congressman for one term, and in that place he achieved no eminence, but the reverse—indeed, it would seem as if his official life in Washington was a series of blunders. His method of attempting to oppose the Mexican War and of trying to exorcise slavery from the District of Columbia was peculiarly *mal-appropos.*

Since then he had done no substantial thing in the way of politics, except to make three speeches in 1854 against the repeal of the Missouri Compromise, and in favor of its restoration. [Whitney footnote: My attention has been drawn to a statement by the usually accurate D. W. Bartlett[2] to the effect that the nomination for governor was offered Mr. Lincoln by the anti-Nebraska party in 1854, but he told his friends, "No, I am not the man. Bissell will make a better governor than I, and you can elect him on account of his Democratic antecedents"; and the writer adds: "So, giving to Bissell the flag it was universally desired that he, Lincoln, should bear," etc.

2. Journalist and travel writer David W. Bartlett (1828–1912) published a campaign biography, *The Life and Public Services of Hon. Abraham Lincoln* (Philadelphia: J. W. Bradley, 1860).

This is erroneous throughout. No candidate for governor was elected or spoken of in 1854, and Lincoln was not mentioned in any responsible way, if, indeed, in any way whatever, for the candidacy in 1856. In fact, no one but Bissell was mentioned, with any emphasis. It was well understood that the candidate must be of Democratic extraction, and Bissell was nominated by acclamation as soon as the temporary organization was effected. I notice another error where it should not be: viz., in Nicolay and Hay's "Lincoln," the distinguished authors name Judge Davis and Senator Trumbull as in attendance at the convention. Neither was. Senator Trumbull was in his seat in the Senate, and Judge Davis was holding court at Danville.]

Such was his political standing on the morning of May 29, 1856, as he and I ate our breakfast together at the residence of Judge Davis in Bloomington, but before night, he had been mentioned by a sage observer and responsible friend as a possible candidate for president, and the statement had been repeated to him by me, and was the germ which first was sown in his mind of hope for, and possibility of attaining, that proud position.

The genesis of the Republican party in Illinois, was as follows, it being also the genesis of Mr. Lincoln's advancement to the supreme headship of the nation: Paul Selby, editor of the *Morgan Journal*,[3] proposed a convention of free state editors on February 22, 1856, at Decatur, and the convention met in the parlors of the old Cassel House, there being about one dozen editors present. Mr. Lincoln was also in Decatur, and in consultation with the members of the convention. Resolutions were adopted in opposition to the extension of slavery, in favor of the restoration of the Missouri Compromise, and the restoration to Kansas and Nebraska of the legal guaranties against slavery of which they were deprived.

The convention also appointed a State Central Committee as follows: S. M. Church,[4] W. B. Ogden,[5] G. D. A. Parks,[6] T. J. Pickett,[7] E. A. Dudley,[8] William

---

3. Journalist and historian Paul Selby (1824–1913) of Jacksonville edited not only the *Morgan Journal* in that town but later moved to Springfield, where he edited the *Illinois State Journal* for many years.

4. S. M. Church of Rockport was a delegate to the Republican national convention in 1856.

5. Railroad promoter William B. Ogden (1805–1877) served as the first mayor of Chicago (1837–1838).

6. Attorney Gavion D. A. Parks (1817–1895) of Joliet served in the Illinois General Assembly in the 1850s.

7. Thomas J. Pickett (1821–1891) edited the Rock Island *Register*.

8. Edward Ambrose Dudley (1897–1879) of Quincy was a prosperous farmer and the leading Republican of Adams County.

Attainment of the Presidency

H. Herndon, R. J. Oglesby,[9] Joseph Gillespie, Gustavus Koerner,[10] and Ira O. Wilkinson.[11] And they recommended the holding of a State convention at Bloomington on May 29 succeeding, and requested the committee to make suitable arrangements. This was done, Koerner, Ogden, and Oglesby not acting with other members of the committee. And this Bloomington convention was of great practical and historical importance as laying the foundations of the Republican party, and as being the distinct starting point of Abraham Lincoln's race for the presidency.[12]

To this convention Lincoln had been made one of the delegates by Herndon, his partner, in his absence, and he attended. Many great politicians were there, among whom I may mention [John M.] Palmer (now U.S. Senator),[13] [Norman B.] Judd, [Burton] Cook,[14] [Ebenezer] Peck, [Orville H.] Browning, [Elihu] Washburne, [John] Farnsworth,[15] [John] Wentworth, [Ozias M.] Hatch,[16] [Jesse K.] Dubois, [Owen] Lovejoy,[17] Herndon, [Archibald] Williams, [T. Lyle] Dickey, and [Leonard] Swett.

By virtue of his political standing alone, Lincoln would not have figured as a leader, either of the convention or of the political moment then inaugurated. He had belonged to the minority party, and had always bestridden the losing horse in **all** political contests, except that he had been once elected

---

9. Richard J. Oglesby (1824–1899) of Decatur was an early backer of Lincoln and served as governor of Illinois for three terms after the Civil War.

10. Attorney Gustav Koerner (1809–1896) of Belleville served as lieutenant governor of Illinois (1853–1857) and was a close friend of Lincoln, who in 1862 appointed him minister to Spain.

11. Ira O. Wilkinson (1822–1894) was the presiding judge of the Rock Island circuit court.

12. Whitney described that convention in *Life on the Circuit with Lincoln*, 73–78.

13. John M. Palmer (1817–1900) was an anti-Nebraska Democrat who, as a member of the Illinois General Assembly, failed to vote for Lincoln for Senate in 1855 but supported him loyally thereafter. He represented Illinois in the U.S. Senate (1891–1897) and served as the state's governor (1869–1873).

14. Attorney Burton C. Cook (1819–1894) of Ottawa was an Illinois state senator who after the Civil War represented his district in the U.S. House of Representatives (1865–1871).

15. Attorney John F. Farnsworth (1820–1897) of St. Charles represented his district in the U.S. House of Representatives (1857–1861, 1863–1873).

16. Lincoln's friend Ozias Mather Hatch (1814–1893) of Pittsfield served as Illinois's secretary of state (1856–1864).

17. Abolitionist Owen Lovejoy (1811–1864) of Princeton was a Congregationalist minister who represented his Illinois district in the U.S. House of Representatives (1857–1864).

220   *Chapter XV*

to Congress, and even then his record was so unpopular that a Democrat was elected as his successor, although the district was a Whig one, as a rule. There were delegates in this convention who had achieved successful political careers, such as Wentworth and Washburne, who had had several terms in Congress, Washburne being a Representative at that time; Judd, who had represented Cook County in the State senate for sixteen years; and many others who controlled the local politics of their immediate localities. But by virtue of his recognized superior *ability*, Lincoln was accorded the post of honor in that convention.

Among human achievements which serve as pivots upon which great events turn, none is more potent than an utterance—a speech or a letter. **Many a poor wretch has been saved from the gallows by force of his advocate's speech on his behalf; other wretches have swung off at the gallows ultimately by the force of the prosecuting speech. Twenty-five years ago, nearly all the land in two entire counties in one of the new states was claimed by a powerful railway company, which claim the government allowed, and issued patents for; but a single speech of a young man, unknown to fame, inspired the settlers on those lands, who were adverse claimants, to maintain their claims, which they did, with ultimate success; and so the title to a scope of rich country large enough for a principality devolved upon the minute pivot of a single speech.**

In 1844, Henry Clay wrote a letter on the subject of the annexation of Texas; it cost him his election. The Mexican War would not have occurred had he been elected, and the whole policy of government would have been different. California, with its rich possibilities, would have remained a Mexican province.

James G. Blaine wrote some letters to one Mulligan of Boston;[18] their promulgation cost him the nomination for president in 1876 and cost him his election in 1884. He also was tempted while in Congress to make a satirical speech directed against Roscoe Conkling;[19] had that speech remained unsaid, he would have been president. **Although the silly and needless public use of three words by one [Samuel D.] Burchard, also cost him his election,**

---

18. James Mulligan was employed by Boston businessman Warren Fisher Jr., who received letters from Blaine indicating that Blaine had abused his power as speaker of the U.S. House of Representatives to promote the fortunes of a railroad. Mulligan had possession of the letters, which Blaine shared with the public in a failed effort to combat charges of corruption.

19. Roscoe Conkling (1829–1888) of Utica, New York, who represented his district in the U.S. House of Representatives (1859–1863), later served as a U.S. senator from New York (1867–1881).

Attainment of the Presidency

and his February election letter (1892) to [James S.] Clarkson[20] cost him the nomination in that year. What shrewd political philosophy there was in Martin Van Buren's remark that he "would rather walk twenty miles to see a man than to write him a letter!"

So, too, with single speeches. [James A.] Garfield's classic speech, in which he nominated John Sherman[21] for the presidency in 1880, caused himself to be selected as the candidate.

At the Bloomington convention I have referred to, Mr. Lincoln made the principal speech; and it was the *chef d'oeuvre* of the convention. That was the initial point of Lincoln's candidacy for the presidency. It segregated him from the political map, and placed him on the pinnacle of Illinois politics. In my "Life on the Circuit with Lincoln," I have given an elaborate account of Lincoln's relation to this convention[22] and which I may here supplement by a few notes.

One conspicuous matter is this, that while Lincoln did not, as a rule, betray enthusiasm under any stress of circumstances, he was in a state of enthusiasm and suppressed excitement throughout this convention; yet he kept his mental balance and was not swerved a hair's breadth from perfect equipoise in speech or action.

We were at Judge Davis' house, a half mile from the focus of political action, and thus out of the whirl of excitement: Archibald Williams and Judge **T. Lyle** Dickey were our companions, the former sleeping with Lincoln, and both were extremely conservative, and had great influence over Lincoln.

The public mind everywhere was in a feverish and excited condition, and this unwholesome condition was emphasized in the minds of the people's representatives assembled at this convention: Lawrence, Kansas, had just been attacked, and the "Free State Hotel" and two printing offices destroyed. Governor Robinson of Kansas[23] had been arrested without legal warrant in Missouri, his house sacked and fired, and himself chained out on the prairie, in default of a jail. Mr. Robinson and James S. Emery, a leading Free State man,[24] and Mrs. Robinson were at the Bloomington convention **arousing and intensifying**

20. James S. Clarkson (1842–1918) chaired the Republican National Committee (1891–1892).

21. John Sherman (1823–1900) represented Ohio in the U.S. Senate (1861–1877, 1881–1897).

22. Whitney, *Life on the Circuit with Lincoln*, 76–78.

23. Charles L. Robinson (1818–1894) served as governor of Kansas (1861–1863). He had been elected governor earlier by the Free State faction, which had no official authority.

24. Attorney James S. Emery of Lawrence (1826–1898) wrote for the *New York Times*.

the indignation. Governor Reeder,[25] who had just escaped from Kansas in disguise, was also there, and all three necessarily, and by design, aroused and excited the delegates' **deep feeling of indignation then already prevalent.** Charles Sumner had been beaten **into insensibility** by "Bully" Brooks[26] in the United States Senate, just one week previously, and was reported to be dying. Word had just come that Senator Trumbull had offered a resolution in the senate having for its aim the prevention of civil war and the restoration of peace in Kansas, which had been received with derision by Douglas and those of his political complexion. Lovejoy and the abolitionists were urging extreme measures and resolutions, which the Kansas colony fomented, and the street **and lobby** talk was all in the direction of **extreme** radicalism. While O. H. Browning was making an excellent speech in the convention, the crowd kept interrupting by calling for Lovejoy, and the former was obliged to yield the floor. The general sentiment was **ultra** radical.

In the seclusion and privacy of our temporary home, Lincoln, Williams, and Dickey discussed the situation earnestly, **and contemplated the jarring elements with deep and earnest solicitude,** all uniting in favor of conservative counsels, and they did more than all others combined in shaping the moderate and conservative course which was finally adopted by the convention. The general sentiment, undoubtedly, was in favor of [the] most radical expressions, but owing mainly to Lincoln's and Williams's monitions, a conservative course was adopted; and the following resolutions, among others, were adopted, chiefly upon Lincoln's suggestion:

> *Resolved*: That we hold, in accordance with the opinions and practices of all the great statesmen of all parties for the first sixty years of the administration of the government, that, under the Constitution, Congress possesses full power to prohibit slavery in the territories and that, while we will maintain all constitutional rights of the South, we also hold that justice, humanity, the principles of freedom as expressed in our Declaration of Independence and our National Constitution, and the purity and perpetuity of our government require that that power should be exerted to prevent the extension of slavery into territory heretofore free.

Lincoln put the situation to Judd and Peck in this way: "Your party is so mad at Douglas for wrecking his party that it will gulp down anything, but our (Whig) **folks are** fresh from Kentucky and **will** not be forced into radical measures; the abolitionists **must** go with us anyway, **they can do nothing else,** and your wing of the Democratic party the same, but the Whigs hold

25. Democrat Andrew H. Reeder (1807–1864) of Pennsylvania was the first governor of the Kansas Territory (1854–1855).

26. On May 22, 1856, Preston Brooks (1819–1857), who represented a South Carolina district in the U.S. House of Representatives (1853–1857), cudgeled Massachusetts Senator Charles Sumner badly with a cane.

the balance of power and will be hard to manage, anyway. Why," said he, "I had a hard time to hold Dubois when he found Lovejoy and [Ichabod] Codding[27] here; he insisted on going home at once."

Governor Reeder was quite a lion to the multitude but no lion to Lincoln. The latter, Williams, and myself were going to our rooms in the evening from the Pike House, and we passed a crowd listening to Reeder, in the Court House square. We listened but for a moment: "He can't overcome me," said Williams. "He would have to do a great deal to overcome my prejudice against him," responded Lincoln, as we all turned away. In fact, Lincoln did not meet Reeder at all. He was deeply prejudiced against him for some reason.

The Convention assembled at Major's Hall in the morning and organized temporarily by electing Archibald Williams as temporary Chairman, when on motion of Leander Munsell, of Edgar County,[28] William H. Bissell was nominated for Governor by acclamation. John M. Palmer was then designated as permanent Chairman, when he made profit of his Democracy thus: "I have always voted a straight Democratic ticket: I voted first for Matty Van [Buren]; then I voted for James K. Polk in 1844; then I voted for Lewis Cass in 1848; and in 1852—let me see" (said he humorously) "who I voted for in 1852."—(voices "Frank Pierce") "Well," (said he) "you may make the charge, but you can't get me to own it." The Committee on Resolutions was then appointed and we adjourned for dinner.

On reassembling, as intimated heretofore, there was a contest about the Resolutions: they were not radical enough for the abolitionists, and some violent speeches were made in opposition, but they were adopted as reported.

Then came the speeches, the first being by Orville H. Browning of Quincy; then came Owen Lovejoy; the next that I remember was Richard Yates; after him, came James S. Emery of Kansas, who made a most thrilling appeal, and then came the arch Enchanter, Abraham Lincoln, who made the most impassioned speech of his whole life.

The morning after the adjournment of the convention, as we came downtown to take the Springfield train, we met several delegates *en route* for the Illinois Central Railroad, and each one had to wring Lincoln's hand and say something complimentary of his speech of the day before. "Lincoln, I never swear," said William Hopkins of Grundy [County],[29] "but that was the damndest best speech I ever heard."

---

27. Abolitionist Ichabod Codding (1810–1866) of Chicago, a Congregational minister, was among the most active of all Illinois lecturers on both slavery and temperance.

28. Leander Munsell (1793–1862) built the Coles County courthouse (1836).

29. Attorney William T. Hopkins (b. 1819) of Morris was a Republican activist and a friend of Lincoln.

224   *Chapter XV*

Of that speech, John L. Scripps, Herndon, and myself each tried to take notes. I succeeded measurably; the others failed ignominiously. My notes are very imperfect, but I reproduce, as best I can, from those notes, the principal parts of that celebrated speech. **It does not do it justice, but is the best version now attainable.** [Elsewhere in the manuscript, Whitney wrote: **As soon as I reached Judge Davis's house, and in the presence of Lincoln, Williams and Dickey, who were discussing some of its features, I enlarged my notes. They are very imperfect, and some of the talk at Judge Davis's may have got entangled with it, but such as it is (and it is the best now attainable) I bestow it on the public, some of the exact language is that of Lincoln, also the general tenor of it, but most of the detail is necessarily mine. (I may state that I also have incorporated Judge Cunningham's recollections and thus improved it: while the Judge endorses my version in many particulars.)]**[30]

On June 17, after the Bloomington Convention, the first Republican national convention met in Philadelphia, and Lincoln polled 110 votes for vice president; and from that time onward, we who were close to him **(in the sanctum sanctorum of his confidence)**—Swett, Dubois, Herndon, Bill Jayne, J. O. Cunningham, and James Somers[31]—used to electioneer each other on his behalf, while politicians of steadier poise looked on askance, if not, indeed, amused.[32]

The first newspaper that mentioned him as a presidential possibility was the *Central Illinois Gazette,* published in Champaign, Ill., by J. W. Scroggs.[33] On May 4, 1859, it printed the following articles, the first in the local column, the second in the editorial. William O. Stoddard, Esq., afterward Lincoln's secretary to sign land patents, and later his biographer, wrote both articles, he being editor of the paper at the time.

30. See the Introduction above for a discussion of Whitney's highly suspect version of the speech.

31. James W. Somers (1833–1904) of Urbana, Illinois, law partner of his uncle, William D. Somers, was appointed by Lincoln to a post in the interior department.

32. "James H. Matheny, one of his life-long friends, has informed me that Lincoln's first real specific aspirations for the Presidency dated from the incident of his being named in the convention as a candidate for Vice-President, at that time, and it is certain, that, from thenceforth, all of Lincoln's energies and finesse were directed to its achievement." Whitney, *Life on the Circuit with Lincoln,* 81.

33. John W. Scroggs (1817–1874) was a physician who established the *Central Illinois Gazette* in 1858.

PERSONAL.[34]

Our Next President,—We had the pleasure of introducing to the hospitalities of our Sanctum, a few days ago, the Hon. Abraham Lincoln. Few men can make an hour pass away more agreeably. We do not pretend to know whether Mr. Lincoln will ever condescend to occupy the White House or not, but if he should, it is a comfort to know that he has established for himself a character and reputation of sufficient strength and purity to withstand the disreputable and corrupting influences of even that locality. No man in the West at the present time occupies a more enviable position before the people or stands a better chance for obtaining a high position among those to whose guidance our ship of state is to be entrusted.

WHO SHALL BE PRESIDENT?[35]

We have no sympathy with those politicians of any party who are giving themselves up to a corrupt and selfish race for the presidential chair, and are rather inclined to believe that the result will be a disappointment to the whole race of demagogues. The vastness of the interests depending on the political campaign now commencing, gives even a more than usual degree of interest to the question: "Who shall be the candidate?" Believing that a proper discussion of this question through the columns of the local papers is the true way to arrive at a wise conclusion, we propose to give our views, so far as formed, and we may add that we are well assured that the same views are entertained by the mass of the Republican party of Central Illinois.

In the first place, we do not consider it possible for the office of President of the United States to become the personal property of any particular politician, how great a man soever he may be esteemed by himself and his partisans. We therefore shall discuss the "candidate question" unbiased by personal prejudices or an undue appreciation of the claims of any political leader. We may add, with honest pride, an expression of our faith in the leading statesmen of our party, that neither Chase nor Seward nor [Nathaniel P.] Banks[36] nor any other whose name has been brought prominently before the people, will press individual aspirations at the expense of the great principles whose vindication is inseparably linked with our success. While no circumstances

---

34. *Central Illinois Gazette,* 4 May 1859.

35. *Central Illinois Gazette,* 7 December 1859.

36. Nathaniel Prentice Banks (1816–1894) of Waltham, Massachusetts, served as speaker of the U.S. House of Representatives (1856–1857) and governor of Massachusetts (1858–1861).

should be allowed to compel even a partial abandonment of principle, and defeat in the cause of right is infinitely better than a corrupt compromise with wrong, nevertheless, the truest wisdom for the Republican party in this campaign will be found in such a conservative and moderate course as shall secure the respect and consideration even of our enemies, and shall not forget National compacts within which we are acting and by which we are bound; and the proper recognition of this feature of the contest should be allowed its due influence in the selection of our standard bearer.

Although local prejudices ought always to be held subordinate to the issues of the contest, it will not be wise to overlook their importance in counting the probabilities of what will surely be a doubtful and bitterly contested battlefield. It is this consideration which has brought into so great prominence the leading Republican statesmen of Pennsylvania and Illinois. If these two states can be added to the number of those in which the party seems to possess an unassailable superiority, the day is ours. The same reasons to a less[er] extent, in exact proportion to its force in the electoral college, affect New Jersey.

From Pennsylvania and Illinois, therefore, the candidates for President and Vice President might with great propriety be chosen. It is true that our present Chief Magistrate is from Pennsylvania, and other States justly might urge that a proper apportionment of the National honors would not give her the presidency twice in succession; but, while there are several good precedents for such a course of action, there is one point which outweighs in importance all others, to-wit: *We must carry Pennsylvania in 1860*, and if we can best do it with one of our own citizens as standard-bearer, that fact cannot be disregarded with impunity. The delegation from the Keystone State will doubtless present this idea with great urgency in the National convention.

Aside from this, there are other points in favor of the two States mentioned, which cannot fail to carry great weight in the minds of all candid and reasonable men. They have both been distinguished for moderation and patriotism in the character of their statesmen, with as few exceptions as any other States. They are among that great central belt of States which constitute the stronghold of conservatism and Nationality. They are not looked upon as "sectional" in their character, even by the South. They, moreover, are, to a high degree, representative States. Where will our manufacturing, mining, and trading interests find a better representative than Pennsylvania? Or what State is more identified in all its fortunes with the great agricultural interests than is Illinois?

The States themselves, then, being open to no valid objection, we come to the question of individual candidates. Pennsylvania has not yet determined her choice from among her own great men, but as for Illinois it is the firm and fixed belief of our citizens that for one or the other of the offices in question, no man will be so sure to consolidate the party vote of this State, or will carry the great Mississippi Valley with a more irresistible rush of popular enthusiasm than our distinguished fellow citizen,

ABRAHAM LINCOLN.

We, in Illinois, know him well, in the best sense of the word, [as] *a true democrat*, a man of the people whose strongest friends and supporters are the hard-handed and strong-limbed laboring men, who hail him as a brother and who look upon him as one of their real representative men. A true friend of freedom, having already done important service for the cause, and proved his abundant ability for still greater service; yet a staunch conservative, whose enlarged and liberal mind descends to no narrow view, but sees both sides of every great question, and of whom we need not fear that fanaticism on the one side, or servility on the other, will lead him to the betrayal of any trust. We appeal to our brethren of the Republican press for the correctness of our assertions.

The next newspaper announcement was in the Aurora *Beacon*, published by John W. Ray,[37] on October 5, 1859, but no one knew how deep and earnest the feeling for him was till the sitting of the convention in 1860.[38]

The truth of history requires me to concede or aver that the proximate and superficial cause of Mr. Lincoln's nomination was adroit and astute political skill and management at the convention, but the ultimate and remote causes were discernable in Lincoln's own political genius, for the unembellished fact is that he was inspired either on May 29 or June 20, 1856, or thereabouts, to compete for this high exaltation, and he wrought this enduring structure of his fame mainly alone. Seward had hundreds of well-trained, astute political henchmen and lieutenants, but Lincoln's few adherents were those whose efforts were, in the main, muscular (running errands and the like) of whom I am proud to have been one.

Alone, he trod the paths of high intent.[39]

Herndon was almost his only mentor; Dubois and Bill Jayne constituted the "Committee of arrangements" in Springfield; Davis and Swett in Bloomington; Lamon and [Alexander Y.] Harrison in Vermilion,[40] etc. Most of them

37. Perhaps John William Ray (1829–1892), who was born in Sangamon County.

38. On November 10 and December 15, the *Beacon* also ran editorials praising Lincoln. Isaac N. Arnold, *History of Abraham Lincoln and the Overthrow of Slavery* (Chicago: Clarke & Co., 1866), 145.

39. "Although I trod the paths of high intent," in Percy Bysshe Shelley, dedication "To Mary [Woolstonecraft]" of "The Revolt of Islam" (1817).

40. Alexander Young Harrison (1821–1862) was killed at the Battle of Shiloh.

228   *Chapter XV*

worked *con amore*, chiefly from love of the man, his lofty moral tone, his pure political morality. In an essay entitled "The Presidential Nomination," appearing in my "Life on the Circuit with Lincoln," the details of how the nomination was directly achieved will be found by those who may be curious to know them.[41]

In the convention of May 29, 1856, Lincoln was, by common consent, placed at the head of the electoral ticket, and he entered actively into the campaign, making speeches in all parts of the State except in Egypt (the southern part of Illinois), **where it would not have been safe for him to present himself at that time.**

In 1858, a legislature was to be chosen in Illinois, upon which devolved the responsibility of choosing a senator to succeed to Douglas's then unexpired term. All eyes were turned to Lincoln as the Republican candidate (and in point of fact, the State convention indicated him by a most radical [i.e., unusual] resolution as "the first and only choice" for senator), and he could not do otherwise than accept the nomination. While, however, his political friends were training him for the senate, he was coaching himself for the presidency, two years thereafter. Disdaining the lesser distinction, and aiming at the greater one, he carefully prepared and read before the convention the celebrated *House-divided against itself* speech of June 16, 1858, which lost him the senatorship and gained him the presidency.

Herndon, who had approved of the speech before it was delivered, said in his bizarre and fantastic style: "*Of that speech, Lincoln instantly died.*" Swett said, "There were ten lines in that speech which killed Lincoln." The keynote of this speech was not suddenly achieved by Lincoln, for in a fugitive speech made during the canvass in 1856 he had enunciated it, and he no doubt would have made it prominent in that canvass had not Judge Dickey, who heard it, implored him to suppress it.[42]

Lincoln claimed no credit for originating the idea of his speech. On the contrary, he said at Cincinnati in 1859: "But neither I, nor Seward, nor [John] Hickman[43] is entitled to the enviable or **memorable** distinction of having first expressed the idea. The same idea was expressed by the Richmond *Enquirer* in 1856—quite two years before it was expressed by the first of us."[44]

41. Whitney, *Life On the Circuit with Lincoln*, 72–89.

42. In the manuscript there appears this passage: "on September 19, he adapted the sentiment in a speech, made also at Bloomington at a mass meeting held there. In deference, however, to the suggestion of Judge [T. Lyle] Dickey, he agreed to use it no further during the canvass."

43. Attorney John Hickman (1810–1875) of West Chester represented his Pennsylvania district in the U.S. House of Representatives (1855–1863).

44. Basler, *Collected Works of Lincoln*, 3:408.

Mr. Lincoln was a constant patron of the Richmond *Enquirer* and obtained his idea of the drift of popular sentiment in the South largely, if not, indeed, chiefly, from that organ. The following editorial article forcibly attracted his attention, the date being May 6, 1856:

"Social forms so widely differing as those of domestic slavery and (attempted) universal liberty cannot long co-exist in the great Republic of Christendom. They cannot be equally adapted to the wants and interests of society. The one form or the other must be very wrong, very ill-suited to promote the quiet, the peace, the happiness, the morality, the religion, and general well-being of communities. Disunion will not allay excitement and investigation, much less beget lasting peace. The war between the two systems rages everywhere and will continue to rage till the one conquers and the other is exterminated. If, with disunion, we could have the 'all and end of all' then the inducement would be strong to attempt it. But such a measure would but inspire our European and American adversaries with additional zeal."

[Whitney footnote: Roger A. Pryor was then editor of the *Enquirer* and probably wrote the article.[45] Lincoln told me that at the Charleston Convention which met at about this time, Pryor obtained his first concrete acquaintance with the Northern Democracy, and that he was perfectly shocked and dismayed at the exhibition. Lincoln said that Pryor was socially a polished gentleman, and that he looked on aghast at the low, profane, and whiskey-drinking crowds that poured out of the Northern cities as convention delegates. I suppose he must have given vent to his feeling of disgust in his columns, and that Lincoln got his ideas there. This would be more probable from the fact that Pryor and his adherents detested the candidate of these Northern "bummers."]

Lincoln read his speech to a little coterie of his friends in advance of its delivery, and Herndon predicted: "Lincoln, deliver that speech, as read, and it will make you president." It was the leaven hid in public opinion, and ultimately it leavened the whole lump; it was bread cast upon the waters to be gathered after many days. Lincoln himself said, "This thing has been retarded long enough. The time has come when these sentiments should be uttered, and if it is decreed that I should go down because of this speech, then let me go down, linked to the truth, let me die in the advocacy of what is just and right." Yet none but Herndon approved of it in advance, and he, chiefly from his belief in the unerring wisdom of Lincoln. Dubois bluntly told Lincoln, in [the] presence of his inner circle of friends, that "*it was a damned fool speech.*" But had Lincoln not made it, he never would have been president. It was a

---

45. Journalist Roger Atkinson Pryor (1828–1919), a fervent secessionist, joined the staff of the Richmond *Enquirer* in 1854 and represented his Virginia district in the U.S. House of Representatives (1859–1861).

"word spoken in season,"[46] and it constituted the turning point in his career. With an astuteness and a political divination superior to all of his fellows, he foresaw the political future and firmly declared, "If I had to draw a pen across my record, and erase my whole life from remembrance, and I had one choice allowed me what I might save from the wreck, I should choose that speech, and leave it to the world just as it is."[47]

The political situation in Illinois was not satisfactory to any class except the discredited politicians who had nothing to lose and everything to gain by [the] abnormal conditions of politics. Judge Douglas had found that the disaffection in the ranks of the Democracy by reason of the enactment of the Nebraska Bill was more than a revolt—that it was, in fact, a radical revolution; and when the administration determined to force Kansas into the Union under the Lecompton Constitution, he made haste to retrieve his past error, and ally himself to the Northern political protestants against the growing aggressions of the awful slave power. This was extremely dangerous ground for even so wily and versatile a politician to assume, for he could hardly hope to retain his standing with the Southern school of politicians if he wavered at all on the slavery question. The condition, however, was desperate; he had lost control of Illinois and must devise some means to regain it, if he would remain in politics, for a legislature was to be chosen in 1858 which was to choose a senator in his place. If he could not succeed himself, his prestige would be gone forever. He must, therefore, recover some at least of the lost ground at home, even at the hazard of losing in the great arena of the whole nation. He therefore placed himself in the field as an avowed candidate for his own succession, and his shibboleth was "Anti-Lecompton."

This was an adroit and wise course and barely succeeded, and that in an entirely unexpected and novel way, for he gained as advocates of his cause, among others, Horace Greeley and John J. Crittenden, both of whom urged his re-election to the senate. The influence of these distinguished men can only be known by an understanding of our local politics, which may be thus stated in general terms: the northern part of the State was peopled by immigrants from the Northern States, which gave a decided "anti-slavery" cast to the politics there. On the contrary, the southern part of the State was peopled by immigrants from Virginia, Kentucky, and Tennessee, whose prejudices and predilections were favorable to the "peculiar institution" and were likewise Democratic in their party affiliations.

But in the center of the State there were several legislative districts, the substratum of whose population was of the "Henry Clay" Whig school of politics, who hated **the** Democracy, with all that the term implied, with

46. Proverbs 15:23.
47. Herndon and Weik, *Herndon's Lincoln,* 400.

religious zeal, but who despised abolitionism in all of its manifestations and modifications, with no less fervor.

The contest promised to be close in the legislature by reason of the fact that since the apportionment of the State into legislative districts in 1850, the southern part of the state had not improved in an equal ratio and consequence with the northern portion, and hence a large numerical majority might be obtained for the Republicans, and yet the legislature be Democratic. The political complexion of most of the districts was in no wise doubtful, but the old Whig districts were extremely so. Ordinarily, they would have sustained the candidates of the Republican party, who would have supported Mr. Lincoln, but in doing so they would be acting in harmony with Lovejoy, Codding, Farnsworth, and the "anti-slavery" cohorts whom their souls abhorred. And Greeley, who had been their political mentor in the era of the Whig party, urged them with the frantic and uncompromising zeal so characteristic of him to support Douglas. Joined to this powerful influence, the Douglas adherents left no means unexhausted to convince them that the tendencies of the Republican party were to the unconditional abolition of slavery and the inundation of the whole nation with free negroes; while to cap all, a letter from John J. Crittenden to T. Lyle Dickey strongly favoring Douglas was published clandestinely and without previous warning in these doubtful districts just on the eve of election and before its views could be counteracted. These several elements elected Douglas, and in my judgment Governor Crittenden's letter was the dominating influence in the election and controlled the result. **It is very lame**, its electioneering tone is plain, **and I may say that Gov. Crittenden was given to volunteering his services intrusively.**

> Frankfort August 1, 1858
> My Dear Sir:
> I read, some days ago, your letter of the 19th of last month, in which you state the substance of a conversation between us in relation to Judge Douglas, said to have taken place in April last at the City of Washington. You ask if your statement is correct and you ask my permission to speak of it privately and publicly as occasion may prompt you. I remember the conversation to which you allude and the substance of it: it occurred at Washington during the last session of Congress, and most probably in April. Your statement of that conversation corresponds substantially with my recollection of it. As you state in your letter I did, in that conversation, speak of Senator Douglas in high and warm terms. I said that the people of Illinois little knew how much they really owed him. That he had the courage and patriotism to take a high, elevated, just, and independent position on the Lecompton question at the sacrifice of interesting social relations, as well as old party ties, and in defiance of the power and patronage of an angry administration

supported by a dominant party disbursing a revenue of some $86,000,000 a year; that for this noble conduct, he had been almost overwhelmed with denunciation; that the attacks made upon him in the debate in the senate were frequent, personal, and fierce; that throughout the entire session, he must have felt the consciousness that he was in daily danger of being so assailed in debate as to force him into altercations and quarrels that might, in their consequence, involve the loss of honor or of life. Notwithstanding all this, he had kept his course firmly and steadily throughout the whole struggle, and had borne himself *gallantly*. I thought there was a heroism in his course calling not only for approbation but for applause.

In the above statement, I have rather confined myself to those particulars of our conversation suggested by your letter, than attempted to detail the whole of it. The above, however, contains the substance of what passed, and whatever else was said in accordance with it. This conversation with you, sir, formed but a part of many others of a like character which I held on the same subject. I often expressed my high opinions of that conduct of Judge Douglas on the "Lecompton" question. I expressed it frequently, fully, and openly, and was careless **with** who might hear or who might repeat it. Under the circumstances I do not feel that it would become me to object, or that, indeed, I have any right to object to your repeating our conversation when I have, myself, so freely and so publicly declared the whole substance of it. I have thus answered your letter as I felt myself bound to do. I must add, however, that I do not wish to be an officious intermeddler in your election, or even to appear to be so. I therefore hope and request that when you have occasion to speak on the subject of this letter, you will do me the justice to explain and to acquit me of any such voluntary intermeddling or of the presumption of seeking to obtrude myself or my sentiments upon the attention of the people of Illinois. I am, sir, with great respect

J. J. Crittenden.

T. Lyle Dickey, Esq.

I note that Mr. Lincoln, **acting from his point of view without reference to me, had the same idea that I had, for he** wrote **thus** to Gov. Crittenden on the day after the election: "The emotions of defeat in which I felt more than a merely selfish interest and to which defeat the use of your name contributed largely are fresh upon me" etc.[48]

I may say further, that after the defection of Judge Douglas from the Democratic party, on account of Lecomptonism, the administration of James Buchanan acted with extreme unwisdom in making an unrelenting war upon Douglas and his friends in Illinois. A strict list was made, and all office holders who adhered to the recalcitrant senator were summarily decapitated and their places filled as a rule by political adventurers without character or standing in the party. The war was even so relentless as to embrace the

48. Basler, *Collected Works of Lincoln*, 3:335–36.

establishment of an ultra-Democratic organ in Chicago to assail Douglas, and even the acquisition of the control of the senator's own organ, likewise to break him down. These schemes, like spitting against the wind, resulted in their authors' discomfiture; the adherents to the "Buchanan" Democracy in Illinois were not so numerous as the accessions which Douglas made from the temporary opposition, chiefly by reason of this unjust warfare upon him for a stand made by him on principle. So Buchanan's efforts, like those of Greeley, for a different reason, aided in the reelection of Douglas.

But the partisans of Douglas were not only sedulous to return him to the senate but likewise to make him the general candidate of the anti-extension-of-slavery party for the presidency. This callow design was broached tentatively in Illinois and elsewhere and gained auditors in unexpected quarters; even my deeply lamented friend, Swett, listened to the voice of the siren, and he and I had a heated discussion about it. Governor Bissell and Jesse O. Norton,[49] in my presence, in January 1859, at the Executive Mansion in Springfield, mutually prophesied that Douglas would be elected president in the succeeding year, partly by Republican votes. This political ghost of the future disturbed Mr. Lincoln very much in 1859. He was then predestined as the candidate of his own State and he viewed with alarm the evidence of the setting of the political tide toward Douglas; Lincoln talked with me about it, and I have heard him talk to others about it, more than once, always with self-deprecation, but likewise always earnestly. But the people remained true to their party allegiance, and while Douglas by an accident retained his technical place in politics, his party remained out of power thereafter for nearly forty years.

I here annex a personal letter from Mr. Lincoln to Governor Chase on the above subject, which shows his opinion of the close straits our party was in in the year 1859.

> Springfield, Ill., April 30, 1859.
> The Hon. S. P. Chase:
> Dear Sir:
> Reaching home yesterday I found your kind note of the 14th, informing me that you have given Mr. Whitney the appointment **he** desired; and also mentioning the present encouraging aspects of the Republican cause and our Illinois canvass of last year. I thank you for the appointment. Allow me also to thank you as being one of the very few distinguished men whose sympathy we in Illinois did receive last year, of all those whose sympathy we thought we had reason to expect.

---

49. Attorney Jesse Olds Norton (1812–1875) of Joliet represented his district in the U.S. House of Representatives (1853–1857, 1863–1865).

234   *Chapter XV*

Of course I would have preferred success; but, failing in that, I have no regrets for having rejected all advice to the contrary and resolutely made the struggle. Had we thrown ourselves into the arms of Douglas, as re-electing him by our votes would have done, the Republican cause would have been annihilated in Illinois and, as I think, demoralized and prostrated everywhere for years, if not forever. As it is, in the language of [Thomas Hart] Benton,[50] "we are clean," and the Republican star gradually rises higher everywhere.[51]

It chanced that Douglas returned to Chicago on July 9, 1858, to take up his canvass for the senate and that Lincoln was there to argue a motion before Judge [Thomas] Drummond, and that he attended and listened to Douglas's harangue at that time. At the request of his Republican friends in the city, he replied the succeeding night.

Just one week later Mr. Lincoln made a speech at his own home in the same tenor.

Mr. Lincoln had with some difficulty induced Douglas to hold a joint debate with him in seven different places in the State, and the first of these joint debates took place at Ottawa on August 21, at which Douglas opened the debate, ***ex abruptio,*** with a violent attack on Lincoln.[52]

It is scarcely necessary to say that there was not one word of truth in Douglas's charges, but the distinguished orator evidently acted on the assumption that "a lie will travel forty leagues before truth gets on its boots." Lincoln kept his temper and made a dignified and conclusive answer. (I may say that I had the honor to be Lincoln's *compagnon de voyage* on this occasion.)

The next debate was at Freeport, August 27, and was made memorable by reason of the trap which Lincoln baited with temporary expediency and caught Douglas's chance of the presidency. It occurred thus: at Ottawa, Douglas had propounded to his competitor a string of not well-considered questions, easy to answer, and which Lincoln cautiously took time to answer, and then turned the tables by demanding "a Roland for an Oliver [tit for tat]."

Lincoln's answers demonstrate conclusively that he was looking beyond the senatorship, for he so answered as to lose votes in that canvass. In fact, he was then in an "Abolition" belt, and his answers were not at all satisfactory

50. Thomas Hart Benton (1782–1858) represented Missouri in the U.S. Senate (1821–1851).

51. Basler, *Collected Works of Lincoln*, 3:378.

52. Whitney footnote: The Chicago *Tribune* thus exhibited the style of Douglas during the debate: "He howled, he ranted, he bellowed, he pawed dirt, he shook his head, he turned livid in the face, he struck his right hand with his left, he foamed at the mouth, he anathematized, he cursed, he exulted, he domineered—he played Douglas."

Attainment of the Presidency

to that element. In his counter questions, however, he compelled Douglas to assert the doctrine of "unfriendly legislation," viz., that by police regulations the States could render the national enforcement of the Dred Scott decision inoperative.

That answer crushed all the life there was out of the Douglas boom for the presidency. When Congress met, the South put [Judah P.] Benjamin, of Louisiana, forward as their spokesman to serve notice on Douglas that he was "not in it" any more as a presidential candidate with any show of success or of getting the Southern vote.

Lincoln summed up Douglas's position as follows: "The Judge holds that a thing may be lawfully driven away from a place where it has a lawful right to be."

At the Brewster House in Freeport, just before the second debate, Lincoln read to Washburne, Uncle Sam Hitt,[53] Tom Turner, Judd, and two or three others, the question he was going to spring on Douglas. Washburne advised against it. Said he: "Douglas will hold that, notwithstanding the Dred Scott decision, the people can exclude slavery. You give him the chance and he'll beat you on it."

"All right," said Lincoln, "then that kills him in 1860, and that canvass is worth a hundred of this. I'm playing for larger game."[54]

It turned out exactly as he said, attesting the wonderful political prescience of Lincoln.

I was also with Lincoln at Jonesboro in September 15th, and the crowd derived great amusement from this little episode which was even more dramatic than is here described. Douglas said at Joliet, speaking of Lincoln, that at Ottawa he "made him tremble in the knees so that he had to be carried from the platform. He laid up some days" &c.

Lincoln **"There was not a word of truth in it."**

Douglas **"Didn't they carry you off?"**

Lincoln **"There, that question illustrates the character of this man Douglas exactly. He says, 'Didn't they carry you off?' . . . Yes, they did. But Judge Douglas, why didn't you tell the truth? And then again: 'He laid up for some days.' He puts that in print for people of the country to**

---

53. Samuel Merritt Hitt (1799–1859) of Mt. Morris was a pioneer settler of Ogle County.

54. Whitney's contention that Lincoln in 1858 knowingly sacrificed his chances to win the senatorship in order to improve his chances of winning the presidency in 1860 is groundless. As Don E. Fehrenbacher observed, "Not only evidence, but logic is against the view that Lincoln deliberately courted defeat in order to deprive Douglas of Southern support for the presidency." Fehrenbacher, "Lincoln, Douglas, and the 'Freeport Question,'" *American Historical Review* 66 (1961): 603.

read as a serious document. . . . I don't want to call him a *liar*, but . . . I don't know what else to call him, if I must tell the truth."[55] **(All there was of this episode at Ottawa is this: Lincoln's friends were so enthusiastic over his speech that they forcibly shouldered him and carried him off the ground, to Lincoln's great disgust.)**

As Lincoln & I went north *en route* to the fourth debate, to occur at Charleston on September 18, he informed me of a plan of attack he was going to spring upon the Little Giant, which was to charge him with adopting the [Robert] Toombs bill, which would not allow a vote on the Lecompton Constitution, Douglas's especial pride and boast being the allowance of a popular vote—popular sovereignty, as he termed it. Douglas's very tame performance there attests the surprise he felt at the shrewd attack.

The remaining debates were held at Galesburg, October 7; Quincy, October 13; and Alton, October 15. Lincoln was successful in securing the popular majority, but, owing to a gerrymandered apportionment, Douglas was elected to the senate to be his own successor. **To me, on the day of Douglas's election to the senate, he said bitterly: "I can't help it, and I expect everybody to leave me." As Emerson says, "Greatness always appeals to the future."**[56]

The joint debates, nevertheless, gave Lincoln a national reputation, and he **was in demand, and** began to get invitations to visit other States. During the ensuing winter, he visited Kansas and was received with "open arms." At Leavenworth, he came like a conqueror; he never had received such an ovation as that before. The whole city joined in the welcome, flags and banners waved, all windows, balconies, and sidewalks were filled with interested humanity, a procession was formed, and he, the central figure in it, was escorted to the hotel amid the loud acclaim of the masses. During that fall, George E. Pugh[57] was run by the Democrats of Ohio for Governor, his competitor being David Tod, and Douglas went there to help Pugh. The Republicans sent for Lincoln, and he spoke at Columbus and Cincinnati. His speeches on those occasions were among the very best speeches he ever made.[58]

In October, 1859, he received an invitation from the Young Men's Republican Association of Brooklyn to deliver an address in Plymouth Church. This he accepted, indicating politics as his theme, and February 27, 1860, as the date. Throughout the winter he made most elaborate preparations, obtaining

---

55. Basler, *Collected Works of Lincoln*, 3:135.

56. Emerson, "Self Reliance."

57. George E. Pugh (1822–1876) represented Ohio in the U.S. Senate (1855–1861).

58. *In the Name of the People: Speeches and Writings of Lincoln and Douglas in the Ohio Campaign of 1859,* ed. Harry V. Jaffa and Robert W. Johannsen (Columbus: Ohio State University Press, 1959).

his facts from "Elliot's Debates,"[59] and writing out the speech in full. Reaching New York on February 25, he found that he had builded his fame better than he knew; that the leading Republican politicians were on the *qui vive* to hear him; and that to cater to this demand the place of the speaking had been changed to Cooper Institute in New York City. When he appeared in this hall of so many stirring memories, he found it packed **full**, standing room being at a premium. The great platform was full of the most renowned Republican political leaders in New York and Brooklyn. After an introduction by the venerable William Cullen Bryant,[60] in fit and complimentary terms, Lincoln delivered his address, the most **ornate and recondite** political speech made during the pro-slavery debate.[61]

This great speech is worthy of study. It was the last elaborate speech he ever made. In it he departed somewhat from his former style. The close political student will notice a system, formalism, precision, and rigidity of logic not apparent in former speeches; a terseness and vigor of language of greater emphasis than was before known; an absolute pruning of all redundancies, both in thought and in expression, **not a redundant word, not a dislocated or irrelevant sentence.** It was a massive structure of unhewn logic, without an interstice or flaw. Singular to say, the style, in some places, is almost precisely that of John C. Calhoun, yet the speech bears the same relation to the slavery issue, as it then presented itself, that Webster's reply to [Robert] Hayne bore to "the Constitution and the Union" in 1830. It was a dignified, stately, solemn declaration of the concrete principles of liberty as they existed in the minds of the American people and as they would be enforced by them at the first opportunity.

It was a genuine revelation and surprise. The conservative *Evening Post* published the speech entire the next day by express order of its venerable editor [William Cullen Bryant], whose warmest commendation Lincoln also received. The entire press of the city eulogized it in the highest terms. On the last day of winter in 1860, Mr. Lincoln awoke to find himself famous; on the first day of winter in 1861, he was president elect of this mighty nation.

I can hardly portray the exhibition which Mr. Lincoln made of himself on the occasion of this trip. Knowing that he would be on dress parade, he went to a clothing store in Springfield before he started and procured a brand new

---

59. Jonathan Elliot, ed., *The Debates in the Several State Conventions on the Adoption of the Federal Constitution* (Washington: Printed by and for the editor, 1836).

60. William Cullen Bryant (1794–1878), an eminent poet, edited the New York *Evening Post*.

61. Basler, *Collected Works of Lincoln*, 3:522–50.

238   *Chapter XV*

suit of ready-made clothes. Of course, they did not fit him—no ready-made suit ever did **fit him**—so, in order to make the trousers appear long enough, they were loosely braced, with the result of bagginess about the waist and thighs. In order that the waist of the coat should be near the right place, a garment was chosen in which the tails were too short, and the rest of it was too full. **Then he bought a new valise, and had this suit packed in it, and when the horse arrived for him to go to the hall, he took out his new store clothes and put them on for the first time, and then he noticed that the creases showed to disadvantage, which** made even Lincoln feel ill at ease, for the audience on the platform contained the *elite* of New York politicians, dressed in the most genteel fashion, **while he was fully conscious of the raw appearance presented by himself**.

Lincoln was more embarrassed at the commencement than ever before on a like occasion, yet being satisfied himself with his speech, and seeing as he progressed that his audience was also satisfied, he was very soon "on his native heath." However much of rusticity there was in his appearance, there was no flavor of the camp or backwoods in his performance, and his auditory entirely forgot the homeliness of the orator in the charm of the oration.

After the meeting was over, Mr. Lincoln was introduced to a great many of the leading men and had quite an ovation. His timidity and embarrassment about his clothes had worn off and he was as "free and easy" as he would have been in an Illinois crowd. The Atheneum Club invited him to its rooms, where they had a fine supper spread, and Lincoln was the lion of the hour. There was no formality, but there was indeed "a feast of reason and flow of soul"[62] which lasted till the "wee sma' hours."

Mr. Lincoln was perfectly at home. He "tauld his queerest stories"[63] with the result that the solemn walls of the club had never before echoed to such hilarity, and when the party broke up, and two gentlemen escorted Lincoln to the Astor House, every one of the party was pleased with himself and with all mankind, **and as for Lincoln,**

> **Kings may be blest, but he was glorious,**
> **O'er all the ills of life victorious**[64]

for the time being, and not with distilled, but with spontaneous, enthusiasm.

62. Robert Burns, "Tam o' Shanter."
63. Burns, "Tam o' Shanter."
64. Burns, "Tam o' Shanter."
   "Kings may be blest,
   But Tam was glorious
   O'er a' the ills o' life victorious."

Attainment of the Presidency

Lincoln was not a Stoic, neither was he an Epicurean, but he *was* human, and on this occasion he acted on the adage, "when you have a good thing keep it." Consequently, this time he remained in the city for several days, seeing it in a judicious, moral way.

Invitations came from many parts of New England to him to stop in their towns and cities and address them. It was known that he was to visit Exeter [New Hampshire], where his son Robert was attending Phillips [Exeter] Academy, and he started on his tour of New England conquest. On March 5, he was at Hartford and was escorted to the city hall by the first company that had been organized of "Wide Awakes," those marching bands that played a conspicuous part in the campaign of that fall all over the country.

Next day, some of the leading citizens formed a committee of escort and showed him all over the city. That evening he spoke at New Haven to an immense audience. Next evening he spoke at Meriden; at Woonsocket, R.I. on March 7; at Norwich, Connecticut, March 8; and at Bridgeport March 10. He met with a continued ovation everywhere. His success was extraordinary, the sledgehammer logic of the Illinois prairies wonderfully pleasing his audience.

At New Haven, the professor of rhetoric at Yale College attended his speech and gave a lecture on its rhetorical style the next day to his class. That evening, taking the train for Meriden, he heard him the ensuing night, for the same purpose. Lincoln was informed of this and was very much astonished at it. Having visited his son, he turned homeward, remaining over Sunday at New York, where he heard [Henry Ward] Beecher[65] preach for the second time that trip.

Then he returned to Springfield, having been absent four weeks. He was perfectly satisfied with his trip, there not having been a single *contretemps* or error in it; it was an unmistakable conqueror's march.

The public man who builds up a career while in official position has infinite advantages over the unofficial one. The former can impress his principles upon laws and measures of legislation, can make himself concretely felt, and of actual use and acquire popularity by deeds. He can also speak in a greater or lesser degree *ex cathedra* with the voice of authority, and gain listening ears. He has access to archives and bureaus and documents, and his utterances, however vapid, will command respect and attention. "Hear me for my cause,"[66] he can say.

65. Henry Ward Beecher (1813–1887) was the eminent pastor of the Plymouth Church in Brooklyn, New York.

66. "Romans, countrymen, and lovers, hear me for my cause, and be silent that you may hear." Shakespeare, *Julius Caesar*, III.2.

The unofficial man **appears in a vast throng, on the level plains of mediocrity; he** must be of exceptional intellectual altitude to tower above his fellows. His voice must have a mighty diapason to be heard above the din. He must be a giant indeed if from his lowly position he can compete with the officially favored. Mr. Seward had been in official position for many years, had been, as it were, the official head of the Republican party, its guide, counselor, and friend. He was the idol of the Empire State and almost equally the idol of New England. His volubility and classicity of speech and profundity of argument were wonderful, and he was a leader of men. His political conscience was pliable and elastic. His principles were indeed bounded, but the corner posts were a great ways apart. He was versatile and prolific of political *finesse*, and also of intrigue. Lincoln was guileless in the lower realms of politics, where Seward was matchless; but in the highest realms, Lincoln brooked no rival. And he had, by unaccredited and independent labors on the hustings, within three years placed himself on a conventional equality with Seward, with the latter's many years of training, with all the auxiliaries of a regency, his countless political friends and sycophants **whose name was legion**. In the whole nation, Seward had barely one "foeman worthy of his steel": it was *Abraham Lincoln*.

At this time the political outlook was cheering for the Republican party. Douglas had been read out of the Southern wing of the Democratic party for the heresy which Lincoln had forced him to **proclaim** at Freeport. As he was the only exponent of his peculiar Democracy among the Democratic hosts at the North, it was **therefore** obvious to even the superficial observer that if that convention nominated Douglas, the South would bolt and set up a candidate of their own; and that if the convention nominated any other than Douglas, especially if it did the bidding of the pro-slavery leaders, there would be no enthusiasm at the North, and the nominee of the Republicans would carry most of the Northern States. In short, no man but Douglas could hope to carry any of the Northern States; and it was apparent that Douglas could not carry any of the Southern States unless it might be one or two of the border States.

Norman B. Judd was the member of the Republican National Committee from Illinois. He was a sly, crafty, shrewd politician. While the Eastern members were assuming as a postulate and foregone conclusion that Seward's nomination was an accomplished fact, Judd's artful eye saw behind the gossamer veil of their assurance a chance for Lincoln, and he commenced his plans far ahead to achieve his nomination. Judd was also a candidate for the gubernatorial nomination in Illinois and hoped that he might achieve both his nomination and Lincoln's. Prior to 1860, all conventions had been held in the East, Baltimore being the great convention city. In fact, nearly

Attainment of the Presidency

all the conventions had theretofore been held there. [William Henry] Harrison, however, had been nominated at Harrisburg, and [John C.] Fremont at Philadelphia. So Judd made the novel proposition in the committee that the convention should be held at Chicago. He argued that the Democrats had departed from the ancient custom of meeting at Baltimore and were to meet at Charleston; now, argued he, let us follow their example and meet in a region where we can make proselytes by the respect we pay to that region. He carefully kept "Old Abe" out of sight, and the delegates failed to see any personal bearing the place of meeting was to have on the nomination. Judd carried his point. He was a railway lawyer and he approached the various railway companies whose lines were in Illinois and persuaded them to make very cheap rates of fare to Chicago during the convention week. **And the result was apparent when the convention met.**

On May 10, the state convention met at Decatur and, selecting delegates to the Chicago convention, instructed them to support Lincoln for the presidency. Judd was defeated for the nomination for governor but was elected as a delegate at large to the convention and chairman of the delegation. The convention met in Chicago on May 16. The railroads had made a cheap excursion rate from all parts of the State, and the city was filled to repletion with Illinoisans, all brimful of enthusiasm for the railsplitter candidate. The Seward *claque* was on hand, too, but not in such force. This was in every way a notable convention. Not until the middle of April was it definitely decided in what hall it should be held. The largest hall of the city was the Metropolitan, at the corner of Randolph and La Salle Streets, and it was expected that the convention would be held there. In March preceding, Mr. Lincoln and I attended an entertainment in that hall and we then talked of the possible scenes to be witnessed there two months later.

But sagacity ruled the hour. An immense crowd would be in the city ready to shout for *Uncle Abe*, and this hall would not contain a tithe of them.

In the early days of Chicago, one of the chief hotels had been the Sauganash, kept by Alderman John Murphy and located at the southeast corner of Market and Lake Streets. **When John Wentworth emigrated west and reached Chicago after a forty mile walk, tired and dusty, he stopped at the Sauganash. A similar experience awaited other architects of Chicago's fortunes, but** the Sauganash had gone the way of all sublunary things and fallen into desuetude, **decay, and dissolution, and** at the time of which I write no structure was left **there at all, but** the site where it had been was low, covered with stagnant water and varied by the appearance of sundry tin cans, hoop skirts, **having no utility except bright reminiscences**, dead cats, and other *debris* attendant upon civic progress. The Market Street front presented a wide expanse **of space**, ample enough to accommodate any probable

242   *Chapter XV*

overflow from a convention hall, **if one should be there erected**. The site was at once secured **after its utility was recognized**, and a two story frame structure erected which was, with no apparent sense or propriety, termed "The Wigwam." The Tremont House, four blocks east, was chosen as the headquarters of the Lincoln coterie, while the Richmond House was the headquarters of the Seward contingent. Right opposite the Tremont House the *Journal*, the evening Republican paper of the city, had its office, which was gay with banners, among which was one with the name *Seward*, **which Mr. Lincoln's men didn't think was a very handsome thing for a Chicago newspaper to foster at that time.**

David Davis, Stephen T. Logan, Leonard Swett, and Jesse K. Dubois were the leaders of the Lincoln forces, and they opened headquarters **at the Tremont House** with a very feeble prospect in view, as things then appeared. The house was mainly filled with the Seward contingent, finely appearing and eminently talented men with national reputations **and also men**

> **"fit for treasons, stratagems and spoils,"**[67]

the leader **of whom** was he of the Mephisphelean visage, Thurlow Weed. There were George William Curtis,[68] William M. Evarts,[69] William Curtis Noyes,[70] Joshua R. Giddings, Horace Greeley, David K. Cartter,[71] John A. Andrew,[72] Austin Blair,[73] Carl Schurz,[74] Caleb B. Smith,[75] Richard Yates, Ozias

---

67. Shakespeare, *The Merchant of Venice*, V:1.

68. George William Curtis (1824–1892) of Staten Island, New York, was a writer and public intellectual who helped found the Republican party.

69. Attorney William Maxwell Evarts (1818–1901) of New York was a prominent Republican who eventually became attorney general, secretary of state, and a U.S. senator.

70. William Curtis Noyes (1805–1864) of New York was one of that city's most powerful lawyers.

71. Attorney David Kellogg Cartter (1812–1887) of Massillon, Ohio, represented his district in the U.S. House of Representatives (1845–1853) and was appointed by Lincoln as minister to Bolivia in 1861.

72. John A. Andrew (1818–1867) of Massachusetts served as governor of his state during the Civil War.

73. Abolitionist Austin Blair (1818–1894) of Michigan helped found the Republican Party and served as his state's governor during the Civil War.

74. Carl Schurz (1829–1906) of Wisconsin was the country's most prominent German-American antislavery champion.

75. Caleb Blood Smith (1808–1864) represented an Indiana district in the U.S. House of Representatives (1842–1849) and served as Lincoln's secretary of the interior (1861–1862).

Attainment of the Presidency

M. Hatch, George Ashmun, William D. Kelley,[76] Edwin D. Morgan,[77] David Wilmot, George S. Boutwell,[78] Frank P. Blair Sr.,[79] John A. Kasson,[80] William T. Otto,[81] Amos Tuck,[82] Andrew Reeder, Thomas Corwin, Columbus Delano[83]—all of national renown. Even the *Times*, the Douglas organ, was forced to admit that it was a remarkably fine looking body of men.

All was bustle and excitement, but everything was done with good nature. The original candidates were William H. Seward, Abraham Lincoln, Edward Bates, John McLean—old line Whigs; and Simon Cameron, Benjamin F. Wade, Salmon P. Chase, and Nathanial P. Banks—old line Democrats. It became early apparent that the struggle would be between the two first named, and, in point of fact, Banks and Wade were dropped out of consideration before the convention met, which still left two Ohio men in the contest, McLean and Chase. Greeley was not an accredited delegate from his own State, but, as Oregon was then a great way off, the party there had delegated Greeley to appear for them, which he did. His efforts were in favor of "anybody to beat Seward," and, considering Edward Bates of Missouri as the one best fitted to do it, he worked with the Blairs and with Maryland and Missouri to achieve that end. Yet on the day the convention met, his paper published a telegram from him saying, "My conclusion, from all that I can gather, is that the opposition to Governor Seward cannot concentrate on any candidate, and that he will be nominated."

Greeley, at that time, was a pariah among the delegates. On the Sunday morning before the convention, I met him in Clark Street coming from the

76. William D. "Pig Iron" Kelley (1814–1890) of Philadelphia represented his district in the U.S. House of Representatives (1861–1890).

77. Merchant Edwin Denison Morgan (1811–1883) chaired the Republican National Committee (1856–1864) and served as governor of New York (1859–1862).

78. George Sewall Boutwell (1818–1905) of Groton, Massachusetts, served as governor of the Bay State (1851–1853) and represented his district in the U.S. House of Representatives (1863–1869).

79. Francis Preston Blair Sr. (1791–1876) of Maryland was a journalist and political power broker in Washington.

80. John Adam Kasson (1822–1910) of Des Moines represented his Iowa district in the U.S. House of Representatives (1863–1867). In 1861, Lincoln appointed him assistant postmaster general.

81. Lincoln appointed William T. Otto (1816–1905) of Indiana assistant secretary of the interior.

82. Amos Tuck (1810–1879) of Exeter, New Hampshire, represented his district in the U.S. House of Representatives (1847–1853), where he befriended Lincoln.

83. Columbus Delano (1809–1896) of Mount Vernon, Ohio, represented his district in the U.S. House of Representatives (1845–1847, 1865–1867) and served as U.S. secretary of the interior (1870–1875).

Lake Shore depot *en route* to the Tremont House, nearly a mile away, lugging a huge leather satchel which he would change from one hand to the other every little while. There were but few people on the street at the time, but he would look into the faces of all whom he met with an air of bucolic simplicity, **as if to say "I'm Jehosaphat Greenham from Lickskillet, and I wonder if yew know where my cousin Jemima mought be found."** He was snubbed in the convention, as he represented no constituency, **really**. There were but few Republicans in Democratic Oregon, and **they had sent him a license to appear for them;** his sole weight in the convention was that of one vote. The New York delegates hardly knew him personally. **I recollect of [David] Cartter of Ohio once saying in the convention: "in reference to what the gentleman from Oregon or New York says" &c. Greeley retorted sheepishly "as to the gentleman from Ohio, or somewhere else" &c.**

Nearly the entire delegation from Indiana came there with the specific design of securing control of the fat Interior Department in case of Republican success. They had agreed on a secretary of that department—Caleb B. Smith; a commissioner of Indian affairs—William P. Dole,[84] formerly of Indiana; and on a candidate for some of the minor offices. They then opened their political huckster shop and spread out their wares for inspection. As there was close intercommunication between Illinois and Indiana, and Lincoln had served in Congress with Smith, it was quite natural that they should give Illinois their support. The bargain was very soon made. Caleb B. Smith was to be secretary of the interior, Dole commissioner of Indian affairs, and the vote of Indiana was to be solid for Lincoln. He therefore started in with **a "big pull":** the **solid** votes of Indiana and Illinois.

The next block of votes that was lying around loose was the Cameron strength in Pennsylvania. This was more difficult to manage. Not having yet been made acquainted with Lincoln's ethical tendencies, Davis got Dubois to telegraph to Lincoln that they could secure the Cameron delegates from Pennsylvania if they might promise Cameron the Treasury. Lincoln replied: "I authorize no bargains and will be bound by none." Just ten words—the normal length of a telegraphic message! **You see—the imperturbable Lincoln!** Not satisfied with this, however, he sent a copy of the *Missouri Democrat* to Herndon with three extracts from Seward's speeches marked, and on the margin of which he had written: "I agree with Seward's 'irrepressible conflict,' but do not agree with his 'higher law' doctrine." And he added, *"Make no contracts that will bind me."*

Everybody was mad, of course. Here were men working night and day to place him on the highest mountain peak of fame, and he pulling back all he

---

84. William P. Dole (1811–1889) served as commissioner of Indian affairs in the Lincoln administration.

Attainment of the Presidency

knew how. What was to be done? The bluff Dubois said: "Damn Lincoln!" **but in this instance "the angel who flew up to Heaven's chancery with the oath blushed as he gave it in, and the recording Angel" etc. etc.**[85] The polished Swett said, in mellifluous accents, "I am very sure if Lincoln was aware of the necessities——"

The critical Logan expectorated viciously, and said, "The main difficulty with Lincoln is——"

Herndon ventured:[86] "Now, friend, I'll answer that," but Davis cut the Gordian knot by brushing all aside with: "Lincoln ain't here and don't know what we have to meet, so we will go ahead as if we hadn't heard from him, and he must ratify it."[87]

And the crowd said, in pantomime, clap! Clap!! Clap!!!

The Cameron contingent was secured for Lincoln on the second vote.

85. "The accusing spirit, which flew up to heaven's chancery with the oath, blushed as he gave it in; and the recording angel as he wrote it down dropped a tear upon the word and blotted it out forever." Laurence Sterne, *The Life and Opinions of Tristram Shandy, Gentleman* (London: T. Cadell, 1794), vol. 6, ch. 8.

86. "By his own statement Herndon was in Chicago during the time of the Convention (May 16–18, 1860) as one of the contingent which had Lincoln's interests in charge. One suspects, however, that in this instance an old man's memory was playing him false. Certainly as late as May 14, when the real Lincoln managers, such as David Davis and Jesse K. Dubois, were on the scene, pulling wires and rolling logs, Herndon was still in Springfield. No contemporary account has been found which mentions Herndon at Chicago or as one of the agitators in the Lincoln-for President movement. With the exception of the belated memoirs of Henry C. Whitney (published in 1907) even delayed reminiscences of the nomination have nothing to say about Herndon's activities. Reliable memoirs, such as those of Gustave Koerner, give elaborate details as to the work performed by David Davis, N. B. Judd, and Orville H. Browning but do not even refer to Herndon." David Donald, *Lincoln's Herndon* (New York: Knopf, 1948), 136.

87. This dramatic statement is omitted in Whitney's account of the nomination in *Life on the Circuit with Lincoln*, 87: "The 'political necessity' which Nicolay and Hay say demanded Lincoln before and during the sitting of the convention, was the necessity of Caleb B. Smith to be Secretary of the Interior; of Wm. P. Dole to be Commissioner of Indian Affairs; of David Davis to be either a supreme judge or a cabinet officer; of Norman B. Judd to be a cabinet minister; and of Simon Cameron to be Secretary of the Treasury. Had not these *political necessities* existed, Seward's great reputation and his acknowledged position as leader of the party would have prevailed and Lincoln would doubtless have been a member of the cabinet, and an obscure one for Lincoln did not shine except as a leader. In a subordinate position, as junior counsel, etc., he was very feeble; as a cabinet officer he would have been a nonentity."

246 *Chapter XV*

The convention met and the Seward *claque* was allowed to fill the hall to repletion. An organization was effected by calling David Wilmot (of "proviso" fame) to the chair. The various committees were appointed.

The second day was consumed in settling the rules and the platform. The Seward *claque* had "open sesame" on this day likewise. The platform was adopted.

When the second plank in the platform was reported, it did not have the quotation from the Declaration of Independence in it, and Joshua R. Giddings moved to put it in, but the convention, somehow, was timid and afraid to do it. Giddings became so disgusted and demoralized at this result that he left the convention. Afterwards, however, the matter was reconsidered, and George W. Curtis made a brief speech in which he shamed the convention for refusing to repeat the sentiments of the Continental Congress, and the quotation was adapted *nem. con.* [unanimously]

Next day the balloting was to take place, and by a political "turn of the wrist," known only to wicked Chicago, when the Seward *claque* were prepared to occupy the main floor of the hall as before, the same was preoccupied by the Lincoln *claque*. To the consternation of the Seward following, they had to be content with their two days' largess, already enjoyed, in which there was no political utility.

The convention was opened and the following candidates were put in nomination: William H. Seward, of New York, nominated by William M. Evarts; Abraham Lincoln, of Illinois, nominated by Norman B. Judd; William L. Dayton, of New Jersey; Simon Cameron, of Pennsylvania; Salmon P. Chase, of Ohio; Edward Bates, of Missouri; Jacob Collamer, of Vermont; John McLean, of Ohio.

Balloting began. On the first ballot, Seward received 173½ votes; Lincoln, 102 votes; Cameron, 50½ votes; Chase, 49 votes; Bates, 48 votes; Dayton, 14 votes; McLean, 12 votes; Collamer, 10 votes; with scattering votes for Wade, Sumner, and Fremont.

On the second ballot Lincoln received the larger part of the votes that had been cast on the first ballot as complimentary to State favorites who stood no chance of being nominated. All of Collamer's came to him, 44 of Cameron's, 6 of Chase's, 6 of McLean's, etc. He gained 79 votes while Seward gained but 11, making the total: Seward, 184½ ; Lincoln 181; the field, 99½.

On the third ballot, the current of votes flowing to Lincoln became a flood, even Seward losing 4½ votes. Of the 465 ballots cast, Lincoln received 231½ and Seward 180. 233 votes were necessary to a choice.

David K. Cartter, of Ohio, then sprang upon his chair and announced a change of four votes from his State from Chase to Lincoln, completing his nomination. Delegation vied with delegation in changing to Lincoln, making

Attainment of the Presidency

his nomination virtually unanimous, and it was formally so ratified on the motion of William M. Evarts of New York.

The nominations were then completed by the selection of Senator Hannibal Hamlin of Maine, and the convention adjourned, while the city was intoxicated with joy.

[Whitney footnote: At the earnest request of Jesse K. Dubois, I hunted up W. R. Arthur,[88] superintendent of the Illinois Central Railroad, whom I found at McVicker's Theatre and got an order for a special train to go *via* Tolono to Springfield in advance of the committee, and to carry Dubois, Bill Butler, Judge Logan, and other of Lincoln's neighbors, so they could fix up things before the committee should reach Springfield.]

During the sitting of the convention Lincoln had been trying, in one way and another, to keep down the excitement which was pent up within him, playing billiards a little, town ball a little, and story-telling a little.

When the news actually reached him, he was in the editorial office of the *Journal*. He got up at once and allowed a little crowd to shake hands with him mechanically, then said, "I reckon there's a little short woman down at our house that would like to hear the news." And he started with rapid strides thither.

The canvass which ensued was spirited, Douglas leading a forlorn hope by canvassing personally and making speeches in all parts of the country where he thought he had any prospect of catching votes. It was a very humiliating and for that time unique spectacle: never before had a man seeking this most exalted position ever gone about personally soliciting votes. The whole country was aroused. The "wide awakes" evoked the enthusiasm of the superficial, and the leading politicians were all active and enthusiastic on the stump, appealing to the patriotism and reason of the thinking masses. The State elections which took place in Ohio, Indiana, and Pennsylvania went so overwhelmingly Republican as to leave scarcely any doubt of Lincoln's election, but when the returns actually came in, they were more than satisfactory.

Popular vote:	Electoral vote:
Lincoln 1,857,610	Lincoln 180
Douglas 1,365,976	Breckinridge 72
Breckinridge 847,953	Bell 39
Bell 590,631	Douglas 12

On February 13 following, John C. Breckinridge himself, resisting all allurements held out to him by those who supported him and by his political

---

88. William R. Arthur (1821–1903) was president of the Illinois Central (1857–1865).

248 Chapter XV

friends, then acting like a true man and a man of honor, presided over the canvass of votes and declared that Abraham Lincoln and Hannibal Hamlin, having received the greatest number of votes for president and vice president respectively, were president and vice president elect.

A crisis was reached at last! The nation had commenced its downward career in 1821 by admitting Missouri as a slave state, then in 1845 by the annexation of Texas; the iniquity of the Mexican war followed; the acquisition of new territory to propagate slavery on; the Fugitive Slave law; the repeal of the Missouri Compromise; the Dred Scott decision; the Lecompton Constitution. *Facilis descensus averno.* **[The road to hell is smooth] "The faithful trembled and sunk in silence, and almost doubted, in the long-continued triumph of wickedness, the reality of the Divine administration of the universe, but the laws of Providence were incessantly acting, and preparing in silence the renovation of the world."[89]**

89. Archibald Alison, *History of Europe, from the Commencement of the French Revolution to the Restoration of the Bourbons* (Edinburgh: Blackwood, 1840), 834.

XVI

Inauguration as President

On the first day of February 1861, Mr. Lincoln and myself left his house and proceeded part of the way "across lots" to the Great Western depot (now Wabash), on which line I had procured a pass for him, **designing to go East for about one hundred miles [to Charleston].** His baggage consisted of an old carpetbag which he had carried on the circuit for several years and which was well worn and was in a state of collapse. No crowd then attended our truly democratic departure.[1] Ten days later he again visited the same depot, but the incidents then were akin to those of a royal progress, for he was then *en route* to the performance of the greatest mission ever entrusted to a mortal man.

A special train was provided, and the following named persons were of the party: Mrs. Lincoln and the three sons, Robert Todd, William Wallace, and Thomas (nicknamed "Tad"); Governor Yates; ex-Governor John Moore;[2] Norman B. Judd; David Davis; Orville H. Browning; Dr. W. S. Wallace (the president's brother-in-law);[3] Ward H. Lamon; **B[urnett] Forbes**;[4] George C. Latham;[5] Elmer E. Ellsworth;[6] **Lockwood** Todd;[7] Colonel E. V. Sumner,

---

1. A fuller description of this episode can be found in Whitney, *Life on the Circuit*, 492–96.

2. John Moore (1793–1866) served as lieutenant governor of Illinois (1842–1846).

3. Dr. William Smith Wallace (1802–1867) was one of the Lincoln family's physicians. He wed Mary Lincoln's sister Frances Todd.

4. Burnett Forbes was an assistant to William S. Wood.

5. George Clayton Latham (1842–1921) was a schoolmate of Robert Todd Lincoln at both Illinois State University in Springfield and Phillips Exeter Academy. He had hoped to continue in that capacity at Harvard but was denied admission. Consoled by Lincoln in a celebrated letter, he attended Yale.

6. Elmer E. Ellsworth (born Ephraim Elmer Ellsworth) (1837–1861), a friend of the Lincoln family, had studied law at the Lincoln-Herndon office and achieved renown as the leader of a military drill team, the "Zouave Cadets of Chicago."

7. Lockwood Marcus Todd (1823–1894) was a cousin of Mary Todd Lincoln.

250   *Chapter XVI*

U.S.A.;[8] Captain John Pope;[9] Major David Hunter;[10] George W. Hazzard;[11] J. M. Burgess;[12] John G. Nicolay; and John Hay. The train was under the charge of General W. S. Wood.[13] [Whitney note: Three of this party were army officers sent by General (Winfield) Scott and two were detectives furnished by Pinkerton. Some of the party left *en route*. Judd left at Harrisburg on the train after Lincoln.]

When the party was embarked, Mr. Lincoln appeared on the back platform and in an abstracted way, gazing mournfully at the little concourse of people who had assembled, **finally** made, **in a husky voice**, a valedictory to his townsmen which was filled with religious emotion.

The train then moved eastward, and the president-elect remained on the platform until the enlarging fields and diminishing houses indicated that he was beyond the limits of the city where he had achieved national fame **and to which he had imparted national fame**; but did not then know, though he did fear, that it was his *last* lingering glance.

On this journey the president-elect spoke at Indianapolis, once to the citizens and once to the legislature; at Cincinnati; at Columbus, before the legislature; at Steubenville; Pittsburgh; Cleveland; Buffalo; Albany (twice); New York City (several times); Trenton (three times, once before the legislature); Philadelphia (twice); and Harrisburg, before the legislature; besides making short formal remarks at stopping places along the route.

Throughout the long journey **thus far**, the highest demonstrations of respect and honor were accorded by the people of all parties and classes toward their future chief magistrate. Even Fernando Wood, then mayor of New York,[14] made an unobjectionable, though not very cordial, speech of

8. Colonel Edwin Vose Sumner (1797–1863) became a major general and the oldest field commander in the Union Army.

9. Captain John Pope (1822–1892) was a career U.S. Army officer and major general in the Civil War.

10. Major David Hunter (1802–1886) was a career U.S. Army officer and major general in the Civil War.

11. Artillery Captain George Whitfield Hazzard (1825–1862) of Delaware graduated from West Point in 1847, served in the Mexican War, and died of wounds sustained during the Peninsular campaign.

12. James M. Burgess of Janesville, a colonel in the Wisconsin State Militia, had been detailed by Governor Alexander Randall to act as a bodyguard on the train journey.

13. The impresario of the train journey to Washington, William S. Wood of New York, was a jeweler, hotel manager, and railroad official who briefly served as the interim Commissioner of Public Buildings in 1861.

14. Democrat Fernando Wood (1812–1881) served as mayor of New York (1855–1857, 1860–1861).

Inauguration as President

welcome. While nearly all the addresses of welcome were couched in such terms of respect and veneration as to leave no doubt of the excellent disposition generally entertained, and the enthusiasm of the masses attested the public devotion alike to the person of their executive and social head and to their government, then believed to be seriously imperiled.

In all places through which the train was to pass, great crowds were assembled, and not a single disparaging remark was uttered audibly; apparently all was amity and good feeling, and those who had cast their votes for another were not at all displeased at the hearty enthusiasm evoked, in which likewise they, in many instances, joined. Business was suspended in many places and a holiday taken. Gay equipages were provided for the presidential party, and the streets through which the cavalcade was to pass were profusely decorated with the highest artistic taste and patriotic design. The star-spangled banner was regnant and exalted.

At Indianapolis, a Republican governor, Morton,[15] greeted him; at Cincinnati, a Democratic mayor. At Buffalo he was welcomed by Millard Fillmore, one of his predecessors; at Albany by Governor Morgan, and at New York City by that *ne plus ultra* of Democrats, Fernando Wood. At several places, **such** as Syracuse and Hudson, platforms were erected, the design being that the president-elect should speak from them; but to accomplish that would have produced an unwarrantable delay, and he was obliged to decline. **But the public enthusiasm was exuberant and hearty, and it might have been said, with the spirit embodied by Tennyson,**

> **"Saxons, and Normans and Danes are we,**
> **But we all are Danes in our welcome of thee."[16]**

The master of a Cunard steamer would be an inefficient skipper of a pleasure yacht—Jared Sparks[17] would have made a naïve performance in teaching an infant school—Washington Irving made a donkey of himself in attempting an after-dinner speech.

The author of "the reply to Hayne" [Daniel Webster] once attempted to make a "by-the-way" speech at Alton, and the editor of the paper reported that "he beat the air and bellowed and said nothing." So again at Rochester, after

---

15. Oliver Perry Morton (1823–1877) served as governor of Indiana (1861–1867).

16. "Come to us, love us, and make us your own

For Saxon or Dane or Norman are we

Teuton or Celt or whatever we be

We are each all Dane in our welcome of thee."

Alfred, Lord Tennyson, "A Welcome, addressed to the Danish Princess Alexandra on her arrival in England, March 7, 1863."

17. Jared Sparks (1789–1866) served as president of Harvard College (1849–1853).

250

Chapter XVI

vainly attempting to say something for a long time, the eloquent defender of
the Constitution abruptly closed by venturing, "I'm told you have a 175-foot
waterfall here; no people ever lost their liberty who had such a high waterfall
as that."

In a similarly false and illogical position was Mr. Lincoln placed when
he made his Eastern tour in February, 1861. His important speeches in prior
canvasses had been widely heralded, and his fame had acquired strength and
momentum by a persistency of iteration and reiteration. Great intellectual
feats were expected from his reported ability and high moral and political
utterances from his unique position, while obvious policy and imperious
necessity demanded that he keep his best thoughts to himself, yet with no
studied appearance of having done so. The net result of all was that he was
expected to entertain the thronging masses, to make a favorable and popular
impression, and yet omit all significant reference to that very line of remark
which the people wanted to hear.

In the first place, Lincoln was that style of orator and man of the world who
could not talk effectively about nothing; he must have something to say and
somebody to convince. **There must be some practical theme involved, or
some practical object to be attained, and then he was** *au fait,* **but "glittering generalities" and** *"smool tawk"* **were not in his intellectual repertoire.**[18]

In view of these drawbacks he spoke **extremely** well, but did not equal
public expectation. The people **wanted to be entertained with those massive chunks of unhewn logic—those cutting shafts of impersonal sarcasm,
which he had hurled with such political effect in former campaigns.** They
longed to hear from his lips the avowal of a defined and trenchant policy
toward the incipient treason which **broke out sporadically in many places,
and** was becoming epidemic in the cotton-growing states. They earnestly
desired that he should exhibit a certificate that even as the crisis had come,

---

18. Whitney note: The masked contempt with which both the "outgoing" and
"incoming" president were regarded in some quarters will be shown by this incident. The Cleveland *Plain Dealer* had a cut representing "Old Buck" resigning the
chair of state to Lincoln. The Chair is in a most dilapidated condition. The dialogue
was thus:

Buchanan: "Mr. Lincoln, sir, it is with infernal satisfaction I surrender to you
the Presidential chair, not so sound, it is true, as when I took it. You will observe,
before *settin'* down, that *I've broke its back and busted its bottom.* Nevertheless,
what is left of it is yours. Take it, and make yourself as happy as you can."

Lincoln. "Thank you, Mr. Buchannon—thank you. I accept this *cheer,* sir, with
pleasure, sir. I see 'nothing the matter' with it, 'Nobody hurt.' If I fail to fill it, sir,
I hope to make up in *length* what I may fall short in *breadth.*"

The expressions, it will be remembered, are some used by Mr. Lincoln *en route*
to Washington **and which sounded so silly and vapid then**.

so also had come the *man*. Had he simply declared, as he did on May 29, 1856, **"we won't go out of the Union and you *shan't*"**—the integrity of the Union, no limit could have been assigned to the spontaneous enthusiasm which he might have evoked. But he knew the dizzy eminence whereon he stood and the gravity of the political situation better than the public, and it was quite clear to him that his paramount duty was to allow no obstacle to intervene between the anomalous political situation and the acquisition of the helm of State; **that he must** not alarm or inflame the conservative Southern mind and the border slave States, nor weaken the alliance or devotion of the Northern Democratic party to the Union, **and yet, then he must not disgust the ultra-Northern element by a too radical display of either moral or intellectual imbecility.**

Accordingly, at Springfield, where he made his first speech, he merely took an affectionate leave of his neighbors, without any exhibition of his political intent. A similar policy controlled him at Tolono, where he, with excellent taste and discretion, said, "I am leaving you on an errand of national importance, attended, as you are aware, with considerable difficulties. Let us believe, as some poet [Henry Wadsworth Longfellow] has expressed it, 'Behind the cloud, the sun is still shining.'"[19]

His second speech at Indianapolis, however, should have satisfied any reasonable, conservative citizen, for he then and there, in an undemonstrative, tentative, and indirect way, gave ample assurance that "the Federal Union must and shall be preserved."

Nor could anything have been **done** in better taste or more neatly done than his almost total self-abnegation and his delegation of the responsibilities of the crisis upon the people themselves. The people are prone to fallaciously reason that a ruler has some occult power and unusual personal interest in the government. The president-elect, at Indianapolis, conclusively dispelled this vain idea in a simple sentence, thus: "It is *your* business and not *mine* if the Union of these States and the liberties of this people shall be lost; it is but little to any one man of fifty-two years of age, but a great deal to the thirty millions of people who inhabit these United States, and to their posterity, in all coming time."[20]

In addition to his elaborate speeches, he spoke at many of the way places briefly; it will be noted that this journey was very shrewdly planned and gave the president-elect an opportunity to impress himself upon the legislatures of the five great states of Indiana, Ohio, New York, Pennsylvania, and New Jersey. I am inclined to think that the public generally was disappointed at

19. Basler, *Collected Works of Lincoln*, 4:190. Longfellow's poem that Lincoln cited is "The Rainy Day."

20. Basler, 4:194.

the reticence manifested by him as to his policy, and at the intellectual feebleness of his speeches. The crisis demanded a great leader, the people wanted assurances that he was one, and, if he had emitted Jacksonian flashes of patriotic fire, enthusiasm would have gathered force, like ocean waves. This, however, would have been of questionable wisdom. As I have said, Lincoln was better informed of the status of affairs than the public, and he knew of the supreme importance of getting control of the government before any *emeute* [riot] or disturbance was made.

On the night of February 22–23 I passed through Harrisburg *en route* for Philadelphia; and, on arising in the morning, was surprised to find my friend, Norman B. Judd, on the train. He informed me that he had come on board at Harrisburg; and in reply to my questions, he indicated that he had grown so nervous at the noise and excitement of the journey with the president-elect that he had concluded to slip quietly away where he could get some rest and tranquility. He questioned me as to what I had heard about the journey so closely as to arouse my curiosity and he whispered to me significantly, "I'll tell you more when we get to Philadelphia." What he had to tell, I will now narrate, **as well as my memory will allow**, substantially as he told it to me. Before I parted with Judd, we both mutually thanked God that our friend the president-elect, was safe in Washington.

Judd said, "You see Pinkerton (our Pinkerton) had been engaged by the Philadelphia [Wilmington] & Baltimore Railroad to watch their road, which there was reason to believe would be assailed at some point by the rebs to destroy communication with the North, and while so engaged, he learned that a plot was being worked up to assassinate Lincoln while he was passing through Baltimore; and he, **accordingly so** wrote me in a letter which was delivered to me at the Burnet House in Cincinnati but which I kept entirely private, not telling any of the party. Pinkerton also stated that he would advise me further during our progress eastward. I promptly replied to him, acknowledging receipt of his note, and urging him to prosecute his research. While we were at Buffalo on Sunday, I received another letter, saying that he was pursuing his investigations and would keep me advised. On reaching the Astor House at New York, I was summoned to a certain room in the upper part of the hotel **by a lady who would be found there. I went and** found there a lady who gave her name as [Kate] Warne[21] (I think) and who had a letter from Pinkerton, introducing her as the chief of his female detective department. Her object in coming was to arrange a meeting for me with Pinkerton himself at Philadelphia. No place was then designated,

21. Kate Warne (1833–1868), one of the first women detectives in the United States, worked with Allan Pinkerton in helping to thwart the planned assassination of Lincoln as he passed through Baltimore in February 1861.

Inauguration as President   255

but we agreed that I should be notified then. It seemed quite unnecessary to send a woman clear to New York to do what a telegram or letter would have done as well. Mysteries increased, for when I got to Philadelphia a man passed through the crowd and gave me a fictitious address at the St. Louis Hotel and **as soon as I could, I took a hack, and going** there, I found Pinkerton under an assumed name awaiting me and with him Mr. Felton, president of the Baltimore Railroad.[22] From their representations I became satisfied that a well-matured and organized plot did exist to kill Lincoln in Baltimore, and I then saw that something must be done. I arranged to have Pinkerton meet me at my room at the Continental, and sent for Lincoln, whom Pinkerton informed of the whole affair, strongly urging that the president go on through secretly that night. Lincoln was fully impressed with the gravity of the situation and the necessity of action; but he was resolute in his purpose, **from which we could not shake him,** to raise the flag over Independence Hall and meet the legislature at Harrisburg the next day. After that, he said, he would do as I said. I then had a conference with the officials of both railways, the telegraph people and Pinkerton, and developed the following plan, which has been strictly followed, so far as I know: Lincoln should fill all his appointments, and leave Harrisburg at 6 o'clock on Friday evening on a special train for Philadelphia, at which hour the telegraph wires should be cut at Harrisburg; the Baltimore train should be held at Philadelphia till Lincoln was aboard, and then go on to Baltimore.

"Hill Lamon should go with Lincoln all the way, and Pinkerton should meet Lincoln and Lamon at Philadelphia, and go with them clear through, and Pinkerton should have someone secure the sleeping car sections from Philadelphia to Washington in the rear of the train, and Lincoln should be represented as an invalid. I was up nearly all night getting these arrangements made, which none of our party as yet knew about, although they saw that something was *up*. When Lincoln got up next morning, he found Frederick Seward[23] there with a message from his father to the effect that he must come to Washington in a clandestine manner, as he had authentic evidence of the existence of a conspiracy to kill him as he attempted to go through Baltimore. This, of course, confirmed the wisdom of my plans, as Seward's information came from other sources than ours. I dismissed young Seward with a message to his father that Mr. Lincoln would reach Washington at six o'clock next morning. I then disclosed the arrangements I had made to Lincoln, who was perfectly unexcited but agreed to all. I told him I wanted

22. Samuel Morse Felton (1809–1889) served as president of the Philadelphia, Wilmington, and Baltimore Railroad (1851–1865).

23. Frederick Seward (1830–1915), son of Lincoln's Secretary of State William Henry Seward, served as assistant secretary of state (1861–1865).

the judgment of others of our party, to which he agreed. Accordingly, I got Davis, Sumner, Pope, and Hunter, and one or two others together and briefly told them what I knew, and what I had done. Davis was quite skeptical, I think, because of the stigma which would rest on Maryland, where he came from, but finally, after insinuations of doubt on his part, both of the facts and wisdom of my plan, he said, 'Well, Lincoln, you have heard the whole story, what do you think about it yourself?'

"Lincoln replied quite carelessly: 'I've thought the matter over fully, and reckon I had better do as Judd says. The facts come from two different and reliable sources, and I don't consider it right to disregard both.'

"'That settles it,' said Davis, a trifle disappointed, I think, first because it was a slight on his State and second, because it was *my* plan, and third because he had a poor opinion of [the] detective business. Sumner was angry **especially** at the selection of Lamon, and he said grimly, 'One thing I want distinctly understood, that *I'm* going to Washington with the president. Such were my orders from General Scott, and I'm going to carry them out.'

"We all tried to reason him out of it, but made no impression at all, and I was then sorry I told him anything about it. In fact, I am sorry I told anybody, for I have got in trouble with Sumner and it has done no good anyway. However, Sumner kept strict watch, and when Lincoln left the dinner table at Harrisburg, just before six, Sumner was on hand. I instructed Lamon what to do. As Lincoln and he got in the carriage to go, I diverted Sumner's attention for a single moment, which threw him off his guard, and when he turned to get in the carriage, as he had intended, it was out of reach, the horses galloping on the way to the train. Sumner, to carry out his program, should have followed, of course, but he was stunned with anger and lost his presence of mind. I never got such a scoring in all my life. I was fearful he would assault me. However, I was so glad that my scheme went through with nothing but a *cussin'* that on the whole, I felt good over it, though I did not get a wink of sleep that night, except what little I got on the train before I saw you. I came on to Philadelphia by the first train to get the news and to be within telegraphic reach and do anything necessary; for of course I could not be certain what might happen. I now see that so much planning and letting so many in the secret, at a time when we were all on public exhibition, was not the right way to do it."

Judd also informed me that his reasons for selecting Lamon were: "First, Lamon was a *Southerner*—had the *Southern* dialect and appearance—and if any parlaying should be necessary, he could ward off suspicion as to his charge better than a Northern man could, since it would not be presumed that a Southerner would have Lincoln in charge. Second, Lamon habitually carried two revolvers in a belt so ostentatiously that I knew it, and I believed he would use them effectively if necessary. Third, Lamon was not known as **well as** Sumner or Hunter was."

Judd also informed me that Lincoln was to be represented as a sick man, and that when the conductor came around one of the party was to give him the tickets which had been bought for the president-elect.

"Lincoln," said Judd, "was disguised no further than this: he wore the bobtail overcoat he had used all winter, and had a shawl **also**, and a soft felt hat that he had borrowed for the trip: **that was all; the design was to get him through clandestinely and safely, and that was part of the plan**. I have no doubt an attempt would have been made to kill him, but I also think **that,** as we knew it in advance, we could have prevented it. But with the warnings we had, it would have been criminal to have let the president-elect be exposed to a needless risk for the sake of appearance. I will say that Lincoln did not show the least excitement or fear throughout, but took a sensible and unexcited view of it, and demeaned himself just as he would had Davis or any other of the party been the person in danger.

"I reached Baltimore," concluded Judd, "in the afternoon of the day Lincoln had passed through, and though it was **decidedly** rainy, I was out on the streets during the rest of that and the next day (Sunday) and was a witness of the deep disappointment felt by the roustabouts, street loafers, and low orders, that the president-elect was safely at Washington. At that time, I felt fully assured that a deep-laid plot for his assassination had been formed. I deem it idle to argue against this theory. It is a well-attested fact."

Just as daylight was breaking on the morning of Saturday, February 23, 1861, the night train from Philadelphia rolled, as usual, into the sole and dingy depot at Washington. The passengers hastily debarked and made their way through the narrow shed towards the exit in front, the last to leave being a party of three, one of whom, attired in a soft felt hat and bobtail overcoat resembling a sailor's pea jacket, would have been noticeable anywhere from the contrast in the length of the man and the brevity of his outward integuments, for his coat and pantaloons were altogether too brief for their wearer. But there were no spectators to take note of these **commonplace** peculiarities **of this little party** except one muffled-up individual who had long been standing in the shadow of a pillar and who hastily emerged as this party came forward, exclaiming, "You can't play that on me, Abe!" The man in the pea-jacket overcoat exclaimed heartily, to all whom it might concern, "It's Washburne." Then the whole party shook hands all around, and all four, getting into a hack, were driven to the ladies' entrance of Willard's Hotel. These, and about three other persons, alone of the whole slumbrous city, were aware that the president-elect, the man whose name was in every newspaper in the entire civilized world, had thus clandestinely and furtively come to assume charge of the government.

Mr. Judd and Judge Davis each assured me afterward that they believed that a well-developed attempt would have been made to assassinate the president-elect had he gone openly through Baltimore; but Mr. Lincoln said to

258   *Chapter XVI*

me afterward: "I do not think I should have been killed, or even that a serious attempt would have been made to kill me, unless some excitement had arisen; but Judd and other cool heads thought I had better take the course I did, and I reckon they were right; it ain't best to run a risk of any consequence for looks' sake."

A suite of rooms had been engaged for the president-elect and his family on the second floor of Willard's, just over the main entrance and fronting on Pennsylvania Avenue, and thither Mr. Lincoln was at once conducted, where he proceeded to make a hasty toilet, **for he was for a whole day relieved, to his comfort, from the exactions of social discipline and the tyranny of his undesirable** *valet de chambre* **[William H. Johnson].** While he was thus engaged, Senator Seward came hastily in, much disconcerted to know that he had misapprehended the hour of arrival and had lost the opportunity to greet his chief at the depot. He was heartily welcomed and sat down to breakfast shortly thereafter in the private parlor in company with the president-elect and Washburne. At table a general view of the political horizon was taken, and the necessities of the hour canvassed **and, as narrated in a New York paper, his first day in Washington was not an indolent one.**

Later in the day the members of the "Peace Conference" visited Lincoln and were **severally** presented to him. One of them, L. E. Chittenden,[24] relates that Lincoln had an apt word for each of them and that he committed no mistake at all; that he answered every Union man in words of cheer and encouragement, and every secessionist according to his folly. Mr. Chittenden says of the incoming president: "He was able to take care of himself. He could not have appeared more natural or unstudied in his manner if he had been entertaining a company of neighbors in his Western home."[25]

On the ensuing eight days, Lincoln was occupied in receiving calls from party leaders, holding consultations on the subject of his cabinet, not yet definitely settled, and other matters of policy in connection with the mighty trust underlined for him on the program of history. Among other privileges which he availed himself of was the making of a visit to the Capitol, which he had not seen since **he left there in** the summer of 1849, when he made a hurried visit to Washington to see President Taylor.

Since then, the plain and somber hall of the lower house had been converted into a gallery for statuary and the senate had left its original hall, so rich with classical memories. Both deliberative bodies now sat in gaudy chambers indicative of the change from the sober days of stagecoach **plainness and**

24. Lucius E. Chittenden (1824–1900) served as a Vermont delegate to the Washington Peace Conference (1861) and as register of the U.S. Treasury (1861–1864).

25. Lucius E. Chittenden, *Recollections of President Lincoln and His Administration* (New York: Harper & Bros., 1891), 71.

Inauguration as President   **259**

simplicity **to the luxurious days of extravagance and meretricious display**. Here the president-elect was received with enthusiasm by the loyal members and with cold disdain and supercilious curiosity by the others—**the rebel and copperhead crew. Many traitors yet remained in Congress: there were [Louis] Wigfall,**[26] **[Robert M. T.] Hunter, [James M.] Mason, [John C.] Breckinridge, and others, North as well as South**. Disguise it as we may, the Southern cause was more popular in Washington than the cause of the Union, while Lincoln and his forthcoming administration were reviled generally in Washington society **and were put on the defensive in social discussions everywhere at the national capital.**

Meanwhile, the city was rapidly filling up with strangers, some animated by the patriotic desire to see the menaced **and jeered at** president-elect safely installed in the White House, some animated by **a merely** idle curiosity **to see the capital and the inauguration**, but the majority, probably, moved by a selfish desire to serve their country in some official capacity.

Caleb Smith and John P. Usher were then at the head of an immense colony of **Indiana** patriots **fatally** bent on expelling the occupants of the Interior Department and rescuing that temple of prolific spoils from the dominion of the enemy. The ponderous and urbane David Davis, judge of the Eighth Illinois Circuit, had engaged the most expensive suite of rooms at Willard's on the second story corner of the Avenue and Fourteenth Street, four apartments distant from the president-elect, so that he might be in a comfortable place to respond to the invitation, which never came, to advise as to the early appointments.

Corydon Beckwith,[27] the suave and distinguished Democratic lawyer from Chicago, with his wife, occupied the next suite, his undisguised object being to secure the promotion of his brother, then already high in the commissary department. Big men and extremely small men were there, with small and great schemes. Most of them had a maximum appointment in view or in incubation, but were willing to take something considerably less. Judd was there, like Joey Bagstock.[28]

> "Sly, sir—de-vil-ish sly."
> His name was on every office-hunter's lips.
> "Where's Judd?"
> "I'll see Judd."
> "Ask Judd."

26. Louis Trezevant Wigfall (1816–1874) of Texas served in the U.S. Senate (1859–1861).

27. Corydon Beckwith (1823–1890) served briefly on the Illinois Supreme Court in 1864.

28. A servant in Charles Dickens's *Dombey and Son*.

"Oh! I know Judd."
"There goes Judd."
"Judd!"
"Judd!!!"
"Judd goes *pop* into the Cabinet."
"What did Judd say about it?"
"Judd looks used up."
"Judd'll do it."
"Judd won't do it."
"That's just like Judd."
"Judd's pretty smart," &c.

Davis vainly attempted alternately to look big with importance and anon to appear like a "looker on in Venice,"[29] but it was no go; he had one of his eyes on any portfolio and the other on the comfortable chair in the Supreme Court room, then draped in funereal crepe. But no message came from the throne room, so near and yet so far, to point the way he was to go.

Mr. Lincoln had written his inaugural in January, in an unused back room in the same building as his office, with no adventitious aids beyond an old desk, one chair, a bottle of ink, a steel pen, a volume of Clay's speeches, one of Webster's, Jackson's nullification proclamation, and the statutes of Illinois, which contained the Constitution of the United States. In this primitive situation, he prepared his first official utterance on plain foolscap paper, carrying it home at night as it progressed, and amending it. He finally engrossed it, and when he started to Washington, he committed it to the custody of the same frail carpetbag he and I had started East with but eleven days before, designing that it should not be out of his reach during the journey, but when he looked for it at Harrisburg, **in order to carry with him on his bizarre journey to Washington**, lo! It was gone! And it contained not only his inaugural address but a large bundle of letters and other papers of indispensable utility at this supreme moment **of time**. Here was a mess! The day of Fate was in plain sight, advancing resistlessly with rapid strides, and here was this vital document, the product of so many free and unexcited hours, out of place. And letters too!—letters whose exhibition might turn the world of politics upside down—besides other almost indispensable and unduplicated documents.

29. A common phrase, meaning *passive observer*, based on a misquotation from Shakespeare, *Measure for Measure*, V:1:
 "My business in this State
  Made me a looker-on here in Vienna,
  Where I have seen corruption boil and bubble
  Till it o'er-run the stew."

Inauguration as President   261

Perplexed almost beyond endurance by the several alarming exigencies which pressed upon him, he privately and without disclosing his anxiety to any but his son Robert, searched everywhere **apparently in vain**, but finally the delinquent satchel turned up in the general baggage room at the depot, in a pile of valises, the least tempting of them all to a thief, but containing one of the great treasures of political literature.[30]

When the president made the journey from Harrisburg to Philadelphia, he kept this satchel by his side, and in the sleeping car from Philadelphia to Washington, it shared his berth and finally, was safely deposited on the velvet carpet in his room at Willard's. He read the inaugural to Seward and one or two others, and to no more. Seward proposed some minor changes, which were adopted, and this document, destined to a classical renown and imperishable fame, was ready for submission to the tribunal of history.

The Fourth of March arrived, bringing in its train a bright sunny day, as if Nature had enrobed itself in spring attire in honor of the renaissance of loyalty to the Union. At 11:05 AM, Messrs Foot[31] and Pearce,[32] the senate committee, called at the President's Room at the Capitol and escorted the venerable outgoing incumbent to a barouche in waiting drawn by six horses. Driving rapidly to Willard's, they took in the president-elect, who, calm and imperturbable, was waiting, arrayed in his new inauguration suit, a new spick-and-span hat, and a gold-headed cane which some admirer had presented to him, and which, apparently, he had not learned to handle.

A procession was formed consisting of military and civic societies and a long line of carriages filled with government dignitaries, which moved in stately and dignified procession through the avenue to the Capitol. The carriage which contained Mr. Lincoln was flanked on both sides by military veterans, heavily armed. Arriving at the Capitol, the president-elect was escorted to the platform which had been erected upon the eastern flight of steps. Here in the presence of an immense concourse of people and attended by the chief dignitaries of the nation, in a clear, emphatic voice and a resolute and impressive manner, and with an air and mien of perfect self-reliance and self-possession, he delivered the inaugural address.

After Mr. Lincoln had concluded the reading of the address, the venerable chief justice administered the oath, which Mr. Lincoln received solemnly

30. This episode, badly garbled by Whitney, took place in Indianapolis. Ted Widmer, *Lincoln on the Verge: Thirteen Days to Washington* (New York: Simon and Schuster, 2020), 138–39.

31. Solomon Foot (1802–1866) represented Vermont in the U.S. Senate (1851–1866).

32. James Pearce (1805–1862) represented Maryland in the U.S. Senate (1843–1862).

262   *Chapter XVI*

and with emotion (**this is no rhetorical figure, as I was an eye-witness**) the chief justice ventured to bestow his benisons **upon him of the imperial purple**: the venerable ex-president offered his congratulations heartily, and the change of administration was accomplished—the renaissance was begun. "Old things had passed away, all things had become new."[33]

Mr. Lincoln re-entered the barouche, the ex-president followed; the carriage was driven rapidly to the door of the White House—the troopers clattering alongside with clanking sabers. The president alighted, sought Mrs. Lincoln, who had preceded him and who now beamed upon him. The family and two or three relatives sat together at lunch. Mrs. Lincoln was perfectly radiant with happiness, the president appeared **somewhat** relieved. Tad and Willie were jubilant, Robert was dignified, **and the waiters were awkward, with all ears open.**

The life at the White House was begun.

33. "Old things are passed away; behold, all things are become new." 2 Corinthians 5:17.

Index

Abell, Bennett H., 68, 68n8, 101–2
Abell, Elizabeth Owens (Mrs. Bennett), 101, 101n6, 102–3
Abraham Lincoln: A History (Nicolay and Hay), 15, 218
Abraham Lincoln: A Life (Burlingame), xii
Abraham Lincoln Encyclopedia, The (Neely), xi
Adams, John Quincy, 192
Aesop's Fables, 40
Allen, John, 69, 69n18, 104
Allen, Robert, 110, 110n17
almanac trial, 75, 75n9, 90n13
Alschuler, Samuel G., 141, 141n17
Alton, IL, 113, 122
Amasis, 188
Anderson, Robert, 85
Anderson's ferry, 43, 46
Andrew, John A., 242, 242n72
Angle, Paul M., xi, xvi–xviii
anti-abolitionists, 231
antislavery legislation, 129–34
Armstrong, Hannah (Mrs. Jack), 75n9, 90, 90n13, 92, 105
Armstrong, John (Jack), 73, 73n5, 74–75, 77, 88, 90–91, 105
Armstrong, William (Duff), 75, 75n9, 90n13
Arnold, Isaac N., 151, 151n8, 154
Arthur, William R., 247, 247n88

Ashley, James M., 188, 188nn37–38
Ashmore, John D., 129, 129n15
Ashmun, George, 188, 243
assassination plot (Baltimore, MD, 1861), 254, 254n21, 255–58
Atchison, David R., 206–8
Aurora (IL) *Beacon*, 227, 227n38

Bacon, Francis, 152, 152n13
Baddeley, John W., 155, 155n20
Badger, George, 208, 208n8
Baker, Edward D., 119, 119n35, 120–22, 127–28
Baldwin, John, 52
Baltimore, MD, 240–41; assassination plot in, 254–58
Bancroft, George, 179, 179n19
bank failures, 119
banks, 123
Banks, Nathaniel P., 225, 225n36, 243
Bartlett, David W., 217, 217n2
Bates, Edward, 243, 246
Beardstown, IL, 64
Beargrass Fort (Louisville, KY), 5–6, 6n15, 7
Beckwith, Corydon, 259, 259n27
Beecher, Henry Ward, 239, 239n65
Bell, John, 128, 128n7, 208, 210
Benjamin, Judah P., 208, 208n9, 235
Benton, Thomas Hart, 234, 234n50
Berry, Polly Ewing, 11n32

Index

Berry, Richard, Jr., 11, 11n32, 12–14, 17
Berry, Richard, Sr., 13, 13n40, 14, 17–18
Berry, William F., 70n20, 80, 80n17, 81, 81n18, 86–87, 104, 116
Berry and Lincoln store, 80–81, 81n18, 84, 86
Berry family, 4, 11, 14–15
Beveridge, Albert J., xvi
Bible, 41
Bissell, William H., 123, 123n40, 137, 217–18, 223, 233
Black Hawk (Mucata Muhicatah), 83–84
Black Hawk War, 83–85
blacks, arming of, 183
Blackstone's Commentaries, 88
Blaine, James G., 192, 200, 216, 220
Blair, Austin, 242, 242n73
Blair, Francis Preston, Sr. (Frank), 243, 243n79
Bloomington (IL) convention (1856), 218–24, 228
Boone, Daniel, 4, 30
Boutwell, George S., 243, 243n78
Brackenridge, John, 45
Brayman, Mason, 153, 153n16
Breckinridge, John C., 247–48, 259
Breese, Sidney, 108, 108n10
Broadwell, Norman, 138, 138n11
Brooks, Preston, 222, 222n26
Brown, Albert Gallatin, 137
Browning, Eliza (Mrs. Orville H.), 103, 103n9
Browning, Orville H., xiv, 109, 109n16, 117, 210, 219, 222–23, 249
Brumfield (Nall), Elizabeth, 5
Brumfield, William, 4–5, 5n11, 6, 8, 14, 19
Bryant, James R. M., 160, 160n27
Bryant, William Cullen, 237, 237n60
Buchanan, James, 100, 178, 217, 232–33, 252n18, 261–62
Bunn, Jacob, 140, 140n16
Burchard, Samuel D., 216, 216n1, 220
Burgess, James M., 250, 250n12
Burkhimer, Michael, xi
Burlingame, Michael, xii–xiii
Burr, Aaron, 209
Bush, Robert, 35

Bush, Samuel W., 35
Bush, William P. D., 35
Butler, William, 138, 138n9, 247

cabin, 28–29, 32–33
Calhoun, John, 90, 90n12, 106, 123, 123n43
Calhoun, John C., 128, 174, 192, 216, 237
California, territorial government for, 132–33
Cameron, John Miller, 67, 67nn3–4, 68, 95–96
Cameron, Simon, 195, 243–45, 245n87, 246
Campbell, David, 166, 166n43
Camp Douglas conspiracy (Chicago, IL), 151, 151n10
camp shelter, 27–29, 32
canals, 108, 114
capitol building (U.S.), 258–59, 261
Carpenter, William, 106, 106n3
Cartter, David K., 242, 242n71, 244, 246
Cartwright, Peter, 127, 127n2, 128
Cass, Lewis, 132, 132n28, 207, 223
Central Illinois Gazette (Champaign), 224, 224n33, 225–27
Champaign County, IL, 156, 162–63, 166
Charleston (SC) convention (1860), 229, 241
Chase, Salmon P., 209, 209n12, 210, 216, 225, 233, 243, 246
Chicago (IL) convention (1860), 241–45, 245nn86–87, 246–47
"Childe Harold's Pilgrimage" (Byron), 203, 203n65
chills and fever. *See* malaria
"chin-fly thesis," xvi, xxiv n36
Chiniquy, Charles, 145
Chittenden, Lucius E., 258, 258n24
Choate, Rufus, 142
"Chronicles of Reuben" (Lincoln), 176
Church, S. M., 218, 218n4
Cicero, 149, 154
Clark, William, 4
Clarkson, James S., 221, 221n20
Clary, William P. (Bill), 72, 72n4, 73–74, 104
Clary's Grove, 68, 72–73
Clary's Grove boys, 73, 79–80, 104, 179

Index

Clay, Henry, xxiv n39, 21n56, 22, 29, 29n4, 30, 40, 60, 116, 151, 174, 192, 200, 208, 212, 216, 220, 230, 260
Clayton, Thomas, 208, 208n7
clergymen, 34, 67, 67n5, 136–37
Cleveland, Grover, 217
Clingman, Thomas, 129, 129n21
Clinton, DeWitt, 117, 117n33, 120
Codding, Ichabod, 223, 223n27, 231
Cofer, Mrs. Martin H., 35
Coleman, Anne C., 100
Colfax, Schuyler, 33, 33n13
Collamer, Jacob, 129, 129n19, 246
Compromise of 1850, 207–9
Confiscation Act, Second, veto of, 183
Conkling, Roscoe, 220, 220n19
contracts, legal, 212
Cook, Burton C., 219, 219n14
Cooper Institute (Union) address (1860), 39, 175, 193, 236–38
Copley, John Singleton (Lord Lyndhurst), 191
corn, shelling and milling of, 21–22
Corwin, Thomas, 128, 128n8, 130, 132, 243
Crawford, Andrew, 32, 32n8
Crawford, Elizabeth Anderson (Mrs. Josiah), 43, 53, 53n9
Crawford, Josiah, 41, 43
Crawford, William H., 216
Crittenden, John J., 128, 128n9, 230–32
Cromwell, Oliver, 174
Crume, Ralph, Jr., 5, 5n12, 8
Cullom, Shelby M., 138, 138n10
Cumberland Presbyterians, 67, 67n5, 95
Cunningham, Joseph O., xix, xxvi nn68–69, 141–42, 224
Curtis, George William 242, 242n68, 246

Davis, David, 140–41, 150, 153, 156–57, 161, 163–65, 201, 218, 221, 224, 249, 256–57, 259–60; and election of 1860, 227, 242, 244–45, 245nn86–87; as judge, 159–60, 162, 166, 189; and Supreme Court, 166
Davis, Henry Winter, 182, 182n26
Davis, Jefferson, 18, 85, 128, 137, 203, 211
Davis, Oliver L., 141, 149, 162, 189

Davis, Rodney O., xxi
Davis, Sarah Woodruff Walker (Mrs. David), 141
Dawson, John, 106, 106n2, 112, 112n27
Dayton, William L., 128, 128n10, 246
Decatur, IL, xv, xix, 56, 113, 241
deer lick, 28
Delano, Columbus, 243, 243n83
Demosthenes, 154
Depew, Chauncey M., 42, 42n27
De Witt, Alexander R., 209, 209n15
DeWitt County, IL, 156, 163
Dickey, T. Lyle, 152, 152n12, 202, 219, 221–22, 224, 228, 228n42, 231–32
Dickinson, Daniel S., 128, 128n11, 207
Dickinson, Edward M., 151
District of Columbia. See Washington, DC
disunion, 229
Dix, John A., 128, 128n12
Dixon, Archibald, 207, 207n2, 208–9, 212
Dole, William P., 244, 244n84, 245n87
Dorsey, Azel (Hazel) W., 32, 32n8
Douglas, Stephen A., 18, 111–12, 114, 116–18, 122, 124–25, 128, 137n5, 140, 178, 222, 230; and anti-Lecompton stand, 230–33; debate style of, 234n52; and election of 1858, xii, xvii, 130, 140, 191–92, 195–96, 199, 209, 228, 230–32, 234–36, 240; hostility toward, 212–13; as Illinois state's attorney, 109; and Kansas-Nebraska Act, 205–9, 211–14; as presidential candidate, 207–8, 233–35, 240, 247
Douglass, Frederick, xvii, 204, 204n68
Douglass, John M., 153, 153n17
Dred Scott decision, 125, 235, 248
Dresser, Charles, 197, 197n54
Drummond, Thomas, 123, 123n41, 234
Dubois, Jesse K., xv, 117, 200, 219, 223–24, 227, 229; and election of 1860, 242, 244–45, 245n86, 247
Dudley, Edward A., 218, 218n8
Duncan, Jason, 69, 69n17, 98, 104
Duncan, Joseph, 107, 107n6
"dung hill thesis," xvi
Dunn, Charles, 107, 107n5

266 Index

Dunn, Jonathan, 69, 69n13, 104
Duthan, John, 53

Eddy, Henry, 108, 108n11
Edwards, Cyrus, 138
Edwards, Matilda, xviii
Edwards, Ninian (governor), 135, 135n1
Edwards, Ninian W., 110, 112, 138, 190, 190n39
Eighth Judicial Circuit (IL), vi, xiv–xv, 156, 161–63, 165–66. *See also* Lincoln, Abraham, on law circuit
elections: of 1831, 71–72; of 1832, 75–76, 76n10, 87–88, 88n8, 106; of 1834, 92, 106; of 1836, 109–11, 127; of 1838, 120–22, 127; of 1840, 127; of 1842, 127; of 1844, 127; of 1846, 127; of 1848, 132, 132n28; of 1854, 125–26, 217–18; of 1856, 197–98, 208, 215, 218, 228; of 1858, xii, 130, 191–92, 195–96, 199, 209, 228, 230–35; of 1859, 236; of 1860, 187, 225–27, 240–44, 247
Elizabethtown, KY, 19, 19n51
Elkin, David, 34
Elkin, William F., 112
Elliott, S. Bernard, 6n15, 9
Ellsworth, Elmer E., 249, 249n6
Emancipation Proclamation (1863), 39
Emerson, Ralph Waldo, 178, 236
Emery, James S., 221, 221n24, 222–23
English Grammar (Murray), 31, 31n6, 78, 78n13
English Grammar in Familiar Lectures (Kirkham), 31, 31n5, 78, 78n11
Erie Canal, 117
Estep, Elijah, 77
Evans (Hank), Sarah (Mrs. John Hank), 17n49, 18
Evarts, William M., 242, 242n69, 246–47
Ewing, William L. D., 123, 123n44

Farnsworth, John F., 219, 219n15, 231
Fehrenbacher, Don E., xvi, xxiv n43, 235n54
Fehrenbacher, Virginia, xvi, xxiv n43
Felton, Samuel M., 255, 255n22
ferry, 43, 46
Ficklin, Orlando B., 128, 128n4, 162

filibustering, 210
Fillmore, Millard, 251
finances, problems of managing, 114–17, 119–20, 123
Flagel, Thomas R., xi
flatboats, 46–48, 61–66, 68, 71–72, 84, 115
Fletcher, Job, 112, 112n26
Foot, Solomon, 261, 261n31
Forbes, Burnett, 249, 249n4
Ford, Thomas, 108, 108n13, 117
Forquer, George, 110, 110n20, 111
Fort Sumter, SC, 183
founding fathers, 212
franking privilege, 134
Freeport Doctrine/Question, 234–35, 240
Frémont, John C., 197, 241, 246
French, Augustus C., 112, 112n23
Friend, Polly Hanks, 20n53
Fulton, Robert, 185

Gaines, Edward, 84
Garfield, James A., 29, 221
Gentry, Allen, 46, 48, 52
Gentry, James S., 46, 46n1, 52
Gentryville, IN, 44, 46, 49, 52; community life of, 49; superstitions in, 49–50
Gibbons, James S., 203n67
Giddings, Joshua R., 129, 129n17, 130–31, 209, 242, 246
Gillespie, Joseph, xix, 124, 124n45, 169, 219
God, justice of, 186
Godby, Russell, 88–90
Gott, Daniel, 133, 133n30, 134
Graham, Mentor, 70, 70n22, 71, 78, 90, 104
Grant, Ulysses S., 53, 63, 195, 217
Greeley, Horace, xiii, 175, 216, 230–31, 233; and election of 1860, 242–44
Green, Bowling, 68, 68n7, 70, 76–78, 88, 91–92, 98, 101, 104; death and funeral of, 105
Green, Nancy Potter (Mrs. Bowling), 76, 78, 78n14, 92, 102, 104
Greene, Lynn McNulty (Nult), 78, 78n12

Greene, William G., xv, 9, 9–10n27, 10, 64–65, 68, 74, 76–78, 80–81, 85, 87, 91, 102, 105, 140; and gambling, 77

Greer, Edmund, 70, 70n21, 92, 104

Gridley, Asahel, 124, 124n46, 141, 156, 162

Grigsby, Aaron, 51, 51n5

Grigsby, Reuben, 44

Grigsby family, 53

Grigsby wedding, 44

grist mills, 21–22, 40, 68, 73, 76

Gulliver, John P., 194, 194n46

Hale, John P., 128n13, 129, 209

Hall, John J., xix

Hall, Levi (Squire), 51, 51n6, 52, 54, 58

Hamilton, Alexander, 29

Hamlin, Hannibal, 247–48

Hanaford, Phebe Ann Coffin, 11, 11n36

Hank(e) (Lupton), Hannah (Mrs. Asa Lupton), 17n49, 18

Hank(e), John, 17, 17n49, 18

Hanks, Dennis, xix, 11, 11n34, 15, 20n53, 29, 34, 36, 51–52, 57–58; migration to Illinois, 52–54, 58, 60; and patronage, 57

Hanks, John, xix, 11, 11n35, 15, 52, 56–64, 66; and patronage, 57–58; and "rail-splitter" title, 57

Hanks, Joseph, 10, 10n29, 11n35, 52

Hanks (Sparrow), Lucey Berry, 11, 11n33, 12–13, 13n38, 13n40, 14–16

Hanks, Nancy. See Lincoln, Nancy Hanks

Hanks, Sophie, xix

Hanks family, vi, xv, xix, 4, 11, 17–18, 21n55

Hannegan, Edward A. (Ned), 162, 162n36

Hardin, John J., 109, 109n14, 111, 127–28; death of, 128

Hardin County, KY, 18

Harding, George F., 151

Harlan, Justin, 108, 108n12

Harmon, Oscar F., 162, 162n29

Harris, Ira, 89n11

Harrison, Alexander Y., 227, 227n40

Harrison, Benjamin, 53

Harrison, William Henry, 53, 83, 241

Hatch, Ozias Mather, 219, 219n16, 242–43

Hay, John, xii, 15, 218, 245n87, 250

Hay, Milton, 138, 138n8

Hayes, Rutherford B., 217

Hayne, Robert, 237

Hazel, Caleb, 22, 22n59

Hazzard, George W., 250, 250n11

Head, Jesse, 17, 17n48

Henry, John, 127, 127n1

Hentz, Caroline Lee, 89, 89n11

Herndon, Archer G., 112, 112n25

Herndon, James, 70n20, 81, 81n18, 87, 104

Herndon, (John) Rowan, 69, 70n20, 81, 81n18, 87, 91, 104–5

Herndon, William H., xvi, xviii–xix, 7, 21n55, 70n20, 136, 138, 184, 189, 197, 218–19, 224, 228; and election of 1860, 244–45, 245n86; and law practice with Lincoln, 153, 155; Lincoln biography by, xi–xii, 103, 181n25; and Lincoln relationship, xii, xv, 189–90, 200, 202, 227, 229

Herndon on Lincoln: Letters (Wilson and Davis), xxi

Herndon's Informants (Wilson and Davis), xii, xxi

Herndon's Lincoln (Herndon), xi–xii, xvi, xxi, xxvi n70

Hickman, John, 228, 228n43

High, George, 198

Hill, John (IL), 91

Hill, John N. (KY), 14, 14n41

Hill, Parthena Williams Nance (Mrs. Samuel), xv, 82, 82n21, 91–92, 105

Hill, Samuel, 69, 69n9, 73, 82n21, 91, 93, 95, 104–5

Hingham, MA, 2

Hitt, Samuel M., 235, 235n53

Holmes, Oliver Wendell, xiii, 202

Hooker, Joseph, 195–96

Hopkins, William T., 223, 223n29

"House divided" speech, 195, 228–30

Houston, Samuel, 210, 210n16

Houston, William, 159n23

Hoyt, Charles, 100n5

Humes, Edwin G., 16

Hunter, David, 250, 250n10, 256

268 *Index*

Hunter, Robert M. T., 129, 129n14, 259
Hutchinson, "Granny," 142

Iles, Elijah, 86, 86n4
Illinois: judicial system of, 124–25 (*see also* Eighth Judicial Circuit); migration to, 52–57; political factionalism in, 137–39, 142, 156, 230–31
Illinois Central Railroad, xiii, 56, 247
Illinois Central Rail Road Company v. McLean and Parke, 152, 152n14, 153
Illinois state legislature: in Springfield, 123–24; in Vandalia, 106–13, 113n31, 114–20, 122
Illiopolis, IL, 113, 122
Indian attack, in Kentucky, 5–7
Indian removal, from Illinois, 83
Indiana: migration to, 24, 26–27, 29; and patronage, 244, 259; settlement of, 38, 40, 48
Inner World of Abraham Lincoln, The (Burlingame), xii
"Inquiry, The" (Mackay), 203, 203n64
Inside the White House in War-Times (Stoddard), xii
Interior Department (U.S.), patronage in, 244, 245n87, 259
internal improvements, 108, 112–17, 120, 125, 129–30
Irving, Washington, 251
Ivanhoe (Scott), 89n11

Jackson, Andrew, 29–30, 53, 75, 106, 109, 117, 119, 121, 183, 200, 209, 254, 260
Jacksonville, IL, 113–14, 122
Jayne, William, xiv, 126, 126n49, 138, 224, 227
Jefferson, Thomas, 3, 183, 192, 209, 219
Jerrold, Douglas, 44, 44n31
Jesus Christ, 20, 168
Johnson, Andrew, xiii, 53, 129
Johnson, Reverdy, 151
Johnson, William H., 197, 197n52, 258
Johnston, Daniel, 35
Johnston, John D., 37, 37n19, 43, 51–52, 54, 58, 61–64
Johnston (Hanks), Matilda (stepsister), 35, 37, 43, 49, 51–52, 54–55, 57

Johnston (Hall), Sarah (stepsister), 35, 37, 43, 49, 51, 51n6, 52, 54–55
Johnston, Sarah Bush. *See* Lincoln, Sarah Bush Johnston
Johnston, William, 37
Johnston children, 35, 37, 43, 49
Jones, James C., 208, 208n11
Jones, John, 45
Jones, William, 52, 52n7
Joy, James F., 153, 153n15
Judd, Norman B., 139, 139n14, 213, 219–20, 222, 235, 249–50, 254–60; and election of 1860, 240–42, 245n87, 246
justices of the peace, 108, 142

Kansas, 221–22, 230, 236
Kansas-Nebraska Act (1854), 137, 137n5, 205–14, 218, 230
Kasson, John A., 243, 243n80
Keckly, Elizabeth, xix
Kelley, William D., 243, 243n76
Kelso, John (Jack), 105, 105n12
Kenton, Simon, 4, 30
Kentucky: Indian attack in, 4–6, 7,17; influence of in Illinois, 107, 135; settlement in, 4–6
Keokuk (Indian), 84
Kirkham, Samuel, Jr., 31, 31n5, 78
Kirkpatrick, William, 63, 85, 85n3
Knob Creek farm, KY, 21
Knox, William, 98–100, 203
Koerner, Gustavus, 219, 219n10

Lamon, Ward Hill, 14, 103, 141, 162, 249, 255–56; and election of 1860, 227; as marshal, 190–91
"Last Leaf, The" (Holmes), xiii, 202
Latham, George C., 249, 249n5
Law, John, 117, 117n34
law circuit, in Illinois, vi, xvi–xv. *See also* Lincoln, Abraham, on law circuit
Lawes, Francis, 2
Lawrence, KS, sack of, 221
lawyers, methods of, 167
lead mines, 107
Lecompton Constitution (KS), 230–32, 236, 248
Lieber, Francis, 191

Index

269

Life of Abraham Lincoln (Lamon), 14
Life on the Circuit with Lincoln
  (Whitney), xi, xv–xviii, xxv n59, 221,
  228
lightning rod, 110–11
Lincoln, Abraham (PA), 3–4
Lincoln, Abraham, III (grandfather), 4,
  4n9, 5–6, 6n15, 11, 14; death of, 5–6,
  6n15, 7, 7n17, 8–9
Lincoln, Abraham, 58; and abstraction, 43, 187, 250; and account
  books, 197; and alcohol, 76–77, 81,
  140, 186; ambition of, 46, 48, 51, 66,
  82, 139; and Ann Rutledge, xii–xiii,
  xvi, 58–59, 94, 97–98, 100–101; and
  antislavery legislation, 130–34;
  antislavery protest of, 112n29, 134;
  antislavery speeches of, 195, 213–15,
  217; background of denigrated,
  29–30, 33–34; and Baltimore assassination plot, 254, 254n21, 255–58;
  and Bible reading, 169; birth of, 13,
  18–20; birth of compared to Jesus,
  20; and Black Hawk War, 84–86, 104,
  106; and blacks, 203–4, 204nn68–69;
  at Bloomington convention (1856),
  218–24; and books, 40–42, 79, 82;
  and business, 187–88; and cabinet of,
  244, 258; as captain of militia, 85–87;
  character of, xii–xiii, xix–xx, 76–77,
  79, 81–82, 91–92, 103, 139–40, 142–43,
  145–47, 154, 163, 172, 178, 182–84,
  186–89, 192–93, 195–96, 200–201,
  225; childhood of, xvi, xviii–xix,
  xxv–xxvi n63, 20–24, 48; and Clary's
  Grove boys, 74–75, 179; as clerk of
  elections, 71; clothing of, 39–40,
  90, 157, 198–99, 237–38, 257, 261; as
  Congressman, 128–34, 140, 155–56,
  217, 219–20, 244; Cooper Institute
  address of, 39, 175, 193, 236–38; correspondence from, 233–34; criticism
  of, 182, 189–91, 196, 252–54, 259; and
  death, xix; debts of, 87, 91, 119, 140,
  197; and depression, xiii, xvi, 35–36,
  98, 100–101, 172–73, 203; diplomacy
  of, 178; dreams and fears of, 51, 51n4;
  and duel with Shields, 124, 124n47;
  education of, 22, 22nn58–59, 23,

23n60, 23n62, 31–32, 39, 65, 78–79,
  175, 184; and election of 1832, 75–76,
  76n10, 87, 87n7, 88, 88n8, 106, 142;
  and election of 1834, 92, 106; and
  election of 1836, 109–11; and election of 1838, 120–22; and election
  of 1842, 127; and election of 1846,
  127–28, 142; and election of 1854,
  125–26, 217–18; and election of 1856,
  197–98, 215, 218, 228; and election
  of 1858, xii, 130, 191–92, 196, 199,
  228, 231–35, 235n54, 236; and election of 1859, 236; and election of
  1860, 225, 227–28, 240, 243–48; and
  emancipation, 182–83; and equal
  rights, 176–77, 191; and family history,
  xv–xvi, 1, 1n2, 2–8, 13, 13nn38 and
  40, 16, 16n47, 18–19; family life of,
  139; farewell address of, 250, 253;
  and fatalism, 92–93; and his father,
  23, 23n62, 181; and ferry boat, 43,
  46; and finances, 116–17, 119–20, 125,
  140, 152, 155, 157, 197–98; financial
  support of relatives by, 37, 59; and
  first year in Illinois, xii, xvi, 59, 61;
  flatboat voyages of, xii, 46–47, 61–66,
  71–72, 84, 103, 115, 121, 179; and
  friendship, 90, 104; friends of, 189,
  199–202; frontier narratives about,
  103; and gambling, 77; and geometry,
  xx, 42, 157, 193–94; as God's agent,
  169–70, 172–73; and grammar study,
  31, 31nn5–6, 78, 78n11, 78n13, 79;
  health of, 40, 125; helpfulness of, 88,
  141–42; heroism of, 195; as "Honest
  Abe," 91; and honesty of, 104, 148,
  153, 163, 183–84, 186, 194–96; horse
  and buggy of, 156–57; and "house
  divided" speech, 195, 228–30; humor
  of, 43, 118, 187–89; in Illinois legislature, 92, 104, 106, 108–13, 113n31,
  114–20, 122–25, 140; and imitating
  church services, 42, 169–70; Inaugural Address of, First, 171, 193, 260–61;
  Inaugural Address of, Second, 171,
  176; and inaugural journey (1861),
  xii, 249–52, 252n18, 253–58; inauguration of, first, 261–62; in Indiana,
  xii, xvi–xvi, 179; intellectual nature

Lincoln, Abraham (*continued*)
of, 175, 180, 184, 186, 192–93; and internal improvements, 104, 114–17, 129–30, 132; and interpersonal relationships, 157–58; as judge substitute, 160; "jumps" out window, 124, 169; and Kansas-Nebraska Act, 212–14, 217; and Kansas visit, 236; kicked by a horse, 40; kindness of, 40, 170, 201; and labor attitudes, 40–41, 61, 81, 83; as laborer, 40–43, 46, 48, 59, 66, 88–89; land warrants of, 86; and law career, xii, 88, 92, 154–56, 159; law cases of, 75, 75n9, 78, 90n13, 100n5, 145–52, 152n14, 153–55, 163–64; on law circuit, vi, xiii–xv, xx–xxi, 140–42, 145, 151, 155–58, 160–66; and law interest, 42, 45; and law studies, 88–89, 92, 97; as lawyer, xx–xxi, 104, 118–19, 144–54, 163–65, 191, 198; literary style of, 175–76; and lodging places, 157; and logical mind of, xx, 144, 156, 163, 180, 183–84, 186, 188, 192–94, 237; manliness of, 189; and Mary Owens, 101, 101n7, 102–3; and Mary Todd Lincoln, xiii–xiv; and melancholy (*see* and depression); and mental perspectives of, 192–93; and mercy, 169, 172, 201, 203; and Mexican War, 128, 130–32, 134, 217; migration of family to Illinois, 52, 54–57; and mill dam, 63–66, 71; and Missouri Compromise, 193, 212, 214, 217; morality of, 175, 180, 184–86, 190, 192; on his mother, 21, 21n55, 181, 181n25; neighbors of, 136, 142; and New England visit, 239; and New Orleans, xii, 64; and New Salem, xii, xx, 65–66, 71–72, 76–77, 90, 103–4, 179; as newspaper reader, 89, 157; note-taking by, 41–42; and novels, 89, 89n11; and oaths, 76, 85; as partisan politician, 178; and patronage, xii, 57–58, 90, 152, 189–91, 244–45, 245n87, 258–60; and paymaster appointments, 190, 190n39; and the "people," 178–79, 203; photographs of, 141; physical description of, xii, 39–40, 72, 76, 90, 142, 154,

157–58, 175, 180–81n24, 189, 198–99, 237–38; physical strength of, 44, 71–72, 74–75, 86, 103, 179–80, 180n24, 181; and poetry, xiii, 43, 98–100, 202–3, 203n64; and political oratory, 59–60, 191–92, 199, 213–15, 221, 223, 252–54, 160–61; and political policies, 182; popularity of, 179–80, 203; as postmaster, 106; and prayer, 170; as president-elect, 248–61; as presidential candidate, 217–18, 221, 224–25, 227–28, 233, 235, 235n54, 243–45; presidential nomination of, xii, 12, 151, 197, 227–28, 240, 246–47; presidential qualifications of, 217–21, 227; and public speaking, 42–43; and racial attitudes, xvii, 146, 146n4; as rail-splitter, 57; and reading, 40–42, 88–89; and Reconstruction, 182, 182n26; and religion, 92–94, 128, 140, 169–73; and satire/sarcasm, 41, 44, 110–11, 188; and séances, 50, 50n3; secretiveness of, 182, 196–97, 200; self-reliance of, 196–97; sensitivity of, 201–2; and servants, 197; shyness of, 92, 101–2, 140–41; and singing, 164; as skeptic, 169; slandered, 110; and slavery 64, 146, 176–77, 184, 185, 185n31, 185–86n32, 186, 191, 214–15; social status of, 49, 102, 135–36, 139–42; as soldier, 84–86; sorrows of, xiv–xvi, xviii–xix, 51, 53, 58–59, 98, 100–101, 181–82, 202; speeches and messages of, 170–71, 193, 215, 217, 223, 228, 234–39, 250, 252–54, 260–61; and "spot" resolution, 130, 134; and Springfield for state capital, 113, 113n31, 114, 122, 125, 135; and stepmother, 38, 181n25; as store clerk, 72, 76–79, 81; as store partner, 80–81, 81n18; as storyteller, 81–82, 92, 156–58, 161, 164, 187, 238, 247; and superstitions, 50; and Supreme Court appointment, 189–90; as surveyor, 90, 193; and sympathy for others, 189; and Zachary Taylor eulogy, 100, 100n5; and temper of, 159n23, 164; and theatre entertainment, 63; and tobacco, 140, 186; as

U.S. Senate candidate, 125–26; as vice-presidential candidate, 224, 224n32; as Whig, 106, 108, 111, 120, 127–28, 130, 156, 199, 219; and women, xii, xx, 39, 43, 92, 101–2, 140–41 (*see also specific women*); and wrestling, 74–75, 86; youth and adolescence of, xii, xvi, 39, 103, 180n24
Lincoln, Bathsheba Herring, 4n9, 5–8, 16n46. *See also* Shipley (Lincoln), Mary
Lincoln, Benjamin, 3, 3n4
Lincoln, David J., 2–3n3, 17n49
Lincoln, Enoch, 3, 3n7
Lincoln, Isaac, 4, 8, 10, 10n29
Lincoln, Jacob, 4, 8
Lincoln, James, 2–3n3
Lincoln, John (son of John), 4, 8
Lincoln, John (son of Mordecai, Jr.), 3–4, 17, 17n49
Lincoln, Josiah, 4, 7–8, 8n20
Lincoln, Levi, Jr., 3, 3n6
Lincoln, Levi, Sr., 3, 3n5
Lincoln (Crume), Mary (Mrs. Ralph Crume), 5, 5n12, 7–8
Lincoln, Mary Todd, 18, 135, 151, 197, 249, 262; behavior of, xiii–xv, 126; and politics, 126, 247
Lincoln, Mordecai (grandfather), 2n3
Lincoln, Mordecai, Jr., 3–4, 17, 17n49
Lincoln, Mordecai, Sr., 3, 3n8
Lincoln, Mordecai, III (uncle), 4–5, 5n13, 6–8
Lincoln (Brumfield), Nancy (Mrs. William Brumfield), 4–5, 5nn11–12, 6–8, 14
Lincoln, Nancy Hanks (mother), xv, 11, 11n32, 12, 14, 16, 18n50, 29, 38, 52; character and description of, 12–14, 20–21, 29, 35, 187; death and grave of, xiii, xv, 19, 33–34, 37, 48, 51, 53, 59, 181, 202; and education, 12, 20, 20n54, 21, 31; marriage of, 12, 14, 14–15n44, 15, 17, 17n48, 18; as mother, 22–24
Lincoln, Robert Todd, 239, 262; and inaugural journey, 249, 261; and mad dog, 50
Lincoln, Samuel, 1, 1n2, 2–3, 9

Lincoln, Sarah (sister), 19, 19n51, 22–23, 33–34, 37, 49; employment of, 43, 48; marriage and death of, 51
Lincoln, Sarah Bush Johnston (Sallie) (stepmother), xv, 12, 12n17, 35, 51–52, 54, 57–58, 60, 64–66, 181n25; domestic duties of, 35, 54; marriages of, 35–37; as stepmother, 37–38, 43
Lincoln, Solomon, 8, 8n21
Lincoln, Stephen, 2
Lincoln, Thomas (cooper), 2–3
Lincoln, Thomas (farmer), 2
Lincoln, Thomas (father), xvi, 4, 8, 11n32, 60, 64; antislavery attitudes of, 53; as carpenter, 10, 52; character and description of, 9, 9–10n27, 10, 10n28, 12, 21, 29–31, 35–36, 64–65; and education of Abraham, 22–23, 23n60, 23n62, 31, 65; finances of, 35–36, 36n17, 48–49, 51; Indiana land claim of, 26–28, 48; in Kentucky, 4–5, 7, 9, 19, 35, 53; marriages of, 12, 12n37, 13–14, 14–15n44, 15, 17, 17n48, 18, 35–37; migration to Coles County, IL, 61; migration to Illinois, 52–57, 60; migration to Indiana, 24, 26–27; and religion, 93; social status of, 53
Lincoln, Thomas (miller), 2
Lincoln, Thomas (Reading, PA), 3
Lincoln, Thomas (Tad) (son), 249, 262
Lincoln, Thomas (son of John), 4, 8
Lincoln, Thomas (weaver), 2
Lincoln, Thomas, Jr. (infant brother), 19, 19n52
Lincoln, Virginia John, 2–3n3
Lincoln, William Brumfield, 19
Lincoln, William Wallace (Willie), 249, 262
Lincoln and the Civil War in the Diaries and Letters of John Hay (Hay), xii
Lincoln-Douglas campaign (1858), xii, xvii, 130, 191, 196, 199, 234–36
Lincoln family, 11, 14, 18
Lincoln in American Memory (Peterson), xi
Lincoln in Lists (Flagel), xi
Lincoln Memorial University (Harrogate, TN), xiii, xxvii
Lincoln on the Eve of '61 (Villard), xii

272   *Index*

Lincoln's Run, KY, 7

Lincoln the Citizen (Whitney), discussed, xi–xiii, xv–xix, xxi, xxvii–xxviii

Lincoln the President (Whitney), xvii–xviii, xxvii

Linder, Usher F., 112, 112n24, 124n47, 162

Locke, John, 194

Logan, John A., 137, 137n7, 138

Logan, Stephen T., xxi, 108, 125, 127, 138, 141, 145, 154–56, 189–90, 197, 200; and election of 1860, 242, 245, 247

Logan County, IL, 156, 163

Longfellow, Henry Wadsworth, 253, 253n19

"Long Nine," 112–15, 118

"Lost Speech," xvi–xvii, xxiv n44, 224

Louisville, KY, 5–7, 7n17

Lovejoy, Owen, 219, 219n17, 222–23, 231

Luther, Martin, 174

lyceum (Gentryville, IN), 45

Mace, Daniel, 162, 162n34

Mackay, Charles, 203, 203n64

Macon County, IL, 52, 156

Madison, James, 3

madstone, 50

malaria (chills and fever), 60–61

Marcy, William, 207, 207n4

marriage bond, 14, 14–15n44, 17

Marshall, John, 154

Mason, James M., 183, 183n28, 259

Matheny, James H., xv, 88n8, 200, 200n58, 224n32

Matteson, Joel, 138, 138n13

Maynard, Nettie, 50n3

McClellan, George B., 183

McClernand, John A., 112, 112n22, 128

McCormick, Andrew J., 112, 112n28

McCormick v. Manny, 151

McDaniels, Stephen, 52

McKinley, James B., 162, 162n32

McLean, John, 152, 152n11, 243, 246

McLean County, IL, 156, 163

McNamar, John (aka John McNeil), 69, 69n10, 73, 95–97, 104, 106

McNeil, John. *See* McNamar, John

McWilliams, Amzi, 149, 149n7, 162

Melanchthon, Philip, 174

Menard County, IL, 90, 155

Mexican War, 127–28, 130, 134, 220, 248; supplies for, 130–31

migration, discussed, 53

"milk sick," 33, 37, 53–54, 60

mill dam (New Salem), 62–65, 68, 71

Miller, Hannah Winter, 16, 16n46

Miller, Joshua, 69, 69n13, 88, 104

Miller, Marion Mills, xi, xiii, xv–xvi, xxvii–xxviii

mills, 21–22, 40, 62–66, 68, 73, 76, 80, 104–5

Miner, Noyes, xix

Mississippi, fiscal repudiation in, 212, 212n18

Missouri Compromise (1820), 193, 206–8, 214, 218, 248; repeal of, 122, 137n5, 191, 207–9, 211–14, 217, 248

Monroe, James, 215

Moore, Clifton H., 156, 156n22, 160, 162

Moore, John, 249, 249n2

Moran v. Baddeley, 155, 155n20

Morgan, Edwin D., 243, 243n77, 251

Morris, Buckner S., 151, 151n9

Morse, Samuel F. B., 185

"Mortality" (Knox), 98–100, 203

Morton, Oliver P., 251, 251n15

Moses, 169–70, 174

Mudd (Lincoln), Mary (Mrs. Mordecai Lincoln III), 7, 7n18

Mulligan, James, 220, 220n18

Munsell, Leander, 223, 223n27

Murphy, John, 241

Murray, Lindley, 31, 31n6, 78, 78n13

music, Civil War era, 203, 203n67

Musick, Samuel, 108

Nall, James L., 4, 4–5n10, 5–8, 14–16, 36

Nall, William P., 5

Nance, Thomas Jefferson, 71, 71n2

Neckar, Jacques, 175, 175n4

Neely, Mark E., xi, xv

Nelson, Daniel P., 72

New Mexico, territorial government for, 132–33

Index

New Salem, IL, xii, 68–71, 76, 78, 94, 103; decline of, 104–5; deserted site of, 104

New York *Evening Post*, 237

Nicolay, John G., xvi, 15, 218, 245n87, 250

Norton, Jesse O., 233, 233n49

Noyes, William C., 242, 242n70

Offutt, Denton, 61–62, 64–65, 68, 71–72, 74, 76–77, 79, 81, 91, 104, 115

Ogden, William B., 218, 218n5, 219

Oglesby, Richard J., 57, 219, 219n9

"Oh! Why should the spirit of mortal be proud?" *See* "Mortality"

Olds, Edson B., 211, 211n17

One Hundred Essential Lincoln Books (Burkhimer), xi

Onstott, Henry, 69, 69n11, 89, 89n9, 104

Ordinance of 1787, 132

Oregon, territorial government for, 132

Orme, William W., 162, 162n33

Otto, William T., 243, 243n81

"Our Government" (Lincoln), 45

Owens (Vineyard), Mary, 101, 101n7, 102–3

Pacheco, Antonio, 133–34, 134n31

Palfrey, John G., 133, 133n29

Palmer, John M., 219, 219n13, 223

Panic of 1837, 119–20, 123

Parks, Gavion D. A., 218, 218n6

Parrott, John H., 17

patronage, xii, 57–58, 90, 152, 189–91, 232, 244–45, 245n87, 258–60

Paul, Apostle, 168–69

Pearce, James, 261, 261n32

Pearson, John, 160, 160n26

Peck, Ebenezer, 123, 123n42, 213, 219, 222

Pennsylvania: and election of 1860, 226, 244; and patronage, 244–45

Peoria, IL, 113, 122

Pepys, Samuel, 103

Peter, Apostle, 168–69

Petersburg, IL, 90, 104–5

Peterson, Merrill D., xi

Phillips, Wendell, xiii

Piatt, Donn, 179, 179n21

Piatt County, IL, 156, 162, 166

Pickett, Thomas J., 218, 218n7

Pierce, Franklin, 207–8, 211, 217, 223

Pike House (Bloomington, IL), 157

Pilgrims, 2

Pilgrim's Progress (Bunyan), 40

Pinkerton, Allan, 250, 254, 254n21, 255

pioneers, 26–31, 34, 53, 84

Polk, James K., 53, 130, 217, 223

Pope, John, 250, 250n9, 256

popular sovereignty, 236

Portrait for Posterity (Thomas), xi

Posey, John F., 59, 59n14, 60

Potter, John, 72, 72n3

Potter, Lucy, 16

Potter, William W., 16

Powell, Elihu N., 163, 163n41

presidential choices, 215–16, 218–20, 225–26, 240

proslavery legislation, 132. *See also* Kansas-Nebraska Act

Pryor, Roger A., 229, 229n45

public lands, 133

Pugh, George E., 236, 236n57

Quakers, 11, 18, 53

Quigg, David A., 160, 160n25

Quintilianus, Marcus Fabius, 194, 194n45

Radford, Reuben, 79, 79n15, 80, 87, 104

railroads, 107–8, 114–15, 152–53, 160–61, 163, 241, 254–55, 257

Ray, John W., 227, 227n37

Real Lincoln, The (Weik), xii

Reconstruction, 182, 182n26

Reeder, Andrew H., 222, 222n25, 223, 243

Regnier, Francis, 69, 69n19

religion, frontier, 42, 49, 136–37

Reporter's Lincoln, A (Stevens), xii

Republican National Convention (Chicago, 1860), xii, 241–45, 245nn86–87, 246–47

Republican Party, in Illinois, 218, 225, 231, 233–34

Reynolds, John, 84, 84n1

274   *Index*

Rhett, Robert Barnwell, 129, 129n20
Richardson, James, 104, 104n10
Richardson, William A., 109, 109n15, 128, 210; and Kansas-Nebraska Act, 205, 210
Richmond (VA) *Enquirer*, 228–29
Richmond House (Chicago), 242
Riney, Zachariah, 14, 14n42, 22, 22n58
Ristine, Joseph, 162, 162n38
river and harbor convention (Chicago, 1847), 199, 199n56
River Timber boys, 73
rivers, navigable, 115, 129–30
roads, 113, 115, 117–18
Robinson, Charles L., 221, 221n23
Robinson, Mrs. Charles L., 221–22
Robinson, John M., 108, 108n8
Robinson Crusoe, 40
Roby, Anna Caroline (Mrs. Allen Gentry), 39
Rogers, Matthew, 104, 104n11
romance, examples of, 94
Romine, John, 53, 53n10
Rutledge, Ann, xii–xiii, xvi, xviii, 58–59, 67n3, 69n10, 94, 104; character and description of, 94–95, 97; engagements of, 95–97; and grammar study, 78; illness, death, and grave of, 97–98, 202; reburial of, 98, 105
Rutledge, David, 96–98
Rutledge, Edward, 67–68
Rutledge, James, 67, 67n3, 68, 91, 94
Rutledge, James McGrady, 105, 105n13
Rutledge family, 95–96

Sac-and-Fox (Indians), 83–84
Salt River, KY, 25–26
Sandberg, Carl, xvi
Sangamon County, IL, 156, 163
Sangamon River, IL, 61–65, 68; navigation of, 87, 115
Sauganash hotel (Chicago), 241
sawmills, 68
Schurz, Carl, 242, 242n74
Scott, John M., 156, 156n21, 162
Scott, Winfield, 250, 256
Scripps, John L., xix, 22n58, 224
Scroggs, John W., 224, 224n33
Selby, Paul, 218, 218n3

Semple, James, 107, 107n4
Seward, Frederick, 255, 255n23
Seward, William H., 151, 208, 208n6, 209, 216–17, 225, 227–28, 240–44, 245n87, 246, 255, 258, 261
Shackford, Samuel, 9, 9n24
Sherman, John, 221, 221n21
Sherman, William T., 195
Shields, James, 124, 124n47, 213
Shipley (Lincoln), Mary, 4, 4n9, 6, 6n14, 8, 14, 16. *See also* Lincoln, Bathsheba Herring
Shipley family, 4, 11, 14–15
Short, James, 91
Sinco, Henry, 69, 69n16, 69n19, 89, 89n9, 104
Sinking Spring Farm, KY, 20, 20n53
slave auction, 64
slavery: in the territories, 131–34, 137, 206–9, 211–12, 214–15, 218, 222, 248; in Virginia, 1
Slidell, John, 183, 183n28
Smith, Caleb B., 242, 242n75, 244, 245n87, 259
Smith, Gerrit, 209, 209n13
Smith, John, 30
Smith, Mrs. Levi, 8
Smith, Robert, 128, 128n3
Smith, Sydney, 44, 44n31
Smoot, Coleman, 92, 92n14
snow, deep, 60–61
Social Darwinism, xviii
Soldiers' Home (Washington, DC), 169
Somers, James W., 224, 224n31
Somers, William D., 165, 165n42, 198
Sparks, Jared, 251, 251n17
Sparrow, Elizabeth Hanks (Betsy) (Mrs. Thomas), 12, 20n53, 29; death of, 33–34, 53
Sparrow, Henry, 11, 11n33, 12, 14
Sparrow, Thomas, 11, 20n53, 29; death of, 33–34, 53
specie payments, 123
Speed, James, 125, 125n48
Speed, Joshua F., xvii, 117, 125, 169, 214
Spink, Peter, 145
Spink v. Chiniquy, 145, 145n3
Springer, Francis, 138, 138n12

Springfield, IL, xii, 96; citizens of, 189–90; described, 61–62, 135; political activities at, 187, 213; becomes state capital, 109–10, 113, 113n31, 114, 118, 122
Standish, Miles, 30
Stanton, Edwin M., 151
state capitol building (Springfield, IL), 122–23
Statutes of Indiana, 42, 52
steamboats, 46
Stephens, Alexander H., 129, 132, 208, 208n10, 211
Stevens, Walter B., xii
Stevenson, George, 185
Stewart, Andrew, 131, 131n24
Stoddard, William O., xii, 224
Stone, Dan C., 112, 112n29
Stuart, John Todd, 88, 106, 127, 135, 138, 154–56, 197, 200, 214
Studebaker, Peter E., 33, 33n12
Sumner, Charles, 207, 209, 222, 246
Sumner, Edwin V., 249–50, 250n8, 256
Supreme Court (U.S.), 206
Swaney, James, 32, 32n8
Swett, Leonard, xv, xix, xxv–xxvi n63, 23, 23nn61–62, 32, 140–41, 146, 151, 156, 160n25, 162, 164, 166, 175, 219, 224, 228, 233; and election of 1860, 227, 242, 245
Sympson, Alexander, xv, 180, 180–81n24

Taney, Roger, 261–62
Tarbell, Ida, xvi, xxiv n36
tariffs, 131, 133
taverns, 165; mealtimes at, 160–61, 163, 165
Taylor, Edmund D., 120, 120n37, 121
Taylor, James, 43
Taylor, Zachary, 53, 100, 217, 258
Tecumseh, 83
telegraph, 163
"Temperance" (Lincoln), 45
Terry, Elias S., 162, 162n30
thanksgiving days, 170–71
Thomas, Benjamin P., xi–xii
Thomas, Jesse B., 121, 121n38, 122
Thompson, Nathan M. (Dow), 86

Thompson, Richard M., 14, 14–15n44, 15
Thompson, Richard W. (Dick), 162, 162n40
tobacco, 81, 140, 186
Todd, Lockwood, 249, 249n7
Todd, Robert Smith, 135, 135n2
toll bridge, 108
Toombs, Robert, 129, 129n16, 208, 236
Toucey, Isaac, 207, 207n5
transportation, 107–8, 114–15, 117, 163
treaties, with Indians, 83–84
Tremont House (Chicago), 242
Trench, Richard C., 191
Trent, Alexander, 86, 86n5
Trent, Martin, 86, 86n5
Trumbull, Julia Jayne (Mrs. Lyman), 123n39, 126n49
Trumbull, Lyman, 123, 123n39, 126, 218, 222
Tuck, Amos, 243, 243n82
Turner, Thomas J., 128, 128n5, 235
Turnham, David, 42, 42n26, 52

Usher, John P., 162, 162n39, 259

Van Atta, Mr., 164
Van Bergen, Peter, 87, 87n6, 91
Van Buren, Martin, 217, 221, 223
Vandalia, IL, 107, 122
Villard, Henry, xii
Voorhees, Daniel W., 162, 162n37

Waddell, Martin, 69, 69n12, 104
Wade, Benjamin F., 182, 182n26, 209, 209n14, 243, 246
Wade-Davis bill, 182, 182n26
Walker, Isaac P., 120, 120n36
Wallace, William S., 190n39, 249, 249n3
Warburton, George, 69, 69n15, 104–5
Warne, Kate, 254, 254n21, 255
Washburne, Elihu, 219–20, 235, 257–58
Washington (Weems), 40–41
Washington, DC: slavery in, 129–31, 133–34, 217; southern sympathies in, 259
Washington, George, 29–30, 174, 182, 188
Washington Peace Conference, 258
Watkins, Thomas, 105, 105n14

276   *Index*

Watt, James, 185

"We are coming, Father Abraham" (Gibbons), 203, 203n67

Webb, Henry L., xv, 86, 113, 113n31

Webster, Daniel, 116, 129, 132, 142, 148, 174, 192, 208, 216, 237, 251–52, 260

Weed, Thurlow, 201, 210n62, 242

Weik, Jesse W., xii, xvi, xxvi n70

Weldon, Lawrence, 162, 162n31

Welles, Gideon, 15–16, 16n45, 16n47

Wentworth, John, 128, 128n6, 130, 213, 219–20, 241

Westward movement, 205–6

Whigs, 222–23, 230–31; decline of, 207–8

whiskey, 73, 79–81

White, Hugh, 216

Whitney, Henry C., 141, 197, 223; advice to Lincoln by, 57; biographical information on, xiii; criticism of, xvi–xix, 147, 159, 159n23; and election of 1860, 245n86, 247; on law circuit, vi, xiii–xv, 157, 165; as lawyer, xxi, 146–47, 149–50, 153, 158–60, 164–65; Lincoln biography by, xi–xii, xix, xxi–xxii n7, 155, 170, 221; on Lincoln marriage, xviii; and Lincoln relationship, vi, xii–xvi, xxiii n23, 146–47, 159, 159n23, 166, 187, 197, 202, 218, 234, 236, 249;

and Lincoln's "Lost Speech," xvi–xvii, xxiv n44, 224; as paymaster, 110, 190n39; racist attitudes of, xvii–xviii, xxv n54

Wide Awakes, 239, 247

Wigfall, Louis T., 259, 259n26

Wigwam (Chicago), 241–42

wildlife, in Indiana, 28, 30

Wilkinson, Ira O., 219, 219n11

Willard's Hotel (Washington, DC), 257–59, 261

Williams, Archibald, 113, 113n30, 152, 219, 221–24

Wilmot, David, 129, 129n18, 243, 246

Wilmot Proviso, 131

Wilson, Douglas L., xxi

Wilson, James, 162, 162n35

Wilson, Robert L. xv, 110, 110n19, 112–14, 118, 190n39

Winthrop, Robert C., 129, 129n22

Wood, Fernando, 250, 250n14, 251

Wood, William (IN), 46, 52, 52n8

Wood, William S. (NY), 249n4, 250, 250n13

Yates, Richard, xiv, xxiii n26, 223, 242, 249

Young, Richard M., 108, 108n9, 113

HENRY CLAY WHITNEY (1831—1905) was a lawyer and personal friend of Abraham Lincoln. His other books include *Lincoln the President, March 4, 1861 to May 3, 1865*.

MICHAEL BURLINGAME is a professor of history and the holder of the Chancellor Naomi B. Lynn Distinguished Chair in Lincoln Studies at the University of Illinois Springfield. He has written and edited twenty-one Lincoln books, among them *The Black Man's President: Abraham Lincoln, African Americans, and the Pursuit of Racial Equality* and *An American Marriage: The Untold Story of Abraham Lincoln and Mary Todd*.

The University of Illinois Press
is a founding member of the
Association of University Presses.

Composed in 10.5/13 Mercury Text
with Weiss display by Jim Proefrock
at the University of Illinois Press
Manufactured by Versa Press, Inc.

University of Illinois Press
1325 South Oak Street
Champaign, IL 61820-6903
www.press.uillinois.edu